Fear in the German-Speaking World, 1600–2000

HISTORY OF EMOTIONS

The history of emotions offers a new and vital approach to the study of the past. The field is predicated on the idea that human feelings change over time and they are the product of culture as well as of biology. Bloomsbury's History of Emotions series seeks to publish state-of-the-art scholarship on the history of human feelings and emotional experience from antiquity to the present day, and across all seven continents. With a commitment to a greater thematic, geographical and chronological breadth, and a deep commitment to interdisciplinary approaches, it will offer new and innovative titles which convey the rich diversity of emotional cultures.

Series Editors: Peter N. Stearns and Susan J. Matt

Published

Emotional Bodies (University of Illinois Press, 2019), Edited by Dolores Martín-Moruno and Beatriz Pichel

Shame: A Brief History (University of Illinois Press, 2017), Peter N. Stearns

The Science of Sympathy (University of Illinois Press, 2016), Rob Boddice

Driven by Fear (University of Illinois Press, 2016), Guenter B. Risse

Doing Emotions History (University of Illinois Press, 2014), Edited by Susan J. Matt and Peter N. Stearns

Fear in the German-Speaking World, 1600–2000

Edited by
Thomas J. Kehoe and Michael G. Pickering

BLOOMSBURY ACADEMIC
LONDON • NEW YORK • OXFORD • NEW DELHI • SYDNEY

BLOOMSBURY ACADEMIC
Bloomsbury Publishing Plc
50 Bedford Square, London, WC1B 3DP, UK
1385 Broadway, New York, NY 10018, USA
29 Earlsfort Terrace, Dublin 2, Ireland

BLOOMSBURY, BLOOMSBURY ACADEMIC and the Diana logo are trademarks of
Bloomsbury Publishing Plc

First published in Great Britain 2020
Paperback edition published 2021

Copyright © Thomas J. Kehoe and Michael G. Pickering, and contributors 2020

Thomas J. Kehoe and Michael G. Pickering have asserted their right under the Copyright,
Designs and Patents Act, 1988, to be identified as Editors of this work.

Cover design: Tjaša Krivec

All rights reserved. No part of this publication may be reproduced
or transmitted in any form or by any means, electronic or mechanical,
including photocopying, recording, or any information storage or retrieval
system, without prior permission in writing from the publishers.

Bloomsbury Publishing Plc does not have any control over, or responsibility for, any
third-party websites referred to or in this book. All internet addresses given in this
book were correct at the time of going to press. The author and publisher regret any
inconvenience caused if addresses have changed or sites have ceased to exist, but can
accept no responsibility for any such changes.

A catalogue record for this book is available from the British Library.

A catalog record for this book is available from the Library of Congress.

ISBN: HB: 978-1-3501-5047-8
PB: 978-1-3502-4045-2
ePDF: 978-1-3501-5048-5
eBook: 978-1-3501-5049-2

Series: History of Emotions

Typeset by Newgen KnowledgeWorks Pvt. Ltd., Chennai, India

To find out more about our authors and books visit www.bloomsbury.com
and sign up for our newsletters.

In memory of Lachie Hill (1946–2019).
This book is for all people who, like her, have boundless curiosity and generosity of spirit.

Contents

List of Illustrations	viii
Acknowledgments	ix
1 Introduction *Thomas J. Kehoe and Michael G. Pickering*	1
2 Political Fear during the Wars of Louis XIV: The Danger of Becoming French *Kirsten L. Cooper*	15
3 Vampires, Ottomans, and the Specter of Contagion: The Intersectionality of Fear on the Periphery of the Habsburg Monarchy *Michael G. Pickering*	41
4 "The Forest is not Everyone's Friend": Fear in an Eighteenth-Century Southwest German Hometown *Dennis Frey*	65
5 Gypsy Hysteria in Nineteenth-Century Germany: A Biopolitical Response *Charissa Kurda*	87
6 Cultivating Fear: The Image of the SA and the Presence of Propaganda in the Late Weimar *Öffentlichkeit* *Jacob Berg and Richard Scully*	123
7 Conceptualizing Gender and Fear: German-Jewish Masculinities in the Third Reich and the Dread of the Unknown *Sebastian Huebel*	165
8 Gangs in the Forest: The Construction of the Criminal Archetype in Post–Second World War Western Germany *Thomas J. Kehoe*	195
9 Fear of Falling: German Discussions of Poverty from 1945 *Christoph Lorke*	227
10 German Angst after 1945 as Fear of the Fear *Pierre-Frédéric Weber*	253
11 Conclusions *Thomas J. Kehoe and Michael G. Pickering*	275
List of Contributors	283
Index	287

Illustrations

1. *Schluss jetzt mit Hitlers Volksverhetzung! Wählt Hindenburg* [Enough now with Hitler's national incitement! Vote Hindenburg], 1932 — 124
2. *Was steckt hinter dieser Maske? Also wählt Marx* [What is behind this mask? So, vote Marx], 1925 — 134
3. *Illustrierter Beobachter* 22 September 1928: *Berlin Voran: Dritter Märkertag 29–30 Sept 1928* [Berlin ahead: Third Berlin-Brandenburg rally 29–30 September 1928] — 136
4. *Bahn frei Für Liste 1 Sozialdemokraten* [Make way for List 1 Social Democrats], 1930 — 138
5. *Fort mit den Stützen des Finanzkapitals—wählt nationalsozialistisch* [Away with supporters of financial capitalism—vote National Socialist], 1931 — 140
6. *Wählt Hindenburg* [Vote Hindenburg], 1932 — 143
7. *Schützt Bayern! Bayerisches Volkspartei Liste 1* [Protect Bavaria! Bavarian People's Party List 1], 1932 — 144
8. *Brüder! Sammelt Euch in der Deutschen Staatspartei* [Brothers! Collect yourself in the German Democratic Party], 1932 — 145
9. *Wir schaffen das neue Deutschland! Denkt an die Opfer Wählt Nationalsozialisten Liste 1* [We create the New Germany! Think of the victims, Vote National Socialist List 1], 1932 — 147
10. *Trotz Hass und Verbot Nicht Tot* [Notwithstanding hate and interdiction, [we're] not dead], 1933 — 148
11. *National-sozialismus: Der Organisierte Wille der Nation* [National Socialism: The Organised Will of the Nation], 1933 — 150
12. *Die Stunde ist da!* [The hour is here] *Völkischer Beobachter: Kampfblatt der national-sozialistischen Bewegung Grossdeutschlands* — 151
13. *Der S.A. Mann ist die sich immer erneuernde Kraft der Bewegung* [The SA man is the self-renewing power of the movement], 1933 — 153
14. *Appell am 23. Februar 1933* [Roll call on the 23 February 1933], 1933 — 155

Acknowledgments

The editors would like to thank the series editors, Professors Peter Stearns and Susan Matt, for their unwavering support of this collection, as well as the editorial team at Bloomsbury for their steadfast professionalism and efficiency in ensuring its smooth path to production. To the reviewers of this book, the editors give their heartfelt thanks for their time and attention to detail. The editors acknowledge the support of their academic institutions, the University of New England and Trinity College, University of Melbourne respectively. The editors thank the contributors for their alacrity for, and patience with, the long project that this book entailed. Michael Pickering would also like to acknowledge and thank the Herzog August Bibliothek, especially the library team and Dr. Elizabeth Harding, for their support of his research endeavors while he was a research fellow in Wolfenbüttel 2018–19. Thomas Kehoe would like to thank all the people who offered such genuine support through an extremely difficult year and who also, in turn, very much helped make this book a reality.

1

Introduction

Thomas J. Kehoe and Michael G. Pickering

Fear is omnipresent in the human experience and as routinely noted by writers—either directly or, more commonly, obliquely—it has been an elemental emotion in many important developments through history. This is of course true for the German-speaking world, which we have defined here as roughly analogous to the Holy Roman Empire. As Kirsten Cooper notes in Chapter 2 of this book, this area was neither purely German, ethnically or linguistically, nor were all the "Germanic peoples" within it. It nonetheless serves as a useful geographic heuristic for the space we are examining and it nearly goes without saying that fear has been a defining emotion of this area's history. Fear—and the fantasies it embodied and with which it intersected—for example, infamously drove the pernicious search for witches, and the perceived links between them and diabolic power, the ritual murder of Christian children, and Jews.[1] Over the approximately four hundred years that this book examines, real and imagined fears of foreign invasion guided many native and official responses to the Ottomans in the south, the French to the west, Poles to the east, and other non-German ethnic groups that pressed at the borders or internally appeared to threaten a certain—albeit at times loose—ethnolinguistic Germanic culture.

Patterns appear from even a cursory inspection of the history of this space. Appearances can be deceiving however, and historians have been reluctant to draw sweeping connections between events often separated by decades or centuries, and which can too readily be attributed to acontextual, generic human emotions. Such reticence has hindered exploration of the interplay between universal human emotions and their contextualized expressions within specific cultural frameworks and a shared historical experience. As the following chapters reveal, in the German-speaking world fear appears to have been constructed in strikingly similar ways. Enemies were imagined to be everywhere, though how these enemies were instantiated in popular imagination was expressed in unique and particular historically and culturally contextualized forms like "the witch" and "the vampire" in the early modern period, "the [racialized] Jew" of Nazism, and "the Polish criminal" in the aftermath of the Second World War. These personifications of fear were frequently imagined living among the "acceptable" Germanic communities (and in the case of Jews and Poles, actually did live in them) yet were believed to be permanently set apart culturally and spiritually, often to the extent of posing an intentional, existential threat to the majority. Such constructions and the logic of an invasive danger drove terrible native and official responses including sporadic violence, ethnic purges, police targeting, and even the Holocaust. These continuities demand closer examination, as do the insights they may potentially provide into the emotional dimensions of Germanic cultural history.[2]

Though the ubiquity of fear is unsurprising, its expression in the particular context we have identified raises questions of whether similarity suggests continuity, or if such patterns are merely generically human expressions of universal emotions? Was the construction of fears in, for instance, post–Second World War Germany connected in some fashion to early modern cultural tropes? If so, may this similarity have been due to the interconnected social, cultural, and political developments in this region? These questions are not easily answered and extend far beyond the capacity of one scholar, or even a team. Our idea has, therefore, been to break initial ground with this book.

If these questions appear to be flirting with a version of the *Sonderweg* argument, let us clarify that we are looking to a subtler connectivity, not one that appeals to some hegemonic notion of "German culture" or a Hegelian idea of the "German spirit" as a teleological explanation for recent events. Rather, we are interested in drawing out how an emotion like fear is in a particular space shaped by geography, history, and socioeconomic conditions, which may together contribute to similarity in expression over time. To that end, we present here a range of early modern and modern historians of the German-speaking world who address how fear was constructed in their respective areas of expertise. Our aim has been to develop a collection that turns around the topic but does not beg the questions we were personally exploring. As will be shown, when examined *in toto*, the chapters of this collection suggest the existence of enduring tropes, such as infiltration/incursion that, while contextualized culturally and historically in each of the periods the chapters address, may speak to broader transtemporal anxieties in Central Europe.

By examining the emotional experience of fear and its expressions, our book sits firmly in the history of emotions, though fear has not received the scholarly attention it deserves. Writing fifteen years ago, Joanna Bourke noted, "Despite the centrality of emotional experience in the past, analysis of emotions such as fear has remained peripheral to the historical discipline."[3] She was speaking broadly, but her observation remains true for studies of early modern and modern history in the German-speaking world. While many historians of this space acknowledge the importance of fear,[4] it is rarely centered and there are currently no books charting its longer history in this space including its construction, instrumentality, and how people coped with it. Indeed, the German-speaking world offers rich emotional territory, and historians of nearly every era touch on the place of fear within it. For instance, nearly every history of the nineteenth and twentieth centuries in Central Europe addresses fear in some fashion. Scholarship on German colonial expansion has noted that the imperative to expand was at least partly driven by various fears including of being outpaced by European neighbors with larger overseas empires and of losing control of trade routes, and by ordinary lower- and middle-class Germans who saw settlement as a solution to economic hardship.[5] Similarly, broadly felt fears about the condition of post–First World War Germany—including economic and social instability, rising communism, and loss of sovereignty—helped drive the rise of ultranationalist movements, both among members and in these parties' political messaging.[6] The fear people felt or was propagated is, in some form, central to virtually every study of Nazi Germany and to the postwar reconstructions of West and East Germany, notably in the construction of new national identities in the divided state.[7] Despite its ubiquity in these histories, most only address the experience of fear obliquely. Xenophobia, for example, is central to Germany's modern history, though rarely addressed on its own as a cultural, social, or societal phenomenon.[8] Jeffrey Herf's thesis of a radical paranoia underpinning Nazi ideology is a notable exception. Yet, even he does not foreground fear as a focus for study in its own right.[9]

There are a few notable exceptions that provide methodological frameworks for analyzing fear in the German-speaking world, although these do not chart the longer history of the emotion in the space. Maria Tatar's exploration of the fetishization of sexual murder in Weimar art and cinema provides an avenue for centering fear in historical scholarship. She shows how the portrayal of sexual murder can be understood as reflection of Weimar's periodized angst. In so doing, she demonstrates the value of exploring fear as a medium for interpreting complex social and historical realities. Adam Zamoyski charts a similar course by showing how conservative anxieties about liberal revolution shaped European governments' policies during the mid-nineteenth century; though, his analysis highlights the conceptual complexities in history of emotions research. At its heart, it is debatable whether we as historians can access "anxieties" or "fears" in the past, or whether these labels when applied to sweeping social forces are anything more than simplistic and subjective descriptors. "Conservative anxieties" may easily be described with other words, such as "outraged" or "resolute." Other emotional concerns—even if pragmatic—likely also apply, for instance: "economic interest." Emotions in historical writing could be little more than a provocative heuristic that gives the past color but has little explanatory value.[10]

In this book we take the view that even if the actual individual experience of fear as an emotion may be obscured, its socially emergent consequences and its impact on history can be meaningfully studied. Consequently, here we make an initial contribution to what should become an important field in the study of Central European history. Two recent edited collections set the broad parameters by demonstrating the salience of centering fear in social, cultural, and historical study. Jan Plamper and Benjamin Lazier bring historians of emotions and science, together with psychologists, sociologists, and members of other disciplines to discuss from a theoretical perspective the constructions and ontology of fear in society, culture, and history, and in turn the importance of making it the focus for study.[11] Michael Laffan and Max Weiss offer an exclusively historical, worldwide exploration of fear from the early modern period through the twentieth century.[12] The contributors in Laffan and Weiss's book show the important role that fear has played as a construction through which events have been understood in world history and as a motivator for historical actors including individuals, countries, and political parties, among others. Our book both extends these works and narrows the focus to a key ethnogeographic space in Central Europe. In so doing, we build upon the social constructionist approach of Plamper and Lazier's collection and the diachronic considerations of Laffan and Weiss's work. We do this through an inquiry into the nature of fear—how fear was understood, developed, and negotiated—and consideration of its instrumentality in various historical contexts in the German-speaking world.

As the scope and conceptual orientation of the works by Jean Delumeau and Zygmunt Bauman suggest,[13] there has been considerable scholarly interest in the diachronic transformations of emotions in Europe spanning the medieval through the modern periods: in essence, how, when, and in what ways have the expressions of emotions and the social "regimes"[14] that structured and organized them changed over time? To what extent can we speak of qualitative differences in terms of what was feared, the intensity of such fears, and the nature of fear itself in the premodern and modern eras respectively? Indeed, Delumeau's pioneering study on the emergence of a Western "guilt culture"—premised, as he sees it, on the development of a doctrine of *contemptus mundi*—takes as its starting point a medieval world filled with both external and internal fears; a nightmarish vista that would only begin to diminish in the eighteenth century.[15] In essence then, the story of modernity in the West becomes, in part, the shift away from such all-pervasive fears.

Two key figures at the center of this debate concerning the premodern and modern dimensions of fear are Peter Stearns and Barbara Rosenwein respectively, and one of the major issues that they engage with concerns the so-called civilizing process articulated in Norbert Elias's eponymous book. In the paradigm suggested by Elias—in large measure an attempt to conceptually unpack the affective normative structures of modernity and their relationship to early modern political power dynamics—the shift from premodern to modern was marked by an increasing "emotional restraint" (*Zurückhaltung der Affekte*).[16] This transformation purportedly began within the centralizing early modern courts and, via a process of socialization and social control, eventually entered in the bourgeois social milieu. Building upon this conceptual framework, some historians have argued that there are important differences between premodern and modern emotional expressions;[17] others have, however, rejected such a division. As Rosenwein wryly notes, belief in such a split constitutes a "grand narrative": "In brief, the narrative is this: the history of the West is the history of increasing emotional restraint."[18] In place of such narratives, Rosenwein (a medievalist) has argued for a focus on that which social communities "define and assess as valuable or harmful to them; the evaluations that they make about others' emotions; the nature of the affective bonds between people that they recognize; and the modes of emotional expression that they expect, encourage, tolerate and deplore."[19] Rosenwein refers to these as "emotional communities."

Appreciating, as Stearns does, that the "grand narrative" in its earlier incarnations was not particularly useful as an interpretative strategy, and at the same time unwilling to "promote emotions history as a series of pointillist inquiries without the possibility of some larger dynamics,"[20] this book does engage with the emotion of fear across a wide time span; but the question of how constructions of fear within the German-speaking world changed over time is another avenue that this collection leaves open for further research. Indeed, this book attempts to draw out connections and common themes rather than differences. Although far from attempting to suggest anything vaguely approximating a psychohistorical approach, we hope to open the way for a consideration of how such connections might speak to resilient cultural commonalities.

A central question at the heart of history of emotions research concerns the extent to which scholars are able to recover anything about emotions at all. While certain source types, such as art works, popular literature, ego documents, legal documents, material culture, and advice literature,[21] for example, are particularly well suited to the examination of how emotions were represented, there is still the question of whether we can really recover individual subjectivities. As Susan Matt indicates with reference to Jean Starobinski, the history of emotions is bound up tightly with the words used to express those emotions.[22] How then to make the transition from "scary sources to real fear?"[23] While the chapters in this collection present various methodological and theoretical approaches relevant to their own case studies, one can discern a general approach that differs somewhat from the dominant focus of emotions research. In place of the question "who was afraid and how do we know that they were afraid?," we address the question "how was fear constructed and represented, and what did this do?" Fear becomes about what-is-to-be-feared rather than necessarily what individuals actually felt. Of course, this casts the conceptual net wide enough to encompass several chapters that focus on the personal and individual dimensions of fear. However, the overall thrust of this collection is to consider the instrumentality of fear.

Indeed, emotions are never politically neutral, and fear is a particularly apt example of this, whether one speaks of high politics or social power dynamics more generally. As Bourke has noted, reframing the discussion in terms of instrumentality shifts the focus of any analysis of fear to its political dimensions: "Crucially, emotions such as fear do not belong only to individuals or social groups: they mediate between the individual and the social. They are about power relations. Emotions lead to a negotiation of the boundaries between Self and Other or One Community and Another. They align individuals with communities."[24] Furthermore, fear is not simply something that people feel but also something that people (sometimes knowingly, sometimes unwittingly) enact. As Jennifer Spinks and Charles Zika note, "Emotions are something that people experience and also do; they are domains of effort exercised by mindful bodies and follow particular social and cultural scripts. Through this exercise, forms of identity can be strengthened and the borders of communities re-formed."[25] This is not to suggest that fear, so understood, is necessarily concretely constructed, stable, and self-consciously deployed by historical actors. Indeed, as several of the contributions in this collection indicate, such constructions were often multifaceted and fluid.[26] Nonetheless, notwithstanding its often-protean nature, fear had the propensity to demarcate boundaries and to maintain (and challenge) political, social, cultural, and economic orders.

There is also the question of what constitutes "fear" and what differentiates it from other related concepts such as "anxiety." It is vitally important to remember that meanings attached to emotions can and do change over time, as has been thoroughly examined in a recent edited collection by Ute Frevert.[27] Frevert makes clear at the outset that the aim of *Emotional Lexicons* is not to examine individual emotions but rather to examine the ways in which emotions generally were constructed, socially regarded, debated, and transformed. Turning to the early modern German-speaking world, we note that the entry on *Furcht* (fear) in the eighteenth-century encyclopedist Johann Zedler's *Universal-Lexicon* refers to it as the feeling of being unable to achieve or fulfill something positive or, alternatively, being unable to stop something negative from happening.[28] *Angst* is this same feeling but at a greater intensity, according to Zedler.[29] Not only is the description of the emotion somewhat different from modern conceptions of "fear" and "angst," but also the relationship between the two terms is, for Zedler, not one of subject–object relations. It is instead one of degree.

In later modern constructions, "fear" and "anxiety" tend to be differentiated according to whether the object inciting the feeling of dread is defined and present or whether it is undefined and absent. Essentially, fear has been imagined as a response to a particular stimulus and anxiety as a subjective experience in the absence of a direct stimulus.[30] Although, as Bourke states, it is important to realize the distinction between fear and anxiety "may reside solely in social, hierarchical responses. In fear states, individuals are consciously able to take measures to neutralize or flee from the dangerous object, while purposeful activity fails individuals whose subjective experience is anxiety. But the ability or inability to 'neutralize or flee' ... is a question of power relations within historical communities—not a fundamental difference between the object or state causing an emotional response."[31] Bauman echoes this notion in his discussion of "liquid fear," conceived of as the generalized fear of societal "implosion" of the late twentieth and early twenty-first centuries. Bauman argues that this pervasive fear of a collapse of civilization—what he refers to as the "Titanic syndrome"—hinges upon an awareness of our dependency upon the structures of civilization itself and of just how fragile these complex structures are. Indeed, it is both a fear of "being evicted from a world where 'elementary staples' go on being provided and there is a holding power that can be counted on"[32] and also one in which "the dangers we fear transcend our ability to act; as yet we have not even advanced as far as to be able to conceive clearly what the tools and the skills adequate to the task would be like—let alone being able to start designing and creating them."[33]

While the various chapters in this collection draw upon individual and particular analytical frameworks and working definitions, questions of how fear was imagined and socially constituted are at the heart of the contributions. Furthermore, this is the first book that has tried to draw connections between disparate constructions of fear in the German-speaking world over a longer period of time. As will become clear, the contributions collected here reveal not only complex constructions of fear specific to their historical and cultural contexts but also an evolving construction of fear in the German-speaking world that is likely in part universally human, and contextualized culturally and historically in this specific space. The chapters cover fear of French cultural incursion in the seventeenth-century Habsburg Monarchy; fear of vampires, pestilence, and military incursion on the border with the Ottomans in the eighteenth century; and fear surrounding "Gypsy" (translated from the German *Zigeuner*) itinerancy. The chapters on the twentieth century address among others national debasement, the shattering of Jewish masculinity through fear during the Third Reich, and fear of criminals.

Important continuities emerge across these seemingly disparate case studies. The dominant forms of these stem from Europe's multiethnic composition and the central location of the German-speaking world, and are addressed here in the first four chapters. A persistent fear of invasion stems from this geography and the German world's porous borders, which Kirsten Cooper explores in the first contributor chapter (Chapter 2). In it, she shows how in the late seventeenth century, the French armies of Louis XIV posed a threat on the border of the Holy Roman Empire. They inspired deep anxiety, which was reflected in political pamphlets as imminent military conquest, religious persecution, and political ruin. Cooper then demonstrates how these genuine geopolitical concerns were transformed into a veritable fantasy of cultural infiltration, represented as a fear of "becoming French."

Chapter 3, by Michael Pickering, elaborates similar themes. Pickering investigates how geopolitical anxieties concerning the loss of territorial sovereignty transformed into fears of incursion, infiltration, and destruction. It was no coincidence, he shows, that fear of vampires was tied to a persistent threat of spreading contagion, or that these anxieties existed on the contentious military border with the Ottoman Empire at the southern extremity of the Habsburg Monarchy.

Pickering's analysis of the fears that vampirism engendered highlight the personification of threat, which Dennis Frey analyzes in more detail in

Chapter 4. Exploring in depth the spiritual and psychological experiences of one ordinary man in a small German town, Frey shows how the struggles of day-to-day life and grander political developments seen through the eyes of regular people could stimulate persistent anxiety. In this particularly fascinating case, Frey explores the man Vahyinger's diarized account of an encounter with a demon in the woods. Refracted through his particular Pietist spirituality, this supposed event reveals the deeply personal, multifaceted and often-contradictory ways in which fear could be expressed.

Charissa Kurda, in Chapter 5, more fully brings out the final key theme of transience and threat that emerges from these collected works. In her chapter, she examines the mass hysteria inside the German Empire and the responses of successive *Kaiserreich* governments to an ostensible *"Zigeunerplage"* ("Gypsy nuisance"). She shows that *Kasierreich* bureaucrats waged a stringent "biopolitical" campaign against Gypsies, which sought to eradicate itinerancy and coerce citizen Gypsies into a sedentary lifestyle commensurate with traditional German culture. In so doing, she also addresses the links between "disease" and perceived incursion into the German body politic that Pickering addresses but further highlights the fear caused by beliefs that the problem was internal rather than at—or near—the border.

The broad themes of the German-speaking world's geography, its mutable borders, and the fear of invasion, along with ethnic transience, and the personification of fear are evident in the later chapters of this book suggesting contextualized continuity. Chapters 6 and 7 explore two sides of the fear that shaped the Nazi period. Jacob Berg and Richard Scully explore the use of the SA as living vehicles for Nazi attempts to propagate fear and in turn establish themselves as the protectors of Germans against foreign racial and ideological invaders, notably (the often conflated) Jews and communists. Sebastian Huebel inverts the lens and examines the fear German-Jewish men experienced during the Third Reich as a result of being targeted by the Nazis and constructed as racial invaders in the "Aryan" state. From these two chapters, we begin to see the reciprocal and contrasting interplay of ethnocentric fears that existing in a specific same time and cultural space.

It is no coincidence that the twentieth-century fears of racial enemies among Germanic peoples and within ethno-German space that Berg and Scully, and Huebel address reflected far older animosities, despite having been constructed around thoroughly modern eugenic and social Darwinian ideas. In an exploration of the racialized and ethnicized fears that led to fear of violent foreign criminals and gangs in post–Second World War Germany, in Chapter 8 Kehoe further highlights that expressions of fear are refashioned, but the base feeling remains constant. The end of the war in 1945 eradicated Germany's sovereignty. Groups including Poles and Russians previously considered racial enemies or simply non-Germanic "others" displaced Germans and held privileged positions in the occupation. Deprived of power, Germans focused on violent foreign criminals and gangs as a way of expressing the deep anxiety they felt at this radical change and the realization of their complete conquest by foreign powers.

The final two contributor Chapters—9 and 10—explore the new fears that emerged in a divided Germany in the wake of the Second World War. Although refashioned, these fears were also contextualized by the German-speaking world's Central European geography and a new fear of foreign incursion resulting from their position on the frontier of the Cold War. For West Germans and Austrians, fear of Soviet and communist invasion became a permanent mode of existence. But East Germany—if not all East Germans—similarly felt the pressure and danger from the West. These tensions were only highlighted by a permeable East-West border, which although ultimately walled was never fully sealed. Christoph Lorke examines aspects of this relational fear, exploring how Germans in the West and the East felt anxieties about poverty in the wake of war and during the resulting economic devastation. Such fears reflected competing political and economic systems that both sought to demonstrate their viability in comparison to the other.

At the book's end, Pierre-Frédéric Weber examines the legacy of the Second World War and Nazi aggression within West Germany as a rump state of the prewar Germany and West Germans' attempt to understand their new position in Europe. He shows how their place at the forefront of the Cold War and the unsettled "German question" affected inter-European and international relations from 1945 until the reunification in 1990. During the Cold War years, other Europeans projected some of their fears onto Germany: fear of loss (concerning territory), fear of asymmetry (in influence), and fear of satellization (regarding sovereignty). These fears were not evenly distributed. Location influenced territorial fear of Germany. Furthermore, these emotions were not present equally or constantly but rather went through rising and falling tides. However, along with fears of communism, and nuclear war and apocalypse, fear of Germany persisted in Europe. West Germans longed to separate themselves from Nazi crimes and a former Germany that had come to instantiate evil, a surrogate for the myriad fears and vexed emotions that dominated Cold War Europe. West Germany in turn took approached international politics cautiously, embracing a mirror fear, or fear of the fear. From Chancellors Konrad Adenauer to Helmut Kohl, West Germany's foreign policy was guided by other counties' potential emotional reactions resulting in a narrative that stressed the collective emotional structure of the political and societal "German Angst."

Together, the contributions to this collection articulate a concept of fear that is at once personal and local, and at the same time also socially and textually emergent; that is, it exists not merely as a reflection of individual anxieties but between people as a broader sociocultural construction. In essence, fear is understood as relational and deeply mediated. The task at hand has been to tease out, from the local and the particular, some of the manifestations of fear in the German-speaking world over the past four hundred years, and then to interrogate these constructions for commonalities. A tentative leitmotif of this collection has been the fear of incursion and consequent change—often perceived as loss, abrogation, or extermination of a political, social, or cultural order. At the heart of this collection, then, is the matter not only of how such orders may be perceived as threatened and potentially eliminated but also the concomitant question of how they are constituted. Such inquiries contribute more broadly to an engagement with the social, political, and cultural dynamics of Central Europe in an age of modernization and transformation.

Notes

1 For the use of "fantasy" in this context, see: Lyndal Roper, *Witch Craze: Terror and Fantasy in Baroque Germany* (New Haven, CT: Yale University Press, 2004). As an expository text to what is a very rich field, see for instance: Marvin Perry and Frederick M. Schweitzer, *Antisemitism: Myth and Hate from Antiquity to the Present* (New York: Palgrave, 2002), esp. chapters 1–3.
2 Michael Burleigh and Wolfgang Wippermann, *The Racial State: Germany 1933–1945* (Cambridge: Cambridge University Press, 1991), 37; Matthew Fitzpatrick, *Purging the Empire: Mass Expulsions in Germany, 1871–1914* (Oxford: Oxford University Press, 2015); Thomas J. Kehoe, "Control, Disempowerment, Fear, and Fantasy: Violent Criminality During the Early American Occupation of Germany, March-July 1945," *Australian Journal of Politics & History* 62, no. 4 (2016): 569.
3 Joanna Bourke, "Fear and Anxiety: Writing about Emotion in Modern History," *History Workshop Journal* 55 (Spring 2003): 112.
4 For instance, in the early modern German context, those contributions by Sigrun Haude and Jeffrey Chipps Smith, *Disaster, Death and the Emotions in the Shadow of the Apocalypse, 1400–1700*, ed. Jennifer Spinks and Charles Zika (London: Palgrave, 2016): 135–54; 247–72.

5 On reasons for German colonial expansion see: Shelley Baranowski, *Nazi Empire: German Colonialism and Imperialism from Bismarck to Hitler* (Cambridge: Cambridge University Press, 2011), 13; Sarah Friedrichsmeyer, Sara Lennox, and Susanne Zantop, *The Imperialist Imagination: German Colonialism and its Legacy* (Ann Arbor: University of Michigan Press, 1998), 9–10.

6 On Weimar see: Detlev Peukert, *The Weimar Republic: The Crisis of Classical Modernity* (New York: Hill & Wang, 1993), on the inflation, 61–2. On the rise of Nazism in relation to sovereignty see: Julia Roos, "Nationalism, Racism, and Propaganda in Early Weimar Germany: Contradictions in the Campaign Against the 'Black Horror on the Rhine,'" *German History* 30, no. 1 (2012): 73. On the impact of the post–First World War peace see: Bernhard Fulda, *Press and Politics in the Weimar Republic* (Oxford: Oxford University Press, 2009), 48–50.

7 On the Nazi Party's deliberate creation of fear in the streets and through propaganda see: Thomas J. Kehoe, "Fighting for Our Mutual Benefit: Understanding and Contextualizing the Intentions behind Nazi Propaganda for the Arabs during World War Two," *Journal of Genocide Research* 14, no. 2 (2012): 137–57; Daniel Siemens, *Stormtroopers: A New History of Hitler's Brownshirts* (New Haven, CT: Yale University Press, 2017); David Welch, ed., *Nazi Propaganda: The Power and Limitations* (London: Croom Helm, 1983). On the regime's use of violent and subversive policing see: Sheila Fitzpatrick and Robert Gellately, *Accusatory Practices: Denunciation in Modern European History, 1789–1989* (Chicago, IL: University of Chicago Press, 1997). Fear was also projected geopolitically and was key to Nazi foreign relations see: Mark Mazower, *Hitler's Empire. Nazi Rule in Occupied Europe* (London: Penguin Books, 2009); Richard Overy, *The Dictators: Hitler's Germany and Stalin's Russia* (London: Penguin Books, 2005). On postwar see: Edith Sheffer, "On Edge: Building the Border in East and West Germany," *Central European History* 40, no. 2 (2007): 307–39.

8 Burleigh and Wippermann, *Racial State*; Ian Hancock, *The Pariah Syndrome* (Ann Arbor, MI: Karoma, 1987); Gilad Margalit, *Germany and Its Gypsies* (Madison: University of Wisconsin Press, 2002).

9 Jeffrey Herf, *The Jewish Enemy: Nazi Propaganda during World War II and the Holocaust* (Cambridge: Belknap Press of Harvard University Press, 2006), 6.

10 Maria Tatar, *Lustmord: Sexual Murder in Weimar Germany* (Princeton, NJ: Princeton University Press, 1995); Adam Zamoyski, *Phantom Terror: Political Paranoia and the Creation of the Modern State, 1789–1848* (New York: Basic Books, 2015).

11 Jan Plamper and Benjamin Lazier, eds., *Fear across the Disciplines* (Pittsburgh, PA: University of Pittsburgh Press, 2012).

12 Michael Laffan and Max Weiss, eds., *Facing Fear: The History of an Emotion in Global Perspective* (Princeton, NJ: Princeton University Press, 2012).

13 Jean Delumeau, *Sin and Fear: The Emergence of a Western Guilt Culture, 13th–18th Centuries*, trans. Eric Nicholson (New York: St. Martin's Press, 1990); Zygmunt Bauman, *Liquid Fear* (Cambridge: Polity Press, 2006).
14 This term refers to: "The set of normative emotions and the official rituals, practices, and 'emotives' that express and inculcate them; a necessary underpinning of any stable political regime." William M. Reddy, *The Navigation of Feeling: A Framework for the History of Emotions* (Cambridge: Cambridge University Press, 2001), 129.
15 Delumeau, *Sin and Fear*, 556.
16 Norbert Elias, *Über den Prozeß der Zivilisation: Soziogenetische und psychogenetische Untersuchungen*, 7th ed. (Berlin: Suhrkamp, 1980), 2:7.
17 Peter N. Stearns, "Modern Patterns in Emotions History," in *Doing Emotions History*, ed. Peter N. Stearns and Susan J. Matt (Urbana: University of Illinois Press, 2014), 17–40.
18 Barbara H. Rosenwein, "Worrying about Emotions in History," *American Historical Review* 107 (June 2002): 821–45.
19 Rosenwein, "Worrying about Emotions," 842.
20 Stearns, "Modern Patterns," 19.
21 Susan J. Matt, "Recovering the Invisible: Methods for the Historical Study of the Emotions," in *Doing Emotions History*, ed. Peter N. Stearns and Susan J. Matt (Urbana: University of Illinois Press, 2014), 48–51.
22 Matt, "Recovering the Invisible," 43.
23 Rosenwein, "Worrying about Emotions," 833.
24 Joanna Bourke, *Fear: A Cultural History* (London: Virago Press, 2005), 354.
25 Jennifer Spinks and Charles Zika, "Introduction: Rethinking Disaster and Emotions, 1400–1700," in *Disaster, Death and the Emotions*, 5. The nexus between emotions and violence further highlights the somatic and performative dimensions of fear: Susan Broomhall and Sarah Finn, eds., *Violence end Emotions in Early Modern Europe* (London: Routledge, 2016).
26 William Reddy's conception of "emotives" works well to articulate the fluid nature of emotions and to emphasise their emergent quality. Reddy proposes that "emotives" (i.e., emotional expressions) encapsulate both performative and constative dimensions of utterances. An emotive is thus a speech act that "both describes ... and changes ... the world, because emotional expression has an exploratory and a self-altering effect on the activated thought material of emotion." Reddy, *Navigation of Feeling*, 128.
27 Ute Frevert et al., eds., *Emotional Lexicons: Continuity and Change in the Vocabulary of Feeling, 1700–2000* (Oxford: Oxford University Press).
28 Johann Heinrich Zedler, *Grosses vollständiges Universal Lexicon aller Wissenschafften und Künste* (Leipzig, 1732–54), 9:2324–5.

29 Zedler, *Grosses vollständiges*, supp. 1: 1476.
30 Ted Honderich, ed., *The Oxford Companion to Philosophy* (Oxford: Oxford University Press, 1995), 35; Arnim Regenbogen and Uwe Meyer, eds., *Wörterbuch der philosophischen Begriffe* (Hamburg: Felix Meiner Verlag, 2013), 43–4; Bourke, *Fear*, 189–90. This distinction is also made in the context of Freudian psychoanalysis, in which *Angst* is a feeling of unease brought about through the generalized threat of castration. See, for instance: Peter Widmer, "Angst und Fucht," in *Angst: Dimensionen eines Gefühls*, ed. Thomas Kisser et al. (Munich: Fink Verlag, 2011), 13–24. This edited collection, unfortunately, offers very little sense of the historical distinction between the terms in the German-speaking context specifically.
31 Bourke, *Fear*, 189–90.
32 Bauman, *Liquid Fear*, 17.
33 Ibid., 20.

2

Political Fear during the Wars of Louis XIV: The Danger of Becoming French

Kirsten L. Cooper

In late June 1672, the cold, salty waters of the North Sea inundated the Netherlands just east of Amsterdam, an act of desperation and fear that resonated across Europe, not least in Germany.¹ The Dutch, who had spent several centuries developing a complex levee system in an effort to keep water *out*, now intentionally opened their dikes. For, on the other side of the water line, a much more terrifying enemy than Mother Nature waited: the armies of Louis XIV. Just five years earlier Europe had watched as Louis's troops marched into the Spanish Netherlands, launching the first of five European wars and numerous international crises that would mark the Sun King's extraordinarily belligerent personal reign.² France was at war for at least thirty of the last forty-eight years of Louis XIV's life and much of this belligerence targeted the Holy Roman Empire.³ Already in 1667, the imperial diplomat François-Paul de Lisola called for a unified European resistance to Louis XIV's expansionism, warning that the monarch would never be satisfied with "the bare conquest of some provinces."⁴ As news of the invasion and flooding of the Netherlands reached German audiences, the fulfillment of Lisola's prophesy and fear of the Sun King's insatiable ambition seemed chillingly real.⁵

Louis XIV's military power reached its height in the 1670s and 1680s. During the War of Devolution (1667–8) and Franco-Dutch War (1672–8), French armies achieved massive and swift victories. The Sun King emerged from the latter conflict in particular at the height of his power and prestige—with his reputation as an unpredictable and ambitious foe solidly established for the fraught decade to follow.⁶ Between the end of the Franco-Dutch War in 1678 and the start of the Nine Years' War in 1688, a string of international crises occurred that fell outside of the recognized boundaries of declared war.

France pursued an extremely controversial policy of "reunions"—the seizure and annexation of claimed territories on France's German border, most notably Strasbourg (1681) and Luxembourg (1684).[7] The shock of these reunions was multiplied by France's refusal to send aid against the Ottoman invasion and Siege of Vienna (1681–3).[8] In 1684 France and the empire signed a twenty-year truce that few in Germany believed would last. In 1685, Louis revoked the Edict of Nantes, officially outlawing Protestantism in France, justifying the persecution and forced conversions that his dragoons had been inflicting, and horrifying protestant and catholic powers alike.[9] In 1686 numerous imperial powers signaled their anxiety about France's future plans when they formed the League of Augsburg—a defensive alliance widely understood as a precaution against future French aggression. Finally, in 1688, German fears were fulfilled when Louis attacked the Palatinate in a "defensive" strike that quickly brought the empire into the Nine Years' War (1688–97).[10]

Princes, armies, and pamphleteers across the empire rose up in opposition to this belligerence, raising a veritable roar of criticism, protest, and outrage.[11] The extent of Imperial unity in countering France was, in fact, remarkable. The Holy Roman Empire, a complicated and confusing mass of overlapping jurisdictions, territories, and levels of authority, was nominally ruled by the Holy Roman Emperor, the Austrian Habsburg, Leopold I.[12] The position of emperor did not, however, guarantee unquestioning support from imperial estates. The empire was an extremely divided entity religiously, politically, and historically and support for the emperor could shift as quickly as the winds of political interest. When confronted with the looming threat of Louis XIV, therefore, the emperor needed to continuously campaign for allies and support within the empire. Political pamphlets were an effective way to do this, and, in the face of the Sun King's repeated onslaughts, more imperial powers lined up behind the Habsburgs than ever before or after.[13]

Both the strength of Imperial coalitions and the number and intensity of anti-French political pamphlets speak to the immense fear of Louis XIV.[14] Pamphleteers harnessed this fear as a way to reach beyond religion, historical loyalties, and dynastic interest to try to unite the fractured empire. A variety of specific anxieties can be gleaned from these pamphleteers' arguments, namely the fear of military conquest, fear of religious persecution, and fear of political ruin. Each of these was tied to specific historical or contemporary developments and embellished with vitriol and polemic. But this rhetoric was more than just a reflection of prevailing concerns; it was an attempt to intentionally stoke fear. In the midst of the open conflict of the 1670s, especially, pamphleteers mobilized fear of conquest, persecution, and destruction as a political tool to garner diplomatic and military support against Louis XIV.

During the 1680s, the ostensible peace between France and the Holy Roman Empire made it more difficult to frame fear-based arguments on the threat of looming invasion and conquest. During this decade of anxiety and insecurity, another of the pamphleteers' strategies proved more useful. Anti-French pamphleteers did not simply exploit existing anxieties of military defeat but also invented a new threat—the danger of becoming French. The conflicts of Louis XIV's reign were undeniably dynastic in nature. German pamphleteers, however, turned these crises into a tale about the danger of French cultural infiltration occurring right under the noses of unsuspecting Germans. By speaking French, consuming French commodities, and adopting French ways, these pamphleteers argued, imperial subjects were aiding Louis XIV in his cultural—and, therefore, his military—warfare. In part, this rhetoric was a response to the actual increase in consumption of French culture and goods that occurred in the late seventeenth century. It was also, however, a conscious attempt to mobilize the member states of the empire through a fear that conveniently sidestepped divisive questions of religion and dynastic politics. While just one of several rhetorical strategies used during the open warfare of the 1670s, the rhetoric of cultural infiltration gained importance during the fraught 1680s. The narrative of pervasive, covert corruption could maintain fear of, and therefore opposition to, France during a time of crisis and precarious "peace." This fear—the danger of becoming French—appealed to a projected sense of cultural and linguistic "Germanness" that was inextricably linked with the future of the empire as a political system. If Germans allowed themselves to be transformed into Frenchmen, French political and military conquest would be inevitable.

This study addresses fear in two ways: the actual fear of Louis XIV's power and ambition, and the political manipulation of fear by pamphleteers and their backers. The first certainly motivated and underpinned the second, but the second was more than just a reflection of the first. Most studies of fear in early modern Europe focus either on personal manifestations of fear in response to daily and supernatural threats or on attempts to assuage fear in a variety of political and theological ways. Fear is discussed as a fact of life that leaders needed to manage to avoid a mass panic.[15] The manipulation of fear for political ends is seemingly only discussed in relation to modern political climates.[16] This is an unnecessary distinction. Instead, as Joanna Bourke has argued, it is more useful to view fear as an historical object of inquiry with a multivalent nature. While certainly physiological and individual, fear can also be understood as a "power relation," mediating within and between different groups. It is important not just to locate and categorize fears but also to ask "what is fear *doing*?"[17] The current chapter analyzes the creation of a discourse of fear in order to achieve specific political goals in early modern Germany. This was not just an example of felt fear in Germany, but was a project of cultivating and harnessing fear as a political tool in the service of dynastic and geopolitical interests. As the Dutch well knew in 1672, the threat of Louis XIV was quite real. But the fear that he inspired across the Holy Roman Empire was in many ways the creation of those confronting the threat, not of the threat itself.

Part I: Reflecting Fear

No matter one's opinion of the Sun King or his government, Louis undoubtedly cut an imposing figure in the political imaginary of early modern Europe.[18] His state apparatus pioneered new strategies of bureaucratic efficiency and effectiveness.[19] He engaged in a multifaceted representational campaign to promote images of his power, wealth, and glory, within and beyond France.[20] This image making was supported by an unparalleled and exceptionally large military.[21] The king was not only ambitious for victory and *gloire*, but he had the military power to achieve it. This combination generated anxiety in the Holy Roman Empire, which political pamphleteers seized upon for their own purposes.[22]

The pamphlet as a genre constituted a fascinating medium that was simultaneously public, official, and usually anonymous. Common since the earliest days of the printing press, political pamphlets served a variety of functions, from simple news reports to sophisticated juridical argumentation.[23] Although difficult to define in terms of form or style, they were uniquely focused on treating contemporary events, particularly in relation to politics, religion, and society.[24] While some tended toward the literary, the majority employed more programmatic argumentation that stitched together a variety of rhetorical strategies. They were intended to be persuasive and polemical—political tools to sway public opinion—and they provided the sort of editorializing that most newspapers and periodicals of the time lacked.[25] The vast majority of pamphlets were published anonymously, with neither location nor publisher. They could be printed on behalf of a ruler, printer, or private individual, from within court circles or beyond.[26] Anonymity allowed for much wider freedom of expression. In contrast to a royal decree or diplomatic correspondence, there was no need to maintain the façade of respect and civility in an anonymous pamphlet. The plausible deniability that stemmed from unclear origins meant pamphleteers could get away with invective wholly unacceptable from more official channels. This translated into more creative argumentation and a wider variety of political rhetoric, as different authors seized on whatever they thought most provocative and persuasive.

It is impossible to say exactly how many pamphlets were published and circulated during the period, but the surviving examples far outpace the incidence of similar sources for any conflict until the Seven Years' War (1756–63).[27] Researching in the *Bibliothèque national de France*, Jeffrey K. Sawyer identified 4,503 pamphlets from the Sun King's reign, most of which were overwhelmingly critical of France. In a survey of eight hundred pamphlets from Dutch libraries, P. J. W. van Malssen found only two or three that contained flattering depictions of Louis XIV. These publication numbers were massive for the period and their consistent condemnation of the French attests to the political anxiety that Louis's belligerence caused.[28] These numbers also tell us something about the audience for these pamphlets. While it is almost impossible to define the exact readership of these pamphlets, from the limited documents that do exist in the imperial archives, it is clear that the Viennese court—and presumably the courts of its allies—put significant effort in granting print privileges, disseminating information, even commissioning authors in order to target politically influential classes across the empire.[29] But pamphlets also reached farther. Analysis of content and style reveals that while some specifically addressed an elite segment of politically important readers, many others aimed at a more general reading public. Pamphlets were a profitable item and constituted a form of popular literature that was accessible to a broad swathe of the literate public, which was relatively large in early modern Germany.[30] Pamphlets were the closest thing to written "mass media" that the late seventeenth century had.[31]

A variety of specific fears can be read from the arguments used by these pamphleteers, all of which were tied to real threats and contemporary crises. The most straightforward was the fear of military conquest. Louis's massive armies and early military successes gave him a fearsome reputation. Pamphleteers both reflected and stoked this reputation by attributing to Louis an insatiable ambition for territorial conquest. Authors accused him of attempting to achieve a dreaded "universal monarchy" by devouring Europe one piece at a time.[32] Even when his immediate goals seemed limited to one territory or one power, "the terrible mass of their gold … and the vast … war preparations" hinted at much more extensive aspirations.[33] No one, they argued, should feel secure in their immunity to the French threat.

To make matters worse, French conquest would not be a benevolent takeover. France "tyrannized, raped, looted and burned" their way through even territories they professed to be allied with.[34] One pamphlet from 1674 recounted story after bloodcurdling story illustrating the "thousands of heinous cruelties" that French troops committed.[35] With horrifying detail the author told of rape by as many as fifty soldiers at a time, the pillage and wanton waste of precious food and resources, destruction of entire villages, and the murder and barbarous mutilation of even those considered the most innocent and feeble of inhabitants.[36] A pamphlet from 1689 described how "a heavily pregnant woman, whom [the French] had stabbed, and whose womb, and with it her unborn child, they had ripped out, was found dead next to her husband," a poor "fisherman from Heidelberg."[37] These horrifying anecdotes, repeated as they were over the course of multiple conflicts, were more than enough to terrify readers on their own. But combined with the prevailing rhetoric of Louis's insatiable ambition and the reality of his immense military power, the effect would have been tenfold. What fear was "doing" here was making the French threat into one of unmatched terror that had to be resisted or the horrors would never stop.

Pamphlets also reflected a set of religious fears. Writers continuously criticized Louis XIV—the "sworn enemy of Christ"—for impiety, specifically his close relations with the Ottoman Empire and seemingly zealous promotion of their designs on Christian Europe.[38] As one pamphlet declared, the French king had made himself "a lovely triple alliance [with] Mohammed, the Most Christian Louis the Great and the devil."[39] Another accused France of being the devil's "earthly paradise," where he had tutored a young Louis XIV.[40] Pamphleteers argued that Louis's impiety posed a threat to all Christendom, particularly in the form of religious persecution. France, a Catholic power, was unsurprisingly seen as a threat to Protestants in the empire, but it was not just Protestants who needed to fear, argued countless pamphleteers. The Sun King posed a religious threat that went beyond confessional division. Like the feared Ottoman Turk, Louis XIV, the "Most-Christian" enemy of Christendom, did not differentiate in his destruction and persecution, harming Catholics just as much as Protestants. This rhetorical strategy turned the Sun King into a biconfessional enemy of all "good" Christians, and, therefore, an enemy of all in the religiously divided empire.[41]

The religious issue also conjured up a concrete historical fear: the memory of bloodshed and disaster caused by religious infighting during the Thirty Years' War (1618–48). This conflict, which has been described as "the most traumatic period in the history of Germany" prior to 1939, was only a few decades gone.[42] As pamphleteers continuously reminded their audiences, the Thirty Years' War was a horrid internal conflict in Germany, the flames of which France gleefully stoked to serve its own interests.[43] Pamphleteers drew on this cultural memory when they lamented the continued religious divisions in the empire—though not, this time, from an evangelical standpoint. Rather, pamphleteers viewed religious bickering as a political weakness that Louis exploited. Spreading "the seeds of disunity" was, after all, one of the many nefarious "stratagems" of the French state.[44] All across the empire, pamphleteers argued, "misunderstandings and fear tear apart the bond of Christian love and society." If allowed to continue, this disunity would "bring the country and people to ruin and death," just as it had "in the confused scramble [of the] Thirty Years' War."[45] Such divisions, pamphleteers argued, could deal a mortal blow to the empire as a whole.[46]

Whether via military conquest or exploitation of internal divisions, pamphleteers repeatedly portrayed Louis XIV as an existential threat to the empire. One author declared his "unwavering opinion, that the French king ... upon splitting off for himself one piece of the empire, already imagined swallowing up control of [all] Germany."[47] Others warned that between Louis's ambition and their own "blindness," the empire would soon fall into "French slavery."[48] These prognostications were extreme—purposefully exaggerated to elicit a strong reaction—but they were loosely based in contemporary realities. Pamphleteers reflected, but also stoked, the fears that French designs generated. Despite their best efforts, however, biconfessional religious arguments could only be so effective and the threat of immediate military conquest evaporated whenever another peace was signed. As Louis's ambition and belligerence continued, in a variety of new forms, pamphleteers needed a different approach. They needed a tool that could bridge the cracks in the empire as well as the vicissitudes of war and diplomacy. They found it in the spectre of cultural infiltration.

Part II: The Danger of Becoming French

The threat of cultural infiltration was particularly disconcerting precisely because it was nebulous, pervasive, and heretofore unrecognized. Consumption of French goods and culture, pamphleteers argued, was ubiquitous in the empire—"one thought, spoke ... desired, saw, heard, smelled and felt nothing but French"—and it was extremely dangerous.[49] Rhetoric against the consumption of French culture and goods presented the issue as a deadly cocktail of "French poison," brewed with three main, interrelated components.[50] Pamphleteers wrote specifically against the mania for French fashion, the preference for France as a destination of Grand Tours (*Kavalierstouren*), and the prevalence of French hobbies in the empire. But this was far more than an issue of taste or cultural chauvinism; it was a question of the future of Germany and the Holy Roman Empire as a political system. Louis's nefarious webs, pamphleteers argued, were infiltrating the courts, communities, even souls of entirely unsuspecting Germans, paving the way for future French domination.

One pamphleteer decried fashion as the wearing of "oft changing, vain, asinine, regularly promiscuous clothing … that one adopts and loves [simply] because the conceited worldlings invent and love it from one moment to the next."[51] This race to constantly keep up with what was new and best seemed like an appallingly frivolous vice to critics. Numerous authors complained about the "peacocks" that strutted around "dressed all in French gallantries and trinkets."[52] The Germans had become so "drunk" on this "bewitching *délicatesse*" that they felt the need to array themselves "even more splendidly and luxuriously than the native [French]," no doubt leading to even higher expenses as they tried to outdress their neighbors.[53] The mania was such that anything French was seized upon, whether "it was seemly and becoming or not."[54] Meanwhile, the French were supposedly fully aware of the damage their fashions were causing. "It is well known," explained one author, "that the Germans always want to have what is new."[55] And so the French "changed and altered" their fashions "almost every month," intentionally keeping the Germans enthralled to French "vanities."[56] According to many writers, the infiltration of French fashions was a concerted effort by Louis XIV to corrupt and enfeeble Germany, while ensuring that German gold continued to flow into French coffers. Cultural fear was also political.

Another way that the French purportedly seduced unsuspecting Germans was through the Grand Tour in France.[57] Pamphleteers seized this "reckless" practice as an explanation for the corruption of German youth.[58] One uniquely literary pamphlet told the story of Parmenio, a hapless 16-year-old who was determined to travel to France in order to become a refined, gallant, gentleman. His parents were not enthused. His mother encouraged him instead to join the military and defend the empire, while his father, subtly named Germanicus, decried the "contemporary abuse" of tours in France. These travels only "led the French Gallantry-Devil into our Germany."[59] Far from contributing to the enrichment of young Germans, their visits to France only encouraged luxury and indolence. Germanicus argued that young Germans should instead visit any number of noble, German cities: "In such places a German can see and get to know his fatherland far better than in France."⁶⁰ But alas, in France they only encountered ruin. "Judge, then, a young person," warned one pamphleteer, "once the spirit is taken in early by such vanities, only rarely do his thoughts then turn to anything proper."⁶¹ Such poor souls could find no remedy to "discharge and drive out the French poison from German blood." France was a "labyrinth" that trapped all who entered.⁶²

French hobbies and pastimes were some of the many traps that ensnared unsuspecting Germans, especially dancing and swordplay. Pamphleteers portrayed these activities as useless vanities that distracted Germans from more important pursuits. While on their Grand Tours, young Germans were far more concerned with studying "French swordplay and dance manual[s]" than with learning any practical knowledge.⁶³ Indeed, as soon as Parmenio reached the relatively unsupervised freedom of Paris, he decided that he had no use for all of his tutor's planned lessons and turned solely to "a bit of French dancing," plus his dancing master's three conveniently attractive daughters.⁶⁴ But, argued the pamphleteers, one could learn to dance just as well in Germany and "save … many thousands every year" in the process.⁶⁵ The same objections were made against the affinity for swordplay. If one insisted on wasting all one's time on mastering the art of sparring "*à la Françoise*" instead of on more practical matters, then the empire already had a surfeit of masters from whom one could learn, and even learn better.⁶⁶ There was no need to go to France or pay for a French instructor to come to Germany.

Even worse, the affinity for swordplay led to a penchant for dueling, portrayed as an absurd and dangerous practice endemic among the "hot-headed" French.⁶⁷ Parmenio learned the dangers of dueling the hard way. First, he was stabbed by his adversary in the arm and left permanently lame. Then, he stabbed his own eye out. Finally, another man hit him so hard in the mouth that he lost his front teeth—leaving him with "a great deformity" whereby the young man resembled "a harried wolf."⁶⁸ When the partially lame, disfigured Parmenio finally returned home to his father, Germanicus could hardly contain his disgust:

> Had you gone to war, and risked your healthy limbs there, it would have been only to the credit of you and me. Instead, I sent a healthy and capable child to France and a half-mutilated and undutiful reprobate returned home to me, which brings neither myself nor the fatherland any advantage or joy.⁶⁹

Had Parmenio returned from war with the same wounds, he would have been celebrated as a hero who had sacrificed his own well-being for the greater good of the empire. Instead, Parmenio chose debauchery and corruption and rendered himself incapable of ever fulfilling his duties, to his father or his fatherland. As a stand-in for an entire generation of supposedly French-obsessed youth, Parmenio had brought harm not just to himself but also to the entire empire.

These arguments against cultural consumption were increasingly connected to an imagined core of "Germanness" that seemed to be under threat.[70] French pursuits distracted from religious devotion and piety.[71] Young Germans were completely ignorant of even the most basic knowledge of their own fatherland.[72] Pamphleteers raised the alarm against the large influx of French dancing, language, and fencing masters, not to mention tailors, dressmakers, wigmakers, and cooks. The blind and unsuspecting Germans allowed these French "agents" and "spies" into their courts, their homes, and their families, to spread corruption and pursue the interests of Louis XIV.[73] Germany was struck by a "consuming illness" that threatened its security and freedom.[74] There was no other explanation for why Germany was constantly the victim of invasion and depredation than their "military and discipline are overwhelmed by so many weaknesses, than that the German youth by and large apply themselves to such weak-hearted exercises and other French vanities."[75] This trickery was subtle but pervasive, and through it France had already pierced farther into the heart of the empire than ever before.[76] Just like marauding French troops or diplomatic intrigues, this was a strategy of attack by Louis XIV. Cultural infiltration was simply warfare by other means.

Pamphleteers argued that Germans were literally *becoming* French due to this cultural infiltration. Whereas Germans were once virtuous, brave, earnest, and constant by nature, they were being transformed into frivolous, volatile, restless Frenchmen.[77] The French language was not just supplanting German but also destroying it.[78] Fashion was not just a problem of expense but was also a question of character. Pamphleteers warned that "foreign clothes become foreign mores, customs and vices."[79] Clothing "turned [one] from a German into a Frenchman" not just from an external perspective "but also in the soul."[80] Running through all of this rhetoric was the contention that Germans were different from the French in every way. To imitate people with such a vastly different character was a dangerous idea: "As long as Germany stuck to its old German virtue and valor, it flourished in great power and happiness. Since it turned to foreign, especially French, vanities and similar lascivious indulgences, it has become more and more enfeebled and almost contemptible."[81] In the words of another writer, "the old German respectability and valor has been many times frozen over."[82] One could barely even recognize true Germans in the empire anymore for all the "German-Frenchmen" that were running about.

The transformation into Frenchmen held serious ramifications. According to pamphleteers, cultural conquest was just the first step in military and political conquest. And, after 1681, this seemed more than an idle threat. In that year, Louis XIV forcibly annexed Strasbourg.[83] This annexation provoked outrage and anguish across the empire, but numerous writers saw this as the inevitable outcome of France's successful cultural offensive.[84] In the words of one writer, "bit by bit the French humour, customs, language, clothing, and other enticing webs of domination slipped into the city and impressed their way into the souls of residents, until their former standing and old German character fairly vanished or was completely forgotten." The Strasbourgers had been so wholly corrupted and transformed that they were practically French already, which, the same author argued, was why the city capitulated so quickly. The change of rule "had very little significance" to a city already French in all other ways.[85]

The use of cultural invasion to lead to military conquest had supposedly been France's plan all along:

> This vigilant and power-hungry crown [Louis XIV] knew very well that the city of Strasbourg [was] a German city, and lay within the borders of the [Holy] Roman Empire, but that the souls of the residents both high and low were mostly French-inclined ... they therefore would not protest very strongly when one held out to them the yoke of French dominion ... that is why France had been concerned for quite some time already ... with how it could acquire this beautiful jewel and splendid citadel of the [Holy] Roman Empire of the German Nation ... To this end it [France] used all imaginable means, at times violent, at times gentle and coaxing, to fulfill its wish.[86]

The French had coveted the strong and strategic city for a long time, but knew that they could not acquire it by any legal or straightforward means, and the strong, German fortress would not have fallen in the face of sheer force. Instead, the French set about a program of infiltration and cultural corruption until the loyalties of the city were so changed and their old German virtues so polluted that the French could take it almost without a fight. What had worked so well in Strasbourg, argued these pamphleteers, was already underway elsewhere in the empire. They warned that "language, customs, and clothing are the first foundation stones of foreign rule," and the French were well on their way to solidifying the first three in Germany.[87] The issue of cultural viability was inextricably linked with the future of the empire as a political system. The fear of cultural infiltration argued that Louis needed to be stopped before his seductive and enchanting strategies came to fruition elsewhere.

Part III: Inventing Fear

This rhetoric of cultural infiltration is remarkable and surprising. This was not an exaggerated reflection of a legitimate contemporary threat or historical memory, but an invention, constructed by the pens of political pamphleteers. As tempting as it is to think of Louis XIV as an all-powerful puppet master pushing French culture to neutralize German resistance, the increasing dominance of French culture was not a carefully orchestrated government plot.[88] Moreover, arguments for cultural invasion and national corruption seem entirely incongruous in the prenationalist seventeenth century. The wars of Louis XIV were nothing but dynastic in nature, three of the four major conflicts stemmed from issues of contested royal successions, and Louis's reign is considered the zenith of divine right monarchy and theories of absolute government in France.[89] Though seemingly out of place, the rhetoric of cultural infiltration was neither an anachronistic anomaly nor "protonationalist" agitation. So how can this rhetoric be explained? To answer this question, we must return to Joanna Bourke's point and think about what the fear of cultural infiltration *did*.[90] First, it allowed pamphleteers—and the political interests they represented—to reach across the internal fractures of a divided empire by appealing to a shared sense of "Germanness," in a way that religious fear could not. Second, this rhetoric became even more useful during the decade of ostensible peace between 1678 and 1688, when the lack of open warfare closed off the easy tropes of imminent invasion and conquest. This rhetoric emerged in response to specific contextual triggers and filled a unique need for those opposing Louis XIV.

Like arguments about religious persecution or military devastation, the rhetoric of cultural infiltration did have a basis in contemporary reality—even if that basis was more tenuous than the others. Since around the mid-seventeenth century, desire for French goods and culture increased rapidly. Even in Vienna, in the thick of war with France, such consumption continued unabated.[91] This was the beginning of a trend that would last through the eighteenth century and beyond.[92] To a seventeenth-century observer, it may well have seemed that Germans across the empire were suddenly obsessed with all things French. But pamphleteers exploited this idea, embellishing the observable into a tale of intrigue, subversion, complicity, and impending doom. And they did so because it served a very particular use.

The Holy Roman Empire was always an extremely divided entity. Composed of well over fifteen hundred semiautonomous states, principalities, cities, and religious territories, politics was always a tricky affair.[93] By the late seventeenth century, certain constellations of dynastic rivalries and power political interests were common, not least being a consistent resistance to growing Habsburg power. Even against the *Reichsfeind*, Louis, a cast of usual suspects continued to refuse to support Habsburg interests.[94] These political divisions were often enhanced by the deep religious fractures that cut across the empire. In the aftermath of the Thirty Years' War and the Westphalian settlement, it was clear to most onlookers that religious unification was unrealistic. But fears of persecution, forced conversion, and loss of rights were real concerns. As much as some pamphleteers tried to make their religious arguments biconfessional, suspicions and confessional antagonisms continued to exist. Between the rock of imperial power politics and the hard place of religious divisions, uniting the empire behind anything was a challenge.[95]

With the rhetoric of "Germanness," however, the pamphleteers found a trope that could ostensibly unite imperial inhabitants. There was already a long conceptual history of the empire as a German institution that this rhetoric drew upon, which allowed pamphleteers to appeal to imperial audiences regardless of their particular family, history, confession, or class.[96] Without denying these other categories of identification, the rhetoric of cultural infiltration urged inhabitants of the empire to put aside their quarrels and their suspicions for the specific and limited task of countering Louis XIV. To follow the logic of the arguments, if they allowed their shared "Germanness" to be destroyed, the entire structure of the empire would inevitably crumble. This would then expose all to the whims and cruelties of Louis's tyranny. Protestants could be sure of merciless persecution, while Catholics would have to live under an irreligious anti-Christ. All imperial states would fall one by one, becoming nothing more than slaves to France. In short, the threat of cultural infiltration was the fear that encompassed all fears. If the members of the empire did not put aside their differences and come together as Germans to protect their fatherland against the French threat, then they would all be doomed.[97]

This rhetoric became especially useful during the period of intense political anxiety from the end of the Franco-Dutch War (1678) to the start of the Nine Years' War (1688). This era posed an interesting problem for opponents of Louis XIV, as there were no major declared Franco-Imperial conflicts. There were, however, a series of other crises that both created intense anxiety about Louis XIV's future plans and required the maintenance of anti-French support in a period of nominal peace. The Ottoman invasion was cast as the work of France, to distract Europe while Louis XIV picked off choice imperial territories as "reunions." Powers across Europe were horrified at Louis's persecution of French

Protestants. Even a truce, signed in 1684, did little to ease suspicions of French intentions, illustrated by the formation of the League of Augsburg just two years later. Finally, all of these fears were legitimized when Louis attacked the Palatinate with little justification and no warning in 1688, sparking the empire's entry into the Nine Years' War.[98] Each of these events played an important role in consolidating critiques of Louis as unscrupulous and insatiable.

The lack of open conflict during this decade, far from assuaging fears of France, only contributed to an atmosphere of anxiety over when—and most importantly how—the Sun King would strike next. Until the 1680s, the Sun King's aggression had manifested itself within the understandable context of outright warfare. Now, however, he pursued his interests by a variety of less straightforward, less predictable, and, therefore, far more "nefarious" means. Pamphlets urged readers not to be fooled by "the golden fruits of peace" that France so temptingly offered.[99] It was important for the opponents of France to remain at the ready, which meant keeping the fires of opposition smoldering. The fear of cultural infiltration satisfied this need. During the Franco-Dutch War, pamphlets arguing against cultural infiltration formed only one piece of a larger discourse of outrage and polemic. During a time of open conflict, fears could just as easily be stoked by stories of violence and depravity.[100] During the 1680s, however, these other rhetorical strategies largely disappeared, while the rhetoric of cultural infiltration not only remained but also increased in severity and depth. The argument for cultural infiltration was uniquely capable of maintaining opposition and a heightened state of fear during a period of ostensible peace. Pamphleteers argued that after failing to achieve his ambitious desires through military might alone, the French king had simply enlisted culture as a foot soldier to sneak behind enemy lines and sabotage imperial defenses from within. For a king already accused of using any means possible to achieve his desires, hiding behind dressmakers and language tutors was hardly surprising.

Anti-French rhetoric mobilized by political pamphleteers was both a reflection and a manipulation of fear. Louis XIV and his massive armies posed a serious threat. It was fear of this monarch's capabilities and ambition that united powers across Europe and in the empire time and time again. But Louis's opponents in the empire also understood the value of fear as a motivational tool. Countless pamphlets told horrifying tales of bloodshed, destruction, persecution, infiltration, sabotage, and defeat in order to spur military and diplomatic support. On top of that, when faced with difficult divisions in the empire and a lack of outright conflict, political pamphleteers constructed a new source of fear: the danger of becoming French.

This cultivation of fear fits what political theorist Corey Robin has called "political fear." He defined political fear as "a people's felt apprehension of some harm to their collective well-being," which becomes "a political tool, an instrument ... created and sustained by political leaders or activists who stand to gain something from it."[101] To be effective, political fear "always preys upon some real threat"—no matter how tenuously—and portrays the threat as an "intractable foe" threatening the very foundation of a community or society.[102] The discourse of cultural conquest did precisely this. From a real foundation in the increase in consumption of French culture and goods, pamphleteers extrapolated a discourse of fear that encompassed a narrative of covert infiltration, moral and political decay, and unwitting complicity. According to pamphleteers, cultural infiltration posed a grave threat to all things German, and, therefore, the future of the empire. The only solution to this intractable problem was to forsake the worship of French culture and unite behind the Habsburgs in the true "interests of Germany."[103]

Thinking about fear as a political tool, a strategy appreciated and used by early modern powers, can help scholars better understand the arguments and rhetoric found in the public political sphere of the late seventeenth century. It makes as little sense to read this rhetoric as nationalist agitation *avant la lettre* as it does to assume it reflects a dire fear that the donning of a French wig would spell the utter destruction of the Holy Roman Empire. Instead, this remarkable rhetoric needs to be read in terms of the political calculations made by the pamphleteers and their backers. Although these ideas were, of course, founded upon significant social and cultural realities, pamphlet propaganda was also warfare by other means. The decisions, strategies, and arguments made therein had a lot riding on them—from justifying military action, to countering French arguments, to mobilizing imperial powers who could just as easily have remained neutral or joined the other side. The early modern period was not simply an age of fearfully cowering populations beset by superstition and disease, while those in power did everything they could to forestall mass panic. Governments and pamphleteers fully appreciated the rich complexities of fear and the political potential it held. In the face of Louis XIV, fear did quite a lot.

Notes

1 Louis XIV's invasion in 1672 and its dire repercussions came to be known as the *Rampjaar* or "Year of Disaster" in the Netherlands, see: Jonathan Israel, *The Dutch Republic: Its Rise, Greatness, and Fall 1477–1806* (Oxford: Clarendon Press, 1995),

796–806. The use of the term "Germany" for the early modern period has, in the past, been controversial to some scholars who argue that the term only applies after 1871. See for example: James J. Sheehan, "What Is German History? Reflections on the Role of the Nation in German History and Historiography," *Journal of Modern History* 53 (1981): 1–23. "Germany" was, however, used synonymously to refer to the Holy Roman Empire throughout the early modern period, a practice that I follow here.

2 See: John A. Lynn, *The Wars of Louis XIV, 1667–1714* (London: Longman, 1999).

3 Major European conflicts of Louis XIV's personal reign include the War of Devolution (1667–8), the Franco-Dutch War (1672–8), the War of the Reunions (1683–4), the Nine Years' War (1688–97), and the War of the Spanish Succession (1701–15).

4 François-Paul de Lisola, *The Buckler of State and Justice against the Design Manifestly Discovered of the Universal Monarchy, under the Vain Pretext of the Queen of France, Her Pretensions* (London: Printed by James Flesher for Richard Royston, 1667), 6.

5 On opinions of Louis in Europe see: Hubert Gillot, *Le Règne de Louis XIV et l'opinion publique en Allemagne* (Paris: Honoré Champion, 1914); P. J. W. van Malssen, *Louis XIV d'après les pamphlets répandus en Hollande* (Amsterdam: H.J. Paris, 1937); Jean Schillinger, *Les pamphlétaires allemands et la France de Louis XIV* (Berlin: Peter Lang, 1999). Tony Claydon and Charles-Édouard Levillain, eds., *Louis XIV Outside In: The Image of the Sun King Beyond France, 1661–1715* (New York: Routledge, 2016).

6 Ian Dunlop, *Louis XIV* (New York: St. Martin's Press, 1999), 304; Lynn, *Wars of Louis XIV*, 161; Martin Wrede, *Ludwig XIV: Der Kriegsherr aus Versailles*, (Darmstadt: Theiss, 2015), 68, 149–50.

7 Lynn, *Wars of Louis XIV*, 161–71.

8 The invasion began in 1681. For more on the Siege of Vienna see: John Stoye, *The Siege of Vienna*, new ed. (Edinburgh: Birlinn, 2006).

9 Roy L. McCullough, *Coercion, Conversion and Counterinsurgency in Louis XIV's France* (Leiden: Brill, 2007), 125–80. Stories of these atrocities circulated throughout Europe in pamphlets such as *Le Dragon Missionaire: Or, the Dragoon Turn'd Apostle. Being a Dialogue between a French Protestant-Gentleman, and a French Dragoon: Wherein the New Way of Converting Hereticks by Dragoons is very Lively and Truly Represented* ... (1686).

10 The scope of this chapter ends with the onset of the Nine Years' War for the simple reason that fear of Louis XIV, and thus the persuasive use of cultivating fear in political pamphlets, receded as French armies increasingly lost their dominance. Both the Nine Years' War and the War of the Spanish Succession (1701–14) were far more troublesome for the French than earlier conflicts had been. See Lynn, *Wars of Louis XIV*, 191–360.

11 Joachim Whaley, *Germany and the Holy Roman Empire*, vol. 2 (Oxford: Oxford University Press, 2012), 31–41, 46–52.

12 For an excellent, concise overview of the structure of the empire see: Peter H. Wilson, *The Holy Roman Empire*, 2nd ed. (New York: Palgrave, 2011).
13 Whaley, *Germany and the Holy Roman Empire*, vol. 2, 27, 28, 53.
14 Not only was there an unprecedented number of pamphlets published during this period, they were overwhelmingly anti-French. See: Martin Wrede, *Das Reich und seine Feinde: Politische Feindbilder in der reichspatriotischen Publizistik zwischen Westfälischen Frieden und Siebenjährigem Krieg* (Mainz: P. von Zabern, 2004), 324–545; van Malssen, *Louis XIV d'après les pamphlets*; Schillinger, *Les pamphlétaires allemands*; Friedrich Kleyser, *Der Flugschriftenkampf gegen Ludwig XIV. zur Zeit des Pfälzischen Krieges* (Berlin: E. Ebering, 1935).
15 Examples include fear of witches and devils, of divine punishment, of warfare, of fire, plague, and natural disaster, and of the night. See: Craig Koslofsky, *Evening's Empire: A History of the Night in Early Modern Europe* (Cambridge: Cambridge University Press, 2011); Andreas Bähr, *Furcht und Furchtlosigkeit: Göttliche Gewalt und Selbstkonstitution im 17. Jahrhundert* (Göttingen: V&R Unipress, 2013); as well as the articles in: William Naphy and Penny Roberts, eds., *Fear in Early Modern Society* (Manchester: Manchester University Press, 1997); and Anne Scott and Cynthia Kosso, eds., *Fear and Its Representations in the Middle Ages and Renaissance* (Turnhout: Brepols, 2002).
16 On the history of fear as a political idea and its use in contemporary American society see: Corey Robin, *Fear: The History of a Political Idea* (Oxford: Oxford University Press, 2004). Modern scholars, for example, have regularly highlighted the use of fear by politicians in cultivating hate and violence in the midst of genocide or to mobilize populist political support. See for example: Allan Thompson, ed., "Part One: Hate Media in Rwanda," in *The Media and The Rwanda Genocide* (London: Pluto Press, 2007), 39–142; Ruth Wodak, *The Politics of Fear: What Right-Wing Populist Discourses Mean* (London: Sage, 2015).
17 Emphasis in original, Joanna Bourke, "Fear and Anxiety: Writing about Emotion in Modern History," *History Workshop Journal* 55 (Spring 2003), especially 123–4. On the history of emotions in general, as well as an excellent attempt to reconcile the humanities and sciences see: Jan Plamper, *The History of Emotions: An Introduction*, trans. Keith Tribe (Oxford: Oxford University Press, 2015).
18 On hagiography of the Sun King see: Daniel Dessert, *Louis XIV prend le pouvoir: Naissance d'un mythe?* (Brussels: Éditions Complexe, 1989). There has also been a substantial revisionist trend that questions the practical "absoluteness" of Louis XIV's "absolute power," see: William Beik, "The Absolutism of Louis XIV as Social Collaboration," *Past & Present* 188, no. 1 (2005): 195–224; Fanny Cosandey, "L'absolutisme: un concept irremplacé," in *Absolutismus, ein unersetzliches Forschungskonzept? Eine deutsch-französische bilanz/L'absolutisme, un concept irremplacable? Une mise au point franco-allemande*, ed. Lothar Schilling

(Munich: R. Oldenbourg Verlag, 2008), 33–51; Lothar Schilling, "Vom Nutzen und Nachteil eines Mythos," in *Absolutismus*, ed. Schilling (Berlin: De Gruyter, 2008), 13–32.

19 Jacob Soll, *The Information Master: Jean-Baptiste Colbert's Secret State Intelligence System* (Ann Arbor: University of Michigan Press, 2009).

20 Jean-Marie Apostolidès, *Le Roi-Machine: Spectacle et Politique Au Temps de Louis XIV* (Paris: Editions de Minuit, 1981); Peter Burke, *The Fabrication of Louis XIV* (New Haven, CT: Yale University Press, 1992); Hendrik Ziegler, *Der Sonnenkönig und seine Feinde: die Bildpropaganda Ludwigs XIV. In der Kritik* (Petersberg: M. Imhof, 2010).

21 John A. Lynn, *Giant of the Grand Siècle: The French Army, 1610–1715* (Cambridge: Cambridge University Press, 1997), 32–64.

22 Wrede, *Das Reich und seine Feinde*, 324–545.

23 On print culture and pamphlets in Germany see: Joachim Whaley, *Germany and the Holy Roman Empire*, vol. 1 (Oxford: Oxford University Press, 2012), 119–21, 186–8, 569–70.

24 Kleyser, *Der Flugschriftenkampf gegen Ludwig XIV*, 9; Van Malssen, *Louis XIV d'après les pamphlets*, 1–3; Jeffrey K. Sawyer, *Printed Poison: Pamphlet Propaganda, Faction Politics, and the Public Sphere in Early Seventeenth-Century France* (Berkeley: University of California Press, 1990), 7–10; Schillinger, *Les pamphlétaires allemands*, 4. On pamphlets as a genre see: Hélène Duccini, "Regard sur la littérature pamphlétaire en France au XVIIe siècle," *Revue historique* 260, no. 2 (1978): 313–37.

25 Regularly published journals and newspapers were just beginning to gain popularity at this time, Jack R. Censer, *The French Press in the Age of Enlightenment* (New York: Routledge, 1994).

26 Gillot, *Le Règne de Louis XIV*, 4. On censorship and the publication process see: Joseph Klaits, *Printed Propaganda under Louis XIV: Absolute Monarchy and Public Opinion* (Princeton, NJ: Princeton University Press, 1976), 3–112; Sawyer, *Printed Poison*; Jutta Schumann, *Die andere Sonne: Kaiserbild und Medienstrategien im Zeitalter Leopolds I* (Berlin: akademie Verlag, 2003), 61–4.

27 Wrede, *Das Reich und Seine Feinde*, 52–3. This fact is made even more astonishing by the otherwise steady increase of print media over the course of the eighteenth century.

28 Sawyer, *Printed Poison*, 1; Van Malssen, *Louis XIV d'après les pamphlets*, 4.

29 Schumann, *Die andere Sonne*, 227–8, 230–1.

30 Schumann, *Die andere Sonne*, 231–2, 234. On literacy rates in early modern Europe see: R. A. Houston, *Literacy in Early Modern Europe: Culture & Education, 1500–1800* (New York: Longman, 1988).

31 Houston, *Literacy in Early Modern Europe*, 181.

32 Universal monarchy was a political insult with a history stretching back to the sixteenth century. See: Franz Bosbach, *Monarchia Universalis: Ein Politischer Leitbegriff Der Frühen Neuzeit* (Göttingen: Vandenhoeck & Ruprecht, 1988). Lisola first used it in reference to the French in his 1667, *Buckler of State* and it quickly became a ubiquitous critique of Louis XIV.

33 "die schreckliche Menge ihres Geldes ... und die gewaltige ... Kriegeszurüstungen," *Der Abgezogene Frantzösischen Staats-Rock, und Teutsche Schutzmantel, Das ist Der ... entlarvte Frantzösische Blaue Dunst und ... Teutschlands Erhaltungs-Kunst ...* (1675), unpag. p. 7. See also Eberhard Wassenberg, *Aurifodina Gallica ... Frantzösische Goldgrube ...* (1672), 4–5.

34 "tyrannisiret, tödtet, schändet, raubet, und brennet," *Die unteutsche Freyheit, Oder Teutsche Gefangenschaft Etlicher Französisch gesinten Subtilen Teutschen ...* (1674), unpag. p. 23.

35 "tausenderley abscheuliche Bosheiten," *Frantzösischen Tyranney. Das ist: Umständlich-waarhaffte Erzehlung, der bißher verborgenen unmenschlichen Grausamkeiten, so durch die Frantzen in denen Niederlanden Zeit hero verübet worden ...* (1674), 13.

36 Ibid. For examples see: 48, 33–4, 45, 46, 49–50.

37 "ein Fischer von Heydelberg, mit seiner hochschwangern Frau befunden, so mit einem Bajonet erstochen, ihr der Leib aufgerissen, und also samt ihrer Leibes-Fruch, bey ihrem Manne todt gefunden worden," *Bericht was die Königl. frantzösische Guarnison zu Heydelberg, ... vom 28. Januar bis den 3. Feb. 1689. Vor erschröckliche Grausamkeiten verübet* (c. 1689), unpag. p. 2. For similar tales see *An die Allerhöchste und unendliche Majestät Himmels und der Erden ... Klage und Bitte ... wider den grausamen Ludwig den XIV. König von Franckreich und dessen unmenschliche, ja! fast über-teuffliche Frantzosen ...* (1689); *Ludovicus der XIV. König in Franckreich, als ein Flagellum Dei zur Warnung vorgestellet ...* (c. 1673/4).

38 "Erbfeind Christi," *Des Aller-Christlichsten Königs Unchristl. Bombardiren und Mordbrennen, oder die grausamste vielfältig wiederholete Frantzös. Tyranney Ludwig des Großen* (Freiburg: Martin Groneman, 1689), 4. On European views of "the Turks" see: Thomas Kaiser, "The Evil Empire? The Debate on Turkish Despotism in Eighteenth-Century French Political Culture," *Journal of Modern History* 72, no. 1 (March 1, 2000): 6–34; Paula Fichtner, *Terror and Toleration: The Habsburg Empire Confronts Islam, 1526–1850* (London: Reaktion, 2008).

39 "eine schöne Tripel-Alliance, Mahomet, der Allerchristlichste Ludwig der Grosse und der Teuffel," *Des Aller-Christlichsten Königs*, 4. This was a play on the traditional moniker of the French monarchs as the "Most Christian Kings."

40 "irrdisches Paradieß," *Der Frantzösische und das Heil. Röm. Reich, verderbende grausame Greuel und Abgott Ludwig der vierzehende, König in Frankreich* (1689), unpag. pp. 1, 28.

41 For more on this see: Wrede, *Das Reich und Seine Feinde*, 361–2, 364.
42 Geoffrey Parker, *The Thirty Years' War* (London: Routledge & Kegan Paul, 1984), 215.
43 *Das Regiersüchtige Franckreich. Worinnen der Europäischen Welt, sonderlich aber Franckreichs Regiersucht und dahero entstehende vielfältige Kriege … her unpartheyisch vorgestellet warden u[sw]* (1684), 18–20, 25.
44 "den Saamen der Uneinigkeit," "Kunstgriffen," Wassenberg, *Aurofidina Gallica*, quotation 14, see also 14–17.
45 "Diese Mißverständnüß und Furcht das Band der Christlichen Liebe, und Geselschafft zerrisse," "die Land und Leute zum Untergang und Todt brachten," "in den 30 Jährichten durcheinander gemischten Krieg," *Der Abgezogene Frantzösischen Staats-Rock*, unpag. pp. 2, 5.
46 *Der Teutsche Frantzoß, worinne mit sinnreichen Lehren und lustigen Exempeln gründlich vorgebildet wird, der Teutschen allzubegierigen Nachahmung in denen Frantzösischen … Vanitaeten …* (1682), 9–10.
47 "unwanckelbaren Meinung, daß der König in Franckreich … schon damahls, als ihm ein Stuck von dem Reich zu theile geworden, die Beherrschung Teutschlandes und gleichsam dessen wahre Besitzung verschlucket zu haben ihme eingebildet," Der Abgezogene Frantzösischen Staats-Rock, unpag. p. 4.
48 "Blindheit," *Curiosorum, nec non politicorum, vagabundi per Europam … Der Ersten Claß Vierdter Theil* [vol. 1.4] (1678), 47; See also: Wassenberg, *Aurofidina Gallica*, 29, 36; *Das von teutschen Geblüth und Frantzösischen Gemüth Leichtsinnige Frauen-Zimmer … allen denen, so diesen Eitelkeiten ergeben, zum sonderbahren Abschrecken vorgestellet …* (1691), 50; "Frantzösisches Sclaventhumb," *Die unteutsche Freyheit*, unpag. p. 11.
49 "Man hat nun so viel Jahre nichts anders gedacht, geredet … begehrt, gesehen, gehöret, gerochen und gefühlet als Frantzösisch," *Der Frantzösische und das Heil. Röm. Reich*, unpag. p. 19.
50 "Frantzösische Gifft," *Teutsche Frantzoß*, 40.
51 "offt veränderten, eitelen, thörichten, offt leichtfertigen Kleider … da man alles was eitele Welt-Kinder darinn von einer Zeit zur andern auffbringen und belieben, mit annimmt und mit beliebet," *Das von teutschen Geblüth*, 28.
52 "Pfauen," "alle in Frantzösische Galanterien und Zeuge gekleidet," *Das von Franckreich verführte Teutschland … Wie Franckreich bißhero … die Teutschen, durch allerhand Ankörnungen, Galanterien, und andere ersinnliche Staats-Streiche, an sich gelocket … dagegen aber seine Monarchische Herrschafft erweitert hat* (Frankfurt: Christian Weidmannen, 1686), 24; see also: *Der Abgezogene Frantzösischen Staats-Rock*; *Curiosorum, nec non politicorum* [1.4].
53 "truncken," "bezaubrende *Delicatesse*," *Der teutsche Frantzoß*, 12; "noch prächtiger und kostbarer als die Inländer," *Das von Franckreich verführte Teutschland*, 24; see also: Wassenberg, *Aurofidina Gallica*; *Das von teutschen Geblüth*.

54 "es sey anst ä ndig und schicke sich oder nicht," *Das von Frankreich verf ü hrte Teutschland*, 33.
55 "weiln es wohl weiß daß die Teutschen immer gerne was neues haben," *Das von Franckreich verführte Teutschland*, 32, see also 8, 34–5.
56 "fast alle Monat changiret, und verändert," ibid., 33; "Vanitäten," *Teutsche Frantzoß*, 12.
57 The Grand Tour had been a staple of elite young men's education since at least the sixteenth century and during the seventeenth France increasingly became the destination of choice, Thomas Grosser, *Reiseziel Frankreich: Deutsche Reiseliteratur vom Barock bis zur Französischen Revolution* (Opladen: Westdeutscher Verlag, 1989), 13, 21–35.
58 "unbesonnene," *Teutsche Frantzoß*, 13.
59 "heutigen Mißbrauch," "den Frantzösischen Galanterie-Teufel in unser Teutschland geführet, verlogene Complementen und etliche leichtsinnige Exercitia," ibid., 27, 28.
60 "ein Teutscher an diesen Orten, seinem Vatterlande zum besten, mehr als in Franckreich sehen und lernen könne," ibid., 29; see also: *Das von Franckreich verführte Teutschland*, 49.
61 "Massen dann ein junger Mensch, wenn das Gemüthe erstlich von solchen Vanitäten eingenommen ist, gar selten seine Gedancken auf was rechtes wenden," *Das von Franckreich verführte Teutschland*, 27.
62 "nicht ein Mittel treffen, damit … der Frantzösische gift auß dem Teutschen Geblüte getrieben und abgeführet wird," *Teutsche Frantzoß*, 40; "Irr-garten," *Das von Franckreich verführte Teutschland*, 3.
63 "Frantzösische … Fecht- und Tantz-Buch," *Teutsche Frantzoß*, quotation 30, also 45, 62, 91, 161, 166–7, 180. See also: *Das von Franckreich verführte Teutschland*, 70.
64 "etwas Frantzösisch Tantzen," *Teutsche Frantzoß*, 160, 166.
65 "jährlich viel tausend erspahren," *Das von Franckreich verführte Teutschland*, 58.
66 *Der Abgezogene Frantzösischen Staats-Rock*, unpag. pp. 26–7, 32, quotation 27; *Teutsche Frantzoß*, 30–1, 45, 221, 116; *Das von Franckreich verführte Teutschland*, 57–65.
67 Dueling was very popular in France, despite repeated royal declarations against the practice: V. G. Kiernan, *The Duel in European History: Honour and the Reign of Aristocracy* (Oxford: Oxford University Press, 1988), 67, 72–6, 95–8. The "hot" French were often argued to possess warmer characters according to Galenic and climatic theory, *Wahrsagerischer Welt-Spiegel … Worinnen wegen der genauer gesuchten Freundschafft und Hülffe den Krieg wider die Teutschen und Holländer fortzusetzen …* (1674), 23; *Der Abgezogene Frantzösischen Staats-Rock*, unpag. p. 40; *Curiosorum, nec non politicorum, vagabundi per Europam … Der Anderen*

Classe Dritter Theil [vol. 2.3] (1679), 10; *Teutsche Frantzoß*, 119; *Das Regiersüchtige Franckreich*, 60; *Curieuser Staats-Mercurius ... insonderheit den gefährlichen Zustand deß H. Römischen Reichs ...* (1684), 50; *Das von Franckreich verführte Teutschland*, 85–6, 91–2.

68 "eine grosse Deformität," "einem gehetzten Wolffe," *Teutsche Frantzoß*, quotation 223. The story spans chapters XXXII–XXXIV. See also: *Der Abgezogene Frantzösischen Staats-Rock*, unpag. pp. 37–8.

69 "Wann du wärest in Krieg gangen, und daselbst deine gesunden Glieder gewaget, würde es mir und dir rühmlicher seyn; so aber hab ich ein gesund un fähig Kind in Frankreich geschicket; hingegen aber kompt mir ein half-zerstümmelt und ungerathener Debauchant wieder zu Hause, welches sowol dem Vatterlande als mir schlechten Nutzen und Freude verursachen wird," *Teutsche Frantzoß*, 238.

70 The empire, of course, was in no way homogenously German, with neither all imperial subjects being German speakers nor all German speakers residing in the empire. Even within the German-speaking regions the diversity—cultural, linguistic, religious, political—was astounding. The imagined nature of this shared "Germanness" cannot be overstated, but imagined communities, of various kinds, can still be extremely influential, see: Benedict Anderson, *Imagined Communities: Reflections on the Origin and Spread of Nationalism* (London: Verso, 1983). The complicated ways in which national categories were understood and used as political rhetoric during this period cannot be fully explored in this chapter but are the subject of my dissertation: "Honest Germans and Perfidious French: The Use of National Ideas in Pamphlet Propaganda during the Wars of Louis XIV" (PhD thesis, University of North Carolina at Chapel Hill, 2020).

71 *Der Frantzösische und das Heil. Röm. Reich*, unpag. p. 20.

72 *Teutsche Frantzoß*, 17–18, 170–1, 250.

73 "Agenten," *Teutschlands Klag- Straff- und Ermahnungs- Rede, an seine untreuen und verräterischen Kinder ...* (1673), unpag. p. 15; "Spionen," *Curiosorum nec non politicorum* [1.4], 35; see also: *Der Abgezogene Frantzösischen Staats-Rock*, unpag. p. 32.

74 "verzehrende Kranckheit," *Der Abgezogene Frantzösischen Staats-Rock*, unpag. p. 29; see also: *Das an der Teutschen Colica danieder liegende Franckreich ... der merckwürdigsten Intrigues des Frantzösischen Hofes aufgelöset und vorgestellet warden ...* (1689).

75 "und woher kompts, daß das teutsche Reich bißhero so wenig wider außwärtige Feinde außgerichtet, das Kriegswesen und Disciplin so vielen Mängeln bey uns unterworffen, als daß die teutsche Jugend sich insgemein auff solche weichmüthige Exercitia und andere Frantzösische Vanitäten leget," *Teutsche Frantzoß*, 7–8.

76 *Der Abgezogene Frantzösischen Staats-Rock*, unpag. p. 31.

77 *Das von Franckreich verführte Teutschland*, 37. See also: *Teutsche Frantzoß*, 132–41.

78 *Der Frantzösische und das Heil. Röm. Reich*, unpag. pp. 20, 22–3.
79 "Fremde Kleider warden frembde Sitten, Gebräuche und Laster," *Der Frantzösische und das Heil. Röm. Reich*, unpag. p. 22. See also: *Das von Teutschen Geblüth*, 21.
80 "wird der Teutsche nicht nur an äusserlicher Kleidung, sondern auch an dem Gemüthe … aus einem Teutschen zum frantzosen gemachet," *Das von Franckreich verführte Teutschland*, 37.
81 "So lange als Teutschland seiner alten teutschen Tugend und Tapfferkeit nachgehangen, hat es in grosser Macht und Glückseligkeit floriret. Nachdem es sich aber auff außländische, sonderlich Frantzösische Vanitäten und dergleichen wolllüstige Verzärtelung geleget, ist es nach und nach entkräfftet und fast verächtlich worden," *Teutsche Frantzoß*, 134. On the dangers of foreign imitation see: *Das von Franckreich verführte Teutschland*, 37, 93–7.
82 "der alten Teutschen Ehrbarkeit und Tugend vielmals zu Glateise worden" *Das von Franckreich verführte Teutschland*, 62.
83 This annexation was part of the policy of "reunions," the seizure of territories along France's eastern border based on legal claims and defensive interests, see: Lynn, *Wars of Louis XIV*, 37, 163–4, 168–9.
84 For an overview of these pamphlets see: Wrede, *Das Reich und seine Feinde*, 463–73.
85 "nach und nach der Französische *humeur*, Sitten, Sprachen, Kleidung und andere ankörnende Beherrschungs-Netze, eingeflösset und in der Inwohner Gemüthern dergestalt eingedrückt worden, daß sie endlich ihres vorigen Standes und alten Teutschen Wesens ziemblich entwehnet oder gar vergessen worden," "so viel nicht zu bedeuten haben," *Das verkehrte Glücks-spiel Europäischen Alliantzen … hingegen aber durch listige Staats-Streiche, Gegen-Alliantzen, auch andere Glücks- und seltzame Zufälle …* (c. 1685), 62–3.
86 "Denn diese wachsame und regiersüchtige Crone [Louis XIV], wuste wol, daß die Stadt Straßburg eine Teutsche Stadt, und binnen des Römischen Reichs Gränze gelegen; jedennoch aber die Inwohner so hohen als niedern Gemüther meist Französisch gesinnet … dannenhero sie sich nicht groß sperren würden, wenn man Ihnen das Joch der Französische Herrschafft vorhalten … Dannenhero ist Frankreich schon vor langen Zeiten darauf bedacht gewesen … wie es dieses schöne Kleinod und herrliche Vestung dem Römischen Reich Teutscher Nation abgewinnen … Zu dem Ende hat es allerhand ersinnliche theils gewaltsame, theils gelinde und liebkosende Mittel gebrauchet, seinen Wunsch zu erfüllen," *Das verkehrte Glücks-spiel Europäischen Alliantzen … hingegen aber durch listige Staats-Streiche, Gegen-Alliantzen, auch andere Glücks- und seltzame Zufälle …* (c. 1685), 61–2.
87 "Die Sprach, Sitten und Kleidung sind der erste Grundstein zu frembder Herrschafft," *Trajani Boccalini Gespräch und Discursen von Gegenwärtiger Staats-Beschaffenheit deß Heiligen Röm. Reichs … und der Cron Franckreich …* (1680), 436.

88 Joan DeJean argued that it was, but the actual content of her analysis presents a much more amorphous process that often began decades earlier, a chronology that fits more closely with other scholarship on the topic, see: *The Essence of Style: How the French Invented High Fashion, Fine Food, Chic Cafés, Style, Sophistication, and Glamour* (New York: Free Press, 2005). See also: Ulrike Graul and Bärbel Zausch, eds., *Frau Hoeffart & Monsieur Alamode: Modekritik auf illustrierten Flugblättern des 16. und 17. Jahrhunderts* (Halle: Staatliche Galerie Moritzburg, 1998); Donna J. Bohanan, *Fashion beyond Versailles: Consumption and Design in Seventeenth-Century France* (Baton Rouge: Louisiana State University Press, 2012), especially 7–29, 114–15. The appeal of this interpretation was nevertheless captured by the *New York Times* review of DeJean's book, which ran with the stunning title of "Style-Obsessed Despot Who Still Dictates to Us," William Grimes, *New York Times*, July 13, 2005, http://nyti.ms/29GpPkZ [accessed: August 6, 2017].

89 On contemporary theories of divine and absolute monarchy see Nannerl O. Keohane, *Philosophy and the State in France: The Renaissance to the Enlightenment* (Princeton, NJ: Princeton University Press, 1980); Arlette Jouanna, *Le Prince absolu: Apogée et déclin de l'imaginaire monarchique* (Paris: Gallimard, 2014); Ronald G. Asch, *Sacral Kingship between Disenchantment and Re-enchantment: The French and English Monarchies 1587–1688* (Oxford: Berghahn, 2014).

90 Bourke, "Fear and Anxiety," especially 123–4.

91 Graul and Zausch, eds., *Frau Hoeffart & Monsieur Alamode*, 4–5; DeJean, *Essence of Style*; Bohanan, *Fashion beyond Versailles*, 1–2, 4; Veronika Hyden-Hanscho, *Reisende, Migranten, Kulturmanager: Mittlerpersonlichkeiten zwischen Frankreich und dem Wiener Hof, 1630–1730* (Stuttgart: Franz Steiner Verlag, 2013).

92 Grosser, *Reiseziel Frankreich*; DeJean, *Essence of Style*; Marc Fumaroli, *When the World Spoke French*, trans. Richard Howard (New York: New York Review of Books, 2011).

93 It is almost impossible to provide an exact number as the territories of the empire were constantly fluctuating. For an overview see: Whaley, *Germany and the Holy Roman Empire*, vol. 1, 41–3.

94 Among others, this cast included Bavaria, Cologne, Münster, and Hanover, though it was not uncommon for them to change alliances from conflict to conflict as their own interests and needs dictated: Whaley, *Germany and the Holy Roman Empire*, vol. 2, 32–41.

95 On the difficulties of overcoming religious division in the empire see: Ibid., 83–7, 439.

96 The conceptual link between the empire and Germany dates back to the late medieval period: Len Scales, *The Shaping of German Identity: Authority and Crisis, 1245–1414* (Cambridge: Cambridge University Press, 2012). In relation

to class or standing, much anti-French discourse arose from *Hofkritik* (criticism of the court), but pamphleteers repeatedly emphasized that the issue of cultural infiltration extended far beyond the courts, *Der Abgezogene Frantzösischen Staats-Rock*, unpag. p. 27, 33; *Teutsche Frantzoß*, 39, 57, 76, 148; *Das von Franckreich verführte Teutschland*, 28; *Das von teutschen Geblüth*, 18; see also: Bohanan, *Fashion beyond Versailles*, 13.

97 See as one example: *Teutsche Frantzoß*, 9–10.
98 Lynn, *Wars of Louis XIV*, 160–90.
99 "der güldenen Friedens-Früchte," *Teutschland, Traue nicht zu viel. Das ist, Was das Röm. Reich Teutscher Nation ... von denen Frantzösischen Messures ... zu besorgen habe: Ob dem Armistitio zu trauen? Und was sonsten ...* (c. 1685), 3.
100 This occurred with the return of large-scale conflict in 1688, when pamphlets recounting military atrocities suddenly reappeared in large numbers.
101 Robin, *Fear*, 2, 16. Robin traces the development of this idea of political fear from Hobbes to the modern era, with his closing remarks on political fear mainly focusing on the contemporary United States. Although the extent and mechanics of political fear in the time of Louis XIV were necessarily more limited than the contemporary examples Robin points to, the core idea was the same.
102 Ibid., 16, 6.
103 "Teutschlandes interesse," *Wahres Interesse des Heil. Römischen Reichs ...* (Osteroda: Barthold Fuhrmann Buchhändeler, 1689), 71–7, quotation 76.

3

Vampires, Ottomans, and the Specter of Contagion: The Intersectionality of Fear on the Periphery of the Habsburg Monarchy

Michael G. Pickering

Beginning in the 1720s, the German-speaking world came into close contact with a purportedly new type of monster: a form of blood-drinking revenant that would eventually become known throughout Europe as the vampire. The background to the vampire "debate" that ensued in the Protestant German lands was the exhumation of one Peter Plagojevitz in the Serbian village of Kisolova in 1725.[1] Plagojevitz had been buried almost two and a half months prior to the official investigation into the incident. In the immediate lead-up to Habsburg Imperial Provisor Frobald's involvement in the case, the denizens of Kisolova had claimed that Plagojevitz had risen from the earth and had murdered nine people.[2] Frombald's report stated that when he inspected Plagojevitz's exhumed body he had noticed that blood had pooled in the mouth. According to the "general acclaim" this was because Plagojevitz had drunk the blood of those he had attacked.[3] In response to the demands of the village inhabitants, Frombald permitted Plogojevitz's body to be staked and then incinerated.[4]

Part one of a second incident took place in 1727 in Medvedja, a Serbian village on the Western Morava River. It had been reported to representatives of the Habsburg administration at Belgrade that a former hajduk[5] named Arnout Paule[6], having broken his neck in a fall from a hay wagon, had returned from the grave twenty to thirty days after his death. It was claimed that he had killed four people and had drunk the blood of several sheep. Following this, his body had been disinterred and was found to be in an uncorrupted state: it contained fluid flood (which exuded from several orifices when the body was manipulated), and there were purportedly new fingernails and toenails in place of the old ones (which had dropped off).[7] The inhabitants of Medvedja took these signs to indicate that Paule had become a vampire, and so they dealt with the body in the following manner:

> True to their habits, they struck a stake through his heart, at which he let out a well audible rasp, and a great amount of blood left him, after which, still on the same day, they burnt the body to ashes and threw them in the grave.[8]

Several years later, in the fall of 1731 a similar incident occurred in Medvedja. This time, a sexaganarian invalid called Miliza had died and then been accused of vampirism. Purportedly, Miliza had passed away after consuming the flesh of the sheep that Paule had attacked.[9] Shortly thereafter, Lieutenant Colonel Schnezzer of the Jagodina District had been contacted by a hajduk leader in the village. In response to what appeared to be a new outbreak of vampirism, Schnezzer sent in a contagious diseases physician from the nearby village of Paraćin. The physician, Glaser, undertook an investigation of the inhabitants and dwellings in Medvedja, only to conclude that there was no indication that the affliction was a contagious disease.[10] Glaser's report was dispatched to Belgrade, and it was decided there that a delegation of Habsburg officials would be sent to Medvedja to conduct a follow-up investigation.[11]

The "discovery" of the vampire by Habsburg military personnel on the southern frontier revealed an intersection of discourses immediately linked to the economic, political, and social stability of the region and the concerns of the state: a concern that vampires were, in one sense, harbingers of impending plague, and that they represented a form of pathogenic infiltration of and incursion into the Habsburg territories; an incursion that would, it was thought, indubitably bring economic harm to affected areas. Indeed, in the eyes of the Habsburg authorities, the threat was, at its core, both a demographic and an existential one: the exhumed bodies of purported vampires—apparently fresh, plump, and pliable months after burial—were not only a possible indicator of the presence of plague; their existence also threatened the stability of the hitherto depopulated buffer zone in which the incidents occurred. Frightened inhabitants purportedly threatened to leave their villages unless the Habsburg military personnel permitted the destruction of the bodies of suspected vampires, as indicated in the Kisolova narrative above.

Geopolitical anxieties regarding contagion and depopulation were strongly rooted in the belief of the Habsburg administration that pestilence was rife in Ottoman-controlled regions; a belief manifested in the construction of the 1,000-mile-long *Cordon Sanitaire* stretching through the Banat and up into Wallachia. This fear of infiltration was also strongly reinforced by the perception of an ever-present Ottoman military threat on the frontier, as evinced by the so-called *Militärgrenze* (military border), which later formed the physical, administrative infrastructure of the *Cordon*.[12] The emergence of the vampire at this particular juncture is readily understandable in the context of the perceived threat to Habsburg territorial sovereignty that military incursion, disease, and depopulation represented. Indeed, beliefs that the dead could potentially rise from their graves and interact with members of the living were in no sense new. However, that several cases of purported revenancy *at this time and in this* place attracted the attention of the Habsburg authorities attests to the capacity of the vampire to articulate these particular geopolitical anxieties.

While the vampire narratives in the Habsburg military sources certainly intersect with a set of concrete anxieties or concerns regarding territorial sovereignty, they also evoke deeper, less prominently articulated fears of incursion/infiltration and destruction. I utilize the term "anxiety" to indicate a construction largely founded on a set of rational concerns; "fear," on the other hand, I use to refer to that which ventures into the realm of the fantastical.[13] The geopolitical anxieties that one discerns in the Habsburg military reports subtly evoke an image or *Feindbild*[14] of a genuinely horrific enemy: one that is dead but also alive; that crosses over unseen—and unstoppable—from the Ottoman lands; that has the capacity to destroy entire villages and, in so doing, to replicate itself with unceasing vigilance. This *Feindbild* is also deeply textual and relational, as the term suggests: *Feind* refers literally to an enemy or adversary, and *Bild* has a variety of meanings, a dominant one of which is "image," both in a figurative as well as a more literal, mimetic sense. "Fear" in this context is, therefore, not about the concrete or the tangible as much as it is about the unseen and the imagined; an order of thought that is at once representational and contingent, forever strung between the possible and the impossible—between accepted, acceptable, "domesticated" knowledge, on the one hand, and a bricolage of tropes, narratives and musings, on the other. Fear, as I deploy the term, exists within the domain of fantasy: it is an evocation of the wondrous and demonic inhabitants of a nightmare landscape beneath the quotidian domain of the effable and familiar. And indeed, we see this in the very figure of the vampire: while purportedly "new," even exciting for the public readership of the early-eighteenth-century treatises and essays on the incidents in Serbia, an examination of the discursive fabric of the vampire itself reveals it to be largely a concatenation of central European folkloric motifs, such as the ambulant corporeal revenant and the *Nachzehrer*, rather than a genuine representation of indigent beliefs.[15] Caught between this reality and its ostensible "foreignness," the vampire, as a creature of purportedly Ottoman provenance, was also imagined as an embodiment of the potential for incursion, whether by force or by stealth: the "first" vampire in the Medvedja case—Miliza—was said to have emigrated from the Ottoman side, as we shall see; and the central character of the Medvedja report—Paule—was in life a mercenary for the Ottomans who had, in the course of his career on the Turkish side, been plagued by a vampire.

That geopolitical anxieties concerning territorial sovereignty could evoke fantasies of decimation by hordes of the blood-drinking undead from the Ottoman lands is to be found via a careful analysis of the archival sources. It is difficult to ascertain whether other instances of vampirism evoked similar fears on the part of the Habsburg bureaucracy, as the term itself was, in the context at hand, an administrative and learned construction.[16] I have no doubt that denizens of other communities in the early eighteenth century likely felt fear at the prospect of the dead returning and harming the living. However, as far as the Habsburg administrative apparatus was concerned, the incidents from Kisolova and Medvedja were unique: indeed, by the 1750 when cases of so-called vampirism emerged in the Transylvanian regions of the Habsburg Monarchy, these were not imagined as uncanny or potentially supernatural occurrences but as indicative of a medical condition.[17] The aim of the present discussion then is to examine the construction of fear on the Habsburg borderlands and to investigate the concomitant normalization of this fear by way of autopsy and the transformation of the vampire into a medical object in the archival material. The key text in this process, that by regimental surgeon Johann Flückinger, would be taken up alacritously in the so-called vampire debate. Many of the texts produced during this time would build upon the medicalization in the military report by Flückinger, transforming the vampire into a thoroughly psychosomatic construct—quite literally, a figment of the (distorted) imagination.

* * *

The most well-known cases of purported vampirism occurred slightly north of the Habsburg–Ottoman border. This border, the *Militärgrenze*, stretched from modern-day Croatia, down and through Serbia, the Banat, then up through Wallachia and into Transylvania. In 1724 Claudius Florimund Graf von Mercy d'Argenteau had developed the idea of staffing the *Militärgrenze* with an unpaid milita derived from the local populations along the border.[18] The aim of this initiative was that the *Militärgrenze* should be largely self-sufficient, the expenses being otherwise too great for the central administration in Vienna to populate it with regular troops.[19] Part of this transformation also involved a concerted effort to shift the local economy from pastoralism to a cereal-based agriculture.[20] In addition to its political and economic functions, the *Militärgrenze* also formed the administrative foundation of the so-called *Cordon Sanitaire*, an institution designed to prevent the entry of plague carriers into the Habsburg territories.[21] At each quarantine checkpoint there was to be "a physician, or at the very least a well-experienced surgeon."[22] Indeed, part of the raison d'être of the *Cordon* was also to protect local inhabitants from epidemic disease, as they provided the material backbone and human capital of the *Militärgrenze* itself;[23] and, through this, to preserve territorial sovereignty in the region.

The events in Kisolova and Medvedja in 1725 and 1731–2 were by no means the only cases concerning revenants in eastern, southeastern, and central Europe, although they were the ones that garnered the most attention in learned circles and the public imagination in the early eighteenth century. In 1718 in the town of Lubló on the Hungarian-Polish border, a famous incident concerning a revenant named Michael Kasparek was purported to have taken place. This appeared in the *Europäischer Niemand*, edited by the Württemberg privy councillor Philipp Balthasar Sinold, in 1719, although it wasn't taken up in the vampire discourse of the early to mid-1730s.[24] Likewise, in the 1720s there were incidents in Késmárk, Brassó, and Déva,[25] none of which made it into the vampire debate. Peter Kreuter has made the point concerning the two decades prior to 1720 that there were likely other such instances in this region that involved the practice of exhuming and destroying the bodies of those suspected of postmortem predations.[26] There is also much further documentation to suggest that such practices took place in the Near East, the Balkan Peninsula, and central Europe.[27]

That it was the Kisolova and Medvedja cases however that garnered the most attention in the early eighteenth century attests to their traction with the geopolitical anxieties of contagion, depopulation and, by extension, the threat of territorial loss. In the former episode the inhabitants of the village threatened to emigrate if they were not allowed to destroy Plagojevitz's body. Peter Plagojevitz had been dead and buried for ten weeks before a series of sudden fatal illnesses struck the denizens of Kisolova. The afflicted claimed that Plagojevitz had lain upon them and throttled them during sleep.[28] The Imperial Provisor Frombald who related the account to the *Staatskanzlei* in Vienna, as Schroeder maintains, expressed his reluctance to allow the exhumation of Plagojevitz to take place, only giving in to the demand when the village inhabitants threatened to emigrate.[29] In the Medvedja case, the physician Glaser, after having found no evidence of a contagious illness, advised the authorities to permit the destruction of the vampire bodies on the grounds that this would appease the villagers and, he implied strongly, help prevent the depopulation of the village through emigration.[30]

The archival provenance of the Frombald text sheds light on the author's rationale for creating the document in the first instance. Schroeder has indicated that the document was most likely not sent initially to the Belgrade administration or to the *Hofkriegsrat* but was instead forwarded directly on to another departmental body in Vienna.[31] This is partially suggested by the fact that the only known surviving manuscript, a copy, appears in the records of the State Chancellery (*Staatskanzlei*) rather than among those of the *Hofkriegsrat*.[32] Essentially, the report is Frombald's justification for not referring the matter on to the administration at Belgrade for a decision on whether to allow the denizens of Kisolova to go ahead with the destruction of Plagojevitz's cadaver. Frombald states that after the series of deaths attributed to Plagojevitz, and after the testimony of the said Plagojevitz's wife that he had returned to her in order to request his shoes, the villagers decided to exhume and examine the body for signs of vampirism. Frombald maintains that he told the villagers that the exhumation would have to wait until a decision came from Belgrade. The villagers, being unwilling to wait, for fear that the destruction would continue during the delay, stated that they would rather emigrate, according to Frombald. It was on this basis that Frombald permitted the investigation and eventual destruction of Plagojevitz's cadaver (which in any case had already been exhumed without Frombald's permission).[33] Although nowhere to be found in the archival source,[34] in the printed report in the *Wienerisches Diarium* Frombald apologizes if he has made a mistake in allowing the proceedings to go ahead without the acquiescence of the Belgrade administration, while at the same time placing the blame on "the rabble, who were out of their minds with fear."[35]

In addition to the threat of depopulation through emigration, another concern was that brought about through pestilence. The next major outbreak of purported vampirism encountered in the Habsburg Monarchy was in the village of Medvedja. Telling is the fact that the first inclination of the regional administration was to send in a contagious diseases specialist. Indeed, in December of 1731, around the time that the Medvedja incident took place, there were official concerns about pestilence in the Banat.[36] The *contagions medicus*, Glaser, was sent in to Medvedja by the lieutenant colonel of the Jagodina District named Schnezzer, and it was there that he undertook a thorough examination of the houses and their inhabitants.[37] Upon the completion of his investigation, Glaser wrote an inconclusive report that was sent to his immediate superiors; a copy was also forwarded on to the Aulic War Council in Vienna. Glaser also penned a letter to his father, Johann Friedrich Glaser, although a copy of this does not survive. The only evidence for the existence of this letter is the published correspondence that Johann Glaser sent through to the editors of the learned journal and mouthpiece of the Leopoldina, the *Commercium litterarium*.[38]

Glaser begins his report by stating that he arrived in Medvedja on December 12, 1731, and "thoroughly and precisely searched through" each house in the village. Within the first few lines of the report he states clearly that he found no evidence of contagious illness such as "tertian- or quartan fever, or pleurisy," which he states were commonly found among Orthodox communities during their fast times.[39] Having inquired about the nature of the symptoms of the deceased during the six-week period, Glaser states that it was explained to him that they had all suffered from chest and side pains as well as terrible aches in their extremities. While Glaser implies that these physical signs may have been the symptoms of an illness, he does not state this clearly. It was further explained to him that the source of the symptoms were two vampires or "bloodsuckers." Glaser maintains that he attempted, alongside several local officers, as well as the corporal of the Stallada company, to talk the Medvedja denizens out of their ideas, but that this was met with stiff resistance. The villagers responded that they would rather emigrate than remain in the village while vampires were attacking people. Glaser mentions that the survivors had banded together in order to keep watch at night, but to no avail. The only possible solution in their view was to receive permission from the administration to find and destroy the vampires responsible.[40] Glaser decided to grant the Medvedja inhabitants permission to open ten graves.

As Glaser was a physician, not a surgeon, he did not officially perform an autopsy on the cadavers for his report. His formal examination involved the exterior parts of the bodies only. While he goes into a little detail concerning the outward appearance of the body of the first vampire after Paule, Miliza, he skims over the descriptions of the other cadavers. He describes Miliza's body as in a "complete" state, its mouth open, and with "light, fresh blood" streaming out of it, as well as out of the nose. The physician explains that the body, which appeared "suspect," was bloated and floating in a pool of blood. The body of Stanno (or Stana, in the Flückinger text), a young woman who died in childbirth, he states, "was of the same nature as the first" (meaning Miliza), and so too was that of her child, who, it is presumed, was buried with her. The bodies of two teenagers, Milloi (Milloe in Flückinger's text) and Joachim, both buried for five weeks, were both "so constituted as the others." A 40-year-old woman named Ruschiza he mentions only as being "half suspect"; a 15-year-old boy named Peter was "very suspect." Following this, Glaser reveals that Milosowa, the wife of a hajduk, 30 year old, and buried for three weeks, was "pretty corrupted, as would be expected." The bodies of a 24-year-old man named Radi and a 9-year-old girl named Wutschiza were both likewise decomposed.[41] The strong implication in Glaser's report is clearly that bodies should begin to decompose after several weeks in the ground. One can see this in his comment about Milosowa's body. He also mentions that Miliza's body, when compared with bodies of those who had been of a plumper constitution in life, who had suffered a shorter illness, and who had been buried for just as long as she had, "would have been necessarily already half decomposed."[42]

Field surgeon of the Fürstenbusch Regiment Johann Flückinger arrived in Medvedja in January 1732, having been called in by the interim commander in Belgrade, Botta d'Adorno, to follow up Glaser's inconclusive investigation of the Medvedja incident. Flückinger was assisted by two adjunct surgeons, Siegele and Baumgarten, as well as one Lieutenant Colonel Büttner and Ensign von Lindenfels from Karl Alexander's regiment.[43] He begins his report with the discussion of the Paule case from five years previously. He explains how the hajduk captain of the Stallada company and its standard-bearer, along with "the oldest hajduks of the village," narrated the case of Paule who broke his neck in a fall from a hay wagon. Twenty to thirty days after his death, people began to complain of having been "plagued" by him, and he purportedly killed four people.[44] It was at this point that his body was exhumed and destroyed. However, the problem continued. In 1731 the invalid Miliza had eaten some sheep from which Paule had sucked blood, and in turn she was reported to have become a vampire after death. At this point in the report, having recounted the brief history, Flückinger states that "on that same afternoon we went to the cemetery, along with the ... eldest hajduks of the village, in order to open the suspected graves and to inspect the bodies therein."[45]

An initial reading of these sources reveals an administrative apparatus dealing with unexplained deaths in several towns across a time span of roughly seven years. A significant concern is depopulation, whether through mortality or emigration, and this can be situated, as discussed, within a broader concern for maintaining the integrity of territorial gains made at Passarowitz in 1718. A further interpretation of these sources tells a somewhat different story. When the vampire narratives are distilled from the military communiqués of Frombald, Glaser, and Flückinger—when the focus shifts from the realm of medical reportage to the secondhand relaying of village narratives and hearsay—what emerges is a construction that at once sits in tension with the quotidian and the readily explainable: a creature that is dead but also alive; one that continues its dark existence through the violent taking of human life; an enemy that cannot be controlled through administrative barriers such as the *Militärgrenze* and the *Cordon Sanitaire*; one that is as much a curse as a disease, and that operates indiscriminately across borders; and one that corrupts but is itself "incorruptible" (*unverwesen* in the military documentation).

This enemy-at-the-gates is constructed in both Medvedja reports as being of Ottoman provenance. In Flückinger's reports, it is stated that during life Paule had been plagued by a vampire in "Cossova in Turkish Serbia."[46] In order to remedy this he had eaten earth from the vampire's grave and had smeared himself with its blood. In Glaser's report, behind the 1731 outbreak two women purported to have been "vampirized" (*vervampÿret*) during life were suspected; it was maintained that they had been fated to "become vampires after death." Glaser narrates a short life history of the first vampire, Miliza, a 50-year-old émigrée from the Ottoman side. He narrates how she emigrated six years previously and was always "neighborly" in her bearing, although it was never known "whether she had believed or practiced anything diabolic." According to Glaser's text, during life she had mentioned to her neighbors that while living on the Ottoman side she had eaten the meat of two sheep killed by vampires, and in so doing was destined to become a vampire herself after death.[47] The other vampire, a 20-year-old woman named Stanno/Stana had died in childbirth. She too had lived on the other side of the border, and it was there that she had smeared herself with the blood of a vampire in order to protect herself from vampires:

> The other woman [purported to be a vampire] was named Stanno, and had died during childbirth. The child had been born, but had also died. The woman was twenty years old and had been buried for one month. During her life she had confessed and narrated to her neighbors that, when she was on the Turkish side, where the vampires also reigned strongly, in order to protect herself from them she had once adorned herself with the blood of a vampire. For this reason she was also destined to become a vampire after her death.[48]

As Peter Kreuter has noted, there are several differences between the Glaser and Flückinger texts. In the former text, Miliza was 50 years old and had settled in Medvedja in the recent past. In the latter document, she had lived in the village all her life and was 60 years old, not 50, when she died. In Glaser's report it is explained that Stana, as we have seen, lived at one point on the other side of the border, and that her vampire troubles began at this time. In the Flückinger text it is never stated that Stanno lived on the Ottoman side. The ambiguity of this narrative—whether the arch-vampires in Medvedja did or did not live on the Ottoman side at one point in their lives—obfuscates the reality that many inhabitants of the southern peripheral zones would have, by default, lived in Ottoman-controlled regions prior to the Treaty at Passarowitz. The fact that this aspect of the narrative is emphasized indicates a conflation of Ottoman 'otherness' with the fundamental 'otherness' of the vampire. Even the word usage, archaic as it may be, in Glaser's relation of Stana's story conjures up the notion that vampires didn't simply *exist* on the other side of the border, but that the Ottoman borderlands were practically teeming with them. Indeed, according to Glaser's report, Stana had maintained that vampires "ruled" or "reigned strongly" ("allwo die vampyres auch sehr starckh *regiereten*" [my emphasis]) on the Ottoman side.

This *Feindbild* took on added potency through the intersection of individual narratives about people (Stana, Paule, Miliza, Plagojevitz) who were purported to have become vampires, or who were seen as likely candidates, and the material reality of their apparently fresh, uncorrupted bodies. Frombald gazes on in surprise at the corpse of Plagojevitz, as he confirms the apparently correct predictions of the "insubordinate" villagers: the cadaver did not emit a bad smell; the body was in a completely "fresh" (*frish* [sic]) state, aside from the nose, which had fallen in; the old white layer of skin had fallen away to reveal a new one, as had the nails from hands and feet; and there was "fresh blood" in the mouth of the corpse. Frombald then details how, when the corpse was staked through the heart, "fresh" blood squirted out of its nose and mouth and, presumably, the cadaver had an erection: upon staking, not only did the blood gush out of the orifices but "rather other wild signs—which I bypass out of high respect—came to pass."[49] Glaser exclaims that one would have expected Miliza's body to have decomposed given the amount of time that it had been interred, even more so given that the bodies of those buried around her who were "younger, [of] plumper constitution in life, and who had suffered a shorter and milder illness" had decomposed.[50] That one can garner a sense of uneasy incredulity on the part of the Habsburg officials Frombald, Glaser, and Flückinger is to be seen in the emphasis on "fresh" blood, which is made throughout their reports. While the impression from the Flückinger text is that this is meant to refer to liquid rather than coagulated blood, that the term "liquid blood" (*liquides geblüet*)[51] is used only once across three texts suggests that the use of "fresh" was a deliberate authorial decision: "fresh" blood in bodies that were likewise unexpectedly, and unexplainedly "fresh." At one level, a strong tension exists in the Frombald, Glaser, and Flückinger texts: what is *purported* to be real is, if not impossible, nonetheless at the fringes of what is plausible; and yet—unearth the corpse!—what appears to be real—indeed, what is observed firsthand—then appears to fully align with and buttress the haunting narratives of the now-dead denizens of Kisolova and Medvedja.

As mentioned previously, the existence of the fantastical relies not on certainty but on uncertainty: it sits on the epistemic knife-edge between what is purported and what is observed. The observations of the Habsburg officials suggested that something highly unusual was happening, and the immediate context was not that of the academy but that of village discourse. The Medvedja outbreak was not—one imagines the members of the community intoning to the *contagions medicus* and the field surgeons—a singular and anomalous instance, but rather, just one in a series of misfortunes of supernatural provenance. The question was thus not simply one of violent incursion across the Habsburg military frontier but of infiltration by way of magical and occult means. To this end, the blood and burial earth of a vampire were shown to be uniquely powerful in the Paule and Stana narratives. They were represented as possessing apotropaic properties but also, conversely, as being a marker of future vampirism in the afflicted. Vampirism was, therefore, not merely an affliction of proximity but chiefly one of affinity: one's life history played a vital part in determining whether one was to become a vampire after death.[52] While a pathogenic outbreak could be avoided or escaped in a spatial, mechanical sense, a magical contagion could not: such an affliction remained attached to the host and in this way could infiltrate borders and cross over into the Habsburg *Erblande* unseen and unchecked.

The hidden connections and relationships carried over from past lives in the Ottoman lands were not limited to apotropaic blood rituals. Indeed, Milizia's narrative involved eating the meat of several sheep who had been purportedly attacked by a vampire. While the Flückinger report states that these sheep had been attacked by Paule several years earlier,[53] Glaser's report mentions that the sheep had actually been consumed during the time when Miliza had lived on the Ottoman side: "During her lifetime [Miliza] had told her neighbors that, when she was on the Turkish [side] she had eaten two sheep that had been killed by vampires, and that therefore when she died, she would likewise become a vampire."[54] While this dimension of the narrative makes sense insofar as vampirism was represented as an affliction of affinity, there is one telling line that suggests another possible interpretation. Glaser states in his report, almost in passing, that "no one knows whether [Miliza], always neighborly in her bearing, ever believed or practiced anything diabolic."[55] Were it not for Glaser's father's letter to the editors of the *commercium litterarium*, one might be inclined to disregard this passage. Two things stand out in Glaser senior's letter: in referring to the purported vampire outbreak that his son had related to him, he refers to it as "a magical pestilence" (*eine magische Seuche*); and he also mentions that his son took part in an autopsy of the vampires. The use of the term "magical" is only interesting in the context of Glaser junior's inclusion of the statement as to Miliza's moral and spiritual conduct. Was this information volunteered, or was it requested? If none of her neighbors had any knowledge one way or the other, it seems unlikely that any of them would have actively raised the matter, thus implying that Glaser had sought this information.

Did Glaser junior harbor the faint suspicion that Miliza could have been a witch[56], or that something genuinely diabolic was afoot in Medvedja? The author of a later anonymous text, referring to the vampire incidents states that a scientist may only resort to witchcraft as a viable explanation once all other possibilities had been exhausted.[57] Glaser's report was certainly inconclusive, and as his father indicates, it was sent to the authorities only after Glaser junior had already "hurriedly" written to him about the incident "promising to add further details [later]." Glaser senior suggests that his son took an off-the-record interest in the case: "My son had the opportunity to conduct an autopsy [on the bodies], and found all internal organs to be healthy and intact; the stomach and diaphragm were full of blood." This autopsy was never mentioned in Glaser junior's report to his superiors. One explanation is that the letter from Glaser senior to the *commercium* had been redacted and partially fictionalized, so as to merge Glaser's account with Flückinger's, although there is no evidence to substantiate this view. Another possibility is that Glaser remained in Medvedja to witness Flückinger's autopsy; however, in the archival copy of Flückinger's report, *Visum et repertum*, there is absolutely no mention of Glaser being in attendance: three military surgeons, Flückinger, Seigele, and Baumgarten were stated as being in attendance, and two officers, one first lieutenant Büttner and one Ensign von Lindenfels confirmed that the surgeons had undertaken the autopsy.[58] Furthermore, Glaser had arrived in Medvedja in mid-December 1731, and the Flückinger visitation occurred in early January 1732. Given that Glaser was stationed at Paracin less than a day's ride away, it is unlikely that he would have remained in Medvedja for several weeks after conducting his investigation. While there is the possibility that Glaser senior had confused the accounts, given that he was writing in February 1732, right at the time that the Flückinger report was making its way into learned circles, it is practically unlikely that he would have done so.

Whether or not Glaser junior had genuinely wondered about the potentially supernatural dimensions of the incidents in Medvedja and had conducted an off-record, unofficial autopsy is difficult to tell. However, in another document, we see a very strong interest in the potentially supernatural dimensions of another case of vampirism on the border. This document was ostensibly a letter from one Ensign von Köttwitz to Michael Ernst Ettmüller, the director of the famous learned society, the Academia Naturae Curiosorum (also known as the Leopoldina). In his letter, von Köttwitz relates a narrative from a town called Kuklina in Serbia in which a woman claimed to have been impregnated by her vampire husband. The brief narrative recounts how he had "used her" in death as he had done in life, except that in this instance "the semen was completely cold."[59] After forty weeks, the woman gave birth to a creature that "had the full proportion of a lad, but not a single member, rather it was like a piece of flesh; and after the third day it wrinkled-up like a sausage." Von Köttwitz then proceeds to ask Ettmüller, given the apparently wondrous nature of the incident, whether it is of "sympathetic, diabolic or astral-spiritual" provenance.[60]

While this source is methodologically problematic, there are some reasons to treat the content of the account as genuine. On the one hand, there is no mention in any other material of von Köttwitz; it has not yet been fully confirmed whether the response to this "letter" really came from Ettmüller; and in any case, it appears in an anonymously authored, printed document claiming a magical origin for vampirism. On the other hand, it is possible that the von Köttwitz in the printed document is actually von Lindenfels in the archival material. Just before von Köttwitz's account, the printed document reproduced Flückinger's *Visum et Repertum*, including three of the five names of those present at the autopsy. Among the names are those of Flückinger, Büttner, and von Köttwitz.[61] When we turn to the archival material, there is no von Köttwitz, Ensign of the Alexandrischen Regiment mentioned; however, there is a von Lindenfels, Ensign of the Alexandrischen Regiment.[62] Why mention Flückinger and Büttner but not von Lindenfels? One possibility is that the anonymous author simply made up a "letter" and fudged the name in order to lend a false sense of credibility to his analysis. Another possibility is that he had access to genuine material—a real letter from von Lindenfels—and purposefully changed the name in order to conceal the Ensign's identity.

In any case, the narrative of the document possesses a degree of verisimilitude: in his research on Orthodox and Muslim Roma from southeastern Europe, including Serbia, T. P. Vukanovic noted the persistent belief that male vampires return to have sex with their living wives, or indeed, other women.[63] Linked with this is the notion that such unions can produce offspring. Indeed, among the communities that Vukanovic studied, it was maintained that children born to a vampire have the capacity, in life, to act as powerful vampire hunters known as Dhampir, although they are fated to become vampires themselves after death.[64] That the von Köttwitz/von Lindenfels account seems to reflect these widespread beliefs—almost certainly far older than the mid-twentieth century when Vukanovic was undertaking his fieldwork—suggests that the account is, at least in part, genuine.

The above account suggests several important things. First, if we assume that its content is mostly genuine, and that it came from the southern frontier, it buttresses the notion that vampirism was likely more widely spread on the border than the Kisolova and Medvedja incidents indicate. Second, if we assume that von Lindenfels was actually the source of the letter to Ettmüller—and the verisimilitude of the account suggests that it came from the front line in any case—then what we have here is evidence potentially indicating an eyewitness at the Flückinger autopsy expressing dissatisfaction with a medical explanation. If von Lindenfels was actually inquiring as to the, as he saw it, magical origins of the vampire incidents, then it is highly likely that others were also asking these sorts of questions: are vampires diabolic, the result of natural magical sympathies, or rather the predations of an astral spirit? The narrative of infiltration takes on greater resonance: the vampire is an enemy of supernatural provenance, one who not only attaches itself to individuals by way of blood rituals, and in so doing crosses borders in an unseen manner; but an entity that can also reproduce, and in so doing continue its line unabated.

* * *

Although neither Glaser nor Flückinger explicitly posited an infectious illness as the cause of the problem in Medvedja, as Peter Kreuter has argued,[65] nonetheless a pronounced discursive link was established in the reports between pathogenesis and the etiology of vampirism, even if neither Glaser nor Flückinger was able to articulate precisely what such an illness might be. Indeed, precisely the wording of Glaser's text (and Flückinger's, as we shall see) indicates a pathogenic basis for vampirism: both repeatedly refer to the afflicted inhabitants of Medvedja as having died after a period of "illness." Any possible spiritual signification of the vampire body hinted at in Glaser's report is largely subsumed to the medical gaze of the physician. The very language of the village inhabitants, their agency in the process of signification, is largely overshadowed by a new language, both figuratively and literally. The textual manifestations of "foreign" signifiers—the names of people and places, and the names of cultural artefacts, such as the "vampire"—are converted into the bureaucratic language of the Habsburg administration. This power dynamic is seen on a different level as well. The web of cultural signification embracing the vampire as liminal creature is replaced with an entirely different form of knowledge production: oral culture is superseded by the written text, and the result is the transformation of the vampire into a medically dead body.

The formal characteristics of the Flückinger text, the *visum et repertum*, do much to shape the construction of the vampire. As a medical document generally, and as an autopsy report more specifically, the text prefigures the nature of the information to be gleaned from the investigation. It situates Flückinger as eyewitness (*visum*) and mediator (*repertum*), thus allotting considerable agency to his position within the group of on-the-ground observers. In much the same way as Glaser's text, the *visum et repertum* medicalizes the body by way of a pathogenic schema. While it is clear in the Flückinger text that the village inhabitants believed the situation to be the result of the predations of several vampires, Flückinger, like Glaser, continually refers to the cause of death as being pathogenic in nature: "A woman named Stana, twenty years old, died two months ago after a three-day illness after giving birth"; "a woman named Miliza, said to be sixty years old died after a three-month illness"; "a heiduc's son Miloe, sixteen years old, was exhumed, [he had] lain in the ground for nine weeks, [having] died after a three-day illness."[66] Intermittently Flückinger continues in this manner. As we have seen, he mentions Paule's "bad death" but does not link this clearly to his transformation into a vampire.

The core significance of Flückinger's text for what has hitherto been the gradual medicalization of the vampire body rests on the autopsies performed on the bodies. The language Flückinger employs does two key things. First, it furthers the construction of a normative framework for the vampire body. By way of incising and opening up the bodies of the potential vampires the text, as a surgeon's knife, lays bare the interior of the cadaver. The organs are "exposed" to the scrutiny of the medical gaze; Flückinger distinguishes between the healthy and the unhealthy, those organs in a fresh state and those in a putrid state. Concerning Stana's body he writes,

> After the opening of the body a quantity of fresh extravascular blood appeared in the pectoral cavity, the vessels as well as arteries and veins along with the coronary ventricles were not, as is otherwise common, filled with coagulated blood, all the viscera, ie. the lungs, liver, stomach, spleen and intestines were completely fresh just as with a healthy person, however I did find the uterus

completely large and very inflamed on the outside, because the placenta as well as the locia had remained inside her and were putrid.[67]

Although Flückinger economizes on space, and in so doing often leaves out specific detail on all the cadavers' internal organs, he nevertheless indicates clearly those that have remained in a pristine internal state. The normative assumptions brought to light in the text are apparent, especially concerning the blood, which is expected to have coagulated. Flückinger is careful to note those bodies showing signs of fluid blood:

> A woman named Russa ... in whom I found fully fresh blood not only in the chest [cavity] rather also in the upper part of the stomach (*fundus ventriculi*) ... a heiduc, 60 years old, died 6 weeks prior, I found a great quantity of liquid blood in the chest [cavity] and the stomach like the others ... Stanjoicka, a heiduc's wife, is 20 years old ... with the removal [of her] from her grave a quantity of fresh blood flowed out of her nose, after the autopsy I found, as already thought, a [quantity of] downright balsamic fresh blood not only in the chest cavity, rather also in the coronary ventricle, [and] all the viscera in a completely healthy and good state.[68]

Further, the language of the report utilizes expressions intended to create a distinct type of knowledge. The utilization of medical terminology, as noted in the quotes above, inscribes the vampire body with medical signification. This act of cutting through the exterior of the body in order to probe the contents of the interior presupposes a hierarchy of knowledge in which exteriority is itself rendered superfluous. This stands in stark contrast to the vampire body as a site of spiritual signification. The uncorrupted features of the vampire, such as new skin and nails, and fresh flowing blood, lose their potential revelatory power; no longer can they offer verification of a world of hidden relations and operations. As a textual representation, the vampire body becomes a taxonomical object of medical scrutiny.

Following the submission of Flückinger's report to Belgrade, a copy was sent to the *Hofkriegsrat* in Vienna. While what might be interpreted as a pay dispute[69] took place throughout 1732 concerning the remuneration of Glaser, Flückinger, the adjuncts, and Büttner, the copy of the report, Schroeder speculates, made its way through Karl Alexander and the court at Stuttgart to the Prussian Academy of Sciences. According to Schroeder, it is plausible that when Karl Alexander, his brother Duke Ludwig-Eberhard, and the Grand Duke Franz Stephan of Lorraine made a trip together to Berlin, a copy of the letter would have been passed on to King Friedrich Wilhelm of Prussia, and then from him on to the Academy of

Sciences, of which he was patron.[70] Another route of transmission could have been through the court at Vienna to the president of the Academia Naturae Curiosorum, Professor Johannes Beier, although there is no documentation to support this.[71]

* * *

In the preceding discussion, I have suggested that we can read the archival sources concerning vampirism as reflective of a set of tangible geopolitical anxieties that contribute to a broader, emergent construction of fear that operates across a discrete stretch of time (1725–32) and across a varied set of documents. Reading the sources "against the grain," one discerns how concrete concerns, such as contagion and depopulation, situated within the context of the threat of military incursion, also intersect with an array of narratives about a new sort of enemy with a distinct *modus*: the blood-thirsty dead and their capacity for unchecked infiltration and destruction. These narratives sit in an uneasy tension with the central reportage of the Flückinger text: the autopsy, which transforms the vampire into a distinctly medical object.

Although it would be stretching my analysis too far to suggest that the process of autopsy represented a concerted fear-allaying strategy, it nonetheless represented one side of the social power relations at play, and in so doing shaped the discourse on vampires: in just over half of the learned treatises that appeared in the several years following the vampire incidents, pathogenesis was the dominant narrative. The question in these texts was (in part) to ascertain what sort of illness the unfortunate denizens of Medvedja had suffered from rather than to genuinely entertain the possibility that the dead had come back to life in Serbia and had attacked the living. I have made the distinction between "anxiety" and "fear" on the basis that the former represents a construction based on rational considerations and the latter refers to the fantastical and the emergent, but one could also situate this within a double-axis model including generalized and specific anxiety/fear respectively. It is then interesting to note how medicalization in this context was able to neutralize "fear" and transform "anxiety" into a specific, localized threat; a threat that could be contained and confronted.

However, the incidents in Kisolova and Medvejda also evoked another, bigger narrative involving a fear of the degradation, fragmentation, and destruction of a political order. The potential loss or gain of territorial sovereignty was a concrete reality for the Habsburg Monarchy, as would become immediately apparent in the closing years of the 1730s with the outbreak of war once more with the Ottoman Empire, and again in the opening years of the 1740s with the invasion by Prussian forces. Indeed, the question of political survival was forever a tenuous one for the Habsburgs. Threats external—France in the seventeenth century under Louis XIV and Prussia in the eighteenth under Friedrich II—coalesced with those of an internal nature, such as the apparent inability of Charles VI to produce a male heir. Nonetheless, while the loss of territory, and the anxieties connected to this were by definition concrete and local, its corollary—the generalized fear of the collapse of a political order (a nightmare not without its own monsters)—was more broadly existential than merely political. Indeed, as the chapter by Kirsten Cooper in this collection has shown, these sorts of existential fantasies also drew upon fears that were deeply cultural. The vampire too could as much represent a generalized threat to a cultural order as to a political one. As Thomas Bohn remarks, the vampire "became an expression of a barbaric world from which civilized Europe could demarcate itself."[72] The encroachment of vampirism from the south, and later in the nineteenth century Bohn continues, from the east, was perceived to represent the "invasion of primitive forces" which were, he states, "bound up with Slavophobic stereotypes."[73] As the vampire debate developed in German university towns such as Leipzig, the vampire began to undergo a transformation in some of the texts: it was psychosomatized as an illness exacerbated by—or even stemming from—a distorted imagination.[74] The true threat was thus the "superstition" (*Aberglaube*) of the Slavic peoples, whether on the southern frontier or, as further cases from the 1750s illustrate, from the eastern provinces. But this was only part of the story. Other texts, while denying the existence of vampires as blood-drinking ambulant corpses, nonetheless ventured into the realm of the diabolic and the numinous to (re-)construct the vampire as a distinctly magical creature.[75]

Notes

1 *Copia des vom Hern Frombald kayl. Cameral Provisore zu Gradiska im König Reich Servien erlassenen Briefes anno 1725*, Haus- Hof- und Staatsarchiv, Türkei I, 191, fol. 25r. All archival collections mentioned in this analysis are in Vienna.
2 *Copia des vom Hern Frombald … erlassenen Briefes anno 1725*, fol. 25r.
3 Ibid., fol. 26r. Although the cause of death was purportedly a twenty-four-hour illness that Plagojevitz had brought upon his victims by (nonfatally) throttling them; the bloodsucking appears to be incidental to the narrative.
4 Ibid., fol. 25v.
5 A type of mercenary soldier.

6   Archival documents indicate this spelling rather than the usual "Arnold" seen in modern scholarly literature.
7   *Visum et Repertum*, Finanz- und Hofkammerarchiv, Hoffinanz Ungarn (HFU), rote Nr. 654, fol. 1138r.
8   *Visum et Repertum*, fol. 1138r–v.
9   Ibid., fol. 1139r.
10 HFU, rote Nr. 654, fol. 1134r.
11 Ibid., fol. 1132r. For details on the routes that the reports from Serbia took through the Habsburg bureaucratic apparatus and into learned community see: Aribert Schroeder, *Vampirismus: Seine Entwicklung vom Thema zum Motiv* (Frankfurt am Main: Akademische Verlagsgesellschaft, 1973), 37–69. For greater detail on the geopolitical and epidemiological contexts of the vampire exhumations see: Michael Pickering, "The Role of Spirit Agency in the Construction of the Vampire in the Anonymous *Acten-mäßige und umständliche Relation von denen Vampiren oder Menschen-Saugern* (1732)," in *Birthing the Monster of Tomorrow: Unnatural Reproductions*, ed. Brandy Schillace and Andrea Wood (New York: Cambria Press, 2014).
12 For general information on this see: Gunther Rothenberg, "The Austrian Sanitary Cordon and the Control of the Bubonic Plague, 1710–1871," *Journal of the History of Medicine* 28, no. 1 (1973): 15–23.
13 I broadly derive my use of "fantasy" from: Lyndal Roper, *Witch Craze: Terror and Fantasy in Baroque Germany* (New Haven, CT: Yale University Press, 2004), 7–12.
14 I take my usage of this term, referring to the construction of a strongly negative image of a perceived enemy, from Róisín Healy's discussion of the construction of an anti-Jesuit Feindbild in early modern Germany: Róisín Healy, *The Jesuit Specter in Imperial Germany* (Boston, MA: Brill, 2003), 21–8.
15 For more on this see: Michael Pickering, "The Birth of the Vampire in Eighteenth-Century Europe" (PhD thesis, University of Melbourne, 2014), chapter 2.
16 See: Pickering, "Birth of the Vampire."
17 For the manuscript version of a famous contemporary report on this see: Georg Tallar, *Obgeforderter Bericht die Blutsauger und derselben Widerlegung in Temesvarer Banat betreff. Verfasst vom Tallar. Zur Ungarischen Geschichte An: 1750*, Finanz- und Hofkammerarchiv, Banaterakten, rote Nr. 53, fols. 1–22.
18 Jutta Nowosadko, "Der 'Vampyrus Serviensis' und sein Habitat: Impressionen von der österreichischen Militärgrenze," *Militär und Gesellschaft in der Frühen Neuzeit* 8, no. 2 (2004): 157.
19 Rothenberg, "Austrian Sanitary Cordon," 17.
20 Nowosadtko, "Der 'Vampyrus Serviensis' und sein Habitat," 156.
21 Rothenberg, "Austrian Sanitary Cordon," 17–18.
22 *Contumaz, und respective Reinigungs-Ordnung, wie solche, sowohl mit denen Personen, als in die Contumz ankommenden Waaren, wie auch Briefschaften*

gehalten werden solle, Kriegsarchiv, Sanitätshofkommission, Akten (1738–1762), [2].
23 Nowosadtko, "Der 'Vampyrus Serviensis' und sein Habitat," 156.
24 Thomas M. Bohn, "Das Gespenst von Lublau: Michael Kaspereks/Kaspareks Verwandlung vom Wiedergänger zum Blutsauger," *Kakanien Revisited* (2009), 4. Although Bohn shows that the Kasparek narrative was taken-up in Eberhard David Hauber's *Bibliotheca sive Acta Scripta Magica* as one of the progenitors of the Serbian vampire cases, the core vampire texts from the early to mid-1730s do not reference this narrative.
25 Gábor Klaniczay, *The Uses of Supernatural Power*, trans. Susan Singerman, ed. Karen Margolis (Cambridge: Polity in association with Basil Blackwell, 1990), 179.
26 Peter Mario Kreuter, "Vom 'üblen Geist' zum 'Vampier': Die Darstellung des Vampirs in den Berichten österreichischer Militärärzte zwischen 1725 und 1756," in *Poetische Wiedergänger: Deutschsprachige Vampirismus-Diskurse vom Mittelalter bis zur Gegenwart*, ed. Julia Bertschik and Christa Agnes Tuczay (Tübingen: Francke Verlag, 2005), 114–17. Kreuter also suggests that other instances were probably known among members of the Habsburg military garrison in Serbia in this period.
27 In addition to the following examples, Stefan Hock provides a detailed overview of cases concerning revenancy in Europe throughout the medieval and early modern periods. Stefan Hock, *Die Vampyrsagen und ihre Verwertung in der deutschen Litteratur* (Berlin: Verlag von Alexander Duncker, 1900), 29–42. For further material concerning revenancy in medieval and early modern central and southeastern Europe see: Z. Krumphanzlová, "Der Ritus der slawischen Skelettfriedhöfe der mittleren und jüngeren Burgwallzeit in Böhmen," *Památky Archeologické* 57 (1966): 285–6; Rudolf Grenz, "Archäologische Vampirbefunde aus dem westslawischen Siedlungsgebiet," *Zeitschrift für Ostforschung* 16, no. 2 (1967): 256; 257–8; Constantin Jirecek, "Das Gesetzbuch des serbischen Caren Stephan Dušan,"*Archiv für slavische Philologie* 22 (1900): 162; Milenko Filipović, "Die Leichenverbrennung bei den Südslaven," *Wiener Völkerkundliche Mitteilungen* 10 (1962): 63–4. For an interesting case from within the Ottoman Empire see: Markus Köhbach, "Ein Fall von Vampirismus bei den Osmanen," *Balkan Studies* 20 (1979): 84–7.
28 *Copia des vom Hern Frombald … erlassenen Briefes anno 1725*, fol. 25r.
29 Schroeder, *Vampirismus*, 45.
30 HFU, rote Nr. 654, fol. 1136r.
31 Schroeder, *Vampirismus*, 41.
32 My research has further confirmed that there are no known copies of the manuscript mentioned in the records of the subcollection "Neoacquistische Subdelegation," Kriegsarchiv, as might have been expected if it had been processed by the Hofkriegsrat.

33 *Copia des vom Hern Frombald ... erlassenen Briefes anno 1725*, fol. 25v.
34 Schroeder speculates that the apologetic ending was added in the printed version of the report as a stylistic improvement. Schroeder, *Vampirismus*, 75–6.
35 *Wienerisches Diarium* (s.l.: July 21, 1725): "dem vor Forcht ausser sich selbst gesetzen Pöfel" [*sic*].
36 Finanz- und Hofkammerarchiv, Ungarisches Kamerale, Ältere Banater Akten, Karton 6, fol. 1032 ff. Also, in 1732 in the village of Trstenik, just southwest across the Morava River from Medvedja, there was an outbreak of pestilence that killed nineteen people: Filipović, "Die Leichenverbrennung bei den Südslaven," 66.
37 HFU, rote Nr. 654, fol. 1134r.
38 Klaus Hamberger, *Mortuus non Mordet: Dokumente zum Vampirismus, 1689–1791* (Vienna: Turia & Kant, 1992), 54–5.
39 HFU, rote Nr. 654, fol. 1134r.
40 Ibid., fols. 1134r–1134v.
41 Ibid., fols. 1135r–1135v.
42 Ibid., fol. 1135r.
43 *Visum et Repertum*, fol. 1140r.
44 Ibid., fol. 1138r.
45 Ibid., fol. 1138v.
46 Ibid., fol. 1138r.
47 HFU, rote Nr. 654, fols. 1134v–1135r.
48 Ibid., fol. 1135r.
49 *Copia des vom Hern Frombald ... erlassenen Briefes anno 1725*, fol. 26r: "sondern andere wilde Zeichen, welche wegen hohen Respect umgehen, vorbeygegangen."
50 HFU, rote Nr. 654, fol. 1135r.
51 *Visum et Repertum*, fol. 1139r.
52 This concept has been widely discussed in ethnographic and folkloric literature, of course. See for example: Dagmar Burkhart, "Vampirglaube und Vampirsage auf dem Balkan," in *Beiträge zur Südosteuropa-Forschung* (Munich: Trofenik, 1966); Harry Senn, *Were-Wolf and Vampire in Romania* (Colorado: East European Monographs, 1982).
53 *Visum et Repertum*, fol. 1139r.
54 HFU, rote Nr. 654, fol. 1134v.
55 Ibid.
56 On the connections between witchcraft and corporeal revenancy see: Karen Lambrecht, "Wiedergänger und Vampire in Ostmitteleuropa – Posthume Verbrennung statt Hexenverfolgung?," *Jahrbuch für deutsche und osteuropäische Volkskunde* 37 (1994): 49–77.
57 Anon., *Schreiben eines guten Freundes an einen anderen guten Freund, die Vampire betreffend* (s.l.: March 26, 1732), [1].

58 *Visum et Repertum*, fol. 1140r.
59 Anon., *Actenmässige und umständliche Relation von denen Vampyren* (Leipzig: Martini, 1732), 17.
60 Ibid., 18.
61 Ibid., 15.
62 *Visum et Repertum*, fol. 1140r.
63 T. P. Vukanovic, "The Vampire," in *Vampires of the Slavs*, ed. Jan Perkowski (Cambridge, MA: Slavica, 1976), 217–18.
64 Vukanovic, "The Vampire," 224.
65 Peter Kreuter, "Krankheit und Vampirglaube. Ein Beitrag zur Phänomenologie des blutsaugenden Wiedergängers in Südosteuropa," *Quo Vadis Romania?* 18/19 (2000-1): 66–7.
66 *Visum et Repertum*, fols. 1138v–1139r.: "Ein Weib Nahmens Stana, 20. Jahr alt so von 2. Monathen nach 3. Tägig krankheit Ihrer niederkunft gestorben"; "Ware ein Weib Nahmens Miliza beylauffig 60 Jahr alt, welche nach 3. Monath Krankheit gestorben"; "Wurde Ein Heyducks Sohn Milloe 16. Jahr alt aussgegraben, so. 9. Woch. in der Erde geleg, und nach 3. Tägiger Krankheit gestorben ..." *Krankheit* has a clear medical connotation.
67 *Visum et Repertum*, fol. 1139r.
68 Ibid., fol. 1139v–1140r.
69 Finanz- und Hofkammerarchiv, Sanitätsakten, rote Nr. 1.
70 Schroeder, *Vampirismus*, 62–6.
71 While it was stated by contemporaries that Karl VI sent a letter to Beier, there is no archival evidence to suggest this. Johann Christoph Meinig, *Besondere Nachricht, von denen Vampyren oder so genanten Blut-Saugern* (Leipzig: Johann Christian Martini, 1732), 4.
72 Thomas M. Bohn, "Vampirismus in Österreich und Preussen. Von der Entdeckung einer Seuche zum Narrativ der Gegenkolonisation," *Jahrbücher für Geschichte Osteuropas* 56 (2008): 161–2.
73 Bohn, "Vampirismus in Österreich und Preussen," 162; 177.
74 See for example: Johann Christian Fritsche, *Eines Weimarischen muthmassliche Gedancken von den Vampyren oder Blutsaugenden Todten* (Leipzig: Blochbergern, 1732); Johan Christoph Harenberg, *Venünftige und christliche Gedanken über die Vampyrs oder Blutsaugenden Todten* (Wolfenbüttel: Meissner, 1733); Johann Christian Stock, *Gründliche Auszüge aus denen Neuesten Theologisch-Philosophisch- und Philologischen Disputationibus*, ed. Johann Boëtii (Leipzig: Gollner 1733); Johann Christoph Meinig, *Besondere Nachrichten von denen Vampyrs* (Leipzig: Martini, 1732); Gottlob Heinrich Vogt, *Kurtzes Bedencken von den Relationen wegen der Vampyren* (Leipzig: Martini, 1732).

75 See for example: Anon., *Actenmässige und umständliche Relation von denen Vampyren* (Leipzig: Martini, 1732); Christoph Friedrich Demelius, *Philosophischer Versuch, ob nicht die merkwurdige Begebenheit der Blutsauger oder Vampyren aus den principiis naturae hergeleitet werden konne* (1732); Michael Ranfft, *Tractat von dem Kauen und Schmatzen der Todten in Gräbern* (Leipzig: Teubner, 1734); W. S. G. E., *Curieuse und sehr wunderbare Relation, von denen sich neuer Dingen in Servien erzeigenden Blut-Saugern oder Vampyrs, aus authentischen Nachrichten mitgetheilet* (s.l.: s.n., 1732).

4

"The Forest is not Everyone's Friend": Fear in an Eighteenth-Century Southwest German Hometown[*]

Dennis Frey

From 1755 to 1784 Ernst Jacob Vayhinger, a worsted-wool weaver (*Zeugmacher*) in the town of Göppingen, kept a chronicle of his household economy, regularly tallying up its yearly profits and losses with a regular invocation of God.[1] While focused mostly on this annual accounting, Vayhinger occasionally offered insights and observations about high politics, local events, weather, and other sundry topics. For instance, in one of his entries for 1782, he wrote,

> The 11th of February was the birthday of our beloved Duke [of Württemberg] Karl, on which day a higher school in Stuttgart was built [and] there were many foreign officials invited from [other] principalities and imperial cities.
>
> About this time, because our Emperor Josef II had closed many monasteries, the Pope himself wanted to come to Vienna in order to control this evil. The Emperor however declined it and [suggested] that the meeting should take place in Florence.[2]

Following these remarks on newsworthy events, Vayhinger subsequently offered:

> An Anecdote
>
> About 12 years ago, as I made my way with a neighbor to Schwäbisch Gmünd[3] to sell my canaries to the dealers there, I took my son, who was about 12 at the time. Following the sale of our birds we headed back. And in the evening we came again to Hohenstaufen.[4] We wanted to continue on, but the baker, Gottlieb, told me, "Vayhinger, stay here. The forest is not everyone's friend." I laughed at this and asked for a torch, but he said, "I will give you a lantern, for if you must continue on, then it is better." I accepted it, and we continued onward. In the forest, we put my son between us, and my fellow burgher carried the lantern. As

we went down the bank of a pit, a strange feeling of doom approached, which I had never before in my life imagined. There came such a storm that the leaves of the bushes fell at our feet. It was as if the forest wanted to collapse in on itself. The wild boars snorted at our feet. About 20 steps from us, someone ran [by], who constantly created sparks and fire with a whetting-steel, [so that] sparks and fire were to be seen and heard down to the ground, and he shrieked "*Hob, Hob, Hob!*" constantly. I shouted after him two or three times, "good friend, wait, let us go together." But he gave me no answer. My son was overcome by such fear [*Angst*] that he screamed. In Hohenstaufen they surely must have heard his far-and-wide screaming. Because the creature who shrieked so and spread fire did not stop, I took it to be a fury and said to my son, "I am telling you, be still. If you keep up your screaming, I will beat you over the head with my walking stick and go on [without you.] That is a damned devil, who will inflict harm on us; let the damned devil run, if he does not want to wait. God will safeguard us!" Then everything went quiet and we came through, thanks be to God.

Now what it was, [and] I am not being too gullible [here], is that about 5 years prior [ca. 1765] a man hanged himself there.[5]

In chronicling nearly thirty years of his life, this particular digression from his usual topics provided the most recognizable representation of fear. From the premonition of evil lurking in the forest to his son's screams that echoed far and wide, Vayhinger's text evoked terror. And, if those elements were not enough, then the "damned devil" thumping the earth and throwing off fire bolts should have put the fright into just about anyone.

Recall though that Vayhinger stated upfront that the events he recounted in 1782 had happened twelve years earlier (*c*. 1770). If the episode was so remarkable, then why did he wait so long to record it in his chronicle? How accurate, or truthful, was his retelling? Did he actually remain calm in this moment of "doom," even calling out to this apparition, before coming to view it as a specter seeking vengeance? Confronted by such a clamor, did Vayhinger use the threat of bodily harm and abandonment to force his son to regain some semblance of composure? Or, was this entire episode simply a good yarn that he had spun over the years with family, friends, and colleagues? And, having perhaps refined this ghost story over the years, had Vayhinger finally decided to put pen to paper and record it for perpetuity? While impossible to answer any of these questions conclusively, a "laborious unraveling" of them will, in Mary Lindemann's words, "lead us closer to an understanding of a historical situation that we can perhaps never fully recreate."[6] And, while deep skepticism might even suggest that Vayhinger's narrative about what transpired on that night in the forest between Hohenstaufen and Göppingen in 1770 was pure fiction, this *Zeugmacher* situated the moment historically as well as spatially. Indeed, once he wrote it down in his journal, it became an artifact of his life, firmly bound by both time and location. As such, a close examination of this supernatural experience in *der Wald*—the clearest representation of fear in his chronicle, but not the only one—will reveal the ways in which anxiety, existential dread, and religion were deeply entangled in Vayhinger's daily, tangible life. Furthermore, those entanglements of the material and immaterial will remind us that the eighteenth century was an era full of flux, nuance, and complexity, especially when it came to emotions among ordinary Swabians.

At first glance, though, Vayhinger's chronicle can hardly be classified as "a proper 'ego document'—the kind of source, such as a diary or personal correspondence, that scholars look to for evidence of a person's thoughts, feelings, and interior struggles."[7] It is, instead, more like another journal, the one kept by Meister Frantz Schmidt in Nuremberg from 1573 to 1618 and analyzed so well in Joel Harrington's book, *The Faithful Executioner*. Although two centuries and some distance separated Schmidt and Vayhinger, both of them seemed to focus primarily on recording their "professional milestones."[8] Over the three decades of record keeping, Vayhinger oftentimes wrote only a handful of lines per year, but those lines always included an annual accounting of his household economy. For instance, in documenting the year from 1764 to 1765, Vayhinger wrote only the following:

> From 1764 to 1765 I worked 22 Centner[9] of wool; but from Micheli [*Michaelis or Michaelmas, Sept. 29th*] until springtime, I was ill; in this year I forfeited 50 fl.[10] Because I was ill, my household economy was quite bad. I got my wool from Lorch, Heidenheim, [and] Herbrechtigen. Bread cost 12, 13, [and] 14 kr., wine 16, 18, 20 kr., and so on. The wine for 16 kr. was soon undrinkable. By God's will, my assets were weakened to 655 fl.; no additional news has happened.[11]

Year in and year out, no matter how long or short his entries were, Vayhinger made sure to state whether his household's net worth had increased or decreased; he missed only the last two years of his chronicle (i.e., 1783 and 1784).

This prominent feature of the "so-called Vayhinger-book" captured the eyes of the late nineteenth-century economic historian, Walter Troeltsch, as he studied closely the worsted wool handicrafts, or *Zeugmacherei*, in early-modern Württemberg.[12] Using "the original, an initially neatly, [but] finally unclearly written *Quartband* of 164 pages" to illustrate the many challenges faced by weavers during the second half of the eighteenth century, Troeltsch argued that this text revealed three distinct periods in Vayhinger's household economy: "In the time of an emerging, young master-craftsman (1755–1764), in the years of setback (1764–1772), [and] finally in the years of success (1772–1782)."[13] Although success came to Vayhinger's household in the 1770s, a citywide fire in 1782 reduced it, along with all the other homes inside the city walls, to ashes. Given these circumstances, Troeltsch concluded his essay with the following remarks: "As we leave our chronicler at a moment of misfortune [i.e., in the aftermath of a city-wide fire in 1782], the impression remains that he had a nature full of energy and constantly strove for progress, which even in his confined atmosphere enabled him to make his life as good as possible. With all of his angularity and sobriety, he is also a reflection of the indestructible strength, even in hard times, of the German middle classes."[14] Much like Harrington's temporal analysis of Schmidt's chronicle—but more than a century earlier—Troeltsch's study of the *Vayhingerbuch* provided "a glimpse of the inner life" of its author.[15] According to Harrington, as an author ages, the tropes in her or his journaling undergo subtle (and sometimes not so subtle) changes, which can offer, when studied closely, insight about that particular author's "thinking and passions."[16] Alas, Troeltsch's brief glimpse came only in his concluding remarks, but given his era and his interests this should not surprise us. Still, though, his concluding remarks alluded to the tropes that pervade Vayhinger's chronicle: "hard times," "misfortune," "sobriety," and "indestructible strength."

To contextualize these early-modern tropes, one must keep in mind that Vayhinger's hometown was located, as argued by Johannes Wallmann, Peter Schicketanz, Hartmut Lehmann, and Martin Brecht, in a hotbed of Pietism.[17] Indeed, nine years after Philip Jakob Spener published his *Pia desideria* in 1675, Eberhard Zeller led several private, devotional meetings, modelled on Spener's notion of "Collegia pietatis," in Göppingen before moving onto other towns in the duchy.[18] Across the entire duchy, Pietism's roots found fertile soil among its denizens, whose faith, according to Albrecht von Haller in 1724, was not only "deeper in the hearts than elsewhere" but also "devoted to piety."[19] The region produced notable Pietist theologians, such as Johann Albrecht Bengel (1687–1752), whose school of thought inspired many Pietist hymnals, and Christoph Oetinger (1702–1782), who was born and raised to 15 in Göppingen and whose work provided the next most significant guiding form (*Leitgestalt*) after Bengel.[20] While radical Pietism remained a minority sect in and around Vayhinger's hometown, the Lutheran ecclesiastical authorities had by 1743 adopted certain elements of Pietism into its official church doctrine.[21] Consequently, during the second half of the eighteenth century, many Lutherans in this region practiced their faith in a largely Pietist fashion, and, as I have argued elsewhere, this faith was undergirded by the many Pietistic hymnals, prayer books, and bibles, found among their personal possessions during much of the eighteenth century.[22] The Vayhingers were no exception to this, owning a collection of books typical for the pious Swabians that they were.[23]

Among early-modern Pietist literature, a noteworthy genre was the conversion narrative. While Vayhinger's chronicle could never be confused for this genre, it shared a lot in common with those texts of more radical Pietists. In his thought-provoking study of this genre, Andreas Bähr argues that fear and anxiety were not just standard tropes in Pietism but "two of the most relevant religious emotions."[24] From his careful analysis of how early Germany Pietists described these emotions, Bähr concludes that fear and anxiety were felt as external affects, as consequences of the arduous path to salvation, and not as feelings or emotions originating from within oneself. These external affects served as evidence of an ongoing journey of pious devotion; indeed, "those who considered accidents, war and the plague not a punishing evil but a trial of the elected and pious, averted the danger of desperation—and thus liberated themselves out of all the abysses and pits of this world. They turned fear into fearlessness, or, to be more precise, the wrong fear into the right: the fearless fear."[25] In Bähr's words:

> Pietist accounts of anxiety do not primarily tell us about anxiety itself but about its overcoming; and they do so in order to illustrate the religious and moral preconditions for this liberation. Thus, from Pietist conversion narratives and (auto-)biographies we may neither conclude that this religion was terrifying nor that anxiety was simply expelled by Pietist piety. In these texts, fear and fearlessness do not constitute two mental occasions being mutually exclusive, but a complex semantic unit which determined the person's relationship with God. What was aimed at here was not coping with feelings of fear—its elimination for the purpose of individual wellbeing—but the transformation of the wrong fear into the right one: overcoming fear so that it becomes the fear of God.[26]

By taking a more historicist approach, Bähr contradicts the older—and in his opinion mistaken—view that Pietism and its introspective nature accelerated the inward turn brought on by the Enlightenment. Instead, as enlightened philosophes grappled with new conceptions of emotions and feelings in the late eighteenth century, Pietist expressions of fear and anxiety remained more externally affective than internally emotional. According to Bähr, "It was not until the late eighteenth century that this fear could be conceptualized as a feeling, especially by critics of religious enthusiasm—initially by orthodox theologians and afterwards by anthropologists, who began to enquire into specifically psychophysical mechanisms of fear and anxiety."[27] Thus, Pietism and the Enlightenment did not go hand in glove, but rather their distinct orientations—external versus internal—conflicted and thus contributed to the sense of flux and nuance that characterized the eighteenth century.

This powerful observation about the ways in which early-modern people experienced fear puts not only the tropes of Vayhinger's chronicle into stark relief but also the entire text. As suggested by Troeltsch, this ordinary *Zeugmacher* reflected the "indestructible strength" and "sobriety" of the *Bürgertum* as they confronted "hard times" and "misfortunes." The early 1770s, for instance, brought hardship, in the form of famine (*Hungersnot*), which Vayhinger discusses in his chronicle. Things got so bad in April 1771 that, according to Vayhinger, "the *Herr Doktor* was sent out, with the [city's] children, into the open countryside in order to show them which roots were good to eat."[28] In August of the same year, he made a special entry on August 5 to record that he "had, through the grace of God, ground a bushel of grain for 6fl. by his cousin; there was joy in [his] house; [and] as [he] came from the mill, the water was already boiling for *Spätzle* [a type of delicate noodle unique to this region]."[29] In good Swabian fashion, Vayhinger further commented that *Spätzle* "taste better than the usual *Dampfnudeln* [steamed yeast dumplings]."[30] Notwithstanding the joy that must have come from those noodles, Vayhinger's "setbacks" were not exclusively due to the famine.

Indeed, tracing them back to their origins in the mid-1760s yields additional, significant insight. In one of his shorter entries in the entire chronicle, Vayhinger wrote that from 1765 to 1766 he had worked even less wool than the year before—only 15 Centner—and that his household's assets had consequently been further reduced to 620 Gulden. While the costs of bread and wine remained the same and once again "nothing new happened," Vayhinger complained bitterly at the very end of this brief entry that he had "never to this point" in his life "suffered such great maladies, [weighing] especially on the chest" and that the "disturbing difficulties," which he would "not name," were due to his wife.[31] In the original text, Vayhinger switched from his native German to Latin when he wrote the word, "wife" (i.e., *Uxor*). Ten years later, in one of his multiple entries for 1777, our weaver explained what the ongoing difficulties were, writing that he "had suffered much because of my wife's drinking."[32] (Interestingly, Troeltsch never points out the alcoholism, couching it instead as "the wife's mismanagement."[33]) Vayhinger's reliance on Latin for the crucial words, "*uxor propter Bibendum*," not only demonstrates that he had learned Latin in his education, but it also suggests that he still felt the need, ten years after hinting at the problem, to mask it somewhat. Still, though, the drinking apparently continued as Vayhinger remarked in 1780: "I have lost 75 Gulden. My wife [*uxor*] had the greatest responsibility for it."[34]

Vayhinger had married Anna Barbara née Schaupp in October 1755.[35] Besides briefly stating her name in the family genealogy that opens his chronicle, Vayhinger's next mention of his wife came when he commented on the year from 1756 to 1757. After complaining that the war (presumably the Seven Years' War—yet another "misfortune") had dried up the market for wool, Vayhinger stated, "My wife has been ill for seven weeks."[36] Anna Barbara would not appear again in his chronicle until nine years later in 1765–6, as mentioned above, when he alluded to her problem with drinking, offering a two-sentence paragraph that combined her troubles with his own physical ailments. The following year (1767) Vayhinger concluded his annual entry with a tally of his household wealth, adding this to his financial statement: "To this date I still have great pains on my body, the Lord sees it."[37] Here, Vayhinger seemed to present himself as a steadfast and resolute subject, encountering his travails unflinchingly. Writing just a year later in 1768 Vayhinger returned to this theme, noting that he could not tell if the "circumstances of his life" were "better or worse."[38] And, in the next sentence he offered perhaps an explanation for his ambivalence: "Yes in this year my wife and I have made three trips, on Easter and St. James Day [July 25th] and after St. Martins Day [November 11th]."[39] To where and why they journeyed was not recorded, but these trips certainly seem related to his equivocation. In his entire chronicle, this three-year stretch from 1766 to 1768 included the bulk of his commentary on his wife and their relationship. Indeed, Anna Barbara would not appear again in Vayhinger's chronicle until nearly ten years later when he finally admitted in 1777 that her drinking was taking a toll. Throughout the chronicle then, nearly every time that Vayhinger mentioned his wife, she was related in one way or another to the themes of household management, his health, and his steadfastness.

Although Vayhinger never explicitly used the term "*hausen*" or "*Haushaltung*" in conjunction with his wife, his comments resemble quite closely the kinds that David Sabean discovered in his classic study of a peasant village not too far from Göppingen. There, in Neckarhausen, such disputes between spouses oftentimes wound up in court.[40] The wife of Andreas Köpple, for instance, complained in a similar fashion, before the magistrates, about her husband "drinking excessively and not caring for his *Haushaltung*."[41] Interestingly though, in his comprehensive study of Neckarhausen, Sabean found "not one case of a woman accused by her husband or the authorities of alcohol abuse," and thus he concluded that "it was simply not a theme for public discourse."[42] This seems to have also held true in the town of Göppingen, for Vayhinger never took Anna Barbara to court and no other evidence of her addiction appears in the public archives. To be sure, Vayhinger recognized it, but he did so only in his private journal. Of course, as argued by Sabean, rumours about "the woman silently tippling at home" were common in the villages of this region where *Most* (cider) could readily be found in most homes.[43] While it remains impossible to tell if Anna Barbara was the target of such rumours, Vayhinger's concentration on the economic implications of his wife's alcoholism suggests that he, like the peasant farmers in Neckarhausen, worried about its deleterious effects on the household economy. This keen awareness of assets developed, as argued by Sabean and others, from both custom and law code in the region, and for close-knit hometown communities this meant that careful household management of all aspects of property was not simply an economic concern but also a cultural, social, and political one.[44]

In the case of Vayhinger, this concern with *Haushaltung* and property ran so deep that when he first described his wife's mismanagement in 1765, he relied on affective language to do so, apparently merging her behaviors with his own physical pain in a brief two-sentence statement. While Vayhinger may have experienced other feelings, such as anger or sadness, over Anna Barbara's drinking, he only records in his chronicle his affective response to it, which suggests that anxiety and fear were at the forefront of his feelings. Since he apparently could not control his wife's predilection for alcohol from 1765 to at least 1780, he may have felt tormented by demons beyond his control. This may explain his attempts to conceal her addiction in Latin, and it may also explain why he never makes mention of Anna Barbara's death at 54 years old on July 11, 1782.[45] This omission is glaring, because he eulogized both of his parents in his journal. Among the nine sentences devoted to his father's death in 1763, Vayhinger wrote that "he was an incomparable man, a good speaker and writer, that few in Göppingen matched."[46] And, while he did not go to such lengths with his mother's death in 1772, writing only a couple of lines, they do include the following: "In this year, eight days after St. Jacobs Day my beloved mother died from a two-year long illness."[47] When Anna Barbara's death came ten years after his mother's, the event coincided temporally with his anecdote about the "damned devil." In fact, Vayhinger reminisced about the encounter in either February or March of 1782 just a few months before his wife died in July. Since Vayhinger offers us nothing about his wife's death, we can only wonder about whether or not her death was somehow entangled with his recorded memory of standing firm and resolute (i.e., "indestructible strength" and "fearless fear") before uncontrollable forces in the forest between Hohenstaufen and Göppingen.

While the full extent of Anna Barbara's alcoholism remains unclear, it clearly affected Vayhinger, and it most likely had an effect on their two sons: Johann Andreas, born on November 30, 1756, and Ernst Jacob the younger, born on November 16, 1758.[48] No direct evidence exists for glimpsing their affective and emotional responses to their mother's addiction. Still, though, they belonged to the household as contributing members, and at the time that their father wrote down his anecdote (February or March 1782) about that frightful night on the road between Hohenstaufen and home, they were, respectively, 25 and 23, or mature young men on the verge of marriage and the establishment of their own households. Indeed, the older son married two years later at the age of 27 in February 1784, while the younger son married in October 1786, also at the age of 27.[49] In 1770, on the other hand, when the encounter with a fire-spewing specter supposedly happened, the boys would have been much younger, with Andreas at 14 and Ernst Jacob the younger at 12. Given these ages and given that Vayhinger mentions travelling with "my son, who was about 12 at the time," it must have been Ernst Jacob the younger who joined his father and a neighbor on that journey to Schwäbisch Gmünd. What also seems clear is that when they made that trip in 1770, Vayhinger was managing a household confronted by numerous significant challenges both from within and without. Indeed, as Vayhinger notes in his chronicle during these difficult years, the famine brought both soaring food prices and a downturn in weaving worsteds, his primary economic activity. As a consequence, Vayhinger looked to his other ventures, like the small business in animal husbandry, to generate lost income. Hence, his statement that the canary "dealers were there" in Schwäbisch Gmünd tells us that this journey was crucial for his Haushaltung.

Here, spatiality becomes significant. The distance between Göppingen and Schwäbisch Gmünd is about 12 miles or 19 kilometers, which on foot should take between four and five hours, with Hohehstaufen lying almost at the midpoint between the two towns. From Vayhinger's account of the journey, it sounds as if this business venture was planned as a one-day, round trip. Accounting for travel time (i.e., eight–ten hours), several hours to conduct business with the canary merchants, and an hour or so for miscellany, such a trip could have been completed in about three-quarters of a full day. This timing would explain why Vayhinger, his younger son, and their neighbor arrived in Hohenstaufen, on the return leg, late in the evening. No wonder then that the baker in Hohenstaufen urged the travellers to stay the night in the village, because "the forest is not everyone's friend." Apparently in some haste, Vayhinger declined the offer, asked for a torch, got a lantern instead, and continued on his way home. Did his wife's alcoholism play a factor in Vayhinger's haste? Since only two years earlier in 1768 he had made three journeys with his wife, why did he leave her at home this time? Did he rush home due to the anxiety about being away for an extended period from someone who apparently lacked self-control? While answers to these questions remain elusive, clearly the late 1760s and early 1770s brought Vayhinger many tribulations ranging widely from the effects of war to famine to health issues to his wife's "mismanagement" of property that would have produced anxiety and fear. Moreover, he carefully situated these tropes of precariousness and resilience—"hard times," "misfortune," "sobriety," "indestructible strength"—frequently in his chronicle as part and parcel of living a pious life.

When he finally wrote the story twelve years later, things were quite different for him, and so too had the tropes subtly shifted. After weathering the difficult years of the early 1770s, his household economy made mostly steady gains through the rest of the decade and into the 1780s by relying on its patchwork flexibility. It had, as suggested by Troeltsch, entered the stage of "success." Indeed, as noted by Vayhinger, the upswing began in late 1772 when he had had "thanks to God a blessed year," after which he then listed his copious harvests of barley, potatoes, and beans as well as the sale of four canary hens for 48 Gulden, which helped push his annual profit to 210 fl.[50] In 1775, when he sat down to tally up his earnings for the year, he discovered that "with God's help" he had made 440 Gulden.[51] And, while his earnings dropped back into the 200-Gulden range a few years later, Vayhinger still thanked God for a healthy profit in 1778. For the most part then, Vayhinger's confidence in his *Haushaltung* must have grown over the years. To be sure, as noted above, his wife's alcoholism could even in 1780 detract from the bottom line, but by this point—fifteen years into her "mismanagement" and eight years into his "successful" years—it most likely seemed less threatening due to strategies that had been developed to weather the tribulations he had faced. As another indication of Vayhinger's successful household management, both of his sons had, notwithstanding their mother's drinking problem, matured seemingly without issue into their young-to-mid-twenties and were on the verge of marriage and full-blown adulthood. Indeed, the chronicler himself (entering his fifties in 1780) had also matured. These temporal changes produced for Vayhinger a quite different space from when he was struggling to make ends meet in his late twenties and thirties. With a prosperous household economy and fewer challenges to it, he was arguably in a safer, more confident space. This is reflected by a noticeable change in the last third of his journal. Not only did his journaling become more reflective, capturing episodes from his youth such as the introduction of potatoes and the mid-century shift to new clothing styles, but it also became much more historically reflexive, placing himself more firmly in time and space. Moreover, his writing, and the tropes he employed therein, took on, in the words of Bähr, "the self-reflection of a rational individual who, in the late eighteenth century, began to discover in the horror of the dream a disturbing potential for moral self-assurance."[52]

With this temporal shift in mind, it pays to take a closer look at how Vayhinger situated his 12-year-old anecdote about the fire-throwing fury. It appears to be inserted halfway through a different narrative about current events in the high politics of 1782. Indeed, before he shares his anecdote, Vayhinger recounts the "birthday celebration of 'our beloved Duke Karl,' as well as the shuttering of monasteries in Austria by 'our Emperor' Josef II." Diverging from this theme and temporal frame, Vayhinger then went back twelve years to his encounter with a shrieking demon. And, in suggesting that it was the ghost of a suicide, he makes the quite reflexive statement: "I am not being too gullible here." Although this self-awareness as an author crops up more and more frequently in the last third of his chronicle, what is most striking here is that immediately following that statement about past events, Vayhinger returns to the present:

Year 1782.

in the sacred Passion Week the Holy Father Pope Pius VI arrived in Vienna. It seems already that he would carry out nothing against the Emperor's will. He is quite praised for his great and beautiful reputation and affability, he only speaks Italian and nothing else, sometimes a little French. The tolerance started by our Emperor Josef, will no doubt remain.

Where the Pope travels next remains to be seen. France wants to introduce Lutherans again. Because [of Emperor Josef's policies] the sacred Holidays [in the Holy Roman Empire] have been abolished among all Catholics and [they now] have two fewer than we Lutherans. At this time according to the newspaper, it has been 245 years since an Emperor and Pope have spoken with one other and that was in Rome and not in Vienna.[53]

Following these comments, Vayhinger once again jumps back into the past, providing a six-sentence overview of those pivotal events from the "Year 1537."[54] Presumably his knowledge of the sixteenth century came either from the newspaper article that he read or perhaps from his own education.[55] Either way, these passages demonstrate that Vayhinger was seamlessly bouncing around in time, from the present (1782) to the past (1770 and 1537) and back to the present (1782). Vayhinger certainly appears to have been manifesting, as Reinhart Koselleck insists, that inherently human compulsion to situate oneself along many different levels of time.[56] In fact, when Vayhinger recorded these events and his anecdote in early 1782, his everyday life at that moment—his present—revolved around managing his household economy, which was plugging along nicely as it navigated manifold challenges, including the growing commercialization and rapidly expanding trade networks of the late eighteenth century. Vayhinger's present was one in which "most communities were becoming increasingly locked into and dependent on regional and even global trade networks, and thus were no longer (if they ever had been) tight, homogeneous, and distrustful little knots of resistance to external pressures or innovations."[57] Throughout his chronicle, Vayhinger acknowledges both implicitly and explicitly the ways in which worlds and worldviews, including time, were becoming ever more entangled.

Clearly this particular moment of entanglement—that is, the meeting of Pope Pius VI and Emperor Josef II—caught Vayhinger's eye, as it must have caught the attention of many of his contemporaries. Vayhinger, though, went a step further than most and crafted (or perhaps copied from his newspaper) a historical narrative about the long rift between these two seats of power. His matter-of-fact reportage of the current state of affairs indicates, with a little bit of reading between the lines, an appreciation and approval of both men and their actions, as well as perhaps a recognition of the parallels between their story and his. The centuries-long rift between the two seats of power appears, in Vayhinger's version, to be on the verge of some sort of resolution. Why then does he insert his fear-inspiring anecdote smack-dab in the middle of this discussion? Did these political events on the world stage somehow jog his memory, taking him back to the difficult days of the early 1770s? Or was this interlude purely coincidental? If we approach these questions with the argument that fear and anxiety manifest themselves differently when approached "from the perspective afforded by a safe place,"[58] then Vayhinger's maturity and success in the early 1780s allowed him to write with more self-confidence and self-reflection. By situating his anecdote not only historically in his own life, but also within the broader events that he read about in the news, Vayhinger succeeded, consciously or unconsciously, in entangling his personal past and present with the broader past and present. In Vayinger's mind, the positive trends in high politics may have mirrored his own upward trajectory from 1760 to 1782, or as Troeltsch put it, from the "years of setback" to the "years of success."

His success and confidence should not, however, be overstated, for shortly after recording these world events and his anecdote, the aforementioned *Stadtbrand* occurred in early August of 1782. Henceforth, his chronicle focused almost entirely and exclusively on the consequences of the fire and the long process of rebuilding and recovery. Since the conflagration started three blocks away from his house, Vayhinger and his sons—his wife had died a month before the calamity—had time not only to "throw much into the ditches ... especially wool, cloth, [and] bedding" but also to fill up their cellar with belongings.[59] Despite all of these efforts, they still lost valuable possessions, like the three "iron ovens" that had heated their house.[60] Even though discouraged by his own situation, Vayhinger observed in his chronicle that many others were clearly in worse shape during the long process of rebuilding the town. Due to the scarcity of resources and the ensuing inflation, the process went slowly, leading Vayhinger to exclaim, "God help us! Everything is so expensive."[61] On the one-year anniversary of the city fire (August 1783), the builders finally began to frame Vayhinger's house, which he duly recorded with a glimmer of hope, followed by: "With so many costs, I often do not know where I am. All the money continually goes to [them]."[62] Besides noting the inflation and stress caused by the costs of the disaster, Vayhinger also mentioned the special fire relief fund put into place by the ducal government in the immediate aftermath of the blaze. On at least two occasions, cash distributions were made from it; after the second one, he exclaimed: "By God's reward, I received 26 fl. 40 kr. This good deed was truly well-received, because I had no more cash left."[63] To be sure, as he chronicled the fire and its aftermath in the last two years of his journal (1782-4), Vayhinger provided multiple representations of fear and anxiety, but they paled in comparison to that from the anecdote about the damned devil.

As argued above, Vayhinger's anecdote—the most explicit representation of fear and anxiety in his chronicle—is an example of temporal heterogeneity and spatiality at work. Written twelve years after the event, from a safer place, Vayhinger could represent, confidently, the phenomena of fear and anxiety. Indeed, as he tells the story, the only member of the party that succumbed to the most primal of fears, sheer terror, was Ernst Jacob the younger. In that instant, Vayhinger threatened his son with bodily harm and abandonment if he did not regain his composure. However, it was not all stick, for he then offered a carrot and a lesson, "God will safeguard us!" Here, with Bähr's insight, it can be argued that Vayhinger had arrived at a point in his life where he could embody the right type of fear. The strange apparition lurking in the forest between Hohenstaufen and Göppingen—"a damned devil" according to Vayhinger—was to be sure a frightful sight but not one to be truly feared.

By applying this lens to his entire chronicle, we come to better understand why Vayhinger regularly invoked God as he annually tallied up his profits or losses. In effect, every time he offered reverence for God's role in the fate of his household economy—for ill or for gain—Vayhinger gave expression to what was most likely the root cause of his affective fear and anxiety: those phenomena, like his wife's alcoholism and natural catastrophes, that were beyond his control and threatened his *Haushaltung*. It must, once again, be emphasized, however, that Pietists were encouraged to view these phenomena not as "punishing evils," but instead as "trials" along the hard, stony path to salvation. In other words, throughout his chronicle, Vayhinger instantiates the "complex semantic unit" of fear and fearlessness described by Bähr. Vayhinger accepted with the appropriate fear and anxiety all that came his way, except for his wife's drinking problem, which he evidently could not control or even influence and which, by custom, could not be addressed in public. This nuanced, complex relationship with fear and anxiety is perhaps best captured in the following statement that Vayhinger made in May of 1783, about a year and a half before the last entries of his chronicle in fall of 1784: "In my life I have now seen everything, except for the plague. To wit, I have experienced war, famine, torrential weather, flood, and last of all, the frightening fire. My God, how will things go for me in the future!"[64] With this statement, Vayhinger seems to express the fearless fear, having navigated "everything" God threw his way while remaining fearful before God.[65]

Among his list of fear-inducing life experiences, however, Vayhinger appears to have made two key omissions: his wife's so-called mismanagement and the fire-throwing fury. In the first case, the omission stemmed most likely from the fact that his wife's behaviors had caused him much consternation over the course of their marriage. Worse yet, he lacked not only control over those behaviors but also a framework with which to make sense of and address them. Anna Barbara and her demons thus remained a constant liability to the household economy, producing plenty of anxiety and fear for Vayhinger throughout much of their marriage but especially during the difficult early years. And, as argued earlier, the gendered nature of this conflict meant, at least in Swabia, that the behaviors could not be resolved in public. Instead, these feelings, like their source, more than likely became internalized rather than being understood as external "trials" sent by God. On the other hand, the second omission of the fire-throwing fury came as a result of Vayhinger's confidence in the complex semantic unit linking fear and fearlessness. As argued above, he did not fear this most frightening representation of fear in his chronicle, because his faith and his secure place in time and space allowed him instead to play with the trope of resolute steadfastness. Whatever he encountered in the enchanted woods on the way home from Hohenstaufen was remembered twelve years later as a winsome anecdote in a vein similar to many German folktales; this treatment had no place among the truly awe-inspiring trials and ordeals that had to be negotiated with fearless fear. Ranging widely from Pietistic conventions to mythical specters inhabiting a dark forest, Vayhinger's representations of fear and anxiety were not at all one-dimensional.

This multivalent and nuanced use of fear by Vayhinger rings true when one considers the recent scholarship on emotions. In various settings, multidisciplinary groups of scholars have come together to study emotions. Two publications from 2012—*Fear across the Disciplines* and *Facing Fear: The History of an Emotion in Global Perspective*—detail the findings of one team that focused exclusively on the emotion of fear.[66] The editors of the former state in their introduction that this emotion must be viewed a complex, temporal phenomenon, one that "involves a manifestation of expectation (the future) and experience (the past) in the present," perhaps even among nonhuman animals.[67] This argument owes much to the contribution of psychologist Arne Öhman (i.e., *The Biology of Fear*), who contends that humans are constantly keeping at bay an existential dread, and while some are able to manage these underlying tensions, others succumb to the overwhelming nature of them. The reality, or "sad truth" in Öhman's words, is that "there is little we can do about the things and events we fear most: illness, death of kin, accidents, terrorist attacks, and so on."[68] The editors of the latter volume echo this position, stating that fear "is the pervading sense of uncertainty about an inherently unknowable condition that could potentially visit pain on the body or loss of what one holds dear."[69] Casting a broader net, the other team of scholars, led by Ute Frevert, investigated the vocabulary associated with emotions in general. They did so by critical analyzing encyclopedias over time and presented their findings in *Emotional Lexicons: Continuity and Change in the Vocabulary of Feeling 1700–2000* (2014).[70] This project makes a compelling case for viewing the late eighteenth and nineteenth centuries as a period in which "the sheer diversity of concepts of emotion ... was unprecedented, existing neither before, nor after it."[71] Since then, however, the diverse and complex vocabulary associated with emotions has been constricted and limited in large measure due to the influence of "the sciences, in particular psychology and the neurosciences, which for their part operate within a standardized model of 'the' human being."[72] Although focused on emotions in general, this team of scholars comes to a similar conclusion as the team focused on fear. That is, in their efforts to create a simple, universalist model of how human beings feel and make sense of the world around them, twentieth-century thinkers ignored all the evidence from the centuries before that pointed out the complexity and nuance of emotions. Thus, these scholars, much like Bähr, view the eighteenth century as a pivotal moment when, in the words of historian Lynn Hunt, a "torrent of emotions"[73] existed.

By laboriously unraveling Vayhinger's anecdote about the "damned devil" haunting the woods near his hometown, we have come closer to understanding the ways in which an ordinary person in eighteenth-century Swabian experienced fear and anxiety. Vayhinger's experiences suggest that he may have been actively engaged in the working out of this new conceptualization of fear as an internalized, complex emotion. After all, for much of his married life he grappled with how to make sense of the trepidation brought on by his wife's intemperance. From their marriage in 1755 to the early 1760s, Vayhinger never mentioned his wife's mismanagement in his chronicle (maybe she had not yet started drinking?). From the early 1760s to the later 1770s, he only hinted at her alcoholism. Then finally in 1777, he put a name on it but concealed it partially through the use of Latin. And, two years before her death in 1782, he blamed her again for the annual losses that afflicted his household economy. His faith, as we have discovered, helped him make sense of the many other, frightful trials, like the famine, weather, and war that he confronted and overcame, but as long as his wife lived, there was no resolution to the constant threat that her behavior posed. This utter lack of control—a terrifying existential dilemma with no apparent resolution—put him in a bind from which he apparently could not escape until the demons died with his wife. All he could do was remain resolute, manifesting his "sobriety" and "indestructible strength." Even if this anecdote was a complete fabrication, its placement in relationship to his wife's death seems more than coincidence; they seem entangled. Written shortly before Anna Barbara died, Vayhinger's anecdote about confronting a terrifying demon twelve years earlier gave meaning and sense to this existential dilemma that seemed to be on the verge of resolution. By playing with the traditional trope of enchanted forests, he simultaneously expressed his fearless fear as well as his own feelings of existential dread, and although he did not approach the complexity and nuance of these feelings with the same language or outlook as an orthodox theologian or philosophe, he was nonetheless navigating them and carving out new meaning.

Notes

* Sincere thanks go to Fred Marquardt and the anonymous reviewers whose thoughtful reading of prior drafts made this chapter much tighter than it was otherwise.
1 Kirchenregisteramt Göppingen (hereafter: KrtG), *Familienregister, 1558–1800, Sch – Z*, 608–36, p. 432. Born on November 7, 1729, Ernst Jacob Vayhinger lived 62 years, dying on December 21, 1791.
2 Stadtarchiv Göppingen (hereafter: StAG), B.I.1.a., *Hauschronik des Zeugmachers Ernst Jakob Vayhinger*, p. 47: [Unless otherwise noted, all translations are mine.] den 11. Februar war der Geburtstag unseres geliebten Herzog Karl, an welchem Tag eine hohe Schule in Stuttgart errichtet wurde, da waren viele fremde Herren eingeladen von Offizieren und Reichsstädten. [¶] Um diese Zeit, da unser Kayser Josef II. viele Klöster in seinem Staat aufgehoben, so wollte der Pabst selbst nach Wien kommen, um diesem Übel zu steuren. Der Kayser aber lehnte es ab und die Zusammenkunft sollte in Florenz geschehen. Der Kayser aber bleibt auf seinem Vorhaben. For an early, almost exclusively economic analysis of this document, see: Walter Tröltsch, "Die Göppinger Zeugmacherei im 18. Jahrhundert und das sog. Vayhingerbuch," *Jahrbuch für Gesetzgebung, Verwaltung und Volkswirtschaft im Deutschen Reich*, ed. G. Schmoller (1896), 165–87.
3 A sizable town about 19 kilometers, or 4 hours walking distance from Göppingen.
4 A small village located almost halfway between the two larger towns: 11 kilometers from Schwäbisch Gmünd, and 8 kilometers from Göppingen.
5 StAG, B.I.1.a., *Hauschronik des Zeugmachers Ernst Jakob Vayhinger*, pp. 47–8 [Here it must be noted that my rather stiff translation of this passage benefited inordinately from Fred Marquardt and Wiebke Reinert, both of whom added nuance and subtlety to it.]: Eine Anekdote. Als ich ungefähr vor 12 Jahren [*c.* 1770] mit einem Bürger von hier mit meinen Kanariaen Vögeln auf Schw. [i.e., Schwäbisch] Gmünd mußte, weil dort die Vogelhändler waren, so nahm ich meinen Sohn Ernst Jakob mit, welcher ungefähr 12 Jahr alt war. Nach unserem Verkauf der Vögel gingen wir zurück. Und am Abend kamen wir wieder auf Hohenstaufen. Wir wollten fort, der Beck Gottlieb sagte zu mir, Vayhinger bleibe er hier. Der Wald ist nicht jedermanns Freund. Ich lachte darüber und verlangte eine Fackel, er aber sagte, ich will euch eine Latern geben, wenn es sein muß, es ist besster. Ich ließ es mir gefallen, ich und der obige Meister gingen. In dem Wald nahmen wir meinen Sohn in die Mitte, der Bürger tragte die Laterne voraus. Wie wir an dem Grub Benkle hinuntergingen, da ging ein wunderlich Schicksal an, welches ich in meinem Leben nicht vermutet hatte. Es kam ein solcher Sturm, daß sich die Wedel von den Buschen zu unsern Füßen begeben und als ob der Wald einfallen wollte. Die wilde Schweine schnarchelten an unseren Füßen. Etwa 20

Schritt von uns laufte einer, der schlug immer Feuer an einem Stahl, welches Schlag und Feuer bis auf den Boden immer zu sehen und zu hören war und schrie: Hob, hob, hob! Beständig. Ich schrie hinter drein zwei dreimal, guter Freund, warte er doch, wir wollen miteinander. Er gab mir aber keine Antwort. Mein Sohn kam eine solche Angst an, daß er schrie. In Staufen hat man ihn wohl hören müssen. Weil der wo so schriee und Feuer schlagt, nicht gehalt, sehe ich es selbsten vor einen Furien an und sagte zu meinem Sohn, ich sage Dir, sei stille, wofern Du mir dein Geschrei fortsetzest, so schlage ich dir meinen Stecken über den Kopf und fahre fort: das ist ein verfluchter Teufel, der uns das Unheil zufüget, laßt den verfluchten Teufel laufen, wenn er nicht warten will. Gott wird uns bewahren! Da wurde alles still und wir kamen Gott Lob durch. [¶] Jetzt was ist das, ich ware sonsten kein Leichtgläubiger, ungefähr vor 5 Jahren hat sich ein Mann da gehängt.

6 Mary Lindemann, *Health and Healing in Eighteenth-Century Germany* (Baltimore, MD: Johns Hopkins University Press, 1997), 74. For a similar argument see: John Arnold, *History: A Very Short Introduction* (New York: Oxford University Press, 2000), but especially p. 119 where he discusses how historians approach "truths in their contingent complexity."

7 Joel F. Harrington, *The Faithful Executioner: Life and Death, Honor and Shame in the Turbulent Sixteenth Century* (New York: Picador, 2013), xxii.

8 Ibid., xxii.

9 A Centner was the equivalent of a hundredweight (approximately 50 kilograms).

10 At this time, the major unit of currency in the Duchy of Württemberg was 1 Gulden (fl.), which equaled 60 Kreuzer (kr.).

11 StAG, B.I.1.a., *Hauschronik des Zeugmachers Ernst Jakob Vayhinger*, pp. 19–20: Anno 1764 bis 1765 habe ich 22 Ctr. wolle verarbeitet; aber von Micheli an bis auf den Frühling krank gewesen; habe in diesem Jahr 50 fl eingebüsst. Indem meine Haushaltung, weil ich krank war, sehr schlecht bestunde. Meine wolle habe gehabt von Lorch, Heidenheim, Herbrechtigen. [¶] Das Brot galt 12, 13, 14 kr, der Wein, 16, 18, 20 kr usw. Um 16 kr wahr er bald nicht zu trinken. Hat dahero Gott das Vermögen geschwächt dass es noch 655 fl gewesen; keine Neuigkeiten sind nicht vorgefallen.

12 Walter Troeltsch, "Die Göppinger Zeugmacherei im 18. Jahrhundert und das sog. Vayhingerbuch," in *Jahrbuch für Gesetzgebung, Verwaltung und Volkswirtschaft im Deutschen Reiche.* ed. G. Schmoller (1896), 1255–77. See also his magnum opus, *Die Calwer Zeughlandlungskompagnie und ihre Arbeiter* (Jena: Gustav Fischer, 1897).

13 Troeltsch, "Die Göppinger Zeugmacherei," 1272, ft. nt. 2, and p. 1275.

14 Ibid., 1277.

15 Harrington, *Faithful Executioner*, xxvii.

16 Ibid., xxv.

17 See Johannes Wallmann, *Der Pietismus* (Göttingen: Vandenhoeck & Ruprecht, 1990), but especially *Ch. VII. Der württembergische Pietismus*; Peter Schicketanz, *Der Pietismus von 1675 bis 1800* (Leipzig: Evangelische Verlaganstalt, 2001), 143–9; Hartumut Lehmann, *Pietismus und weltliche Ordnung in Württemberg vom 17. bis zum 20. Jahrhundert* (Stuttgart: Kohlhammer, 1969), passim; and Martin Brecht and Klaus Deppermann, eds., *Geschichte des Pietismus. Band 2: Der Pietismus im achtzehnten Jahrhundert* (Göttingen: Vandenhoeck & Ruprecht, 1995), but especially *Ch. IV. Der württembergische Pietismus* by Martin Brecht.
18 Wallmann, *Der Pietismus*, 125.
19 Schickentanz, *Per Pietismus von 1675 bis 1800*, 140.
20 Ibid., 150.
21 See: Wallmann, *Der Pietismus*, 123. For more specific details on the *Pietistenreskript* of 1743, see Brecht, *Ch. IV. Der württembergischen Pietismus*, 245–7, in *Geschichte des Pietismus, Band 2*.
22 See Dennis Frey Jr., "Wealth, Consumerism, and Culture among the Artisans of Göppingen," *Central European History* 46, no. 4 (2013): 741–78.
23 See StAG, B.II.2.g., *Zubringens Inventuren vom 23. Jan. 1750 biß 20. Febr. 1756*, p. 490, and *Inventuren & Teilungen*, 23.2–209.5 (1789) and 24.2–405.5 (1792). According to the marriage and death inventories for Vayhinger and his wife, classic Pietist literature, such as a copy of *Scrivers Seelenschatz* and bibles, were found among their possessions. See Hartmut Lehmann, ed., *Geschichte des Pietismus. Band 4: Glaubenswelt und Lebenswelten* (Göttingen: Vandenhoeck & Ruprecht, 2004), passim, but particularly *C. Frömmigkeit und Gebet*, where the author, Johannes Wallmann, discusses the significance of Scriver's contributions (pp. 86–8).
24 Andreas Bähr, "Fear, Anxiety and Terror in Conversion Narratives of Early German Pietism," *German History* 32, no. 3 (2014): 355. Here, Bähr provides a long list of scholars whose work sheds light on our understanding of "affect." See also, of course, Bähr's *Furcht und Furchtlosigkeit: Göttliche Gewalt und Selbstkonstitution im 17. Jahrhundert* (Göttingen: V&R unipress, 2013).
25 Bähr, "Fear, Anxiety and Terror," 364.
26 Ibid., 369. For further insight on "God's power and fear" see: Bähr, *Furcht und Furchtlosigkeit*, 54–183.
27 Bähr, "Fear, Anxiety and Terror in Conversion Narratives," 369.
28 StAG, B.I.1.a., *Hauschronik des Zeugmachers Ernst Jakob Vayhinger*, p. 26: Diese Woche (1771) ist auch der Herr Doktor mit den Kindern auf das Feld gesandt wordern, um ihnen Wurzeln zu zeigen, welche gut zu essen sind.
29 Ibid., 31: Den 5. August habe ich durch die Gnade Gottes ein Scheffel Korn gemahlen von meinem Vetter Schuler a 6 fl. Da war Freude in meinem Haus. Das Wasser hat schon gesotten zu Spatzen, ehe ich von der Mühle gekommen. [1 Scheffel = 8 Simri = 1.77 hectoliters].

30 Ibid.: Diese schmecken besser als sonsten Dampfnudeln.
31 Ibid., 20: Anno 1765 bis 1766 habe ich 15 Ctr. wolle verarbeitet, habe solche von Lorch, von Heidenheim, vom Stadtschäfer gehabt. Das Brot galt 13, 14 kr, der Wein 16, 18, 20 kr usf. Neues geschahe auch nichts. In diesem Jahr habe wieder eingebüsst 35 fl, dass mein Vermögen, welches Gott erhalten wolle, 620 fl ist. [¶] Und ich seit dato große Beschwerlichkeiten an meinem Leibe habe, besonders auf der Brust. Es ereignen sich aber betrübte Unannehmlichkeiten wegen meinem *Uxor*, welches ich aber nicht nennen will. [¶]
32 Ibid., 36: ... habe vieles ausgestanden wegen meinem *uxor propter bibendum*.
33 Troeltsch, "Die Göppinger Zeugmacherei im 18. Jahrhundert und das sog. Vayhingerbuch," 184.
34 StAG, B.I.1.a., *Hauschronik des Zeugmachers Ernst Jakob Vayhinger*, p. 41: Anno 1780 den 20. Mai habe ich gerechnet, habe 75 fl. eingebüßt, mein Uxor hat den größten Teil daran.
35 KrtG, *Familienregister, 1558–1800, Sch – Z*, 608–36, p. 432, and StAG, *Zubringens Inventuren vom 23. Jan. 1750 biß 20. Febr. 1756*, p. 490, which is dated October 8, 1755.
36 StAG, B.I.1.a., *Hauschronik des Zeugmachers Ernst Jakob Vayhinger*, p. 9: Da ist eine grosse Not mit unserem Handwerk gewesen, niemand hat keinen Zeug wollen wegen dem Krieg. ... Und das Gesind ist entsetzlich ohnwerth gewesen; dieweil ich ausgewesen, habe keine Wolle mehr gehabt; mein Weib ist sieben Wochen krank gewesen.
37 StAG, B.I.1.a., *Hauschronik des Zeugmachers Ernst Jakob Vayhinger*, p. 20: Bis dato habe ich noch große Schmerzen an meinem Leibe, der Herr sehe darein.
38 Ibid., 21: Was die Umstände meines Leibs betreffen, so weiss ich nicht, ist es besser oder ärger.
39 Ibid.: Ja diesem Jahr habe 3 Reisen getan, ich und mein Weib um Ostern und Jakobi und nach Martini.
40 See: David Sabean, *Property, Production, and Family in Neckarhausen, 1700–1870* (New York: Cambridge University Press, 1990), passim, but especially pages 101–16. Neckarhausen lies about 31 kilometers to the west-southwest of Göppingen. See also his discussion of "Patterns of Drinking," 174–9.
41 Ibid., 107.
42 Ibid., 176.
43 Ibid.
44 Among many fine studies see: Anja Benscheidt, *Kleinbürgerlicher Besitz: Nürtinger Handwerkerinventare von 1660 bis 1840* (Münster: Lit, 1985); Hildegard Mannheims, *Wie wird ein Inventar erstellt? Rechtskommentare als Quelle der volkskundlichen Forschung* (Münster: F. Coppenrath, 1991); Ian F. McNeely, *The Emancipation of Writing: German Civil Society in the Making, 1790s–1820s*

(Berkeley: University of California, 2003); Hans Medick, *Weben und Überleben in Laichingen 1650–1800: Lokalgeschichte als Allgemeine Geschichte* (Göttingen, 1997); Sheilagh Ogilvie, *A Bitter Living: Women, Markets, and Social Capital in Early Modern Germany* (Oxford: Oxford University Press, 2003); David Sabean, *Property, Production, and Family in Neckarhausen, 1700–1870*, as well as his *Kinship in Neckarhausen 1700–1870* (Cambridge: Cambridge University Press, 1997); Sylvia Schraut, *Sozialer Wandel im Industrialisierungsprozeß, Esslingen 1800–1870* (Esslingen: Stadtarchiv Esslingen am Neckar, 1989); and Jonathan Sperber, *Property and Civil Society in South-Western Germany, 1820–1914* (Oxford: Oxford University Press, 2005).

45 KrtG, *Familienregister, 1558–1800, Sch – Z*, 608–36, p. 432.
46 StAG, B.I.1.a., *Hauschronik des Zeugmachers Ernst Jakob Vayhinger*, p. 16: Er ist unvergleichlicher Mann gewesen, ein guter Redner und ein Schreiber, dass in Göppingen wenig seinesgleichen gewesen. According to KrtG, *Familienregister, 1558–1800, Sch – Z*, 608–36, Vayhinger's father died on October 5, 1763.
47 KrtG, *Familienregister, 1558–1800, Sch – Z*, 608–36, 32: In diesem Jahr ist 8 Tag nach Jakoby meine liebe Muter gestorben an einer langwierigen Krankheit von 2 Jahr. According to KrtG, *Familienregister, 1558–1800, Sch – Z*, 608–36, Vayhinger's mother died on August 5, 1772.
48 KrtG, *Familienregister, 1558–1800, Sch – Z*, 608–36, 32.
49 Ibid.
50 StAG, B.I.1.a., *Hauschronik des Zeugmachers Ernst Jakob Vayhinger*, p. 32: Dieses Jahr habe ich Gott Lob ein gesegnetes Jahr.
51 Ibid., 34: Anno 1775 [¶] habe zusammengerechnet, da habe mit der Hilfe Gottes gewonnen 440fl.
52 Bähr, *Furcht und Furchtlosigkeit*, 534–5.
53 Ibid., 46: Anno 1782. [¶] in der hl. Charwoche ist doch der hl. Vater Papst Pius VI. in Wien angelangt. Es scheint schon, er werde wider des Kaysers Willen nichts vornehmen. Er wird sehr gerühmt um seines großen und schönen Ansehens und seiner Leutseligkeit, er spricht nur italienisch und nichts anders, bisweilen etwas französisch. Die Toloranz, wie unser Kayser Josef angefangen, wird wohl bleiben. [¶] Wo der Papst hinreist, wird sich zeigen. Frankreich will auch die Lutheraner wieder einführen. Wegen der hl. Feiertage sind bei den Katholiken alle abgeschafft und haben zwei weniger als wir Lutheraner. Dato laut der Zeitung sind es 245 Jahr, daß sich kein Kayser und Pabst miteinander besprochen haben und doch in Rom und nicht in Wien.
54 Ibid., 47: Anno 1537. [¶] zu Nizza Paul III. und Kayser Karl V. und Franz I. König in Frankreich.
55 For more details on early-modern education, especially among Pietists, see: Kelly J. Whitmer, "Eclecticism and the Technologies of Discernment in Pietist Pedagogy,"

Journal of the History of Ideas 70, no. 4 (October 2009), pp. 545–67. And, for a more general overview turn to the following: Arnold Weller, *Sozialgeschichte Südwestdeutschlands: unter besonderer Berücksichtigung der sozialen und karitativen Arbeit vom späten Mittelalter bis zur Gegenwart* (Stuttgart: Konrad Theiss, 1979); McNeely, *Emancipation of Writing* (2003); Richard van Dülmen's three-volume *Kultur und Alltag in der Frühen Neuzeit* (Munich: C.H. Beck, 1990, 1992, and 2005).

56 Reinhart Koselleck, *The Practice of Conceptual History: Timing History, Spacing Concepts*, trans. Todd Samuel Presner and Others (Stanford, CA: Stanford University Press, 2002), 111.
57 Lindemann, *Health and Healing in Eighteenth-Century*, 108. Lindemann mentions the groundbreaking work of Heide Wunder here.
58 Jan Plamper and Benjamin Lazier, eds., *Fear across the Disciplines* (Pittsburgh, PA: University of Pittsburgh Press, 2012), 10.
59 StAG, B.I.1.a., *Hauschronik des Zeugmachers Ernst Jakob Vayhinger*, p. 52.
60 Ibid., 53.
61 Ibid., 60.
62 Ibid., 62.
63 Ibid., 66.
64 StAG, B.I.1.a., *Hauschronik des Zeugmachers Ernst Jakob Vayhinger*, p. 60: In meinem Leben habe ich nun alles erlebt, nur keine Pestilenz. Als Krieg, Hunger, Wetterschlag, Wasser, zuletzt den erschrecklichen Brand habe ich alles erlebt. Mein Gott, wie wird es mir weiter ergehen!
65 For further analysis from Bähr see: *Furcht und Furchtlosigkeit*, 185–312 (*4. Natur-Gewalten*).
66 See Michael Laffan and Max Weiss, eds., *Facing Fear: The History of an Emotion in Global Perspective* (Princeton, NJ: Princeton University Press, 2012) and Plamper and Lazier, *Fear across the Disciplines* (2012).
67 Plamper and Lazier, *Fear across the Disciplines*, 7–8.
68 Ibid., 50.
69 Laffan and Weiss, *Facing Fear*, vii.
70 Ute Frevert, ed., *Emotional Lexicons: Continuity and Change in the Vocabulary of Feeling 1700–2000* (Oxford: Oxford University Press, 2014).
71 Ibid., 17.
72 Ibid., 31. For additional insight on the power of existential dread in modern society see: Zygmunt Bauman, *Liquid Fear* (Cambridge: Polity Press, 206).
73 See: Lynn Hunt, *Inventing Human Rights: A History* (New York: W.W. Norton, 2007).

5

Gypsy Hysteria in Nineteenth-Century Germany: A Biopolitical Response

Charissa Kurda

Known collectively by the press, politicians, and ordinary people as "Gypsies" (a translation of the catchall term used in German, *Zigeuner*), this itinerant ethnic group was one of the most feared and mistrusted in Germany prior to the First World War.[1] By the end of the nineteenth century, Gypsies were commonly viewed with apprehension as a criminal subpopulation believed to pose a serious threat to German public safety, their nomadic tendencies were likened to a plague (*Zigeunerplage*). The increasing presence of this peripatetic group coupled with the perceived failure of the bureaucratic efforts to control them initiated widespread fear.

Despite knowing very little about their culture, Gypsies have been traditionally branded with recurrent images as work-shy parasites, criminals, and romantic outcasts. As a result, the Gypsies were regarded with a mixture of fascination, fear, suspicion, and alienation. According to Gilad Margalit, German chroniclers from the fifteenth and sixteenth centuries have typically described the Gypsies as: "vagrant people, black in appearance, dirty and clad in rags, and wandering without purpose or aim throughout the country ... [they] lived by pick pocketing, thievery, robbery, palm reading, witchcraft and magic."[2]

However, German literary works produced in the seventeenth century had also romanticized the Gypsy nomadic lifestyle as free from moral constraints and responsibility. The 1670 picaresque novels, *Die Lebensbeschreibung der Ertzbetrügerin und Landstörtzerin Courasche* and *Der seltsame Springinsfeld* by Hans Jakob Christoffel von Grimmelshausen, are two well-known examples that reflect this depiction.[3] Kirsten Martins-Heuß confirms this romanticization in her study of the mythical character of the Gypsy: "A Gypsy is a dark person, always travelling, work-shy, living for the day without any plans, indulging in sensual pleasures. He delights the population with his artistic offerings."⁴ This romantic motif was highly popularized because it arguably reflected a stark contrast to German society: the Gypsies attained a state of freedom that the Germans did not have. At the same time, the vagrant lifestyle of the Gypsies drew the suspicion and hostility of their sedentary hosts. Their traditional itinerant professions as peddlers, musicians, actors, crafters, animal traders, fortune tellers, and healers were believed to serve as a cloak for petty crime, such as begging and stealing. The following passage from Alfred Dillmann's *Zigeunerbuch* makes this view clear:

> Aside from begging, [committing] crimes of hunting, [using] fields, forests and pastures, spreading dangerous epidemics, [using] fire precariously and their jugglery, these people are very inclined to thievery. Here opportunistic theft and shoplifting play a roll, as does planned larceny through counterfeiting. ....
> Alongside this are dishonest horde trading. ... and the swindling of money for the healing of "cursed" cattle and for assurances regarding the ascension of troubled souls.⁵

By the late nineteenth century, many Gypsies had successfully assimilated to their environment by holding regular employment in ordinary trades or intermarrying with German partners. However, a large number of Gypsies still followed a nomadic lifestyle, which clashed with the values held by their sedentary hosts, and facilitated continuous friction between the two populations.⁶ As a result, the Gypsies were not only viewed as a nuisance for rural communities, but their nomadic way of life was branded with criminalization, leading German authorities to conclude that their plague-like presence posed as a danger to public safety. Dillmann writes, "The 'Gypsy plague' from which we are now suffering is characterized by the fact that a large number of bands of Gypsies and Gypsy individuals, who ... endanger public safety by their vagrant lifestyle."⁷

Fears of Gypsy hordes threatening rural communities with property abuse, begging, stealing, and violent clashes had also begun to manifest in the local press. An example of this can be seen in the *Münchner Neueste Nachrichten* from 1900, which reported,

> For years Gypsy gangs have made their presence felt though a true plague. The pure Gypsies [*echten Zigeuner*] ... have almost disappeared and in their place gangs have appeared, who live as vagabonds and generate terror [*den Schrecken*] towards peasants. Under the guise of professions, these gangs live by begging, fortune-telling, divination, cheating and stealing.⁸

This hysteria largely reflects how the German rural population felt exposed and unprotected against the so-called threats posed by the Gypsies and their nomadic behavioral traits—which, as Ian Hancock points out, were often the result of discrimination and poverty. Thus, the authorities were urged to effectively deal with the Gypsy plague that was allegedly terrorizing local residents.[9]

In the government response to the societal fears of the ostensible *Zigeunerplage*, we see the beginnings of a discernible biopolitical persecution of Gypsies.[10] *Kaiserreich* officials employed strict measures of expulsion against foreign Gypsies and assimilative regulations against domestic ones in order to end itinerancy and force a sedentary lifestyle. Procedures of expulsion often involved refusing the entry of foreign Gypsies into Reich territory, as well as deporting noncitizen Gypsies. Efforts to sedentarize the Gypsy population, by contrast, entailed preventing the issuance of itinerant trading licenses to travelling workers; the incarceration of convicted Gypsies into workhouses; the forced removal of Gypsy children from their parents; the collection of biometric data (photos, fingerprints, descriptions of bodily features) and mandatory reporting and registration to local officials. It was hoped such policies would disrupt Gypsy nomadic culture by further criminalizing and stigmatizing it, resulting ultimately in their disappearance.[11]

Explaining these anti-Gypsy measures remains contested. Scholars such as Gilad Margalit, Wolfgang Wippermann, and Marion Bonillo suggest persecution was racially motivated.[12] Pointing to the fear and antipathy whipped by popular fiction, the media, and in pseudoscientific discourse, they argue that the image of the criminal Gypsy had a decisive influence on the state policies and police attitudes.[13] By contrast, others like Leo Lucassen have more compellingly argued that prior to Nazi Germany, anti-Gypsy policies depended less on racial attitudes than on systemic economic, social, and political factors.[14] This analysis highlights instead the focus on Gypsies' peripatetic lifestyle, which was deemed a threat to public order and the safety of German citizens. As Lucassen convincingly suggests, the Gypsy persecution should be understood as a by-product of the growing linkage between the poor relief system and the processes of state formation. The reorganization of this system, based on the principle of residency (*Heimatprinzip*), in his opinion, "not only created a class of itinerant people who were permanently excluded" but also brought about a widespread increase of vagrancy, beggary, and criminality, which required swift action by local authorities.[15]

Scholarship in the field of *Antiziganismus* (anti-Gypyism) has recently embraced a systems-based approach that links the development of the modern bureaucratic state with the increased prejudice and marginalization of the Gypsies. Instead of rooting the nineteenth-century Gypsy persecution in the later exceptions of fascism, the most recent research by Jennifer Illuzzi has sought to explore how a modern nation-state committed to the liberal concept of equality before the law can sanction a pernicious criminalization of the Gypsy population and deliberately place their lives outside the law by the state and its apparatus.[16] Illuzzi develops this framework by utilizing Giorgio Agamben's reworking of the concept of biopolitics. Following Carl Schmitt, Agamben stresses the importance of sovereign power, arguing that the sovereign both produces and dominates bare life (*zoé*), separating it from political existence (*bíos*).[17] For Agamben, it is the sovereign who decides which life is considered "valuable" versus "not worth living."[18] Agamben calls the figure that lives in this "state of exception" the *homo sacer*; a being who "is simply set outside human jurisdiction without being brought into the realm of divine law."[19] Illuzzi argues that the Gypsies living under the *Kaiserreich* offer a paradigmatic example of the *homo sacer*. In her opinion, the emergence of bureaucratic control and policing methods during the *Kaiserreich*, coupled with increasing pressure for executive officials to devise effective solutions for combatting the ostensible "Gypsy plague," caused the Gypsies to be gradually pushed into a juridical "state of exception," which tied their existence intrinsically to the sovereign and positioned them as outside of the realm of law and justice.[20]

While Illuzzi's thesis breaks new ground by reconceptualizing the historical mechanisms undergirding Gypsy persecution, her analysis and Agamben's theory fail to consider the relational, decentralized, and productive aspect of power within the *Kaiserreich*—features that are far more pronounced in Michel Foucault's model of biopolitics. Throughout the late nineteenth century, regulations against the Gypsies mirrored the state's decentralized power structures. Notwithstanding several attempts from *Kaiserreich* bureaucrats to coordinate a national approach to the "Gypsy question" (*Zigeunerfrage*), policies remained strictly within the jurisdiction of local and state authorities.[21] Archival material revealing that executive bureaucrats purposely avoided imposing "exceptional laws" against citizen Gypsies creates another difficulty for Illuzzi's analysis. These new findings render the core of Agamben's theory inoperative for Gypsies living under the *Kaiserreich*.[22] A more Foucauldian approach centered on the concept of technologies of the self might be more useful. For Foucault, biopolitics aims "to administer, optimize and multiply [life], subjecting it to precise controls and comprehensive regulations."²³ That is to say, biopolitics regulates and controls the life of the state's social body by nurturing the type of life it wishes to produce. It was this manner of administering the population that was arguably manifested in the treatment of Gypsies living in the *Kaiserreich*, as the state's executive authorities employed a set of legal restrictions and regulations, which criminalized and stigmatized the Gypsies' itinerant way of life.

The Racial Construction of the Amorphous Gypsy Image

The state's security apparatus was crucial to its biopolitical intervention and regulatory control of Gypsies in order to eliminate mass hysteria from German rural populations. The police operated as an instrument of the state, protecting its citizens from the feared threat of nomadism, by categorizing, criminalizing, and monitoring vagrant groups such as the Gypsies. However, the definition of "Gypsy" remained ambiguous meaning that their categorization was often a complicated and confusing process for authorities.[24] Although an authoritative, legal definition of "Gypsy" did not emerge until the Munich Conference in 1911, racial theorists and anthropologists repeatedly attempted to construct a distinctive image for the Gypsies prior to it. This thinking was important to their later racial categorization and status as a feared group of German society.[25]

Heinrich Grellmann offered one of the first attempts. In his *Dissertation of the Gipsies*, Grellmann consolidated the exemplar of the asocial Gypsy, whose lifestyle was an inversion of sedentary norms. Crucial to Grellmann's thesis was crystallizing contrasting Gypsy stereotypes: he glamourized their putatively exotic beauty and alterity and simultaneously described them as "cruel" and "savage" people, whose profound laziness increased their "propensity to stealing and cheating."[26] He placed his assessment in nineteenth-century criminal biology writings, asserting that Gypsies were descendants of the lowest and most despised inhabitants of society and could only reach a higher degree of civilization through careful guidance.[27]

Grellmann's treatise made a considerable impact on the pseudoscientific construction of the Gypsy image. Many German scholars at the time adopted his criminalized archetype.[28] One of the first was Richard Liebich who similarly labeled Gypsies as criminals.[29] But in contrast to Grellmann, Liebich was harsher and believed that the Gypsies' lifestyle was an immutable, inborn trait. As a result he writes, "To a certain degree, the [Gypsy] lifestyle becomes innate [which] can neither be totally forgotten, nor completely suppressed."[30] Liebich's belief illustrates the early origin of intrinsic, biological inferiority claims about Gypsies. There were others with similar views, notably Cesare Lombroso who argued in *L'uomo delinquente* (Criminal Man) that criminality was a biological condition, identified by specific "signs of degeneration." Although he paid little mention to Gypsies, Lombroso nonetheless viewed them as a "living example of a whole race of criminals."³¹ While many other contemporary scholars initially rejected Lombroso's thesis, Nazi criminal biologists such as Robert Ritter adopted his idea of inherited moral defects and applied them during the Third Reich.³²

Civilian police chief, Alfred Dillmann, further contributed to developing a racial image of Gypsies. In his 1905 *Zigeunerbuch*, Dillmann associated Gypsies with crime, claiming they often committed crimes under the guise of trading professions.³³ In contrast to Liebich and Lombroso, however, Dillmann viewed Gypsies' criminality as a socially influenced behavioral trait rather than being biological. He nevertheless maintained the dangers of a mixed German and Gypsy gene pool as a source of mutual degradation of German and Gypsy blood.³⁴

Hermann Aichele, too, depicted the Gypsies as "uncultured" beings who "belonged to the lowest economic class" and were compelled to live as social parasites at the expense of the host community.³⁵ In his study, *Die Zigeunerfrage mit besonderer Berücksichtigung Württembergs* (1912), he argued that their peripatetic lifestyle was a result of the intrinsic "lack of intellectual capacity of the uncivilized."³⁶ Concurring with Dillmann, Aichele labeled Gypsies using the racial-anthropological term "half-breeds" (*Mischlinge*) and argued that racially pure Gypsies were rare among Germans.

While these were certainly racist attitudes during the empire, biopolitical regulations targeting undesirable Gypsy behaviors—itinerancy and vagrancy—were more important. Such behaviors were often likened to the biological in the press, which continuously equated criminality with Gypsy itinerancy, in turn describing a feared "Gypsy plague" (*Zigeunerplage*) present in German society. In August 1903, for example, the *Neue Bayerische Landeszeitung* stated: "The Gypsies are for us a true menace. The farmers, whom are situated in the outdoor fields, must always live in fear, that hordes of dangerous riff-raff are stealing something … The question arises whether the State authorities are truly incapable of handling the Gypsy plague."³⁷ As in this example, the media often exaggerated their criminality, paralleling the suspicion, fear, and mistrust of Gypsies in regular society. Spurred by the press and a common sense of threat, executive authorities hardened their approach toward Gypsies and their peripatetism.

Several scholars of the Gypsies including Grellmann, Liebich, and Aichele considered state intervention vital for shaping and optimizing a sedentary population.³⁸ In response to the increasing calls to combat the feared "Gypsy nuisance," these experts believed it was necessary to eradicate the Gypsies' nomadic lifestyle by implementing strict regulations, such as assimilation, expulsion, surveillance, and deterrence, which were to be carried out by the police. Although *Kaiserreich* bureaucrats and scholars alike debated the effectiveness of these biopolitical strategies, they were nonetheless utilized by authorities to tightly control the Gypsy population.³⁹

Grellman was a strong advocate for Gypsy assimilation. Even though he complained that Gypsies' criminal behavior was a burden on the state, he did not view expulsion as a suitable solution. It would only drive them into neighboring countries. He believed instead that Gypsies' peripatetic lifestyle could be corrected and they could be transformed into productive citizens through education. He therefore proposed "civilizing" them and integrating them through State intervention.⁴⁰ Economics provided the primary rationalization for this biopolitical solution. He believed that civilizing the Gypsies could be advantageous to the financial growth of the State by generating higher tax revenues.⁴¹

Not all scholars shared Grellmann's view that Gypsies could be transformed into useful citizens through assimilation. Owing to his belief that the Gypsies' manner of living was biologically determined, Liebich was strongly against their integration into German society and instead championed expulsion, tighter passport control, and interrogation of foreign Gypsies at border entry points. Once their genuine country of origin (*Heimat*) was ascertained, instead of mere border removal, Liebich recommended Gypsies be repatriated to their point of provenance to prevent their return.⁴² Although Liebich believed that expulsion was the only way to cleanse Germany of the ostensible "Gypsy nuisance," his proposal was difficult to implement. In most cases, uncovering Gypsies' identity and returning them was almost impossible, and unwanted Gypsies were more often pushed onto neighboring German states.⁴³

Given the difficulties associated with the deportation, some German scholars argued that assimilation remained the easiest path to making Gypsies sedentary, though its success depended on stringent regulation. One expert who particularly held this view was Aichele.⁴⁴ In his opinion, a combined strategy of deterrence (*Abschreckung*) and corrective institutions (*Fürsorgeerziehung*) would most effectively encourage Gypsy assimilation. Local authorities were to surveil and police them, as well as forcibly remove Gypsy children from "the harmful influence of [their] parents."⁴⁵ From Aichele's perspective, an interventionist biopolitical approach was required to correct Gypsies' vagrancy and force them to "[remain] inside the limits of order."⁴⁶

These ideas shaped policy in the *Kaiserreich* in the late nineteenth century. A suite of severe state regulations intended as a biopolitical intervention were implemented to disrupt and strictly control the lives of Gypsies and eradicate their feared nomadism from German society. A racial image of the Gypsies certainly existed at this time. Reinforced by pseudoscientific anthropological discourse, the Gypsies were often regarded as a criminal subpopulation whose idleness and laziness hindered their ability to partake in regular (wage) labor. Their vagrancy was viewed with suspicion, as well as a burden to the regular population, as their itinerant professions as traders, peddlers, craftsmen, and entertainers were often depicted as a pretext for begging and stealing. Though Wilhelmine scholars did not universally accept that Gypsies were innately criminal, the notion of Gypsy criminality as a biological condition, as well as the ideas of "racial mixing" eventually became the basis for anti-Gypsy racial doctrine in the Third Reich.⁴⁷

Biopolitical Beginnings of Gypsy Assimilation, Deterrence, and Expulsion in Bavaria

Bavaria spearheaded the campaign against the Gypsies after formation of the Empire in 1871, targeting a feared "Gypsy plague" that was threatening the safety of its citizens. According to Albrecht, the Reich-wide economic crisis at the end of the 1870s significantly intensified Bavarian anti-Gypsy policy by creating high unemployment and leading to an influx of migrants, including vagrants. The increasing presence of itinerant groups such as Gypsies in provincial communities led to a spreading fear among rural Germans. The media and district officials issued several complaints about the "Gypsy plague," in which unchecked hordes of Gypsies were depicted roaming throughout the Reich, conspicuously begging and stealing. Viewing their presence as a threat to their financial development and citizen safety, the Bavarian government sharpened its measures against them.⁴⁸ Expanding on the Bavarian ministerial decrees of 1867 and 1868, on January 12, 1871, the Bavarian Interior Ministry distributed a circular to the police and local authorities, ordering them to restrict the issuing of itinerant trading licenses to wandering bands of Gypsies, and to expel any Gypsies of non-German nationality found residing within Bavarian territory.⁴⁹

The directive stated that upon their entry into Bavarian state territory, Gypsies were, "to provide a reliable and complete proof of nationality (*Staatsangehörigkeit*) and place of origin (*Heimat*) regarding not only the group leader but also the accompaniment of men, women and children and in cases when proof of these relations is found to be insufficient, they should be immediately sent over the state border (*Landesgrenze*)."[50]

Despite these measures, the Bavarian government argued that "large numbers of beggars, vagrants and Gypsies" continued to threaten "public safety in rural areas," which in turn could be resolved through tighter management by the security police and immigration authorities.[51] To that end, a ministerial decree was issued on January 23, 1878, ordering the Bavarian police to scrutinize "beggars, vagrants, Gypsies or otherwise questionable individuals." Those who provided insufficient identification papers (*Ausweispapiere*) were subjected to further treatment by the local police authorities. Additionally, to assist with their investigations, the Bavarian police were strongly advised to acquire and utilize the "Central Police Journal" (*Zentralpolizeiblatt)*, which contained information about "dangerous or otherwise questionable individuals of any kind, in particular scammers, vagabonds [and] Gypsy bands."[52] In 1881, the Bavarian Ministry continued its efforts to aid the process of repatriating foreign Gypsies back to their native country. An official journal (*Amstsblatt)* of the State Ministry from July 12, 1881 ordered that any Gypsy groups encountered by police were to be subjected to a thorough investigation in order to ascertain their personal information, such as their name, place of origin, occupation/trade, citizenship status, and current residence—a measure reinforced on March 13, 1882.[53]

At this point, however, biopolitical government policies primarily targeted foreign Gypsies. In 1885, the biopolitical campaign against the feared "Gypsy plague" intensified. Owing to the accumulation of grievances from fearful Bavarians concerning "Gypsy bands and … their dangerous wandering," the Bavarian bureaucracy hardened its stance toward them, reinforcing existing measures to expel foreign Gypsies, and in a directive issued on April 11, 1885, implementing strict new policies against the German-born. This direction aimed to "purge (*säubern*) the land of wandering bands of Gypsies" and "turn [domestic Gypsies] towards a sedentary lifestyle."[54] To control them, the police were further authorized to conduct a thorough examination of bands they found in Bavarian territory. Those unable to prove their German citizenship or who lacked sufficiently convincing identification papers (*Legitimationspapiere*) were to be detained and held in police custody until they could be deported. Even those who were cleared were nonetheless kept under "stringent police surveillance."[55]

Additionally, to prevent itinerant trading, authorities were ordered to withdraw the trade licenses (*Wandergewerbscheine*) granted to travelling workers and to deny any new issuances. All Gypsy owned horses were inspected for possible disease and any infected were confiscated, presumably to restrict the movement of travelling bands of Gypsies.[56] To achieve both an assimilative and a deterrent effect, this law called for the prosecution of petty crime committed by the Gypsies and decreed that convicted Gypsies were to be transferred to workhouses. In cases of incarceration, welfare establishments were instructed to remove Gypsy children from their families and place them into correctional reformatories (*Erz iehungsanstalten*).[57] This decree not only reinforced the criminalization of the Gypsies, but it also shows how the Bavarian authorities deliberately adopted a strongly interventionist and biopolitical approach toward eradicating feared nomadic elements from German society. Through the continued expulsion of foreign Gypsies from the empire, as well as the increasing assimilation and rigorous surveillance of domestic ones, Bavaria utilized regulatory mechanisms to disrupt and discipline the lives of Gypsies and to coerce them to conform to the state's dominant lifestyle, so as to halt societal fears of this peripatetic group.[58]

Notwithstanding that these stringent biopolitical measures resulted in a general decrease in the number of foreign Gypsies and the behavioral improvement of domestic ones, the Bavarians were unable to completely eradicate the feared threat of vagrancy. On January 24, 1889, Bismarck enquired about whether the existing Bavarian regulations had been successful.[59] Although the Bavarian Interior Ministry responded in a letter from April 14, 1889, that they had not yet achieved a "complete cleansing [*Säuberung*] of the empire," they believed that with "constant and strict control and surveillance of Gypsy bands," as well as by implementing an "energetic persecution of all perpetrated, comprehensible transgressions," they could achieve a "further reduction" of foreign Gypsies and the "improved behavior" of German-born ones.[60] In a ministerial resolution on October 5, 1889, Bavarian executive administrators declared that they would "gradually reduce this scourge," and implement even stricter measures that intended to make an itinerant lifestyle impossible for Gypsies. The entry of foreign Gypsies into Reich territory was even more stringently prohibited and itinerant trading licenses for domestic Gypsies were again cancelled. In addition, police were required to ascertain the identity of current Gypsy residents and to monitor those who led a vagrant lifestyle through the collection of personal information, such as birth and health certificates, marriage licenses, and military documents.[61] While this decree primarily sharpened existing measures against the Gypsies, it demonstrates how the Bavarian state exercised increasing biopolitical control over the lives of the Gypsies to prevent the growth of nomadism and address the concerns regarding the feared Gypsy plague.[62]

The Culmination of Bavaria's Biopolitical Management of Gypsies: The Creation of the *Zigeunerzentrale* and Dillmann's *Zigeunerbuch*

Despite the conscious efforts of the Bavarian bureaucracy to tighten its control over the Gypsy population and eliminate societal fears of their nomadic behavior, the process of criminalization proved more difficult than authorities intended. This resulted in an incomplete and unsatisfactory implementation of regulations by the police force, which not only led to the increasing frustration of executive authorities but also caused growing criticism, fear, and hysteria from the public.[63] In August 1897, for example, the *Pfälzische Presse* reported on the "great nuisance and harassment of the Gypsy population, who are passing through government districts, begging and stealing," raising the question of "whether the police authorities always pursued the correct method to effectively counter this threat to national security, which should not be underestimated." It bluntly advised that "in the interest of public safety and the reassurance of a fearful population, especially in the rural areas, it seems necessary to target all Gypsies, whether domestic or foreign, with the full rigor of the law" and demanded for the state to prosecute and scrutinize encountered groups of Gypsies, as well as confiscate their property, including animals, to achieve "a cleansing of the region from Gypsy bands."[64]

Pressure to stiffen Bavaria's approach toward this "plague" also emanated from political discussions within the Bavarian state assembly in 1898. The general opinion from parliamentary members was that police officials were not in a position where they could guarantee the safety and security of the population against small groups of Gypsies. One representative recalled a recent situation in Swabia, where a "dangerous horde" of approximately one hundred Gypsies engaged in petty crime, stealing wood, chickens, hay, and straw from residents, and were subsequently found inhabiting a nearby farming property. Allegedly, it was only after the landlord's firm disapproval that the authorities were summoned to the scene, which called into question the professionalism of law enforcement officers and whether they could actively prevent the occurrence of these types of "spectacles." In response to this criticism, the Interior Minister Feilitzsch insisted that because of current legislation, the "Gypsy plague has diminished considerably"; however, he admitted that despite enacting the strictest regulations against this peripatetic group, the Bavarian government "cannot entirely dispose of the matter," since most Gypsies are Bavarian subjects who cannot be deported under the Freedom of Movement Act (*Freizügigkeitsgesetz*).[65]

To respond to the increasing demands from a fear mongering media, as well as to address the accusation of police inadequacy, in 1899 the civilian police chief, Alfred Dillmann, created a special central office for handling Gypsy affairs in Bavaria, called the *Zigeunerzentrale*. Through the systematic collection and utilization of biometric data, such as fingerprinting and photography, this center aimed to gather intelligence and coordinate actions against the Gypsies. The police were required to report itinerancy to the Gypsy headquarters and to collect information of known Gypsies, including photographs, identity papers, animal ownership, place of origin, registered birth, marriages, deaths, and any criminal transgressions.[66]

Owing to the extensive statistical information that had been collected by the *Zigeunerzentrale*, a report from Dillmann, dated January 10, 1900, indicated that the process of expelling and prosecuting Gypsies was becoming much smoother.[67] In a second report, from January 21, 1902, Dillmann had compiled a list of specific cases of Gypsies who had been expelled by the police and those who were arrested for conducting criminal activity, such as murder, theft, fraud, begging, and vagabondage.[68] Despite making "significant progress" against the "Gypsy nuisance," in May 1904, Dillmann admitted to the Bavarian Interior Ministry that that their current system of surveillance to "control" the Gypsies was insufficient. Thus, he proposed to publish the identities and descriptions of Gypsies who had been reported to the Gypsy headquarters and to circulate this among the police force.[69] In 1905, this became the *Zigeunerbuch* (Gypsy Book). With the purpose of assisting in the "reduction of the Gypsy nuisance and the raising of public safety," this book was used as a key policing tool for identifying and dealing with any Gypsies encountered in Bavarian territory. It contained detailed information about those classified as Gypsies, including their names, personal details, criminal records or behaviors (e.g., begging, theft, or expired travelling trade licenses), and even photographs. Additionally, Dillmann specified the laws and administrative regulations affecting Gypsies, albeit these were mostly a reinforcement of existing stringent measures, and ordered for the police authorities to actively report on any Gypsy activity or arrests to the Munich headquarters.[70] A closer analysis of the *Zigeunerbuch* indicates that itinerancy was heavily criminalized and prosecuted, and that Bavaria's anti-Gypsy policy was being guided toward an increasingly strict regime of control and surveillance. Dillmann's reasoning was simple; if officials had access to personal information of every Gypsy they encountered, their identity could be ascertained, the level of threat that they posed to other German citizens could be established, and the appropriate course of action could be determined. Furthermore, the increasing cooperation and exchange of intelligence with Württemberg officials demonstrate the initial attempts made by the Bavarian government to build a national biopolitical approach toward combatting the ostensible "Gypsy plague."[71] The *Zigeunerbuch* is arguably the most prominent pre–First World War example, which shows the culmination of Bavaria's biopolitical management of Gypsies. Thus, Bavaria's strict surveillance measures for regulating Gypsies and eradicating the feared threat of vagrancy were widely adopted by other German states, as they also made attempts to coordinate action against their respective Gypsy populations.[72]

A Bavarian Counterpart: The Prussian Response to an Ostensible "Gypsy Plague"

Beyond Bavaria, Prussia too expressed its fears of Gypsy itinerancy and the state's desire to protect its citizenry from their alleged criminal activity. After the unification of the Reich, Prussian authorities had also begun to implement an increasingly harsh regime of biopolitical regulations against the Gypsies. Similarly to Bavaria, on October 23, 1870, the Prussian Interior Ministry issued a circular, which primarily targeted foreign Gypsies. It blocked their entry into Prussian territory "whether or not they provided travel documents," prohibited authorities from issuing them with itinerant trading licenses, and forcibly expelled those found without a valid permit across the state border—measures which were reiterated on October 31, 1883.[73]

As Illuzzi and Fitzpatrick make clear, the deportation procedure of Gypsies was increasingly becoming an issue of jurisdiction for border officials.[74] Since German-born Gypsies were granted basic protections by the state, which exempted them from deportation, Prussian officials often found it increasingly difficult to expel Gypsies across the German border, resulting in repeated delays and complaints about "the prevalence of wandering bands of Gypsies."[75] In an attempt to resolve this problem, the Prussian interior minister, Robert von Puttkamer, advised Bismarck to coordinate national action against the Gypsies, which would improve and accelerate the process of deportation. Supporting his recommendation, Bismarck ordered Puttkamer to draft a decree, which would make a clear distinction between foreign and citizen Gypsies. This became official on April 30, 1886 and was divided into two segments.[76]

The first section regularized the procedures concerned with the immigration of foreign Gypsies. It reinforced the 1870 and 1883 directives and additionally ordered officials to identify foreign Gypsies by their "outward appearance," though these external characteristics were not specified and depended upon the judgment of authorities. The second section of this circular defined domestic Gypsies as those "who have continued to reside in the territory of the German Reich and [have] temporarily abandoned their regular residence to roam Germany in great numbers." As such, to "work towards a solution of public safety and safety from dangerous mobs," this decree stated that domestic Gypsies would require more stringent regulation, that is, "turning [them] towards a sedentary lifestyle."[77]

Despite this distinction between foreign and domestic Gypsies, complaints about the "mischief" caused by wandering bands of Gypsies continued. In an advisory statement from Bismarck to the Prussian Interior Ministry on July 1, 1886, Bismarck called for an "exceptional law" (*Ausnahmengesetz*) for domestic Gypsies, which should exclude them from exercising their legal rights to practice their traditional occupations. For constitutional reasons, namely to preserve the Gypsies' rights to their freedom of movement and trade, this general ban could not be issued; however, Bismarck did propose a more stringent regime of control, which was officially enforced in a decree issued by Puttkamer on September 29, 1887.[78] The goal of this decree was simple; it intended to impose even stricter conditions for Gypsies wishing to obtain an itinerant trading license, to strongly discourage a vagrant lifestyle. The consequences for those attempting to obtain a travelling work permit without sufficient proof of German citizenship was expulsion—a requirement that was renewed on September 3, 1889.[79] Even in cases where Gypsies could prove their nationality, applicants for travelling permits were subjected to rigorous examination by police authorities and were required to have a permanent residence and sufficient finances to support their family—an instruction that was reiterated on December 8, 1892, and again on December 30, 1901.[80] Additionally, those Gypsies found guilty of "vagrancy, begging, loss of residency" or other "criminal" transgressions were subjected to harsh punishments, such as incarceration in workhouses and with their children institutionalized in correctional reformatories. Finally, to give Gypsy children a "sedentary lifestyle," those under the age of 14 were forbidden from itinerant trading and applicants were disqualified from obtaining a travelling work permit if their children did not have a regularly attend school—a measure that was reinforced on October 23, 1889, and once more on May 1, 1904.[81]

Despite the existing measures against Gypsies, government officials continuously reported on their plague-like presence in the *Reich*, which instilled fear in their rural communities, and subsequently urged the executive authorities to devise new "preventative police measures."[82] This is exemplified in a missive dated February 5, 1900, from the district president in Koblenz to the Prussian Interior Ministry. Declaring their presence as a "nuisance," the governor reported on how his community lived in "great fear of Gypsy vengeance" and how local inhabitants are rarely able to stop Gypsies from "begging, stealing and camping on foreign property." In addition to its fear mongering contents, his letter is instructive for understanding how the increasing presence of the Gypsies was a result of the core difficulties concerned with the execution of anti-Gypsy policy. He complained that small groups of Gypsies continued to enter the district, despite regulations to the contrary. He bemoaned that the fear of incurring costs for the transport and surveillance of Gypsies repeatedly resulted in "Gypsy dumping"; that is, pushing unwanted Gypsies over various state borders within the Reich and shifting the responsibility of identification, research, and repatriation onto police officials in neighboring districts. Moreover, the registration of Gypsies proved difficult, as, in his opinion, police forces were not equipped with the knowledge to clearly identify encountered Gypsies and their place of origin, as the papers they carried were often false. Finally, he protested that the district Gendarmes and police forces were greatly understaffed, given the increasing presence of Gypsies. As a solution, he advised strengthening the responsibilities of police authorities and for the government to implement even stricter measures against the Gypsies. He called for the prohibition of Gypsies camping in public places, the allocation of adequate employment and housing for Gypsies—to ensure their sedentariness—and he further suggested that itinerant trading licenses should be valid only in the district in which they were first issued.[83]

To resolve the increasing difficulties associated with implementing anti-Gypsy policy, in 1906 Prussia renewed its biopolitical approach to the feared "Gypsy nuisance" by releasing its publication of *Anweisung zur Bekämpfung des Zigeunerunwesens* (Directions for the Combating of the Gypsy Nuisance) by the interior minister Bethmann Hollweg. Offered as a complementing counterpart to Dillmann's *Zigeunerbuch*, this circular publicized the legal measures used for dealing with both foreign and German-born Gypsies within Prussian territory. Crucially, this publication did not specify any new legal initiatives; rather, it reiterated existing anti-Gypsy policy to combat their peripatetic tendencies. Nonetheless, Hollweg's *Anweisung* arguably initiated a decisive step toward regularizing Prussia's biopolitical approach to dealing with the "Gypsy plague."[84] As with Bavaria, rather than creating an exceptional legal framework for dealing with the Gypsies, Prussia favored a stringent regulatory regime, which utilized vigorous methods of policing to continuously reinforce the expulsion of foreign Gypsies and the refusal of travel permits to domestic ones. This included imposing heavy restrictions for obtaining itinerant trading licenses (such as: holding a permanent residence, being in possession of sufficient funds to support their family, and making sure that their children of school age were sufficiently educated), energetic prosecution of law infringements, particularly vagrancy, and strict police surveillance that targeted Gypsies, their children, and their animals. The explanation for this biopolitical intervention was to halt the nomadic lifestyle of the Gypsies, which was considered as a "burden on the population."[85] In the hopes of building a Reich-wide solution to the "Gypsy question," Prussia circulated its *Anweisung* to other German states. However, rather than following a nationally coordinated approach, several German states adopted aspects of Prussian policy and created their own initiatives for dealing with their respective fears of nomadic Gypsies.

Centralization and Transnationalism: A Failed Political Attempt to Combat the Feared "Gypsy Nuisance"

Despite the efforts of State governments to place severe regulatory pressure on Gypsies, by 1911, executive authorities received an upswing in complaints about the increasing appearance of Gypsies within several districts. The failure to totally eradicate Gypsy itinerancy from German society stoked the fears of rural communities. Officials lay the blame for this apprehension on the difficulties associated with enforcing the existing laws, thus urging the authorities to take harsher, national action against the Gypsies. A useful illustration of this can be seen in a letter from 1910 written by the governor in Breslau to the Prussian Interior Ministry. Claiming that the rural population was imperiled by the "Gypsy plague" and lived in "fear of [the Gypsies'] revenge," he reported that groups of Gypsies continued to roam the area, allegedly using their itinerant trading licenses as a disguise for pilfering and stealing. In his opinion, the source of this problem was the inability of officials to clearly identify encountered Gypsies, resulting to mistaken issuances of travelling certificates. As a solution to this problem, the Breslau president recommended for authorities to be more vigilant of the conditions for granting permits. He further stated the difficulty in prosecuting Gypsies for crimes of vagabondage, since many groups of Gypsies held sufficient finances upon their arrest, and destitution was a mandatory condition for their conviction. Also, he bemoaned the difficulties associated with ascertaining the nationality of Gypsies. To resolve these issues, he suggested coordinating Gypsy intelligence on a national level, so that officials could perform thorough criminal and background checks for Gypsies in question, thus allowing authorities to more efficiently prosecute Gypsies, as well as ascertain their identity and citizenship. In addition, he accentuated the importance of Gypsy incarceration, as this would assist in their transition toward sedentariness. Finally, he recommended a more strenuous regulation of the Gypsy social segment and a more concentrated effort to separate families, so that their children could receive a sufficient education.[86]

Another significant issue concerned with anti-Gypsy policy that was not specified in this report, but nonetheless continued to garner attention, was the jurisdiction regarding the procedure for the expulsion of Gypsies. The fact that the German states had no uniform legislation for dealing with the Gypsy "nuisance" complicated the practice of expelling unwanted individuals to a neighboring state. Each jurisdiction sought primarily to get rid of its own Gypsies as quickly as possible; in practice, this meant that states would routinely push Gypsies back and forth across the empire's frontiers.[87] In this sense, a letter from a district authority in the Bavarian province, Gemünden, dated January 26, 1910, is particularly illuminating. In one case from May 11, 1903, a group of Gypsies arrived from the Prussian frontier, and although the scrutiny of their papers proved that they were indeed Prussian subjects, they had been rejected by their home state and expelled across to Bavarian territory. To resolve this issue of cyclical expulsion, he urged for the executive authorities to take "radical action against the Gypsy plague" through the creation of a nationwide law (*Reichsgesetz*).[88]

The insistence for the *Kaiserreich* authorities to coordinate national action against the Gypsies also spilled into parliamentary discourse within the *Reichstag*. Because of the growing complaints about the problem community fears of the "Gypsy plague," the bureaucrats grew frustrated by the perceived lack of progress in controlling the Gypsies and called for Reich-wide regulations. In the sessions of 1905–6, 1907, 1909–10, and 1912, political representatives, too, discussed the constant cycling of Gypsies between state, national, and international borders. As a solution, some called for a federal agreement to combat the "Gypsy nuisance" in a "collective, national and effective" manner, while others urged for an exceptional legal framework for controlling Gypsies, which would introduce a Reich-wide ban on their vagrancy and movement. Although Prussian representatives continuously rejected the suggestion for an exceptional law against Gypsies, authorities certainly made other attempts to deal with Gypsies in a unified manner.[89]

Given the difficulties associated with Gypsy expulsion across national borders, the Bavarian government believed that international cooperation with their neighboring countries, including Austria-Hungary and Switzerland, was necessary to achieve a centralized approach to combatting the "Gypsy question." Although from 1890, Bavaria and Austria-Hungary had maintained an agreement to deport foreign Gypsies who were found residing in their respective states, by 1911 this treaty had deteriorated. A report from Lindau officials, dated February 6, 1907, can offer a useful insight to the complexities of international border jurisdiction between Germany and Austria-Hungary. It describes how a German Gypsy family arriving in Lindau via railway from Friedrichshafen was denied passage onto their connecting train to Bregenz by Austrian immigrations authorities. Despite carrying legitimate registration papers, a German passport, and a valid permit for overseas travel, the entire family was refused entry to Austria on the grounds of being perceived as foreign Gypsies. After failing to secure alternative transportation via ship and being refused a longer layover, the family was sent back across the Württemberg border. According to Article 11 of the 1870 Treaty between Austria-Hungary, Germany, and Switzerland, "each state is responsible for the railroads within their own territory." Thus, since the family was denied entry while still on Bavarian soil, the German authorities viewed this action as a clear violation of Bavarian sovereignty. However, they recognized that the leader "Jakob Pfister" was registered in the *Zigeunerbuch* under the alias "Jakob Reinhardt"—an individual who had incurred several penalties and whose citizenship status and place of origin was unknown.[90] What this case illustrates is that despite having proper identification, anti-Gypsy policy in Austria-Hungary, too, was unapologetically severe and strictly denied the entry of suspect foreigners. It further demonstrates how international border jurisdictions were further complicated by state policy, solidifying the need for transnational cooperation.

Swiss cooperation with Bavaria, too, declined by 1911. In 1906, Switzerland had adopted strict policies against foreign Gypsies and informed Bavarian authorities that all Gypsies would be denied entry into Swiss territory and subsequently deported back to Germany, regardless of their identification papers and citizenship. The Swiss further sought Bavarian assistance for tighter frontline border controls operations at sea and rail ports. To halt the border crossings between Swiss and Bavarian territory, Dillmann's *Zigeunerbuch* was circulated among Swiss officials. This cooperation grew into a proposal in 1909 from the Swiss authorities to attend an international conference, discussing a seventeen-point program that aimed to implement a Central European approach to combatting the ostensible "Gypsy plague." It proposed for all individuals "considered to be Gypsies" to be apprehended and rigorously interrogated about their date of birth, place of origin, religion, marital status, occupation, and current residence. Furthermore, the Swiss recommended the collection of biometric data, such as descriptions of bodily features, fingerprints, and photographs. Crucially, the Swiss program also included a plan for each government to create a national Gypsy registry, which would serve as a cumulative database for the international exchange of Gypsy intelligence.[91] Finally, the most controversial aspect of this proposal was the suggestion of forced Gypsy naturalization in the state corresponding to their origin, and it was largely due to Prussia's strong objections to this that the Swiss dropped the proposal, thereby shattering the efforts for an international solution to the Gypsy problem.[92]

Notwithstanding the deterioration of international cooperation between Switzerland, Austria-Hungary, and Germany, the Bavarian government continued its efforts to develop a systematic, nationwide approach to the "Gypsy question." On December 18 and 19, 1911, the Bavarian Interior Ministry convened a conference in Munich, which was attended by representatives from larger German states affected by the feared "Gypsy nuisance."[93] The main topic of discussion concentrated on solidifying the biopolitical control of Gypsies by tightening the collection and use of biometric data, such as photographs and fingerprints, of known Gypsies and establishing a centralized Gypsy intelligence service (*Zigeunernachrichtsdienst*). The introduction of the of the *Denkschrift über die Bekämpfung der Zigeunerplage,* authored by Theodor Harster, states,

> The solution of the "Gypsy question" cannot be undertaken through legislation on the level of the Reich or the individual states, but that this goal is best achieved through the creation of unified, administrative regulations ... Furthermore, the establishment of an intelligence agency to report on the presence of Gypsies is necessary, [as is] the collection of all intelligence by a central office, which receives recorded fingerprints of Gypsies and acts as a central database for all state parties.[94]

In Harster's view, a centralized Gypsy intelligence service would achieve a Reich-wide solution to the "Gypsy question." Nominating Munich's *Zigeunerzentrale* as the basis for its prototype, this center would allow authorities to more stringently control and coordinate action against the Gypsies by building a national cataloguing system that housed all biometric and personal data, including fingerprints and photographs, of citizen Gypsies. These measures, Harster argued, were crucial for performing the continued expulsion of foreign Gypsies, the strict certification, registration, and licensing of domestic Gypsies and the prosecutions of criminal transgressions.[95] The discourse employed at the conference illustrates how it was impossible for the representatives to agree upon an executive solution to the "Gypsy question," as they hotly debated whether a centralized intelligence agency for Gypsies should be created. The Prussian representative voiced strong objections to this proposal. Although he personally welcomed the establishment of such an agency, he was uncertain of the extent of Prussia's involvement within this reorganization. Until their role was clearly defined, he was unable to endorse the plan for a national Gypsy headquarters. He further conveyed doubts as to whether the efforts and costs arising from such an implementation were justified. Prussia's reluctance to create a center for Gypsy control in Bavaria did have some impact on the decisions of others, particularly Saxony, as their representative stated that their approval rested upon Prussian participation. Despite this, several representatives expressed their support for a federal Gypsy headquarters in Munich, including those of Hessen and Baden. Owing to their close cooperation with Bavaria, Württemberg too supported Harster's proposal but stressed the importance of the involvement of all states to ensure success.[96]

Harster's *Denkschrift* additionally called for the intensification of existing biopolitical measures against foreign and domestic Gypsies. The entry of noncitizen Gypsies into Reich territory continued to be blocked. In the case where foreign Gypsies were found residing inland, influenced by the Swiss proposal, Harster suggested that they should be granted German citizenship, so that they could become sedentary. Unsurprisingly, due to the strong objections from the Prussian representative, this controversial recommendation was not implemented. It did, however, initiate heated discussions of sending foreign and stateless Gypsies to penal colonies, even though an official legislation did not eventuate.[97] Additionally, regulations within this document reinforced Munich's ambitious goal to turn citizen *Zigeuner* into a sedentary population via mechanisms of strict regulation and surveillance. Harster clarified that policies of sedentarization targeted "the parasites on the national body who refused to accept the best efforts of the state to assimilate them to the culture of our people."[98] As such, he believed that the civilization of domestic Gypsies was possible and urged authorities to renew their efforts for regularizing education for school-aged Gypsy children and placing them into correctional reformatories. As well as this, Harster recommended extending the use of new biopolitical tools, such as fingerprinting and photography, to all areas of the Reich, as a means of combatting identity fraud and building a more extensive cataloguing system.[99]

Furthermore, Harster proposed for the conference delegates to create an administrative category for the term "Gypsy." The development of a legal, comprehensive definition proved difficult, as representatives heatedly discussed what constituted a "Gypsy" and to whom the label should be applicable. Based largely on the characterization offered by Dillmann's *Zigeunerbuch*, Munich officials proposed a behavior-based definition, which stressed "outer appearance, occupation and nomadic lifestyle" as determining factors rather than a racial-based definition, which would be determined by their membership in a tribe or race.[100] The Prussian representative agreed that a broad definition was necessary, as it would be impossible to create a definition, which encompassed every case. In disagreement with this, the representative from Hessen criticized Munich's definition as too broad and suggested that the classification of the Gypsies should heavily focus on their trading profession. He believed those who practiced a trade were still considered to be Gypsies, unless the trade was sufficient to provide "support for them and the people travelling with them."[101] This suggestion was rejected, as it assumed that all Gypsies were poor, and it failed to consider that those who could sufficiently support their families with their trading profession could easily escape scrutiny. The representative from Alsace-Lorraine pointed out that "any precise determination of the concept would mean a restriction for the authorities; in any case, the suggested definition of the concept went too far, since harmless people would fall under the definition." And, he suggested avoiding the creation of a definition of the Gypsies altogether.[102] The representative from Württemberg, Hermann Aichele, on the other hand, proposed to use social science as a basis for their definition.[103] Eventually, they agreed on a compromise: "Gypsies, in the eyes of the police, are those who are Gypsies according to the teachings of ethnology as well as those who roam about in the manner of Gypsies."[104] Thus, the legislative definition of the term "Gypsy" remained a social and behavioral category rather than a racial one.

The events following this meeting demonstrated that the Munich Conference was only a partial success. Baden and Hessen were the only two states that had agreed to sign the proposal generated at the conference, while a missive from the Bavarian Interior Ministry on December 31, 1913, indicates that Prussia—and subsequently Saxony—refused the establishment of a national center for controlling Gypsies in Bavaria, on the grounds that it would undermine state jurisdiction, since the severity of the "Gypsy nuisance" differed in each district.[105] The outbreak of the First World War further diverted attention from the "Gypsy plague" and delayed practical follow-ups.[106] While a stable definition of the term "Gypsy" allowed authorities to more rigorously control and monitor known Gypsies, as well as build their cataloguing database through the collection of comprehensive biometric data and intelligence, the attempt for a unified approach to the "Gypsy question" ultimately failed. Rather than creating a centralized Gypsy intelligence service, based in Munich, authorities opted to deal with their respective Gypsy populations within their own legal frameworks. Nonetheless, the Munich Conference of 1911 demonstrates how biopolitical policy against the Gypsies continued to be rigorously applied, with behavior-based measures of assimilation, expulsion and the collection of biometric data seeking to assist authorities in preventing the feared threat of nomadism from flourishing in German territory and to coerce the Gypsies to conform to a sedentary lifestyle.

Conclusions

The widespread fear about an ostensible *Zigeunerplage* reflected in media and political discourse consequently initiated a stringent biopolitical campaign against the Gypsies. Since nomadism was viewed as a putative threat to a modern society, which instilled fear among German sedentary communities, the *Kaiserreich* executive authorities made several attempts, without much luck, to build a national approach that dealt with eradicating these unwanted and feared behaviors. While the bureaucratic regulations for controlling Gypsies were not as biologically intrusive as those implemented during the Third Reich, legislation during the *Kaiserreich* period nonetheless made several attempts to control and optimize the type of life that they wanted to produce. To deal with foreign Gypsies, German state governments prohibited their entry into Reich territory and expelled any Gypsies without proven citizenship found residing on German soil across the empire's frontier. German-born Gypsies, on the other hand, were subjected to strict measures of assimilation, surveillance, and deterrence, which intended to criminalize Gypsy itinerancy and coerce them to adopt a sedentary lifestyle. Through an acute degree of policing, *Kaiserreich* officials were responsible for restricting the traditional way of life and movement of Gypsies as much as possible. These regulations imposed stringent rules for obtaining or renewing itinerant trading licenses and mandated strict conditions for registration upon arrival in a new district. To combat identity fraud and to strengthen their intelligence database, the usage of biopolitical tools, such as the compulsory recording of Gypsy fingerprints and photographs, was ordered. Encountered bands of Gypsies also faced constant scrutiny, and in some cases, their wagons and animals were confiscated. To achieve both an assimilative and a deterrent effect, those Gypsies found convicted of criminal transgressions were incarcerated in workhouses, while their children were threatened with forcible removal from their families and placement into corrective reformatories. Despite the *Kaiserreich's* unapologetically severe approach to dealing with the Gypsy problem, these laws in practice were difficult to enforce. Its effect was twofold: the perceived failure of the executive efforts to cleanse the population of the alleged "Gypsy plague" facilitated mass hysteria within media and political discourse, which consequently expedited the push for more rigorous preventative measures, such as a national Gypsy law. Though such a law never eventuated, the German states nonetheless continued to vigorously enforce state and local biopolitical regulations for controlling the Gypsies. Its ultimate objective was to eradicate Gypsy itinerancy from Germany—a lifestyle that was often equated with criminality and feared by the rural population.

Notes

1 Throughout this article, several groups will be included under the generic term "Gypsy." According to Milton, the largest group of Gypsies that existed in Germany were called the Sinti, while the core group which lived in Austria were known as the Roma. Another linguistic subgroup of the Sinti was called the Lalleri, who resided primarily in Burgenland, though in Switzerland, the predominant group were known as the Jenisch. From the late 1970s, the traditional term "Gypsy," which translates to "Zigeuner" in German, was believed to bear derogatory connotations. Therefore, it was replaced with the phrase "Sinti and Roma." Although the term "Gypsy" is currently loaded with derogatory connotations, it will be used throughout this article as the historically applicable term for the Gypsies living in Germany. The rationalisation for using this word is to maintain historical continuity and authenticity, as during the nineteenth-century German authorities, the media and public did not know or use the terms "Sinti" and "Roma." The terms "Sinti," "Roma," and "Gypsy" will only be used in cases where they are specifically cited from secondary sources, Sybil Milton, "Hidden Lives: Sinti and Roma Women," in *Experience and Expression: Women, the Nazis and the Holocaust*, ed.

Elizabeth Roberts Baer and Myrna Goldenberg (Detroit: Wayne State University Press, 2003), 53–5.
2 Gilad Margalit, *Germany and Its Gypsies* (Wisconsin: University of Wisconsin Press, 2002), 8.
3 Hans Jakob Christoffel von Grimmelshausen, *Die Lebensbeschreibung der Ertzbetrügerin und Landstörtzerin Courasche* (Nuremberg: Felsecker, 1670); Hans Jakob Christoffel von Grimmelshausen, *Der seltsame Springinsfeld* (Stuttgart: Reclam, 1976).
4 Kristen Martins-Heuß, *Zur mythischen Figur des Zigeuners* (Frankfurt am Main: Hagg Herchen, 1983), 93.
5 Alfred Dillmann, *Zigeuner-Buch* (Munich: Dr Wild'sche Buchdruckerei, 1905), 6.
6 Guenter Lewy, *The Nazi Persecution of the Gypsies* (New York: Oxford University Press, 2000), 14.
7 Dillmann, *Zigeuner-Buch*, 6.
8 GStAPK, I. HA Rep. 77, Ministerium des Innern, Tit. 423 Nr. 53 adh/2 Bd. 2, *Münchner Neueste Nachrichten*, 1900.
9 To explain why Gypsies often engaged in begging and stealing, prominent Gypsy scholar, Ian Hancock writes, "Forbidden to do business with shopkeepers, the Roma have had to rely upon subsistence theft to feed their families; and thus stealing has become part of the stereotype." See: Ian Hancock, "Introduction," in *The Gypsies of Eastern Europe*, ed. David Crowe and John Kolsti (New York: M.E. Sharpe, 1991), 5.
10 The "long nineteenth century" is a term coined by the British Marxist historian Eric Hobsbawm and is featured in his trilogy book series titled, "The Age of Revolution: Europe 1789–1848" (1962); "The Age of Capital: 1848–1875" (1975); and "The Age of Empire: 1875–1914" (1987). It refers to the period between the years of 1789 and 1914 and is thought by Hobsbawm to have crucially formed the cultural and economic foundation of the modern world. Accordingly, it began with the creation of bourgeoisie capitalism and egalitarian citizenship in France, manifested in the French Revolution, and ended with the outbreak of the First World War, which culminated in the collapse of western liberal bourgeois society in Europe.
11 Angelika Albrecht, *Gypsies in Altbayern 1871–1914: Eine sozial, wirtschafts und verwaltungsgeschichte Untersuchung der bayerischen Gypsiespolitik* (Munich: Kommission für Bayerische Langesgeschichte, 2002); Matthew Fitzpatrick, *Purging the Empire: Mass Expulsions in Germany, 1870–1914* (Oxford: Oxford University Press, 2015); Tara Zahra, "'Condemned to Rootlessness and Unable to Budge': Roma, Migration Panics, and Internment in the Habsburg Empire," *American Historical Review* 3, no. 1 (June 2017): 702–26.
12 Other scholars who have supported this position include Angus Bancroft, Angus Fraser, Ian Hancock, Joachim Hohmann, Donald Kenrick, Grattan

Puxon, and Michael Schenk; see their respective works: Angus Bancroft, *Roma and Gypsy-Travellers in Europe* (England: Ashgate, 2005); Angus Fraser, *The Gypsies* (Oxford: Blackwell, 1992); Ian Hancock, "The 'Gypsy' Stereotype and the Sexualisation of Romani Women," in *Gypsies in Literature and Culture*, ed. Valentina Glajar (Basingstoke: Palgrave-Macmillan, 2007), 181–91; Joachim Hohmann, *Geschichte der Zigeunerverfolgung in Deutschland* (Frankfurt am Main: Campus Verlag, 1988); Donald Kenrick and Grattan Puxton, *The Destiny of Europe's Gypsies* (London: Sussex University Press, 1972). Michael Schenk, *Rassismus gegen Sinti und Roma: Zur Kontinuität der Zigeunerverfolgung innerhalb der deutschen Gesellschaft von der Weimar Republik bis in die Gegenwart* (Frankfurt am Main: Peter Lang, 1994).

13 Furthermore, these historians have concluded that racist attitudes and regulations implemented against the Gypsies during the *Kaiserreich* were a prelude to the Gypsies' persecution in Nazi Germany. For them, the ideologies in the works of Heinrich Grellmann, Richard Liebich, Cesare Lombroso, and Alfred Dillmann laid the foundation for the racial mistreatment of the Gypsies during Nazi Germany. Margalit, *Germany and Its Gypsies*; Wolfgang Wippermann, *Wie die Zigeuner: Antisemitismus und Antiziganismus im Vergleich* (Berlin: Elefanten Press, 1997); Marion Bonillo, *"Zigeunerpolitik" im Deutschen Kaiserreich 1871-1918* (Frankfurt am Main: Peter Lang, 2001); Heinrich Moritz Gottlieb Grellmann, *Dissertation on the Gipsies, Being an Historical Enquiry, Concerning the Manner of Life, Economy, Customs, and Conditions of These People in Europe, and Their Origin*, trans. Matthew Raper (London: Elmsley, 1787); Richard Liebich, *Die Zigeuner in ihrem Wesen und in ihrer Sprache* (Leipzig: Brockhaus, 1863); Cesare Lombroso, *Der Verbrecher in anthropologischer, ärztlicher und juristischer Beziehung*, trans. M. Fränkel (Hamburg: Richter, 1887–90); Dillmann, *Zigeuner-Buch*.

14 Others who argue similar views to Lucassen include: Guenter Lewy, Angelika Albrecht, Rainer Hehemann, and Herbert Heuss. See: Annemarie Cottaar, Leo Lucassen, and Wim Willems, *Gypsies and Other Itinerant Groups* (Great Britain: Macmillan Press, 1998); Lewy, *Nazi Persecution of the Gypsies*; Leo Lucassen, "A Blind Spot: Migratory and Travelling Groups in Western European Historiography," *International Review of Social History* 38, no. 2 (1993): 209–35; Leo Lucassen, "Eternal Vagrants? State Formation, Migration and Travelling Groups in Western Europe, 1350–1914," in *Migration, Migration History, History: Old Paradigms and New Perspectives*, ed. Leo and Jan Lucassen (Bern: Peter Lang. 1997), 225–52; Angelika Albrecht, *Zigeuner in Altbayern 1871-1914* (München: Kommission für Bayerische Landesgeschichte, 2002); Rainer Hehemann, *Die „Bekämpfung des Zigeunerunwesens" im Wilhelminischen Deutschland und in der Weimarer Republik, 1871-1933* (Frankfurt am Main: Haag + Herchen Verlag, 1987); Herbert Heuss, "'Anti-Gypsyism Is Not a New

Phenomenon.' Anti-Gypsyism Research: The Creation of a New Field of Study," in *Scholarship and the Gypsy Struggle*, ed. Thomas Acton (Hertfordshire: University of Hertfordshire Press, 2000).

15 With the intention of improving the regulation and control over the labor reserves, as well as excluding alien beggars from cities, urban authorities initiated a change in Germany's poor relief system during the mid-nineteenth century. Under the reformed poor relief system, the *Heimatprinzip* (principle of residency) stipulated the restriction of relief to local inhabitants and the exclusion of "aliens" or noncitizens. This meant that if poor aliens, such as the Gypsies, could not prove that they were permanent residents in their communities, they were refused rights to poor relief. Further details of Lucassen's argument can be seen in Leo Lucassen, "'Harmful Tramps': Police Professionalization and Gypsies in Germany, 1700–1945," in *Gypsies and Other Itinerant Groups*, ed. Annemarie Cottaar, Leo Lucassen, and Wim Willems (Great Britain: Macmillan Press, 1998), 80–2; Leo Lucassen, "Eternal Vagrants? State Formation, Migration and travelling Groups in Western Europe, 1350–1914," 229–331; Leo Lucassen, "Between Hobbes and Locke: Gypsies and the Limits of the Modernisation Paradigm," *Social History* 33, no. 4 (2008): 423–41.

16 Jennifer Illuzzi, *Gypsies in Germany and Italy, 1861–1914* (New York: Palgrave Macmillian, 2014), 14–18.

17 Giorgio Agamben, *Homo Sacer: Sovereign Power and Bare Life* (Stanford, CA: Stanford University Press, 1998).

18 Ibid., 142.

19 Ibid., 82.

20 J. Illuzzi, "Negotiating the 'State of Exception': Gypsies' Encounter with the Judiciary in Germany and Italy, 1860–1914," *Social History*, 35, no. 4 (2010): 421.

21 Illuzzi, *Gypsies in Germany and Italy*, 99–100; Fitzpatrick, *Purging the Empire*, 184.

22 Illuzzi has argued that the bureaucracy purposely sought to push citizen Gypsies into a foreign category—a "state of exception"—where the protections of the *Rechtsstaat* was denied to them. Bonillo and Fitzpatrick have each pointed out that this was not the case, as casting out domestic Gypsies, either juridically or physically, from society was purposely avoided by executive authorities and doing so would violate their constitutional rights. Constantine, too, states that the system of transferring vagrants and beggars into workhouses was not exclusively applied to Gypsies, as it was a regulation that was embedded in the *Rechtsstaat*. See, Fitzpatrick, *Purging the Empire*, 181–4, 204; Bonillo, *Zigeunerpolitik im Deutschen Kaiserreich: 1871–1918*, 104, 111, 126; Simon Constantine, "Particularities of Persecution. The Policing of Gypsies in Saxony 1871–1914," *Immigrants and Minorities: Historical Studies in Ethnicity, Migration and Diaspora* 32, no. 1 (2013): 40–1.

23 Michel Foucault, *The History of Sexuality: Volume 1: An Introduction* (New York: Random House, 1978), 136–7.
24 Both Illuzzi and Luccasen have discussed the "fuzzy" image of the Gypsies and its impact upon the implementation of anti-Gypsy policy. Before the late eighteenth century, the category "Gypsy" was often used as a derogatory term which applied to those who led a nomadic lifestyle, including vagabonds, travelers, and beggars. Though nomadism and criminality were increasingly viewed as central attributes of "Gypsy" character, after the unification of the Reich, the police faced the problem of distinguishing between "foreign" and "native" Gypsies, as the "homelessness" of the Gypsies often prevented them from obtaining official identification papers. Fitzpatrick further states that " 'Gypsy' was an organizing concept used for the categorizing and policing of a subaltern social segment perceived as having a particular mode of social transgression in common rather than a stable description of a recognizable ethnic or national community." See: Illuzzi, *Gypsies in Germany and Italy*, 51–2, Lucassen, "Eternal Vagrants? State Formation, Migration and travelling Groups in Western Europe, 1350–1914"; Fitzpatrick, *Purging the Empire*, 180.
25 One of the most important debates associated with recent Gypsy scholarship is concerned with portraying an authentic and accurate representation of Gypsy ethnicity and culture. Some historians, such as Angus Fraser, Ian Hancock, and Thomas Acton, have argued that Gypsies were an ethnic group, which was historically shaped by outsiders. Others, namely Leo Lucassen, Wim Willems, and Anne-Marie Cottaar, have correctly argued that the idea of the Gypsies as a unified group is incorrect. Their identity was shaped by their travelling occupations, such as hawking, peddling, and trading, and their increasing marginalization from European communities, which forced them to develop distinctive cultural traits to ensure their survival. To investigate this debate further see: Thomas Acton, "Modernity, Culture and 'Gypsies': Is There a Scientific Method for Understanding the Representation of 'Gypsies'? And Do the Dutch Really Exist?," in *The Role of the Romanies: Images and Counter-Images of "Gypsies"/Romanies in European Cultures*, ed. Nicholas Saul and Susan Tetbutt (Liverpool: Liverpool University Press, 2004); "The 'Gypsy' Stereotype and the Sexualization of Romani Women"; Leo Lucassen, *Die Zigeuner: die Geschichte eines polizeilichen Ordnungsbegriffes im Deutschland, 1700–1945* (Köln: Böhlau, 1996), 8, 177; Cottaar et al., *Gypsies and Other Itinerant Groups*.
26 Grellmann, *Dissertation on the Gipsies*, 22, 66 and 67.
27 Ibid., 80.
28 While several scholars have praised the cultural importance of Grellmann's thesis, including August Pott, Martin Block, and Hermann Arnold, some contemporary researchers have critiqued the reliability and historical accuracy of his portrayal

of the Gypsies. Willems points out that Grellmann's image of the Gypsy was often fabricated, as his observations and interpretations were usually not his own. Rather, they were heavily borrowed from the texts of previous writers, whose ideas derived from earlier chronicles. For further information about the reception of Grellmann's thesis see: August Friedrich Pott, *Die Zigeuner in Europa und Asien: Ethnographisch-linguistische Untersuchung, vornehmlich ihrer Herkunft und Sprache, nach gedruckten und ungedruckten Quellen* (Halle: Heynemann, 1844), 14–15; Martin Block, *Zigeuner. Ihr Leben und ihre Seele, dargestellt auf Grund eigener Reisen und Forschungen* (Leipzig: Bibliographisches Institut, 1936), 24; Hermann Arnold, *Die Zigeuner: Herkunft und Leben im deutschen Sprachgebiet* (Breisgau: Walter-Verlag AG Olten, 1965), 253; Wim Willems, *In Search of the True Gypsy: From Enlightenment to Final Solution* (Great Britain, Routledge, 1997), 301–2.

29 Referring to them as a "plague," Liebich characterized the Gypsies as work shy, lazy, and careless, and believed that their traveling lifestyle was sustained through criminal practices. Liebich Begging argued that it was "ensconced in [the Gypsies'] nature" and was considered to be the most common of their criminal tendencies, as it provided a major source of income, though the Gypsies were also known to commit crimes of robbery and document forgery, see: Liebich, *Die Zigeuner in ihrem Wesen und in ihrer Sprache*, 3, 28, 72, 78, 80, and 107.

30 Liebich, *Die Zigeuner in ihrem Wesen und in ihrer Sprache*, 3, 28, 72, 78, 80, and 107.

31 Influenced by the work of Charles Darwin, Lombroso claimed that the "born criminal" could be identified as a distinctive anthropological type which could be recognized by specific physical characteristics, or "signs of degeneration." In addition to physical stigma, the "born criminal" possessed moral abnormalities, manifested in "asocial" behavior, such as the usage of slang and a lack of "moral sense," see: Cesare Lombroso, *Der Verbrecher in anthropologischer, ärztlicher und juristischer Beziehung* (Hamburg, 1887–90); Cesare Lombroso, *Die Ursachen und die Bekämpfung des Verbrechers*, trans. Hans Kurella (Berlin: Bermuhler, 1902).

32 Richard Wetzell, *Inventing the Criminal: A History of German Criminology, 1880–1945* (Chapel Hill: University of Carolina Press, 2000).

33 Dillmann, *Zigeuner-Buch*, 6.

34 Furthermore, Dillmann claimed that the "racially pure Zigeuner ... ceased to exist" in German society, and that the Gypsies living in Bavaria either derived from racial mixing with Germans or had arisen "autochthonously" from European soil. See: Dillmann and Alfred. *Zigeuner-Buch*, 5–6.

35 Hermann Aichele, *Die Zigeunerfrage mit besonderer Berücksichtigung Württembergs* (Dissertation, Stuttgart: University of Tübingen, 1911), 7 and 35.

36 Ibid., 25.

37 Other references of Gypsy criminality are also mentioned, as the newspaper article states: "In some parts of the country, mysterious aliens move in hordes up to 100 from place to place. In addition, many are heavily stealing, begging [engaging in] fraudulent horde trade and sometimes have substantial sums of money. Our country's population is suffering greatly." BayHStA MInn 66436, "Die Zigeunerplage." *Neuen Bayerische Landeszeitung,* No. 191, 26. August 1903.

38 Grellmann, *Dissertation on the Gipsies,* Liebich, *Die Zigeuner in ihrem Wesen und in ihrer Sprache*; Aichele, *Die Zigeunerfrage mit besonderer Berücksichtigung Württembergs.*

39 Illuzzi, *Gypsies in Germany and Italy*; Lucassen, "'Harmful Tramps': Police Professionalization and Gypsies in Germany, 1700–1945"; Albrecht, *Zigeuner in Altbayern 1871–1914.*

40 Grellmann states, "Let the state teach him and keep him in leading strings till the end is attained. If the root of this depravity lies so deep, in the first generation, that it cannot be removed immediately, a continuation of the same care will, in the second or third descent, be sure of meeting its reward. When [a Gypsy] has discontinued his Gipsy life, consider him with his fecundity and numerous family, who being reformed, are made useful citizens." See: Grellmann, *Dissertation on the Gipsies,* 80.

41 Ibid., 80–1.

42 Liebich, *Die Zigeuner in ihrem Wesen und in ihrer Sprache,* 107–10.

43 Illuzzi, *Gypsies in Germany and Italy,* 137–8.

44 Aichele's systemization of anti-Gypsy policy demonstrates how German executive administrators tried a range of biopolitical approaches to deal with Gypsy itinerancy. Described as the "period of paternalism," prior to 1862, Aichele states that attempts were made by German governments to assimilate the Gypsies and integrate them into German colonies, with the intention that they could become "orderly citizens," who conformed to a sedentary lifestyle. In the subsequent period (1862–79), governments were motivated by individualism, in which domestic Gypsies could exercise the same rights of freedom of movement and trade (*Freizügigkeit und Gewerbefreiheit*) as other citizens. For Aichele, this sanction was a "baby step" toward fashioning the Gypsies into "an upstanding and civilized population." However, after the unification of Germany, Aichele argues that the increasing complaints of Gypsy "harassment" caused the Chancellery to increase their control over Gypsy immigration, particularly through prohibiting the entry of foreign Gypsies into the German Reich. From 1879 onward, measures against citizen Gypsies sharpened, as the *Kaiserreich* authorities implemented strict policies of legal control, which focused on the eradication of their vagrant lifestyle, See: Aichele, *Die Zigeunerfrage mit besonderer Berücksichtigung Württembergs,* 8, 62–70, 101–2.

45 Ibid., 8, 101–2.
46 Ibid., 102.
47 Lucassen, "'Harmful Tramps': Police Professionalization and Gypsies in Germany, 1700–1945."
48 Albrecht provides a comprehensive overview of the decrees and issues concerned with Zigeuner and vagrancy prior to the unification of Germany, see: Albrecht, *Zigeuner in Altbayern 1871–1914*, 81–4; for additional media reports regarding an ostensible "Gypsy plague" see: Hehemann, *Die „Bekämpfung des Zigeunerunwesens,"* 153–84.
49 For a detailed analysis of the 1867 and 1868 edicts see: Albrecht, *Zigeuner in Altbayern 1871–1914*, 81–4; BayHStA Minn 66433 Ministerium des Innern an Regierungen Kamer des Innern, January 12, 1871.
50 BayHStA Minn 66433 Ministerium des Innern an Regierungen Kamer des Innern, January 12, 1871.
51 The reports of increasing complaints and Bavaria's recommendations for resolving these issues are mentioned in the introduction of the decree "Ministerialentschließung von 23. Januar 1878" in Werner Höhne, *Die Vereinbarkeit der deutschen Zigeunergesetze und verordnungen mit dem Reichsrecht insbesondere der Reichsverfassung* (PhD Dissertation, Heidelberg University, 1929), 130.
52 "Ministerialentschließung von 23. Januar 1878" in Höhne, *Die Vereinbarkeit*, 130.
53 BayHStA MA 5999, *Amstsblatt des K. Staatsministeriums des Innern* 12 July, 1881 "Bekanntmachung. Das Verfahren bei Ermittlung und Festgestellung der Identität und Zuständigkeit von Personen unbekannter Herkunft betr. Kgl. Staatsministerium des Kgl. Hauses und des Aueßern, der Justiz und des Innern"; Albrecht, *Zigeuner in Altbayern 1871–1914*, 87–8.
54 The full quote in the directive issued by the interior minister, Freiherr von Feilitzsch, reads, "ohne zu erhebliche Belastung der Staatskasse das Land von den herumzeihenden Zigeunerbanden dauernd zu säubern." (Without straining the Bavarian Treasury, to continually purge the State of wandering bands of Gypsies.) A circular from the Chancellery to the Bavarian Interior Ministry on July 1, 1886, revealed that another intent of the April 1885 decree was to turn the Gypsies toward a non-sedentary lifestyle, see: BayHStA MA 5999, *Amtsblatt des K. Staatsministeriums des Innern*, München, 16. April 1885 "Ministerialentschließung vom 11. April 1885, Die Handhabung der Sicherheit in Bezug auf Zigeuner"; BayHStA MA 5999 Der Reichskanzler (Reichsamt des Innern) an das K.B. Staatsministerium des Königl. Hauses und Äeußern, Berlin, den 1. Juli 1886.
55 BayHStA MA 5999, *Amtsblatt des K. Staatsministeriums des Innern*, München, 16. April 1885 "Ministerialentschließung vom 11. April 1885, Die Handhabung der Sicherheit in Bezug auf Zigeuner."
56 Ibid.

57 It is also mentioned that police authorities were permitted to incarcerate Gypsies into workhouses for "the purpose of breaking up a Gypsy gang," see: BayHStA MA 5999, *Amtsblatt des K. Staatsministeriums des Innern*, München, 16. April 1885 "Ministerialentschließung vom 11. April 1885, Die Handhabung der Sicherheit in Bezug auf Zigeuner."

58 BayHStA MA 5999, *Amtsblatt des K. Staatsministeriums des Innern*, München, 16. April 1885 "Ministerialentschließung vom 11. April 1885, Die Handhabung der Sicherheit in Bezug auf Zigeuner."

59 BayHStA, MInn 66434, Der Reichskanzler (Reichsamt des Innern), Berlin den 24. Januar 1889.

60 Ibid., Reichskanzler an MA 24.1.1889, Kammer des Innern an das Staatsministerium des Innern, München, den 14. April 1889.

61 BayHStA MA 5999, *Amtsblatt des K. Staatsministerium des Innern*, München, No. 28, 12. Oktober 1889 "Ministerialentschließung vom 5. Oktober 1889, die Handhabung der Sicherheitspolizei in Bezug auf Zigeuner," In the October 5, 1889 decree, the following points report: "1. die Zahl der ausländischer Banden sich vermindert hat, und 2. die inländischen, wenn auch eine wesentliche Abnahme ihrer Zahl nicht allenthalben ist, doch schüchterner in ihrem Auftreten geworden sind." It further states, "Wenn hiernach eine völlständige Säuberung des Landes noch nicht erreicht ist, so darf bei steter und fortgesetzter strenger Kontrolle und Ueberwachung der Zigeunerbanden und bei energischer Verfolgung aller durch sie verübten Uebertretungen doch allmählig eine weitere Minderung derselben und gleichzeitig eine bessere Zügelung ihres Auftretens erhofft werden."

62 Ibid., *Amtsblatt des K. Staatsministerium des Innern*, München, No. 28, 12. Oktober 1889 "Ministerialentschließung vom 5. Oktober 1889, die Handhabung der Sicherheitspolizei in Bezug auf Zigeuner."

63 Illuzzi, *Gypsies in Germany and Italy*, 28, 51–5.

64 BayHStA MInn 66435, *Pfälzische Presse* Nr. 225, am 15. August 1897. Similarly, the *Augsburger Postzeitung* in 1895 urged "in our complaints, we need not anxiously differentiate between real Gypsies and pseudo-Gypsies. Both hordes of pests are the same in their intention to unabashedly beg and brazenly steal" in BayHStA MInn 66435, *Augsburger Postzeitung*, 16. März 1895.

65 Ibid., Kammer der Abgeordneten, Sitzung 295 vom 2. März 1898.

66 Ibid., "Bekämpfung des Zigeunerunwesens," *Bayerische Gemeindzeitung*, 10th Mai, 1899, Nr. 14, 209–16. According to Illuzzi, Dillmann believed that the key to fighting the "Gypsy plague" was "legibility." That is, if the fingerprint of a Gypsy would match their name, age, physical description, and place of origin, the authorities would have strong grounds for expelling and repatriating foreign Gypsies back to their "homeland," thus creating a sedentary and upstanding society. See: Illuzzi, *Gypsies in Germany and Italy*, 55–6.

67 BayHStA, MInn 66435, Königl. Polizeidirektion München an das kgl. Staatsministerium des Innern, München, den 10. Januar 1900.
68 Ibid., Königl. Polizeidirektion München an das kgl. Staatsministerium des Innern, den 21 Januar 1902.
69 BayHStA, MInn 66436, Königl. Polizeidirektion München an das kgl. Staatsministerium des Innern, München, den 13. Mai 1904.
70 An English translation of Dillmann's "sixteen points" can be viewed in Fitzpatrick, *Purging the Empire*, 192–4. Dillmann, *Zigeuner-Buch*, 8–14. The circulation of Dillmann's *Zigeunerbuch* to Bavarian police is confirmed in BayHStA, MInn 59999 K. Staatsministerium des Innern an das K. Staatsministerium des Königlichen Hauses und des Aeussern, München, den. 7 Juni 1905.
71 Dillmann, Alfred, *Zigeuner-Buch*, 10–14.
72 Given their long history of close cooperation, Württemberg naturally followed Bavaria's approach to dealing with Gypsies. In 1905, Dillmann's *Zigeunerbuch* was adopted by Württemberg officials as a standardized policing tool, and, much like Bavaria; their regulations reflected a stringent regime of deportation, surveillance, assimilation, and restrictions of movement and trade. However, prior to this, rather than following a nationally coordinated approach, Württemberg's system for regulating Gypsies operated strictly at state and local levels. Württemberg's measures against foreign Gypsies matched those of Bavaria, as executive administrators continued their efforts to restrict Gypsy immigration to Reich territory. Württemberg's policies for citizen Gypsies were also in line with that of Bavaria, as regulations sought to turn the Gypsies toward a sedentary lifestyle by imposing tight restrictions upon movement and trading, as well as increasing the surveillance and data collection of known Gypsies. For an extensive overview of regulations implemented against Gypsies in Württemberg see: Aichele, *Die Zigeunerfrage mit besonderer Berücksichtigung Württembergs,*; Thomas Fricke, *Zwischen Erziehung und Ausgrenzung: zur württembergischen Geschichte der Sinti und Roma im 19. Jahrhundert* (Frankfurt am Main: Peter Lang, 1991) and Höhne, *Die Vereinbarkeit der deutschen Zigeunergesetze*, 165–72.
73 GStAPK, I. HA Rep. 77, Ministerium des Innern, Tit. 423 Nr. 53 adh/2 Bd. 1, Zircularerlaß des Innenministers vom 22. Oktober 1870, Bl. 9. A reference of the 1883 decree can be cited in GStAPK I.HA Rep. 77, Ministerium des Innern, Tit. 423 Nr. 53 adh/2 Bd. 1, Zirkularerlaß des Innenministers vom 30. April 1886, Bl. 119–27.
74 Jennifer Illuzzi, "Negotiating the 'State of Exception,': Gypsies' Encounter with the Judiciary in Germany and Italy, 1860-1914," *Social History* 35, no. 4 (2010): 421; Fitzpatrick, *Purging the Empire*, 182–5.
75 GStAPK, I. HA Rep. 77, Tit. 423 Nr. 53 adh/2 Bd. 1, Bericht der Königl. Regierung in Minden an den Innenminister, vom 3. März 1885, Bl. 106–9.

76 GStAPK, I. HA Rep. 77, Ministerium des Innern, Tit. 423 Nr. 53 adh/2 Bd. 1 Erlaß des Innenministers an die Oberpräsidenten der preußischen Provinzen vom 22. Februar 1885, Bl. 100–5; GStAPK, I. HA Rep. 77, Ministerium des Innern, Tit. 423 Nr. 53 adh/2 Bd. 1, Schreiben des preußischen Innenministers an den Reichskanzler vom 1. Mai 1885, Bl. 110–11; GStAPK, I. HA Rep. 77, Ministerium des Innern, Tit. 423 Nr. 53 adh/2 Bd. 1, „Zirkularerlaß des Innenministers vom 30 April 1886," Bl. 119–27.

77 GStAPK, I. HA Rep. 77, Ministerium des Innern, Tit. 423 Nr. 53 adh/2 Bd. 1, "Zirkularerlaß des Innenministers vom 30 April 1886," Bl. 119–27.

78 GStAPK, I. HA Rep. 77, Ministerium des Innern, Tit. Nr. 53 adh/2 Bd. 1, Der Reichskanzlers (Reichsamt des Innern), Berlin den 1. Juli 1886, Bl. 151–4; Der Reichskanzler an das Ministeriums des Innern, Berlin, den 12. März 1887 Bl. 174–5; Das Ministerium des Innerns an den Reichskanzler Bismarck, Berlin, den 24. Juni 1887 Bl. 179–83; Das Ministerium des Innern "Erlaß des Innminisers vom 29. September 1887," Berlin, den 29. September 1887, Bl. 205–7.

79 GStAPK, I. HA Rep. 77, Ministerium des Innern, Tit. Nr. 53 adh/2 Bd. 1, Ministerium des Innern "Erlaß des Innenminisers vom 29. September 1887," Berlin, den 29. September 1887, Bl. 205–7; GStAPK, I. HA Rep. 77, Ministerium des Innern, Tit. Nr. 53, adh/2 Bd. 2, Der Reichskanzler an das Ministerium des Innern, 3. September 1889, Bl. 36–7.

80 GStAPK, I. HA Rep. 77, Ministerium des Innern, Tit. Nr. 53 adh/2 Bd. 1, Ministerium des Innern "Erlaß des Innenminisers vom 29. September 1887," Berlin, den 29. September 1887, Bl. 205–7; GStAPK, I. HA Rep. 77. Ministerium des Innern, Tit. 423 Nr. 53 adh/2 Bd. 2, Erlaß des Innenministers vom 8. Dezember 1892. Bl. 122–3; GStAPK, I. HA Rep. 77, „Ministerium des Innern, Tit. 423 Nr. 53 adh/2 Bd. 3 Zusammenfassung der Ergebnisse des Innenministers vom 30. Dezember 1901. Bl. 107–8;

81 GStAPK, I. HA Rep. 77, Ministerium des Innern, Tit. Nr. 53 adh/2 Bd. 1, Ministerium des Innern "Erlaß des Innenminisers vom 29. September 1887," Berlin, den 29. September 1887, Bl. 205–7; Erlaß des Innenministers vom 29. September 1887; Rundschreiben des preußischen Innenminisers und des Kultusministers vom 23. Oktober 1889 in Bonillo, M., *Zigeunerpolitik im Deutschen Kaiserreich: 1871–1918*, 242–6; Preußische Ausführungsanweisung zur Gewerbeordnung, 1 May 1904 in Hohne, 105–6.

82 Despite the urging from media and government officials to devise new policies for combatting the "Gypsy nuisance," some provincial regions voiced their satisfaction and successful implementation of current anti-Gypsy measures. A report from Königsberg to the Prussian Interior Ministry, for example, indicated that the number of Gypsies living in the district were consistently low and declining; the largest presence being a Gypsy horde of approximately fifty in the Labiau area,

while the smallest was a family of six in the Wehlau district. It further reported that those few German Gypsies who remained in the area were sedentary, as the families had obtained a permanent residence and their children were attending school regularly. Thus, the Königsberg governor believed that current policy was effective, and that newer, more stringent measures against citizen Gypsies were not necessary. See: GStAPK: I.HA Rep. 77 Ministerium des Innern. Tit. 423 Nr. 53 Adh. 1, Der königliche Regierungs-Präsident, an den Herrn Minister des Innern, Königsberg 23 Januar 1900, Bl. 252–3; Der Polizei Präsident an den Herrn Minister des Innern, Berlin 6 Januar 1900, Bl. 261.

83 GStAPK: I.HA Rep. 77 Ministerium des Innern. Tit. 423 Nr. 53 Adh. 1, Der Regierungs Präsident Koblenz an den Herrn Minister des Innern zu Berlin, den 5. Februar 1900, Bl. 352–5.

84 Bethmann Hollweg, *Ausweisung zur Bekämpfung des Zigeunerunwesens vom 17. Februar 1906* (Berlin: Carl Henmans Verlag, 1906), 3–6.

85 *Ausweisung zur Bekämpfung des Zigeunerunwesens*, 5.

86 GStAPK, I. HA rep 77 Tit. 423, nr. 53, adh. 2 Heft 1, Regierungs-Präsident Breslau an den Minister des Innern, Berlin, Oktober den 9. 1910, Bl. 20–4.

87 Illuzzi, "Negotiating the "State of Exception," 421; Fitzpatrick, *Purging the Empire*, 182–5; Lewy, *Nazi Persecution of the Gypsies*, 7.

88 Similar complaints of cyclical expulsion between northern and southern Germany can be seen in BayHStA MInn 66436, Königliche Regierung von Oberfranken, Kammer des Innern an das K. Staatsministerium des Innern, Bayreuth, den 24. Mai 1906; GStAP I.HA Rep. 77 Ministerium des Innern, Tit. 423 Nr. 53 adh/2 Bd.5, Königliches Bezirksamt Gemünden an die Königliche Regierung von Unterfranken und Aschaffenburg Kammer des Innern, Gemünden, am 26. Januar 1910, Bl. 348–50.

89 One who briefly spoke on the issue of cyclical expulsion in 1905, and again in 1907, was the anti-Semite Max Liebermann. To resolve this issue he "urged the *Reichstag* to establish an agreement between the federal governments, which would make it possible to counteract the "Gypsy nuisance" in Germany in a collective, national, and effective manner." GStAP I.HA Rep. 77 Ministerium des Innern, Tit. 423 Nr. 53 adh/2 Bd.5, Reichstag Nr. 28, 12. Legislatur Periode. I. 1907. (19. Feb 1907), Bl. 76 One who particularly championed the idea of an exceptional law for Zigeuner was the wartime chancellor, Georg von Hertling. For a comprehensive analysis of the debates within the Reichstag, concerned with the expulsion of Zigeuner and developing an exceptional legal framework, see: Fitzpatrick, *Purging the Empire*, 185–9.

90 BayHStA, München Abt. II, MA 92791 K.Staatsministerium des Innern an die K.Staatsministerien, des Königlichen Hauses und des Aeußern, der Finanzen, für Verkehrsangelegenheiten, München, den 3. November 1906; K. Gesandtschaft

in Wien an das K. Staatsministerium des Innern, Lindau, den 6. Februar 1907; K.Staatsministerium des kaiserlichen und königlichen Hauses und des Äußern an den königlich bayerischen außerordentlichen Gesandten und bevollmächtigten Minister, am 23 Mai 1908; K.Staatsministerium des Innern an das K.Staatsministerium des Königlichen Hauses und des Aeußern, München, den 12. November 1908.

91 The full 17-point program can be viewed in GStAP I.HA Rep. 77 Ministerium des Innern, Tit. 423 Nr. 53 adh/2 Bd.5, Der schweizerische Bundesrat an die Schwizerischen Gestandschaften in Berlin, Paris, Rom und Wien, Bern, 2. Juli 1909, Bl. 326–34.

92 GStAP I.HA Rep. 77 Ministerium des Innern, Tit. 423 Nr. 53 adh/2 Bd.5, Der schweizerische Bundesrat an die Schweizerischen Gesandtschaften in Berlin, Paris, Rom und Wien, Bern, 2. Juli 1909, Bl. 326–34. BayHStA, MA 92791 K.Staatsministerium des Innern an die K.Staatsministerien, des Königlichen Hauses und des Aeußern, der Finanzen, für Verkehrangelegenheiten, München, den 3. November 1906; BayHStA, MA 92790 Kgl. Bayerische Gesandtschaft in Bern an des K.B. Staatsministerium d. Kgl. Hauses u.d. Aeußern, Bern, 10 September 1907; K.Staatsministerium des Innern an das K. Staatsministerium des Königlichen Hauses und des Aeußern, München, den 8. September 1907; Kgl. Bayerische Gesandtschaft in Bern, an das K.B. Staatsministerium d. Kgl. Hauses und des Aeussern, Bern 5 September, 1907; Kgl. Bayerische Gesandtschaft in Bern an das K. Staatsministerium d. Kgl. Hauses und des Aeußern, Bern 15 März 1907; BayHStA Minn 66436 Kgl. Bayerische Gesandtshaft in Bern an das K. Staatsministerium Kgl. Hauses und des Aeußern, Bern, den 13. August 1906.

93 Representatives present at the Munich Conference included those from Prussia, Saxony, Stuttgart, and Alsace-Lorraine, Württemberg, Baden, and Hessen. BHStA, MA 92790, *Niederschrift über die Besprechung im K.B. Staatsministerium des Innern am 18. Und 19. Dezember 1911*, betreffend die Bekämpfung der Zigeunerplage, Munich 1911, 1–2.

94 BayHStA, MA 92790, *Denkschrift über die Bekämpfung der Zigeunerplage,* Munich 1912, 4.

95 Ibid., 3–5.

96 BayHStA, MA 92790, *Niederschrift,* 10–14.

97 Fearing that the costs associated with civilizing stateless Gypsies would greatly strain their finances, Prussia opposed Harster's notion. As a solution, the Alsace-Lorraine representative suggested that "foreign and stateless Gypsies ... should be sent to colonies"—a recommendation that did not become a reality, despite support from Hessen and Württemberg. Ibid., 22–4.

98 BayHStA, MA 92790, *Denkschrift*, 42.

99 Ibid., 18–24.

100 Ibid., 7.
101 BayHStA, MA 92790, *Niederschrift*, 5–6.
102 Ibid., 6.
103 Ibid., 7.
104 Ibid., 5.
105 BayHStA, MF 67417, K. Staatsministerium des Innern an das K. Staatsministerium des Königl. Hauses und des Aeußern, Dezember 31 1913, München.
106 Fitzpatrick, *Purging the Empire*, 197; Illuzzi, *Gypsies in Germany and Italy*, 150.

6

Cultivating Fear: The Image of the SA and the Presence of Propaganda in the Late Weimar *Öffentlichkeit*

Jacob Berg and Richard Scully

On March 19, 1928, Joseph Goebbels affirmed in *Der Angriff* that the "lords of money are preparing their final blow. They have robbed our people of faith and will; they have shamed and dishonored us, and now want to grab us around our neck. No speeches, no begging, can stop that—only resistance, battle, attack!"[1] Goebbels—who was eventually appointed Reich minister for Popular Enlightenment and Propaganda—had, in a few words, briefed his fellow ideological soldiers on just how to deal with the enemies of National Socialism, namely: violence and aggression. This violent and belligerent approach to politics was not unique to the NSDAP but was derived from, and helped to reinforce, an ongoing, systemic culture of fear in Germany. Throughout the 1920s and early 1930s (a time later known by Nazis as the *Kampfzeit*; or "time of struggle"), social disorder and chaos—political upheaval, street violence, and even bloodshed— marred the public sphere in Germany.[2] During this period the Nazis in particular learned to use their paramilitary force—the *Sturmabteilung* (SA)—as a means of instilling fear into political and ideological rivals through a very real physical, violent and intimidating presence in German towns and cities.[3] However, the SA was also used to promote fear—by both the Nazis and their political opponents— through a different medium not commonly examined: visual propaganda in the form of posters. This threatening, fear-provoking presence of the SA is illustrated nicely in a pro-Hindenburg election poster of 1932 (Figure 1), entitled *Schluss Jetzt mit Hitlers Volksverhetzung! Wählt Hindenburg* (Enough with Hitler's Incitement! Vote Hindenburg).[4] The image shows a colossal, yet distressed, German worker with a gigantic broom attempting to sweep up and contain a seemingly uncontainable civil war (*Bürgerkrieg*) between the SA and members

Figure 1 *Schluss jetzt mit Hitlers Volksverhetzung! Wählt Hindenburg* [Enough now with Hitler's national incitement! Vote Hindenburg], 1932, courtesy of the Bundesarchiv, Plak 002-016-007/Artist: Anon.

of the *Roter Frontkämpferbund* (RFB)—the paramilitary organization of the *Kommunistische Partei Deutschlands* (KPD). With knives pulled and groups of brawling paramilitary soldiers, accompanied by communist and Nazi banners, the image accentuated the violent political climate of 1932.[5] More importantly, it represents how political propaganda posters of the time reflected—but also sought to foster—a very real and deep-seated fear of SA and paramilitary violence among the German population. The ubiquitous political violence that characterized German streets during the later Weimar period instilled a fear into people.[6] A fear—so capably explored by Dirk Schuman—that such violence would lead to civil war.[7] This was a fear that was held as much by the paramilitary groups and extremist parties themselves, as well as by the general public or more moderate groups. Nazi propaganda was effective in reenforcing fears and prejudices about supposed enemies of Germany.[8] During the early time of struggle this meant painting political opponents as enemies of the state, while later (founded on more racialized principles) it meant the demonization of the Jews above all.[9]

Fear was undoubtedly a valuable tool in the propaganda kit of German political parties in the late Weimar *Öffentlichkeit*.[10] Various political parties exploited this civil war hysteria for their own advantage.¹¹ Indeed, the aim of much Nazi propaganda in this time was to awaken ordinary Germans to the fears the Nazis held for Germany's future. In this, a good deal of Nazi poster art sought not to deny the existing or feared state of civil war epitomized by the *Wählt Hindenburg* poster, but rather to subvert the simple caricature of the SA and NSDAP produced by their ideological opponents, and "sell" the movement as the solution to this state of affairs. They sold themselves as the needed antidote to this fear, at the same time as fostering it.

The SA was the most visually obtrusive segment of the NSDAP (especially in the years leading up to the seizure of power in 1933).¹² Without SA violence, and their ubiquitous presence in the streets (including via motorized propaganda support), the Nazi party would have been hard-pressed to secure its political authority.¹³ Hitler's Stormtroopers were, as described by Conan Fischer, the "foot soldiers of the Nazi movement and the spearhead of day-to-day propaganda campaigns."¹⁴ They were the marchers, flag bearers, and bodyguards of the NSDAP, and they performed many functions of vital importance. Remembered mostly for their active involvement in political violence and intimidation during the 1920s and early 1930s, from as early as 1921, the NSDAP leadership used the SA to contest control of the streets and public spaces with their leftist political opponents (and thereby assert that the Nazi party would eventually rule the state).¹⁵ Through the use of staged brawls against communist "aggressors" in the beer halls of Southern Germany (in particular in the Nazi homeland of Bavaria), along with various other displays of physical violence and intimidation, the SA not only asserted its collective strength but increased Nazi public appeal in a democratic mass market.¹⁶ As Daniel Siemens has noted, Goebbels believed that reproducible acts of violence could increase the public's awareness of National Socialism and make the party "politically relevant."¹⁷

Scholars tend to agree that the SA played a decisive role in the Nazi seizure and consolidation of power through acts of brutality, terrorism, and intimidation.¹⁸ There is similar consensus over the Stormtroopers' eventual fall from grace: the very factors that had made it a valuable entity prior to and immediately following the seizure of power in 1933 (the propensity for hooliganism and terror directed against political opponents), together with the military ambitions of *Stabschef* [Chief of Staff] Ernst Röhm, ultimately meant that the SA became dangerous to the regime. It increasingly threatened to employ its violence in a way that was no longer in line with the policy of the new regime and thus placed the building the new Germany in jeopardy.¹⁹ In order to solve this problem of a "revolutionary" SA, in June 1934, Hitler eventually ordered the SS to arrest and assassinate SA leaders (as well as old political rivals) in what has come to be known as the "Röhm purge" or "Night of the Long Knives."[20] The underlying motivation for this event was undoubtedly an internal fear held by the NSDAP of the SA and their capabilities, given their size and still-revolutionary ideology.

Despite the apparent consensus in the scholarship, and the vast amount of literature that has been produced on SA violence and intimidation (up to and including the seizure of power), there remains no dedicated study on another key role of the SA, and the one which complemented its real, physical role: its visual and symbolic role in propaganda, especially in poster art. These were images of Stormtroopers that proliferated in German public spaces and sustained the SA's presence long after the last brawl had been broken up, the sound of jackboots and marching songs had faded into the distance, and the last Stormtrooper had gone home to his otherwise mundane life. Posters hung in the public spaces were an inescapable and overpowering optical form of indoctrination, regardless of whether passersby viewed them in an active or passive, incidental fashion.[21] The Stormtroopers' claim on public space was sustained by posters that they themselves often posted, the content of which functioned to perpetuate and extend a multilayered sense of fear: fear of the SA itself in the minds of its opponents; and fear of existing or impending civil war in the minds of the German electorate.

Social and Economic Disorder

As historian and social scientist Eric Johnson argues, an overall sense of "political turbulence and economic uncertainty" had been building in Germany since the end of the First World War.[22] This manifested itself in phases of heightened tension, followed by relative calm. Germany was riddled with widespread dissatisfaction against the republican leaders for signing the Treaty of Versailles.[23] The Weimar Republic did, however, manage to weather what Richard J. Evans calls the "storms of the early 1920s" and had entered a period of comparative social, economic, and political stability from late 1923 until the end of the decade.[24] However, even in that period—the so-called golden years of the Weimar government—memories were still fresh of the time of seemingly constant upheaval: the disastrous end to the First World War; the revolution that toppled the monarchy and ushered in the republic; separatism in the *Länder*; the *putsches* from both the left and then right of the political spectrum; the Franco-Belgian occupation of the Ruhr; and the subsequent hyperinflation of 1923; as well as the loss of the old prewar (or, indeed, wartime) certainties.[25]

Fear is variable; it presents itself as a disassociated feeling in peaceful societies that have seemingly no basis for disorder, yet in other societies becomes endemic in times of chaos and upheaval. Extremist political groups who rely on fear for their political advancement are, therefore, somewhat at the mercy of events, even if they seek also to foster irrational fears through propagandistic means. As Evans has noted, even in the unsettled conditions of Weimar Germany, there would need to be a "catastrophe of major dimensions if an extremist party like the Nazis was to gain mass support."[26] The catastrophe is well known: on October 24, 1929, the *Brooklyn Daily Eagle* printed its front-page headline: "Wall St. in panic as Stocks Crash."[27] As a result of US loans to Germany's agricultural, steel, and chemical firms, the stock market crash had major repercussions for Germany and its struggling economy. Prior to the crash, the German economy had been essentially reestablished by loans from the United States of America. German industry had accelerated as a direct result of foreign investment.[28] However, with the Wall Street crash, short-term foreign loans had been recalled and German industries—along with their long-term investments—were forced to downsize or even close.[29] This in turn meant that the German economy was forced to rely on its own resources to sustain itself—at the same time as repaying debt—and thus was hurled into deep economic depression.

The failing German economy had a significant impact on millions of the country's workers. Masses of urban civilians became unemployed; as a result, less money was available to spend on food, which in turn, heightened the already widespread agricultural crisis, forcing agricultural businesses into bankruptcy.[30] Agricultural workers were also now out of work, spreading unemployment from the cities into the rural areas of Germany. By January 1931, the economic crisis in Germany had reached new heights with a total of 4,886,925 people unemployed.[31] President Paul von Hindenburg—under powers granted by Article 48 of the Constitution and with the connivance of his favored candidate for the chancellorship, Heinrich Brüning—had issued emergency decrees that severely reduced social welfare outlays, federal support to local and state governments, and civil service salaries.[32] This not only heightened the effects of the economic crisis but also aggravated the frustration of the middle classes.[33] In this context, street violence and protests gained much more significance than they had in the early 1920s.[34] In Berlin itself, unemployment rose from 133,000, in 1928, to 600,000, by 1932.[35] Between 1930 and 1933 the average national unemployment rate was over 30 percent.[36] In 1932, there were nearly thirteen million Germans (workers and their dependents) suffering from an inability to find employment and the resultant psychological and social stresses this placed on a society defined by the male breadwinner and an associated work ethic.[37]

Economic difficulties, although primarily a working-class phenomenon, had started to deteriorate the morale of other social groups, creating an atmosphere of anxiety and disillusionment toward the Weimar Republic.[38] Many young men who had gone through adolescence and early adulthood expecting a well-paid and secure future were left jobless, deprived, and miserable.[39] But even more importantly, it fostered a fear in those as yet unaffected by unemployment who realized they might very well be next. Although hotly debated among historians, Conan Fischer has repeatedly shown that the economic crisis following the 1929 crash played a decisive role in funneling civilians from the working classes into the SA (even as they were also joining other political movements in larger numbers).[40] As Daniel Siemens has pointed out, this was a result of many Germans being gripped with a fear of social decline.[41] Many of the young men that began saturating the SA in the late 1920s and early 1930s were born in the first decade of the twentieth century, thus into a world shaped by a war that they had "missed," and the associated revolution, economic crisis, and social upheaval.[42] Many politically unaffiliated, working-class males were looking for a radical solution to their own destitution—or *potential* destitution—along with a solution for the guilty parties who had placed them and the nation in such a position.[43] As anthropologist and cultural historian Geoffrey Skoll has argued: "Nothing motivates like fear, and gratitude is accorded to those who promise protection."[44] In Germany at this time, society had fundamentally transformed as a result of impoverishment and class boundary disintegration. Social stability had essentially dissolved.[45] As a result of growing middle-class resentment toward the Weimar Republic and the ongoing Depression, large numbers of middle-class citizens thus also began to see the youthful dynamism and physicality of the Nazi party as a solution to their ongoing problems.

SA Violence and Terror

On April 30, 1928, Joseph Goebbels asserted that "we are coming not as friends, also not as neutrals. We come as enemies! As the wolf attacks the sheep, so come we."[46] In light of the impending German Federal Election in May of that year, Goebbels in this statement was providing his audience with another clear message about National Socialism. At its core, Nazism was founded on principles of violence and belligerence. Although ill-defined, the Nazis' ideology sought to locate scapegoats and enemies on whom their wrath and outrage could be expended.[47] Nazism sought to confront political and ideological enemies both psychologically and physically.[48] The politics of violence as used by Hitler's SA was propaganda.[49] The Stormtroopers were the brown-shirted political soldiers of the movement, the physical manifestation of National Socialism.[50] The very presence of a group of seemingly passive SA members who could resort to violence instantaneously instilled fear into "potential dissidents and bystanders alike."[51]

As early as 1921, the SA had been used for the protection of NSDAP meetings and to fight political opponents.[52] It was a small organization in the early years, with a membership of only one thousand by the end of 1922.[53] The first major display of public physicality and violence that received significant publicity was at the *Deutsche Tag* (German Day) held in Coburg on October 14 and 15, 1922. Against the requests of the Social Democrats, Communists, and trade union leaders, the SA—preceded by a marching band—tramped through the town engaging in clashes with the left throughout the day and into the evening.[54] This was followed in 1923 by the "Beer Hall Putsch," which ultimately led to the outlawing of the Nazi party (Hitler being sent to Landsberg Prison; and the nationwide banning of the SA).[55] Although it survived in Bavaria—under the covert name of *Frontbann*—the SA was not fully revived until Hitler called for the organisations' refounding on the February 26, 1925.[56]

From the beginning of its existence, the SA was involved in battles over public space in cities and towns all over Germany and ultimately aimed at the control and domination of that public space (essentially, to put an end to a bourgeois *Öffentlichkeit*).[57] The most common contexts for SA violence were political rallies and marches. In the larger cities and industrial areas of Germany—especially in places where the SPD and the KPD could claim higher levels of support—the Nazis used these rallies and marches as deliberate provocations.[58] As Stormtroopers marched through major city or town centers and main streets, they could be heard singing in unity *Die Rote Front, schlagt sie zu brei/ SA marschiert. Achtung, die Straße frei* ("Beat the Red Front to a pulp. The SA is marching: Keep off the streets").[59] Riccardo Bavaj has noted that the top priority of SA propaganda was the "physical conquest and symbolic occupation of public space."[60] SA marches through German city centers acted as a demonstration for both power and dominance. Bavaj describes "the road" as a "stage for the rehearsal of the conquest of power."[61] As mentioned earlier, through the conquest of the streets, the SA also became an instrument for working-class recruitment (and repression).[62] The territorial organization of the SA made it adept to such acts of violence; as small *Sturmbanne* units, brigade-sized *Standarten* (or even larger *Brigaden*) from neighboring territories competed with one another in the attacking and destroying of communist strongholds.[63] As Pamela Swett has described the desire for territorial control was perhaps the most common source of neighborhood violence.[64] The SA through the use of intimidation and terror isolated "racial enemies" and disrupted political rival groups and their campaigns.[65]

The original SA consisted primarily of members from the *Freikorps*: private right-wing militia that engaged in political violence and social revolution in Weimar Germany after the war (and who were used by Weimar authorities to suppress ideological enemies).[66] By 1927, acts of aggression and violence—particularly towards Communists and Social Democrats—had become ubiquitous. One such event occurred in March 1927. The SA had gathered in the town of Trebbin to take part in a series of mass rallies and marches as part of Goebbels' "Battle for Berlin." From Trebbin, Stormtroopers traveled by train to Lichterfelde Ost, located on the south side of Berlin, to begin their march toward West Berlin in the evening.[67] It was here that SA members encountered a group of individuals from the Red Front Fighters League, on their way home from a political demonstration in Leuna (in Saxony).[68] At Lichterfelde Ost station, the two groups clashed in what is described as "an open fire fight."[69] As Siemens has noted, the SA destroyed the windows of train carriages, bashed the communists with flagpoles, hurled stones at them, and also shot at them.[70] Detectives investigating the brawl discovered 230 rocks, empty bullet cartridges, and teeth aside pools of blood.[71]

The early 1930s saw intensified political struggle as a result of both the Depression and the contentious 1930 German Reichstag elections (which occurred at a time when unemployment was high). Taxes in Germany had been increased, salaries decreased, and there was a widespread feeling of dissatisfaction throughout German society.[72] Chancellor Heinrich Brüning appealed to the country to return him with a majority, however his government was severely attacked by other political groups such as the SPD for being a presidential puppet; by the nationalists for his support of the Young Plan; by the KPD on general principles; and also by the NSDAP.[73] Via the SA, the Nazis—primarily a Bavarian movement—set out to challenge the left in its own territory, in working-class districts, by heightening its use of physical violence.[74] By this stage, the SA had grown into an organization of sixty thousand Stormtroopers with a more national membership rather than just a Bavarian one.⁷⁵ Members of the SA were terrorizing towns, assaulting the offices of left-wing organizations, and attacking prominent members of the SPD and KPD (which prompted these organizations to adopt similar tactics for defense).⁷⁶ Historians have argued that Hitler himself had grown concerned about the destructive activism associated with the SA, due to the danger this posed to his presentation of the Nazi movement as a legal and responsible, anti-republican force.⁷⁷

From June 1930, the state [*Lander*] governments decided on measures to impede the growth and violence of the SA.⁷⁸ In the following month, a series of restrictions were imposed on the organization in Bavaria, Prussia, and Baden.⁷⁹ One of those restrictions was a ban on wearing the brown-shirted uniform.⁸⁰ Prohibitions on the SA uniform repeatedly limited the propagandistic self-portrayal of the NSDAP.⁸¹ Uniforms had become a potential source of violence. For the SA soldier, the uniform served as a symbol of the fight against the republic and for a larger, free and more powerful Germany.⁸² Goebbels had noted in his diary on the May 8, 1932, that "if the SA marches again in the Brown shirt, then the whole Depression would be overcome, and the enemy will sink from our blows to meet the bottom."⁸³ Despite the ban there was a general fear among the German populace that SA and Communist violence would escalate into civil war.⁸⁴ This is somewhat due to the fact that such bans actually had very little effect on the terroristic and public activities of the SA as they simply marched in white shirts and maintained their controversial and militaristic character.⁸⁵ This was especially true after the ban on the SA had been lifted. In August 1931, the newspaper *Magdeburgische Zeitung* noted that Germany had been "in a civil war … for years."⁸⁶ SA violence was no longer just something read about in newspapers but rather something that occurred in every town and city throughout Germany and—where it did not occur—was present as an imagined threat in the minds of everyday Germans, reinforced by the virtual, visual presence of the SA in poster art. The ever-increasing presence of the SA in towns and cities—heightened by an impressive number of motor vehicles that enabled the SA to appear omnipresent—contributed to heightened feelings of fear.⁸⁷

Fear is often fueled by propaganda but also built on very real threats. The imaginary threat of civil war, as presented by propaganda and the very real threat of civil war as a result of the presence, disruption, and violence of the SA in all working-class areas in 1932, was heightened.⁸⁸ This was a year characterized by an increasing use of "civil war like clashes," brawling and terror between the SA and their political opponents.⁸⁹ In July 1932, the *Reichstag* elections, and the surrounding competition for popularity among the electorate led to an unprecedented number of violent clashes as the SA willingly applied "terrorist pressure."[90] The increasing intensity of electoral campaigning at local, state, and national levels also meant that the NSDAP and the SA were consumed by an overall feeling of being overstretched.[91] The contemporary fears expressed in the *Magdeburgische Zeitung* and other papers go to some length in demonstrating the violent reality that was taking place between the SA, the police and other political opponents. Such confrontations have given historians like Daniel Schmidt the impression that by the summer of 1932, the "manageable" levels of radicalization and terror "became part of everyday life during the civil war-like final phase of the republic."[92] Bessel concurs and identifies numerous examples of SA violence that characterize the atmosphere of 1932. On Sunday July 10, 1932, in the town of Ohlau (now part of modern-day Poland) Stormtroopers and SPD sympathizers collided on their way back from their respective party rallies. Upon their meeting in the center of the town, a fight ensued that immediately involved hundreds of people.[93] By 11:00 p.m. that evening the conflict had concluded and order was restored, but only thanks to the intervention of the army. The clash had left dozens dead and many others in a serious medical condition.[94]

One month later, in August 1932, the East Prussian capital of Königsberg became the epicenter of what Bessel calls "the most brutal terror campaign carried out by members of the SA before 1933."[95] On the day before the election, a red terrorist group attacked an SA man. According to Goebbels diary entry of August 1, a communist cut his throat in broad daylight in the street with a razor.[96] Additionally, after the *Reichstag* elections were completed, SA troops in Königsberg were advised that communist radicals elsewhere had ambushed Stormtroopers early on August 1. The results of the election go to some length in explaining why the Communist Party attacked the SA, with the National Socialists receiving 13,732,779 votes, while the Communist party only received 5,278,094 votes.[97] After hearing of these attacks, the local *Sturmführer* in Königsberg responded with retaliation. As Iris Helberg and Yves Müller have identified, after the Nazis seized power, *Rache* (revenge) of such events was a central motive of Stormtrooper violence.[98] However, Stormtroopers in Königsberg in August 1932 did not wait for revenge. They had taken it immediately. Over the course of several days, petrol pumps throughout the city were set alight to distract police and fire crews while the brownshirts looted ammunition and weapon stores, bombed prominent SPD and KPD headquarters; murdered *Reichsbanner* and communist members (such as Gustav Sauf and Otto Braun); assaulted Jewish members of the community; and destroyed Jewish businesses by throwing grenades into their shops.⁹⁹ In one, particularly terrorizing event, a Nazi sympathizer was said to have fired into a crowd with a machine gun. Events such as these were not isolated incidents but formed part of a broader trend of political violence that instilled a rising level of the fear of civil war into Germans throughout 1932. The very reportage of these events brought them uncomfortably close to those who had no direct experience of them.¹⁰⁰

Posters and the Distribution of Fear

It was in this violent and aggressive context that Nazi artists—as well as opponents of Nazism—used propaganda posters to build upon the authentic angst associated with real paramilitary violence at the hands of the SA, in order to instill fear in the German population in an attempt to win popular support. It is a common idea that authoritarian regimes, such as Nazi Germany, identify enemies who present a danger to the national community (in this case the specifically racial *Volksgemeinschaft*) and then seek to control, alienate, and eliminate those designated as undesirable.¹⁰¹ Such regimes then shape and manage the opinions and attitudes of the public through instruments of the state, namely: propaganda.¹⁰² The SA, as the physical manifestation of Nazi ideology, became the outwardly visual symbol of the party and a catalyst for propaganda dissemination.¹⁰³

It was initially however, the anti-Nazi—largely liberal-democratic—parties that first used the image of the SA in poster propaganda to instill fear in the electorate. And indeed, perhaps as a result of the negative image the SA had among respectable voters, the SA presence in the NSDAP's own propaganda posters prior to 1930 was somewhat sparse. *Was steckt hinter dieser Maske? Also wählt Marx* (Figure 2) was designed by republican campaigner Walter Reimar, for the second round of voting in the presidential election of 1925, when the war hero and victor of the Battle of Tannenberg, Paul von Hindenburg faced off against Wilhelm Marx, a Bavarian Catholic, who was supported by the Social Democrats (SPD).¹⁰⁴ On April 7, Hindenburg announced his willingness to represent the coalition of conservative interests known as the *Reichsblock* in the presidential election.¹⁰⁵ According to the propaganda of the opposing *Volksblock*—developed behind Marx, and consisting of the Social Democratic Party, *Zentrum Partei* [Centre Party] and the German Democratic Party—a Hindenburg victory would mean military rule and violent repression; an idea represented in the Reimar poster by a machine gun (specifically, a *Maschinegewehr*

Figure 2 *Was steckt hinter dieser Maske? Also wählt Marx* [What is behind this mask? So, vote Marx], 1925, courtesy of the Bundesarchiv, Plak 002-014-018/ Artist: Walter Reimer.

08), bayonet, and a pair of jackboots with spurs. The image cleverly displays a giant Hindenburg mask shielding a group of dangerous right-wing characters represented in a malevolent fashion.

Most notably, a Nazi Stormtrooper, wearing the brassard of the Nazi movement on his left bicep, is prominent among the right-wing characters represented. The SA figure has been drawn wielding a handgun, emphasizing the violent and militaristic nature of the Stormtroopers.[106] In 1925, opposing political parties were well aware of the violent capabilities of the SA and the Nazi party they represented and Reimar's use of such an image exemplifies this broader context. However, the SA had only just been reestablished in February of that year and Hitler had made it clear that this new SA should no longer carry weapons.[107] As Siemens has pointed out, this was counterintuitive to limit the "new SA" from striking with physical force considering their opponents seemed to be organizing themselves along such lines.[108] Although, this context increases the likelihood of Reimar's imagery being based on the memory of the revolutionary SA from the Munich Putsch rather than from any episodes of violence that the SA was involved with between its reestablishment in February and Hindenburg's victory on April 27, 1925. By presenting the SA in this fashion, the artist negatively and cleverly utilizes the already-existing fear and stigma attached to Nazi Stormtroopers to manipulate public opinion in an attempt to swing the vote away from a Hindenburg presidency.

Likely in response to this misuse of a National Socialist symbol—as a means of reasserting control over their own image—the Nazis themselves propagated an image of the Stormtroopers via posters. However, they did not initially seek to allay fears of the SA but rather favored the use of an image that would evoke a sense of fear, not only in the minds of their political enemies but also the general public. Pro-Nazi artists indeed built upon the physical and violent trademarks of the SA as a means of reinforcing the morale of the brownshirts themselves and celebrating them to the wider Nazi movement. In so doing, the images themselves provided the members of the SA with a visual guide as to how they might behave.

Berlin Voran: Dritter Märkertage, 29–30 Sept 1928 (Figure 3) illustrates the physicality, unity, and violent nature of Hitler's Stormtroopers. The image was created in 1928 to advertise and celebrate the *Dritter Märkertag* (Third Berlin- Brandenburg Rally) set to take place on September 29–30.[109] The image appeared on Saturday, September 22, 1928, in the nationally produced pictorial tabloid, *Illustrieter Beobachter* (published weekly, on a Saturday).[110] The poster displays a band of SA men, carrying Nazi flags on banner poles, charging

Figure 3 *Illustrierter Beobachter* 22 September 1928: *Berlin Voran: Dritter Märkertag 29–30 Sept 1928* [Berlin ahead: Third Berlin-Brandenburg rally 29–30 September 1928], courtesy of the Wiener Library, P830 [1926–30]/Artist: Anon.

forward as if charging into combat. Goebbels believed that a flag's value was higher than that of a newspaper in regard to propaganda value, because flags did not appeal to critical intellect but to the simple emotions of viewers.[111] The men are depicted in a style typical of SA images drafted prior to 1933: unnaturally strong, muscular, and square-jawed with a violent disposition. The men are all sketched in uniformity with fists clenched symbolizing the SA's willingness to engage those who oppose them with physical aggression. By September 1928, the ban on the SA, as a result of escalating SA violence in 1927, had been lifted.[112] An account written by Ingeborg Wessel (sister of the SA "martyr" Horst Wessel) describes the events that took place on September 29 and 30 1928.[113] She recalls that "after a meal," the SA "marched into Berlin," joined by "crowds of people" and other Nazi sympathizers. Writing in the present tense, she highlighted the physical size of the group stating that the column "does not end" and detailed the public engagement with the propaganda parade highlighting that "all windows are occupied." On October 6, 1928, *Illustrierter Beobachter* reported on the marching columns of the SA and provided more concrete details of the event. The paper stated that ten thousand brownshirts marched under swastika flags through Berlin.[114] The Berlin SA at this point only had eight hundred members compared to the eleven thousand members of the Berlin RFB.[115] Being part of the National Socialist press apparatus meant the paper most likely exaggerated the scale of the event, or that advertisements (like the one that appeared in *Illustrierter Beobachter* itself) and effective mobilization attracted more SA troops from other regions in Germany. In either case, the parade gives an impression of the dynamism associated with the Nazi party; and Ingeborg Wessel went on to describe how the "Giant Sport Palace" was "completely filled for the first time by the NSDAP." What is also important about her account in this instance is that she notes that the SA became involved in "*Schlägereien*" (brawling). The *Illustrierter Beobachter* likewise commented that the SA under the directives of Goebbels had purposefully marched through "Red Berlin" as a demonstration of its strength and force.[116] Goebbels favored street battles and demonstrations in the "left" districts of Berlin to make the NSDAP a top topic of conversation.[117] Although it is difficult to make concrete connections between the poster and the actual events that had taken place, at the very least *Berlin Voran* with its violent connotations undoubtedly set a visual precedent for the event that was clearly met by the SA.

If, by the late 1920s, the Nazis were seeking to take control of the SA image for their own purposes, this did not prevent their opponents from caricaturing the brownshirts in a more negative style. The Social Democratic Party—another victim of SA radicalism—used images of an unruly SA as a deliberate means of contrasting the Nazis with their own professed dedication to peace and good order. In August 1930 (just prior to the September *Reichstag* elections) the SPD was the strongest party in the Reichstag having won 29.8 percent of the votes in the 1928 Reichstag elections ahead of the NSDAP at 2.6 percent and the KPD at 10.6 percent.[118] The SPD in seeking to shatter the rising support for extremist

Figure 4 *Bahn frei Für Liste 1 Sozialdemokraten* [Make way for List 1 Social Democrats], 1930, courtesy of the Bundesarchiv, Plak 002-020-115/Artist: Anon.

parties following the onset of the economic crises released an election poster titled *Bahn frei! Für Liste 1 Sozialdemokraten* (Figure 4). Published in Berlin, the image encourages German citizens to vote for the SPD in order to establish a "Free Road" clear of the political extremist parties like the NSDAP on the right and the KPD on the left. Although the artist remains unknown for this poster, the wording chosen to accompany the image is significant. As Bavaj has noted—and as alluded above—"the road" or the street acted as the stage for the conquest of power.[119] The "battle of the streets" was defined by both the communists and the SA as a fight for gaining control over neighborhoods, which according to Eve Rosenhaft fitted particularly well with the KPD.[120] The desire for territorial control and power was perhaps the most common source of neighborhood violence during the early 1930s.[121]

The poster, adopting very similar imagery to that of Nazi artists, presents a strong, shirtless man elbowing two separate figures in the face, knocking them out of his way as if breaking up a street brawl. On the left, a Nazi Stormtrooper is identifiable by the Nazi brassard being worn on his right upper arm, and on the right a member of the Red Front Fighters League is also identifiable by his communist arm band. The knife falling out of the right hand of the RFB man symbolizes the aggressive nature of the Red Front Fighters League and this adopted imagery further signifies that the NSDAP and the KPD were continuously involved in violent brawling at the time. By breaking up the conflict between the more radicalized political parties, and by knocking both the extreme right and the extreme left out of the road, the SPD claim to be opening a clear path to a more honorable and peaceful future. The image undoubtedly played on the fears of everyday Germans toward violent and radicalized political parties and the artist presents the SPD as the peacekeepers of the street and the ones to bring about a solution to the rising levels of violence in Germany.

By 1931, the Nazis sought to combat such negative projections of their SA through ever greater use of the Stormtroopers in their own poster art, and Nazi propaganda became even more explicit in its use of violent symbolism and the dissemination of the concept of fear. In one key example from that year, Nazi cartoonist Eulau Hofmann used the SA as shorthand to represent the idea that the NSDAP would—allegorically and physically—smash financial capitalism, in his poster *Fort mit den Stützen des Finanzkapitals—wählt nationalsozialistisch* (Figure 5). The guilty parties in the poster include an overweight financial capitalist on the left (with pinstriped trousers, frock coat, and a top hat), along with the then-chancellor Brüning on the right (also wearing pinstriped trousers). The continuously escalating economic crisis and growing unemployment obviously played an integral role in the formation of this poster. With Nazi propagandists seeking to highlight Germany's internal enemies, Hoffmann makes a clear accusation of blame toward financial capitalists and chancellor Brüning for the ongoing situation in Germany. Hofmann's poster connected the strength and physicality of the SA with the anti-capitalist ideology of the

Figure 5 *Fort mit den Stützen des Finanzkapitals—wählt nationalsozialistisch* [Away with supporters of financial capitalism—vote National Socialist], 1931, courtesy of the Bundesarchiv, Plak 003-006-012/Artist: Eulau Hofmann.

NSDAP, as a revolutionary means of smashing the capitalist system, and its *Reichstag* component in Brüning's government. This is particularly important given the need to appeal to and subvert the equally revolutionary credentials of the KPD. In addition, the muscular figure with chiseled facial features, a raised fist and a square jawline, lends to the SA connotations of power, strength, and violent activism; a prime example of the Nazis reappropriating the SA image and giving it a positive spin by reframing something civilian populations would already have been familiar with and undoubtedly viewed negatively. The Nazis used imagery like this not just to explicitly identify enemies of the *Vaterland* but also to implicitly foster a sense of fear toward such enemies and the ongoing financial problems that such enemies were subjecting the population too: a fear that they themselves experienced and banded together in order to combat. Simultaneously, this also sent a very subtle message of fear to the German population that the methods used against these adversaries may also be used against them if they stood in opposition to the NSDAP.

As the idealized SA man in Hofmann's poster indicates, throughout 1931–3, propaganda poster artists sought to turn the SA's connection with violence into a positive attribute by representing them as the battered soldiers of the German nation; fighting internal enemies, in support of ethnically true German values.[122] The SA represented an embodiment of the social values that the NSDAP had supposedly instilled in its young men: they were tough, they did not shy away from violence, they stood united and fought when confronted, and proved themselves worthy, over and again.[123] Their representations in poster art, to a large extent, mirrored the broader Nazi movement and its associated ideology. Unlike the bourgeois party organizations—such as the *Wirtschaftspartei, Deutsche Demokratische Partei*, and the *Deutschnationale Volkspartei*—the NSDAP set out to present itself as a fighting, fanatical mass movement, a *national* alternative to the *international* communist movement.[124]

In the context of 1932 the economic crisis had led to more than 6 million unemployed. This combined with two Reichstag elections (July and November), the presidential elections with two ballots and in some regions parliamentary elections meant other political parties also adopted NSDAP- and KPD-style tactics, producing a period of heightened political activity and street violence as parties attempted to destabilize the Weimar Republic.[125] As noted above (and also by Bernhard Fulda along with other historians such as Dirk Blasius), 1932 was definitely a year haunted by the "specter of civil war," and this idea certainly played on the fears of those who had lived through the violent early years of the Weimar Republic.[126] The brawls, fistfights and radical hooliganism on

German streets (mostly at the hands of the SA), was used by both politicians and propagandists alike to play on public fears and contributed to what was arguably developing into a full-blown "civil war psychology."[127] As Siemens has notably remarked the SA in 1932 had grown substantially in strength with at least fifteen thousand SA men being present in the capital. Their strength combined with their political soldier mentality in propaganda turned Berlin into a battleground.[128] The media largely built upon this notion of civil war and, therefore, heightened the fear associated with this message. SA violence against Red Front Fighters would have certainly been a contributing factor to such fear, having increased substantially since 1927 (as shown in the compulsory insurance scheme for SA men that covered physical injury suffered during SA duties: in 1927 there were only 110 claims made for physical injury; by 1932 the total number of claims had risen to over 14,000).[129] Newspapers of the period make increased specific mention of the notion of civil war and provide a valuable connection to the fear of such an event in relation to the SA. On Thursday, June 30, 1932, a leading Social Democratic newspaper—*Volksstimme*—warned its readers in Magdeburg that it is "necessary to prevent the SA from becoming the master of the street" and that the "last remnant of the civil war" needs to be crushed. The article urged that a "struggle against these enemies" was a struggle "for your freedom."[130]

A series of posters created by opposing political parties for the March/April 1932 presidential elections utilized the theme of civil war to increase their own resonance with a civilian mass gripped with fear. Two pro-Hindenburg election posters use imagery of civil war to encourage voters to find safety under Hindenburg's leadership. This was in many ways a throwback to the earlier presidential election of 1925. Figure 1 (analyzed at the beginning of this chapter) utilized the imagery of civil war at the feet of a colossal German worker. However, given the about-face in political orientation by 1932 (the moderate and centrist parties such as the SPD now supporting the president, their former opponent), this time members of the SA and the KPD are violently brawling at the feet of a colossal Hindenburg (who is holding onto a large anchor—a symbol of stability amidst turbulence) rather than—as in 1925—the SA being a covert supporter of a militaristic Hindenburg (Figure 6). Numerous other posters of 1932 depicted armies of both Stormtroopers and communists either engaged in fighting one another or together fleeing, vanquished, from a battlefield. Figures 7 (created by the Bavarian People's Party) and 8 (a German Democratic Party poster) show how fear of SA violence and the idea of an impending civil war remained a major theme in anti-Nazi poster imagery, although in much more intensified form.

Figure 6 *Wählt Hindenburg* [Vote Hindenburg], 1932, courtesy of the Bundesarchiv, Plak 002-016-001/Artist: Anon.

Figure 7 *Schützt Bayern! Bayerisches Volkspartei Liste 1* [Protect Bavaria! Bavarian People's Party List 1], 1932, courtesy of the Bundesarchiv, Plak 002-024-014/ Artist: Anon.

Figure 8 *Brüder! Sammelt Euch in der Deutschen Staatspartei* [Brothers! Collect yourself in the German Democratic Party], 1932, courtesy of the Bundesarchiv, Plak 002-037-027/Artist: Anon.

In response, the Nazi party took up the notion pioneered by Hofmann—and which had underpinned the imagery of their opponents—by claiming that they were actually the solution to the state of civil war. Artists in late 1932 and early 1933 again drew on the violence and brutality associated with the SA to design posters that showed the SA's willingness to engage physically against the internal enemies of Germany. This also conveyed in a very subtle fashion a message that warned civilians of the wrath that will be unleashed on them if they did not cooperate with the National Socialist agenda.[131] Peter Merkl argued that political violence and upheaval on the streets at the hands of the SA was, for Hitler, symbolic of the ideological struggle between National Socialism and Marxism.[132] The notion of struggle was intrinsic to every aspect of Nazi ideology, as "struggle"—in Nazi parlance—meant fighting to the death against internal and external enemies.[133] Nazi ideology aimed at ridding Germany of all its defects and creating a new *Volksgemeinschaft* (national community) that had transcended social and class divisiveness through ethnic unity and true German values.[134] Goebbels merged this nationalist and defensive notion of struggle with the political activism of the SA to present to the masses the idea that the NSDAP was fighting for a new and improved German nation (just as Hitler had commented in *Mein Kampf* that "the SA … had risen to the level of a living organization of struggle for the erection of a new German State").[135] The Stormtroopers were the first to represent in visual form the idea of the *Volksgemeinschaft* by presenting themselves as self-sacrificial, working for the common good and by placing the national socialist will first.[136]

Nazi propaganda poster artists further built on the theme of struggle by propagating the image of the SA as a dedicated soldier, prepared to suffer injury, or even death, in order to secure a new German nation (Figure 9).[137] In October 1932 (ahead of yet another set of Reichstag elections scheduled for November) Hermann Witte designed the poster *Wir Schaffen das neue Deutschland! Denkt an die opfer Wählt Nationalsozialisten Liste 1* ("We create the New Germany! Think of the victims, Vote National Socialist List 1"). Depicting two members of the SA, unlike the caricatured or idealized SA men of earlier years (where they were depicted as the aggressor), Witte showed a soft, human side to the Stormtroopers. This reflects a move by the Nazis to present multiple different images in order to appeal to different constituencies. One of the men is shown to be injured with a bandage swathed around his head and his arm wrapped around the shoulders of the other SA figure for support; in the manner of another national symbol beyond reproach: a wounded soldier of the First World

Figure 9 *Wir schaffen das neue Deutschland! Denkt an die Opfer-Wählt Nationalsozialisten Liste 1* [We create the New Germany! Think of the victims, Vote National Socialist List 1], 1932, courtesy of the Bundesarchiv, Plak 002-042-108/ Artist: Hermann Witte.

Figure 10 *Trotz Hass und Verbot Nicht Tot* [Notwithstanding hate and interdiction, [we're] not dead], 1933, courtesy of the Bundesarchiv Plak 003-005-010/Artist: FTZ.

War. The purposeful placement of the word "*Wir*" ["We"], over the legs of the SA men, is used to merge the figures visually with the slogan.

The solid, square-jawed SA man continued to appear, although in something of a new form; as in a January 1933 poster (Figure 10: *Trotz Hass und Verbot Nicht Tot* ["Notwithstanding hate and interdiction, [we're] not dead"]). The overall message of the image seeks to convey that despite the ban on the SA and the measures placed against the organization, it was still very much alive and willing to defend Germany against internal enemies. The size of the Stormtrooper by comparison to the other figures in the image furnishes the impression of strength and superiority, despite technically being the victim of repressive measures. The SA man is standing in a purposeful pose, fists clenched, looking sternly at a series of caricatured individuals that are designed to represent the "real" enemies of National Socialism. It is clear to see that the artist has constructed the entire image around the already-founded fear associated with the SA. Artistically, the enemies depicted in the image (moving from left to right) include the SPD, the KPD, the Centre Party, and the Bavarian People's Party. These supposed real enemies of Germany are placing a series of symbolic rocks in the path of the SA man so as to block any further progress by the party. But to no avail. What is additionally notable is the way in which the enemies have been drawn to display a strong sense of fear of the SA man. All of the representatives, apart from the

Centre Party who has for lack of a better term been caught red handed, are either cowering or retreating away or completely denying responsibility. In Either case, none of them have backs turned toward the SA man. This not only paints the SA in an authoritative light but also seeks to portray the SA as a group to be feared.

The artist used the SA as an allegorical icon to represent the entire NSDAP. This was not uncommon among political poster art of the time. The SA, from as early as 1925 right through to 1944, was used in propaganda posters as shorthand to represent the entire Nazi movement.[138] The rocks are depicted with engravings that represent the measures used by the state against the SA and the Nazi party. The stones include "terror," "lying," "emergency decrees," "censorship of the press," and the banning of the SA. "Terror" in this instance is something of which the artist accuses the state, and ideological opponents, of employing against the NSDAP and the SA; thus, any use by the SA of brutality and violence is simply a measure of defense against that sort of terror. This notion of self-defense translated directly into the courtroom with most SA men being acquitted due to their actions being deemed as "self-defense." Because Communist strongholds were usually located in the poorer regions, which often were marked by higher rates of criminal activity, the Communists had become representative—at least in the eyes of the law-as hostile toward the state. This certainly helped the SA and their chances of acquittal in the courtroom.[139] Although judges accused SA men of exceeding their limits in regard to self-defense, often SA men were acquitted in courtroom proceedings because of self-defense.[140] While the SA was depicted in posters as strong, superior, and a willing defender of the German people, the ideological enemies were depicted as not.

It was the cartoonist Hans Schweitzer (or "Mjölnir") who perfected the new imagery—of the battered, but resolute soldier fighting for the will of the German nation—by early 1933. Just prior to the accession of Hitler to the chancellorship the well-known poster "*National-sozialismus: Der Organisierte Wille der Nation*" (Figure 11) was released. The image depicts three SA men drawn with jutting jawlines and chiseled facial features; they are battle-ready despite having only recently been involved in violent conflict.[141] Having worked on such imagery for several years prior, the particular way in which Schweitzer drew the SA men became a constant image in Third Reich propaganda from this moment onward; eventually endorsed officially by the movement itself.[142] The bandage around the head of the foregrounded figure signifies the SA's willingness to engage physically with the NSDAP's opponents and harkens back to the Witte poster of the previous year, while combining with the same theme as *Nicht Tot*. The SA in this poster embodies the essence of Nazi ideology as

Figure 11 *National-sozialismus: Der Organisierte Wille der Nation* [National Socialism: The Organised Will of the Nation], 1933, courtesy of the Bundesarchiv, Plak 003-002-043/Artist: Hans Schweitzer.

outlined by Goebbels in 1928 and also highlights the notion of struggle, heroic sacrifice, and defense in a way that is much more defensible to more moderate audiences.[143]

The Antidote to Fear

On January 31, 1933, the Nazi newspaper *Völkischer Beobachter* printed a Mjölnir cartoon (Figure 12) of parading columns of idealized, militaristic, SA men, marching through the Brandenburg gate in front of the watchful eyes of President Hindenburg (the embodiment of the unvanquished German national

Figure 12 *Die Stunde ist da!* [The hour is here] Völkischer Beobachter: Kampfblatt der national-sozialistischen Bewegung Grossdeutschlands, courtesy of the Wiener Library, P499 [1/1–31/3/1933]/Artist: Hans Schweitzer.

spirit and head of the republic).[144] Hans Schweitzer's image is a culmination—at the moment of Hitler's accession to the chancellorship—of the evolution of a righteously violent SA, eliding it with the German nation-in-arms; making it clear that the Nazi movement is not a revolutionary force, *per se*, to be feared but rather a defense against impending revolution and a force for the restoration of a true German national ethos. While a culmination of earlier developments, it also represents a visual shift in how the SA was represented in NSDAP propaganda. After Hitler had obtained high office in January 1933, propaganda posters were altered in their emphasis: from portraying the SA as a band of battered brawlers (Figure 11) to depictions of a respectable, disciplined, orderly, and trustworthy organization—more so than ever before, the antidote to fear.

Following Hitler's assumption of power, the appearance of the SA became characterized by respect, discipline, devotion, and order. Propaganda artists sought to alter the mentality of the masses by attempting to remove the fear associated with the SA and replacing it with trust. This can be seen in a poster designed in 1933 by L. Diebitsch (Figure 13) entitled *Der S.A. Mann ist die sich immer erneuernde Kraft der Bewegung*. Propagandists had clearly abandoned, at least for a time, the representation of the SA as a band of fighting National Socialists.[145] Instead, the poster depicts a portrait of a senior Stormtrooper dressed immaculately in his fully equipped SA uniform, standing in front of two large swastika flags. The artist appears to have been inspired by well-known SA public symbols such as Horst Wessel or Heinz Klingenberg from SA *Mann Brand*, as the image bears resemblance to both these figures. Additionally, he has been depicted in a far less aggressive manner by comparison to its pre-"seizure of power" counterparts.[146] Political posters, and other forms of mass media, such as film, depicted the SA in this respectable way as a self-renewed organization to divert the attention away from, or at least counterbalance, the unruly behavior of the real SA. As Longerich has remarked, after the seizure of power the uncontrollable and unpredictable elements of the SA including their violence (along with abduction of political opponents, murder, torture, indiscriminate arrests, and so on) created an atmosphere of insecurity and fear that made all forms of opposition to the regime incredibly difficult.[147] Siemens noted that after Hitler's appointment as Reich chancellor, the Nazis and more specifically the SA chose to be engaged in "barely disguised terrorism" instead of following more legal pathways.[148]

The presentation of the SA as a respectable, trustworthy, and well-mannered organization became widespread in Nazi poster art during 1933. One example

Figure 13 *Der S.A. Mann ist die sich immer erneuernde Kraft der Bewegung* [The SA man is the self-renewing power of the movement], 1933, courtesy of the Bundesarchiv, Plak 003-010-011/Artist: L. Diebitsch.

is by Wilhelm Emil Eber—commonly known as Elk Eber—who was an early member of the Nazi movement and had won Hitler's approval as a result of participating in the 1923 *putsch*.[149] In 1933, he designed an advertisement (Figure 14) for the "Roll Call of the SA": a national rally that gathered on the third anniversary of the death of party icon, Horst Wessel (after whose assassination in 1930, February 23 became a seminal date for the NSDAP).[150] Eber modeled his SA men on the myth of Wessel ideal type: as respectable and orderly members of the movement, expressed most explicitly through the immaculate presentation of their uniforms and sharp facial features.

The irony of this shift in imagery is palpable. From mid-February 1933, institutional prohibitions upon SA violence were removed; and additionally, Hermann Göring—in response to supposed left-radical and communist disturbances, such as the Reichstag fire—formed the *Hilfspolizei* (Auxiliary Police) out of SA members, thus providing a legalized framework for their activities.[151] The SA now acted as "defenders of the state."[152] This allowed for an unprecedented increase in violent political acts against the SPD, KPD, and trade unions.[153] Stormtroopers arrested trade union officials, wrecked the offices of their Marxist political enemies, ransacked archives, stole property and money, and turned the headquarters of their political opponents into their own torture chambers; and all was done *legally*, in the name of the state.[154] Now that Hitler was chancellor, SA violence could barely be contained. Ian Kershaw described this SA brutality as "orgies of hate filled revenge against political enemies and horrifically brutal assaults on Jews."[155] Other commentaries have observed that this violence was used by the NSDAP deliberately to intimidate opposition and create a public sphere that was characterized by terror, even as the propaganda imagery promoted an image of calm and good order, and all in a bid to remind those of what might befall them if anyone stepped out of line or failed to show loyalty to the new order.[156] In May 1933, recruitment to the Nazi party was ceased as a result of the explosive growth in party membership following Hitler's ascension to power.[157] However, the SA imposed no such restrictions on size and continued to grow into a formidable organization of 4,500,000 men (absorbing many of those opportunists who were denied membership of the party).[158] Thereafter, and increasingly, the SA—the instrument of Nazi terror—now threatened the stability that Hitler desired to build and threatened to confound its representation in propaganda as the face of the Nazi party. This was an image that had taken several years to perfect, via the necessary artistic and ideological juggling of the concept and reality of fear.

Figure 14 *Appell am 23. Februar 1933* [Roll call on the 23 February 1933], 1933, courtesy of AKG images, AKG5697230/Artist: Elk Eber.

Conclusion

Fear was a highly valuable instrument in the propaganda tool belt of political parties throughout the later stages of the Weimar Republic. The *Kampfzeit* period was defined by its social disorder, political upheaval, street violence, and bloodshed. Although it is debated about whether Germany, especially during 1932, even came close to approaching what would be defined as a "civil war," the fear associated with this concept plagued the minds of German citizens like a disease and even shaped the politics of the time. It was during this period that the Nazis used the *Sturmabteilung* as a means of instilling fear into its political and ideological opponents, not only through the use of violence, terror, and the contestation for public space but also through pervading the public sphere with visual images that in the form of political posters. Such visual artifacts served as a reflection of the very real and deep-seated fear associated with the SA and paramilitary violence among the German population. Within the context of the Weimar *Öffentlichkeit*, Nazi poster art sought not to deny the cultivated and existing state of fear but rather tapped into and highlighted these existing fears and altered the caricatures of the SA and NSDAP produced by their ideological opponents to sell the Nazi movement as the solution to that fear. This chapter has revealed that the SA played an important role in the creation of fear not only in party poster propaganda but also in oppositional propaganda as well. Reactionary parties used posters as a modern tool to cultivate fear in an attempt to win electoral support.

Notes

1 Joseph Goebbels, *Der Angriff: Aufsätze aus der Kampfzeit* (München: Franz Eher Nachf, 1935), 335.
2 Sven Reichardt, *Faschistische Kampfbünde. Gewalt und Gemeinschaft im italienischen Squadrismus* (Köln: Böhlau Verlag, 2002), 129; Richard Bessel, *Political Violence and the Rise of Nazism: The Storm Troopers in Eastern Germany 1925–1934* (London: Yale University Press, 1984), 9; Conan Fischer, *Stormtroopers: A Social, Economic and Ideological Analysis, 1929–1935* (London: George Allen & Unwin, 1983), 167; Dirk Schumann, *Political Violence in the Weimar Republic, 1918–1933: Fight for the Streets and Fear of Civil War*, trans. Thomas Dunlap (Oxford: Berghahn Books, 2009), 261.
3 Paula Diehl, *Macht-Mythos-Utopie: Die Körperbilder der SS-Männer* (Berlin: Akademie, 2005), 155.

4 For information on the image of President von Hindenburg in propaganda consult: Richard Scully, "Hindenburg: The Cartoon Titan of the Weimar Republic, 1918–1934," *German Studies Review* 35, no. 3 (2012): 541–65.
5 Heinrich Bennecke, *Hitler und die SA* (München: Günter Olzog Verlag, 1962), 192.
6 Dirk Blasius, *Weimars Ende. Bürgerkrieg und Politik, 1930–1933* (Göttingen: Vandenhoeck und Ruprecht GmbH, 2005), 13.
7 Schumann, *Political Violence in the Weimar Republic*, 312. It is important to note that although violent clashes and incidents were taking place across the Reich, that even in 1932 "Germany was not in imminent danger of drowning in an uncontrollable flood of violence, let alone a real civil war."
8 Ian Kershaw, "How Effective Was Nazi Propaganda?," in *Nazi Propaganda: The Power and the Limitations*, ed. David Welch (New York: Routledge, 1983), 200.
9 Diane Kohl, "The Presentation of 'Self' and 'Other' in Nazi Propaganda," *Psychology and Society* 4, no. 1 (2011): 17.
10 The most useful formulation of the *Öffentlichkeit* concept [roughly, the "public sphere" of Jürgen Habermas] comes from Geoff Eley. Characteristic of bourgeois liberal democracies, it is "the structured setting where cultural and ideological contest or negotiation among a variety of publics takes place." See: Geoffrey Eley, "Nations, Publics, and Political Cultures: Placing Habermas in the Nineteenth Century," *Habermas and the Public Sphere*, ed. Craig Calhoun (Cambridge, MA: MIT Press, 1992), 306.
11 Blasius, *Weimars Ende*, 13.
12 Gerhard Paul, *Aufstand der Bilder: Die NS Propaganda vor 1933* (Bonn: Verlag J. H.W. Dietz Nachf, 1990), 138.
13 Stefan Hördler, "SA-Terror als Herrschaftssicherung: 'Köpenicker Blutwoche' und öffentliche Gewalt im Nationalsozialismus," in *SA-Terror als Herrschaftssicherung: "Köpenicker Blutwoche" und öffentliche Gewalt im Nationalsozialismus*, ed. Stefan Hördler (Berlin: Metropol Verlag, 2013), 9; Bruce Campbell, "The SA after the Röm Purge," *Journal of Contemporary History* 28, no. 4 (1993): 659.
14 Conan Fischer, *The Rise of the Nazis* (Manchester: Manchester University Press, 1995), 58.
15 Peter Longerich, *Die Braunen Bataillone: Geschichte der SA* (München: C.H. Beck, 1989), 116.
16 Riccardo Bavaj, *Der Nationalsozialismus: Entstehung, Aufstieg und Herrschaft* (Berlin: be.bra Verlag, 2016), 26.
17 Daniel Siemens, "Prügelpropaganda: Die SA und der nationalsozialistische Mythos vom Kampf um Berlin," in *Berlin 1933–1945*, ed. Ch. Kreutzmüller and M. Wildt (Munich: Siedler Verlag, 2013), 36.
18 Richard Bessel, "The Nazi Capture of Power," *Journal of Contemporary History* 39, no. 2 (2004): 182; Bruce Campbell, *The SA Generals and the Rise of Nazism*

(Kentucky: University Press Kentucky, 1998), 2; Fischer, *Stormtroopers*, 161; Irene von Götz, "Die Frühen Konzentrationslager in Berlin," in *Bürgerkriegsarmee: Forschungen Zur Nationalsozialistischen Sturmabteilung (SA)*, ed. Yves Müller and Reiner Zilkenat (Frankfurt am Main: Peter Lang GmbH Internationaler Verlag der Wissenschaften, 2013), 132–3; Longerich, *Die Braunen Bataillone*, 121; Otis Mitchell, *Hitler's Stormtroopers and the Attack on the German Republic, 1919–1933* (Jefferson, NC: McFarland, 2008), 2; Detlef Mühlberger, *The Social Bases of Nazism, 1919–1933* (Cambridge: Cambridge University Press, 2003), 5; Sven Reichardt, "Violence and Community: A Micro Study on Nazi Stormtroopers," *Central European History* 46, no. 2 (2013): 279. For a comprehensive and excellent discussion on the role of the SA in consolidating power through "street politics" consult: Daniel Siemens, *Stormtroopers: A New History of Hitler's Brownshirts* (Cornwall: Yale University Press, 2017), 32–74.

19 Longerich, *Die Braunen Bataillone*, 179. Also see: Eleanor Hancock, *Ernst Röhm: Hitler's SA Chief of Staff* (Basingstoke: Palgrave Macmillan, 2008), esp. 131 ff.
20 Campbell, "The SA after the Röhm Purge," 659.
21 Birgit Witamwas, *Geklebte NS-Propaganda: Verführung und Manipulation durch das Plakat* (Berlin: Walter De Gruyter GmbH, 2016), 3; Jeffery Herf, *The Jewish Enemy: Nazi Propaganda during WW2 and the Holocaust* (Cambridge: Belknap Press, 2006), 28–30.
22 Eric Johnson, "The Crime Rate: Longitudinal and Periodic Trends in Nineteenth- and Twentieth-Century German Criminality, *from Vormärz to Late Weimar*," in *The German Underworld: Deviants and Outcasts in German History*, ed. Richard J. Evans (London: Routledge, 1988), 180.
23 Jürgen Falter, *Hitlers Wähler* (München: C.H. Beck, 1991), 26; Fischer, *Rise of the Nazis*, 7.
24 Richard Evans, *The Coming of the Third Reich* (London: Penguin, 2003), 230.
25 Robert Gerwarth and John Horne, "Vectors of Violence: Paramilitarism in Europe after the Great War, 1917–1923," *Journal of Modern History* 83, no. 3 (2011): 489–512.
26 Evans, *Coming of the Third Reich*, 230.
27 Front page headline, *Brooklyn Daily Eagle*, eighty-ninth year, no. 295, 1929, 1.
28 Richard Overy, *The Nazi Economic Recovery, 1932–1938* (London: Macmillan Press, 1982), 17; Nicola Garcia, "The Republic between Two Reich's," *Hindsight* 15, no. 2 (2005): 10.
29 Overy, *Nazi Economic Recovery*, 20.
30 Ibid., 14–16; Evans, *Coming of the Third Reich*, 236.
31 Donna Harsch, *German Social Democracy and the Rise of Nazism* (North Carolina: University of North Carolina Press, 1993), 127.
32 Ibid.

33 Conan Fischer, "'The SA of the NSDAP;' Social Background and Ideology of the Rank and File in the Early 1930s," *Journal of Contemporary History* 17, no. 4 (1982): 657.
34 Siemens, *Stormtroopers*, 73.
35 Dietmar Petzina, "The Extent and Causes of Unemployment in the Weimar Republic," in *Unemployment and the Great Depression in Weimar Germany*, ed. Peter D. Stachura (London: Palgrave, 1986), 35.
36 Petzina, "Extent and Causes of Unemployment," 33.
37 Richard Evans and Dick Geary, *The German Unemployed: Experiences and Consequences of Mass Unemployment from the Weimar Republic to the Third Reich* (New York: Routledge, 2015), 7.
38 Evans, *Coming of the Third Reich*, 243.
39 Fischer, "The SA of the NSDAP," 657.
40 Conan Fischer, "The Occupational Background of the SA's Rank and File Membership during the Depression Years, 1929 to mid-1934," in *The Shaping of the Nazi State*, ed. Peter D. Stachura (New York: Routledge, 1978), 152; Fischer, *Stormtroopers*, 155; Conan Fischer and Carolyn Hicks, "Statistics and the Historian: The Occupational Profile of the SA of the NSDAP," *Social History* 5, no. 1 (1980): 132; Peter Stachura, "The NSDAP and the German Working Class, 1925–1933," in *Towards the Holocaust: The Social and Economic Collapse of the Weimar Republic*, ed. Michael Dobkowski and Isidor Wallimann (Westport, CT: Greenwood Press, 1983), 138.
41 Daniel Siemens, *The Making of a Nazi Hero: The Murder and Myth of Horst Wessel* (London: I.B. Tauris, 2013), 73.
42 Bavaj, *Der Nationalsozialismus*, 44.
43 Oliver Reschke, "Die soziale Zusammensetzung der Berliner SA in der Kampfzeit im Vergleich mit ihren Kontrahenten vom Berliner RFB. Ein Diskussionsbeitrag," in *Bürgerkriegsarmee: Forschungen zur Nationalsozialistischen Sturmabteilung (SA)*, ed. Yves Müller and Reiner Zilkenat (Frankfurt am Main: Peter Lang GmbH Internationaler Verlag der Wissenschaften, 2013), 125.
44 Geoffrey Skoll, *Social Theory of Fear: Terror, Torture and Death in a Post-Capitalist World* (New York: Palgrave MacMillan, 2010), 58.
45 Skoll, *Social Theory of Fear*, 59.
46 Goebbels, *Der Angriff*, 73.
47 Robert Gellately and Nathan Stoltzfus, "Social Outsiders and the Construction of the Community of the People," in *Social outsiders in Nazi Germany*, ed. Robert Gellately and Nathan Stoltzfus (Princeton, NJ: Princeton University Press, 2001), 4; Fischer, *Stormtroopers*, 178.
48 Siemens, *Making of a Nazi Hero*, 66.
49 Richard Bessel, "Violence as Propaganda: The Role of the Stormtroopers in the Rise of National Socialism," in *The Formation of the Nazi Constituency, 1919–1933*, ed. Thomas Childers (Sydney: Croom Helm, 1986), 135.

50 Longerich, *Die Braunen Bataillone*, 32; Paul, *Aufstand der Bilder*, 135; Diehl, *Macht-Mythos-Utopie*, 153.
51 Siemens, *Stormtroopers*, xxxvi.
52 Longerich, *Die Braunen Bataillone*, 22–3.
53 Mühlberger, *Social Bases of Nazism*, 58.
54 Bennecke, *Hitler und die SA*, 42. See also: Peter Merkl, "Approaches to Political Violence: The Stormtroopers, 1925–1933," in *Social Protest, Violence & Terror in Nineteenth- & Twentieth-Century Europe*, ed. Gerhard Hirschfeld and Wolfgang J. Mommsen (London: MacMillan Press, 1982), 370.
55 Martin Broszat, *German National Socialism 1919–1945* (Santa Barbara: Clio Press, 1966), 134.
56 Siemens, *Stormtroopers*, 30.
57 Reichardt, *Faschistische Kampfbünde*, 14; Daniel Schmidt, "Die Sturmabteilung und die Staatsgewalt. Zum Verhältnis von SA und Polizei in Preußen 1930–1934," in *Bürgerkriegsarmee: Forschungen zur Nationalsozialistischen Sturmabteilung (SA)*, ed. Yves Müller and Reiner Zilkenat (Frankfurt am Main: Peter Lang GmbH Internationaler Verlag der Wissenschaften, 2013), 299.
58 Bessel, *Political Violence and the Rise of Nazis*, 79.
59 Deutsche Volksgemeinschaft, *SA marschiert durch Deutsches Land*, 1929. Avail.: https://youtu.be/pyMqLkYjwzg [accessed March 11, 2017].
60 Bavaj, *Der Nationalsozialismus*, 26.
61 Ibid.
62 Fischer, *Stormtroopers*, 5.
63 Eve Rosenhaft, *Beating the Fascists? The German Communists and Political Violence, 1929–1933* (Cambridge: Cambridge University Press, 1983), 19.
64 Pamela Swett, *Neighbors & Enemies: The Culture of Radicalism in Berlin, 1929–1933* (Cambridge, Cambridge University Press, 2004), 235.
65 Hördler, "SA-Terror als Herrschaftssicherung," 9.
66 For the *Freikorps* in a Europe-wide context of paramilitarism see: Robert Gerwarth, *The Vanquished: Why the First World War Failed to End* (London: Allen Lane, 2016).
67 Joseph Goebbels, *Kampf und Berlin. Der Anfang* (München: Franz Eher Nachf, 1934), 50; Rosenhaft, *Beating the Fascists*, 19.
68 Goebbels in *Kampf und Berlin* notes that members of the Red Front Fighters League were returning from a political demonstration in Leuna (50–1), while Daniel Siemens, commenting on the same event notes that these members were returning from a demonstration in Jüterbog (67). The authors are unsure of the correct location.
69 Goebbels, *Kampf und Berlin*, 50.
70 Siemens, *Making of a Nazi Hero*, 67.

71 Ibid.
72 Ernst Otto Bräanche, Rainer Gutjahr, Hanspeter Rings, and Andreas Schenk, "Politische Plakate: Von der Weimarer Republik bis zur jungen Bundesrepublik," *Politik & Unterricht* 35, no. 2/3 (2009): 34.
73 James Pollack, Jr., "The German Reichstag Elections of 1930," *American Political Science Review* 24, no. 4 (1930): 989–95; Rosenhaft, *Beating the Fascists*, 71–3; William L. Patch, Jr., *Heinrich Brüning and the Dissolution of the Weimar Republic* (Cambridge: Cambridge University Press, 1998), 54–69.
74 Bessel, *Political Violence*, 77.
75 Fischer, *Stormtroopers*, 5.
76 Bessel, *Political Violence*, 79.
77 Fischer, *Stormtroopers*, 5.
78 Ibid.
79 Michael Hechter, Karl-Dieter Opp, and Reinhard Wippler, *Social Institutions: Their Emergence, Maintenance and Effects* (Berlin: De Gruyter, 1990), 256.
80 Bennecke, *Hitler und die SA*, 146.
81 Paul, *Aufstand der Bilder*, 174.
82 Ibid., 175; Schumann, *Political Violence in the Weimar Republic*, 187.
83 Joseph Goebbels, *Die Tagebücher von Joseph Goebbels*, Entry 8 May, 1932, vol. 2 (München: K.G. Sauer Verlag, 1987), 166.
84 Blasius, *Weimars Ende*, 13.
85 Yves Müller and Reiner Zilkenat, "'Der Kampf wird über unserem Leben stehe, solange wir atmen!' Einleitung," in *Bürgerkriegsarmee: Forschungen zur Nationalsozialistischen Sturmabteilung (SA)*, ed. Yves Müller and Reiner Zilkenat (Frankfurt am Main: Peter Lang GmbH Internationaler Verlag der Wissenschaften, 2013), 15.
86 *Magdeburgische Zeitung*, No. 436, August 12, 1931. Quoted in: Schumann, *Political Violence in the Weimar Republic*, 282.
87 Siemens, "Prügelpropaganda," 38; Schumann, *Political Violence in the Weimar Republic*, 226.
88 Rosenhaft, *Beating the Fascists*, 22.
89 Siemens, "Prügelpropaganda," 37–8.
90 Anke Hoffstadt, "'Eine Frage der Ehre-Zur 'beziehungsgeschichte' von Stahlhelm Bund der Frontsoldaten' und SA," in *Bürgerkriegsarmee: Forschungen zur Nationalsozialistischen Sturmabteilung (SA)*, ed. Yves Müller and Reiner Zilkenat (Frankfurt am Main: Peter Lang GmbH Internationaler Verlag der Wissenschaften, 2013), 279.
91 Campbell, *SA Generals*, 80.
92 Schmidt, "Die Sturmabteilung und die Staatsgewalt," 299.
93 Bessel, *Political Violence*, 86.

94 Ibid.
95 Ibid., 87.
96 Joseph Goebbels, *Die Tagebücher von Joseph Goebbels, Entry 1 August, 1932*, vol. 2 (Munich: K.G. Sauer, 1987), 212.
97 "Der Neue Reichstag: Vorläufige amtliche Stimmverteilung," *Volksstimme*, No. 179, August 1, 1932.
98 Iris Helberg and Yves Müller, "'Die 'Köpenicker Blutwoche' 1933-Über Opfer und Täter," in *Bürgerkriegsarmee: Forschungen zur Nationalsozialistischen Sturmabteilung (SA)*, ed. Yves Müller and Reiner Zilkenat (Frankfurt am Main: Peter Lang GmbH Internationaler Verlag der Wissenschaften, 2013), 192.
99 Bessel, *Political Violence*, 88–9.
100 "Nazi Putschversuch in Königsberg: Mit Brandbomben, Mord und Totschlag," *Volksstimme* No. 179, August 1, 1932, 2.
101 Gellately and Stoltzfus, "Social Outsiders," 4.
102 Skoll, *Social Theory of Fear*, 59.
103 Bessel, "Violence as Propaganda," 131; Reichardt, *Faschistische Kampfbünde*, 131; Longerich, *Die Braunen Bataillone*, 123.
104 Falter, *Hitlers Wähler*, 173. The previous incumbent—the SPD leader, Friedrich Ebert—had died in office on February 28, necessitating an election several months before the end of his seven-year term.
105 Heinrich Winkler, *Germany: The Long Road West, 1789–1933* (Oxford: Oxford University Press, 2000), 409.
106 The SA commonly used weapons in street clashes and terroristic activities. Daniel Siemens has notably pointed out that in 1930 police reports revealed that there were no fewer than eighty-three incidents involving the collection of weapons. See: Siemens, "Prügelpropaganda," 37–8. Also see Reichardt, *Faschistische Kampfbünde*, 2002.
107 Siemens, *Stormtroopers*, 30.
108 Ibid.
109 Nazi regional assemblies in Berlin and Brandenburg were called "Märkertage."
110 *Illustrierter Beobachter*, September 22, 1928 (München: Franz Eher Nachf), p. 234, WL P830, P01246.
111 Paul, *Aufstand der Bilder*, 170.
112 Reichardt, "Violence and Community," 279.
113 Ingeborge Wessel, *Mein Bruder Horst-Ein Vermächtnis*,1933, 36. Avail.: https://archive.org/details/Wessel-Ingeborg-Mein-Bruder-Horst-Ein-Vermaechtnis/page/n36 [accessed May 24, 2017].
114 "Der 3. Märkertag in Berlin," *Illustrierter Beobachter*, Folge 20, October 6, 1928, Franz Eher Nachf, München, p. 242, WL P830, P01246.
115 Rosenhaft, *Beating the Fascists*, 19.

116 Ibid.
117 Reichardt, *Faschistische Kampfbünde*, 117; Paul, *Aufstand der Bilder*, 139.
118 Falter, *Hitlers Wähler*, 25.
119 Bavaj, *Der Nationalsozialismus*, 26.
120 Rosenhaft, *Beating the Fascists*, 25.
121 Swett, *Neighbors or Enemies*, 235.
122 Broszat, *German National Socialism*, 7.
123 Bessel, *Political Violence*, 153.
124 Broszat, *German National Socialism*, 61. For commentary on bourgeois political parties in Germany during the rise of Nazism see: Peter Fritzsche, *Germans into Nazis* (Cambridge: Harvard University Press, 1999), 160.
125 Bernhard Fulda, *Press and Politics in the Weimar Republic* (Oxford: Oxford University Press, 2009), 169; Von Götz, "Die Frühen Konzentrationslager in Berlin," 133; Falter, *Hitlers Wähler*, 34.
126 Fulda, *Press and Politics*, 173; Blasius, *Weimars Ende*, 13.
127 Fulda, *Press and Politics*, 173.
128 Siemens, "Prügelpropaganda," 38–40.
129 Bessel, *Political Violence*, 76.
130 "Schart euch um das Freiheitsbanner! Kämpfer und Kämpferinnen der Eisern Front!" *Volksstimme* No. 152, Juni 30, 1932, 1.
131 Skoll, *Social Theory of Fear*, 99.
132 Merkl, *Making of a Stormtrooper*, 163.
133 Adolf Hitler, *Mein Kampf*, trans. Ralph Manneheim (New York: First Mariner, 1999), 285–9. Hitler dictated extensively on the notion of an eternal struggle between the superior and the inferior. Ian Kershaw, "Ideology, Propaganda and the Rise of the Nazi Party," in *The Nazi Machtergreifung* (London: Routledge, 1983), 165; Michael Burleigh and Wolfgang Wippermann, *The Racial State: Germany, 1933-1945* (Cambridge: Cambridge University Press, 1991), 37–41.
134 David Welch, "Nazi Propaganda and the *Volksgemeinschaft*: Constructing a People's Community," *Journal of Contemporary History* 39, no. 2 (2004): 213.
135 Hitler, *Mein Kampf*, 552.
136 Paul, *Aufstand der Bilder*, 135.
137 Fischer, "The SA of the NSDAP," 651.
138 Werner Von Axster-Heudtlaß, 1944 *Wehrkampftage Schiesswehrkämpfe*, 1944, B/ Arch Plak 003-010-048; Jacob Berg, "The Face of Nazism: Representations of the *Sturmabteilung* in Nazi Propaganda Posters, 1925–1945" (Honours thesis, University of New England, 2016), 104.
139 Johannes Fülberth, "'Bürgerkriegsarmee in permanenter 'Notwehr'?," in *Bürgerkriegsarmee: Forschungen zur Nationalsozialistischen Sturmabteilung (SA)*, ed. Yves Müller and Reiner Zilkenat (Frankfurt am Main: Peter Lang GmbH Internationaler Verlag der Wissenschaften, 2013), 41.

140 Ibid., 43.
141 Peter Paret, "God's Hammer," *Proceedings of the American Philosophical Society* 136, no. 2 (1992): 230.
142 Hans Sponholz, "'Die SA'- Wandplakate." In *SA-Wandplakat 1940–1944*, NS 23/942, Bundesarchiv Berlin-Lichterfelde.
143 Witamwas, *Geklebte NS-Propaganda*, 67.
144 Hans Schweitzer, *Die Stunde Ist da!*, *Völkischer Beobachter*, January 31, 1933, 2; On Hindenburg's status see: Scully, "Hindenburg," 2012.
145 This type of imagery would not reemerge among NSDAP propaganda until the war years, 1939–45.
146 Welch, "Nazi Propaganda and the Volksgemeinschaft," 215.
147 Longerich, *Die Braunen Bataillone*, 172.
148 Siemens, *Stormtroopers*, 123.
149 Klaus Fischer, *Hitler and America* (Philadelphia: University of Pennsylvania Press, 2011), 23.
150 Siemens, *Making of a Nazi Hero*, 17. Goebbels stated in his diary on February 23, 1930, that Horst Wessel was the "new martyr for the Third Reich." For more information on Goebbels' views on Horst Wessel see: Goebbels, *Die Tagebücher von Joseph Goebbels*, vol. 1, 504–5.
151 Schmidt, "Die Sturmabteilung und die Staatsgewalt," 308–9; Hördler, *SA-Terror als Herrschaftssicherung*, 10.
152 Zbynek Zemen, *Nazi Propaganda* (Oxford: Oxford University Press, 1973), 39.
153 Bessel, "Nazi Capture of Power," 181.
154 Von Götz, "Die Frühen Konzentrationslager in Berlin," 144. See also: Christian Goeschel and Nikolaus Wachsmann, "Before Auschwitz: The Formation of the Nazi Concentration Camps, 1933–9," *Journal of Contemporary History* 45, no. 3 (2010): 532.
155 Ian Kershaw, *Hitler* (London: Penguin, 2009), 302.
156 Hördler, *SA-Terror als Herrschaftssicherung*, 11; Bessel, "Nazi Capture of Power," 182; Siemens, *Stomrtroopers*, 128.
157 Mühlberger, "The Social Basis of Nazism," 58.
158 Magnus Brechtken, *Die Nationalsozialistische Herrschaft, 1933–1939* (Darmstadt: WBG, 2004), 35; Fischer, *Stormtroopers*, 161.

7

Conceptualizing Gender and Fear: German-Jewish Masculinities in the Third Reich and the Dread of the Unknown

Sebastian Huebel

"Dread of the downfall. Fearing the Unknown, against which one is powerless." (Furcht vor dem Untergang. Bangen vor dem Ungewissen, dem man machtlos gegenüber sitzt).

Paul Steiner, Diary Entry 11.3.1938[1]

"Troubled times ..., especially for us Jews. We are sitting in a mouse trap."

Willy Cohn, Diary Entry 30.1.1933[2]

"I was to be sure, outwardly courageous and strong but inwardly disheartened and forsaken. ... I cried."

Edwin Landau, Memoir[3]

Historians have relatively recently discovered the role of emotions in the making and experiencing of history. We still know far too little about emotions of the past, people's concerns and affections in history, though historians have begun to use emotions as an analytical category.[4] With the more recent incursions into the intimate, private sphere of people's past lives, cultural historians seek to untangle some of the emotional nettings—the attitudes, behaviors, perceptions—and bring them into interpretive, meaningful historical contexts. One such basic emotion—fear—is the subject of this essay.

The leitmotiv, as Thomas Kehoe and Michael Pickering assert in the Introduction of this volume, is to obtain a more nuanced understanding of fear as an emotion, especially fear of incursions and consequential change throughout German history. As the other chapters in this volume illustrate, fears often manifested themselves in forms of cultural discourses that constructed real or imagined images of threatening "others"—such as French invading soldiers, Soviet-communist occupiers, or even vampires and demons. This chapter instead concentrates on one of the "outsider" groups that Germans throughout history had (allegedly) come to fear: Jews. We will investigate the types of fears experienced within this outcast group during the era of the Third Reich and see how German Jews processed and negotiated these fears. Though the "outsider" group thus becomes the focal point in this chapter, the volume's leitmotivs of feared incursion and change in German lands throughout history—in this case enforced by a racist, genocidal regime—still apply as German Jews felt and came to fear the dramatic changes and incursion into their everyday lives.

As part of a cultural history of emotions, I intend to paint a more comprehensive picture of German-Jewish life during the period of the Third Reich by drawing a coherent link between the concept of gender and the concept of fear. Specifically, my argument is based on the premise that the cultural construct and social experience of fear—real and imagined—need to be better understood in its gendered dimensions, especially among groups that were forcefully isolated from mainstream society and subsequently persecuted. Of course, fear is a basic and universal emotion that inescapably affects every human being and that therefore transcends ethnicity, class, and race but also gender. Yet, the experience, perception and representation of fear can differ significantly in gender-specific contexts.

Following a steady growth in anti-Semitic discrimination and persecution, German Jews were ridden by personal fears following the Nazi takeover. Starting in 1933, these fears emerged not only in quite unexpected and unprecedented ways, but they were also perceived and processed in gendered terms. In this chapter, I will analyze specific forms of fear and link them to understandings of German-Jewish identity by examining a selection of primary sources written by German-Jewish men and women in which three manifestations of gendered fears were evident and at times rather openly expressed and at other times more indirectly and implicitly addressed.

To start with, in the prewar years of the Third Reich, economic fears of facing unemployment and a resulting reduction in income which was needed to support themselves and their families distressed Jewish men. Gendered masculine fears also pertained to the growing likelihood of facing social humiliation, symbolic degradation, and the concomitant loss of status in public society to which middle-class Jewish men since the nineteenth century had access to and in which they had established themselves as respected citizens. Third, with the beginning of a process of singling out, imprisoning in concentration camps and violently maltreating their psyches and bodies, fears of the physical integrity and inviolability of Jewish men also began to surface.

It is my argument that significant inroads into a more nuanced understanding of the social and private emotional life of German Jewry during the Nazi years can be made if the cultural concept of fear is illuminated and positioned in a more gendered matrix. German-Jewish men, like women, experienced fear in specific gendered terms and gendered spaces. The increased concerns for a potential loss of status and respect in society, economic survival and subsistence for themselves and their families, as well as concerns for the physical safety of themselves and their dependents were often emblematic male-specific experiences and pressures as both were closely tied to contemporary gender norms and expectations of men in their roles as provider and protector, as well as holder of status, respect, and honor in the public sphere.[5]

Over the last three decades, many historians of the Third Reich have adapted their methodologies and directed their research toward previously under-examined historical sources, especially ego documents such as diaries and memoirs that allow insight into individuals' internal world of perceptions and emotions.[6] This essay examines a series of diaries and memoirs, with an emphasis on the former. Diaries are an especially useful medium for my historical analysis. Jochen Hellbeck argues, "In its ideal form the diary is imagined as a receptacle for private convictions expressed in spontaneous and un-coerced fashion."[7] In addition to convictions and held beliefs, one could add the realm of emotions; diaries constitute a reservoir of personal feelings and sentiments translated into words. Diaries can be particularly insightful as the diarist's reflections on his or her day-to-day observations and experiences are typically recorded in an unfiltered and unrestrained manner. Diarists generally (but not exclusively) keep records for their own sake; most diaries are not meant for publication or a wide readership. Consequently, the words of the diarists may lack eloquence, proper diction, and grammar; on the other hand, they are rich with immediacy, honesty, and self-reflection, benefits that can help the historian recapture and comprehend some of the internal turmoil and fears that German Jews confronted in the Third Reich.

Yet, how can fear as an ontological paradigm be uncovered and then dissected by the historian? Fear as a conceptual reality is obviously quite different from material realities. It is one thing to reconstruct events based on the materiality of historical evidence; it is another to find evidence that establishes the historicity of emotions, such as fear. Alexandra Garbarini in her work on Holocaust diaries has analyzed this methodological conundrum. She argues,

> Many diarists believed their experiences to be unprecedented and conveyed the fear that they were potentially unrepresentable to the outside world. On the one hand, they sought to ensure that the outside world would learn about the horrors to which Jews had been subjected. On the other hand, they feared that language would efface or misconstrue the particularity of their experiences. These Jewish diarists thus called attention to the lack of transparency of their own representational endeavors at the same time that they insisted on the ethical, historical and juridical value of the writing.[8]

Because the term fear itself is frequently not directly mentioned—as the exemplary quotes at the beginning of this essay illustrate—an analysis of fear needs to rely to a large degree on a careful reading between the lines that seeks to empathize with the author and his or her emotions. I contend that important conclusions can be still drawn from a skillful reading of and justified by bringing individual sources into a larger comparative context.[9] As Keith Oatley has succinctly pointed out, emotions like fear are evaluations, judgments of what is important to us: our goals, our concerns, our aspirations.[10] Emotions, unlike moods, are thus reactive, and as Ute Frevert has shown, they create relationships and facilitate social bonding.[11] Emotions like fear are founded upon reciprocity and gain meaning only in relational contexts. For the purpose of my study, I define fears by German-Jewish men as the (anticipated) loss of the socioeconomic, cultural, and physical-bodily status quo. Thus, although the term fear might not have explicitly been used or addressed by the authors whom I will analyze below, it becomes clear that many diarists used expressions of serious concerns pertaining to the loss of the male provider and protector roles within their families and their ostracism from public society where they had held honorable positions as respected and integrated citizens. In the sources, fears then can be excavated and understood as gendered fears as they related to male-specific responsibilities and pressures. As David Gilmore and George Mosse have explicated, the gender conventions and responsibilities of men being breadwinners and protectors of their families are embedded in universalist and historical traditions. German-Jewish men's fears of their gendered identities being eviscerated by their inability to perform such roles are thus not a specific predicament that pertains to German-Jewish men in the Third Reich only but to masculinity in general. The fears this paper looks at are rather grounded in feared scenarios and realities, such as facing unemployment or physical brutality by Nazi camp guards. Though these fears take on a less personified character than in the other chapters, it is clear that these fears are still the consequence of the Nazi regime and individual Nazi behaviors and, as such, they also represent personal fears of invasions and incursions.

The focus of this study is on men and on the Third Reich for several reasons. Jewish masculinities are an understudied topic. While much progress has been made in women's history over the last four decades,[12] men's studies lag behind, particularly in the case of German-Jewish men, who as a group have not yet been systematically studied.[13] The 1930s, moreover, represents a time period when fears came into existence in a more unexpected and unprecedented way. Though fear is a universal basic human emotion, it becomes even more pronounced at certain times—in our case the era of the Third Reich—when a significantly large group of people experience a sudden and drastic reduction in their quality of life.[14] I concentrate on the 1930s, furthermore, because unlike the years of the Holocaust itself, 1941–5, which have arguably received much more scholarly attention, the prewar years constitute a time when the early stages of Nazi persecution were not yet based on extermination policy but rather on discursively humiliating, economically impoverishing, and socially isolating Germany's Jews. These phases (which ultimately led to genocide) affected and were experienced differently by German-Jewish men and women.[15]

It needs to be emphasized, though, that fears were not an exclusively male experience. As gender theories rely on the concept of gender being a relational category of social relationships, it would be false to analyze Jewish men and their fears in isolation and separated from women. To fully understand the construction of German-Jewish masculinity, it is imperative to bring the constitutive elements of masculinity into a relational context of Jewish women and their lives. The production of masculinity and femininity, in other words, occur codependently and social understandings and constructions of masculinity can only be revealed and become meaningful in a context that pays equal attention to femininity.

Gendered Themes of Fear

Before we scrutinize how German Jews represented fear in historical documents, we must start by asking how German-Jewish men avoided showing signs of fear. When the Nazis gained power in January 1933, the radical parts of the movement lost little time in translating their rabble-rousing anti-Semitic rhetoric into action. Besides taking on the battle against political enemies, the Nazis sought to immediately and visibly demonstrate their intentions to ostracize and discriminate against German Jews. As part of their discursive strategies, German Jews were branded as racial outcasts and were stigmatized as greedy capitalists, profiteers, and as dishonest, shady businessmen who were alien in character and deed to honest, German workmanship. On April 1, 1933, the Nazis, in one of their first demonstrations of new national prowess, called for a national boycott against Jewish businesses. Nazi formations, typically Stormtrooper men, were placed in front of Jewish stores to prevent customers from shopping. Jewish stores were desecrated with Jewish emblems and slandering phrases. The boycott was amplified by specific forms of harassment, physical intimidation, and violence against Jewish business owners. Strikingly, the Jewish reactions to the boycott were gendered. Analyzing these responses requires a gender-aware approach to historiography.

In 1933, it was generally Jewish male business owners who in public spaces were confronted with the direct impacts of the Nazi boycott. Hermann Tuggelin (b. 1908) recalls how he was brutally beaten in his family store requiring subsequent hospitalization:

> I went to the store because I did not want to leave [my] mother alone there. I was reading a newspaper, [when] SA thugs entered the business. "Today we can settle scores with the Jewish pigs." I did not fall for the provocation. In this moment, I received a terrible punch below my left eye. The blood splashed. I fell to the floor ... The SA men fell onto me, beating me. I do not know how long I was beaten. ... I was brought to the Jewish hospital. Afterwards, I did not walk to my mother. I did not want to jeopardize her.[16]

Though memoirs and diaries are not replete with references to Nazi violence in the first year of the Nazi dictatorship, many sources delineate how Jewish men reacted in defiance to the Nazi-sanctioned boycott and threats of violence. Since it could be assumed that the Nazis would disturb Jewish businesses on April 1— as the boycott was preceded by massive propaganda campaign in the media—it is noteworthy that most Jewish store owners had decided in advance to open their stores; what is more, many Jewish business owners resorted to a public counterstrategy to respond to and in fact resist Nazi intimidation. In several cases Jewish men put on their First World War uniforms and decorated their stores with wartime memorabilia, medals, and other symbols. Edwin Landau vividly recalled the day of the boycott:

> I took my war decorations, put them on, went into the street and visited Jewish shops where at first I was also stopped. But I was seething inside and most of all

I would have liked to shout my hatred into the faces of the barbarians … This land and this people that until now I had loved and treasured had suddenly become my enemy. So I was not a German anymore, or I was no longer supposed to be one. … I approached … one guard whom I knew and who also knew me and I said to him, "When you were still in your diapers, I was already fighting out there for this country."[17]

Others like Erich Leyens even went further and approached the passersby on the street, handing out pamphlets that detailed their families' historical roots as German citizens, and their loyalty to Germany, its culture, and its government.[18] Such declarations of Germanness like Leyens' were typically performed through active reference to past military service. The resultant Jewish male self-portrayals not only symbolized a gendered response that reflected these men's understanding and affirmation of true German soldierly manhood—but through their constructions of Jewish military masculinity, they simultaneously also demonstrated a visible and conscious lack of external fear. As former soldiers, many Jewish men performed the role of the stoic, steadfast, and disciplined man who stood his ground at a time of crisis and confronted his adversary face-to-face.

Commemorating the First World War and referencing past heroic battlefield sacrifices and risks they had endured, German-Jewish men resorted to a public anti-fear campaign that not only presented them in a symbolically potent, militarized context that disseminated notions of physical and moral strength, willpower, discipline, and bravery but also denoted a defensive strategy that was meant to prevent men from being emasculated, looking unmanly and appearing fearful. Taking action into their own hands, these Jewish men adopted a gendered strategy that closely reflected accepted social gender norms of German gentile society in which "Aryan" manhood was defined by being strong and fearless.[19]

Over the course of the Third Reich, Jewish public demonstrations of perseverance, bravery, and strong will continued, albeit with decreasing frequency and success. The Jewish World War One veterans' organization, for instance, published a number of commemorative books with the implicit intention to uphold the masculine image of the fearless Jewish soldier.[20] It was also successful in winning a number of concessions from the government—most notably a delay in the forced dismissal of Jewish government employees. But over time, the public sphere was lost to Jewish men and women as an arena for performing acts of building and maintaining recognition. Unemployed and expelled from associational public life, many men became depressed. With their social, public status destroyed as formerly respected citizens, and the loss of patriarchal influence at home due to forced unemployment and the resulting inability to uphold gender norms of being the breadwinner, over the course of the 1930s many German-Jewish men moved into a private sphere where public acts of defiance and demonstrations of fearless bravery, such as those still committed in April 1933, had an increasingly limited meaning.[21] So we must now turn to the world of diaries and memoirs to show how German-Jewish men recognized, acknowledged, and processed fear within the private sphere.

Economic Fears

Despite initial public acts of defiance by some German Jews, one of the first and immediate repercussions of the Nazi takeover in 1933 was an economic deterioration of living standards due to the loss of employment.[22] In Germany's patriarchal society, with men being the legal heads of their households and typically the primary income-makers, un- and underemployment, either through direct dismissals by their employers or more gradually through a declining income generated from self-employment, led to serious fears about economic survival. At some point, starting in 1933, the great majority of German-Jewish men—often in the coinciding role as husbands and fathers—began to worry about sustaining a level of economic subsistence. Some groups, such as civil servants, lawyers, and physicians, were dismissed in 1933 if they did not qualify for an exemption; others, such as the self-employed, struggled to make a living, sometimes until 1938. Yet, regardless of profession, even with a sustained income, the existential fear of being unable to secure a living in the future intensified.[23]

Willy Cohn, father of four children, was a public-school teacher in Breslau (now Wrocław) until 1933 when he was dismissed from his position. Unemployed, he struggled to make an income for his family. Living off a diminishing salary and his dwindling savings, Cohn noted in his diary on September 22, 1935: "I am thinking about how I might earn some money, but unfortunately, the possibilities are limited. It is very hard to keep up the household like this. … As long as I can work on my own, I will do so, but how long will my strength hold out?"[24]

Yet, Cohn's situation did not improve over time. In December 1938, he noted: "I'm short on money … and I don't know how we are going to get through this. I don't want to ask anyone either. It is very difficult for a father when he is unable to do what he would like to do."[25]

In a similar vein, Victor Klemperer (1881–1960), dismissed from his professorship and forced into retirement in Dresden in 1935, confided his economic troubles to his diary in 1934: "There are moments at which I am almost suffocated by money worries. I force myself not to think about a bill which must be paid in the coming month."²⁶ A year later, he grieves: "From Easter, I shall have no more students, have to retire, i.e. be reduced from 800 Mark to 400. But even now I can hardly meet my obligations. How to keep going with half an income?"²⁷ Max Krakauer (1888–1965), formerly in the movie business in Leipzig, remembered how dire the deprivations due to his loss of income were:

> I had to feed (*ernähren*) my family and the question how I should do this tortured me and many, many other men who shared my fate (*Schicksalsgenossen*) day and night. Whatever I tried, and I tried everything conceivable, failed due to the Nazi agitation against us Jews. The losses and disappointments followed. Soon we had to find smaller living quarters.²⁸

In postwar memoirs, German Jewish children recall how in the Third Reich their fathers struggled to keep a façade of normal family life but in reality, despaired in their attempts to continue making an income for their families. Hans Winterfeldt remembered how his father, after being dismissed, took on a salesman's job, left before sunrise every morning with a heavy bag of merchandise and toured the countryside villages outside of Berlin, only to return at night without having sold a single item.²⁹ Heinz Abrahamson recalled how deeply shaken his father was the day after the anti-Jewish boycotts of April 1, 1933. He became so depressed and fearful that he had to stop working as a shoemaker, falling into a passive state. Eventually, it was his mother who had to sell the business and provide for the family herself.³⁰ Inge Deutschkron remembered how her father, after becoming unemployed, only spent time with other men who were in similar situations, playing cards all day long.³¹

Undeniably, German Jews, both women and men, young and old, experienced existential struggles and fears in the Third Reich. Yet, they perceived, internalized, and processed these fears differently and in gendered terms. It was men, whose lives were based on the gendered role expectation of being the providers, who felt primarily responsible for their failures and in turn came to experience the fears for the future in more pressing ways. According to Monika Richarz, starting in the late eighteenth/early nineteenth century, Jewish men had came to identify themselves increasingly with their occupations and the status and respect that emanated from their professions.³² Simone Lässig reinforces the notion that masculinity was unequivocally defined by gainful employment (*Erwerbstätigkeit*), which in turn made men the heads (*Oberhaupt*) of their families.[33] Though many contemplated emigrating from Germany to leave economic fears behind, not everyone was prepared to do so. Alfred Meyer remembered that emigration from Germany was not possible for his father. Like many other Jewish husbands and fathers, Alfred's was "not skilled in languages and legal knowledge as an attorney was not useful abroad. Nor did he possess any entrepreneurial skills."[34] Securing employment abroad in advance to leaving your old job and your home behind was, therefore, a complicated and often daunting challenge for German Jews. Paul Steiner noted in his diary on March 12, 1938, a few days prior to Austria's annexation, that many Jews were contemplating escape from their homeland but without knowing how to make an income in the future. He predicted that if he should lose his position, he would have to look for prospects in another country.[35]

Steiner was not alone in linking economic prospects abroad to the growing unlikelihood of continuing to live in Germany. What is revealing in Steiner's case, however, is not so much his intention to leave his home for better economic opportunities in some other country but rather the actual fear that was driving his emotions and thoughts at the time he translated his fears into words. His diary entries show that the author had not yet faced unemployment; yet, the underlying fear is keenly noticeable. Like Krakauer, Klemperer, and Cohn, Steiner was driven by economic fears. All felt the need to reflect on them in their diaries and memoirs, and writing was a vitally important means to communicate their fears. For these authors, the medium of the diary and the process of diary-writing both served as release valves needed to treat their anxieties. Relating the innermost private feelings of existential fear to their diaries resembled a symbolic contract of trust between the written words and the authors. The secretive aura that orbited around these fears would be locked into the diary in exchange for the authors' open acknowledgment of their fears.

The excerpts above demonstrate how German-Jewish men were pressured by cultural gender discourses to fulfill the gender norm of providing for themselves and their dependents and resorted to means of negotiating their failures in the utmost private, intimate sphere. From the documents analyzed, I have not come across any evidence that fathers and husbands openly revealed their economic fears in front of their loved ones.[36] Victor Klemperer wrote in his diary that on numerous occasions, he had to control his emotions in his wife's presence. "I have gradually become a master of suppressing all my worries."[37] Presumably, these men shied away from admitting their fears in front of their wives and children, partially in order to spare them similar pain. The loss of employment was not only indicative of a decline in living standards due to a declining income but also a loss of masculinity and concomitant loss of status and recognition. Acknowledging such to the people who were most important to these men, their families, and to whom their masculine roles and achievements were performed, would have resulted in a more dramatic humiliation for these men. Instead, some chose diaries as a medium to which they entrusted their fears and humiliations.

In the early years of the Third Reich, German-Jewish men tried to uphold the masculine images of being in control in the presence of their families and wives and thereby maintain the virtues of male willpower and guardianship for as long as possible. Felix Fechenbach (1894–1933), journalist, husband, and father of three children, was taken into protective custody in March 1933. In the surviving correspondence between him and his wife, Fechenbach expressed confidence that upon his release he would be able to resume working and providing for his family; in the meantime, a smaller residence would have to suffice. Strikingly, the language he used to give directives to his wife was bereft of fear. His language was one of economic rationalizing and steadfast coolness. He wished "to get out of this protective custody so that I can again provide for my family."[38]

Ludwig Marum (1882–1934), lawyer by profession, father of three children, was deported to the concentration camp Kislau in May 1933. In his letters to his wife, he too tried to console his wife about her economic worries. He stated that if he no longer could work as a lawyer, he would find something else. For this reason, she should not cancel their rental agreement.[39] Again, the absent husband seemed to continue performing the gender role of the active decision-maker and head of the family. In another letter, he wrote that he had the courage to continue with his life and as before, provide for them and their children. "Once I am free again, I am going to earn our bread. Don't be afraid!"[40]

In prewar Nazi Germany, when Jewish men still pursued the conventional path of being the breadwinner, economic concerns were not intimately shared. The examples of Klemperer, Fechenbach, and Marum indicate that discussing fear with their wives and within the family was not commonly practiced. Instead, in their self-construction as heads of their families and households, fears were suppressed or downplayed. These men convincingly relay an impression that they were in control of their own and their families' affairs and their judgment carried decisive weight. The fears that undeniably must have existed were shifted into and processed in specific spaces—the private sphere. German-Jewish men felt confident to address their economic fears in more direct ways only to themselves and through the written words they used to communicate their anxieties. As Willy Cohn noted in his diary in April 1933: "True we are not being killed, but we are being tortured mentally and our ability to make a living is being systematically undermined."[41]

Fears for the Family

Closely tied to economic fears were Jewish men's ever-mounting concerns for the physical well-being of their families. In addition to the provider responsibility, Jewish men developed serious concerns about their abilities to perform the protector roles.

Since the early days of the Third Reich, for most German-Jewish families the issue of emigration became ever more pressing. Even though many families, by decision of the *pater familias*, decided at first against it, the issue itself became more salient over time. While the decision-making process pertaining to leaving their homeland (*Heimat*) behind and starting a new life in a foreign country was a burdensome, uneven and time-consuming process, by 1938/1939, most German Jews were determined to leave Germany.[42] In their decisions to move abroad, German-Jewish parents had, among other priorities such as job prospects, as their top priority the strong intention to keep their families together. Jewish men saw it as their primary objective to preserve their families as a collective unit and bring them out of the country safely. While economic fears for a future existence in Germany were certainly a major motive for emigration, a more general pull-factor for Jewish men to migrate was the potential well-being of their dependents in another country, where they would not be constantly confronted by a virulent, aggressive anti-Semitism (such as in schools); where they were not being subjected to social harassment and legal discrimination; and where their personal safety was guaranteed. Alfred Elbau (1911–2006) recalled in his memoir-diary that his father, who for years had been reluctant to emigrate, eventually consented only under the condition that the entire family would move together.[43] Alfred's father's decision prevailed and the entire family was able to leave Germany in May 1938. Based on the father's refusal to emigrate prior to 1938, it is plausible to speculate that a partial emigration, by the parents only for instance, or in combination with one child, would not have been acceptable for the father, who clearly felt responsible for *all*, even for his adult children, who were financially independent and self-supporting. The fear that would arise from leaving their children behind during such dire times with an uncertain future was not an option for Elbau's father.

In a different case, the 58-year-old Salomon Riemer (1880–?), after having settled in Palestine together with his wife in 1936, sent the following letter to his sister-in-law, who lived either in Britain or North America:

Tel Aviv, October 1, 1938

My dear, faithful Sister-in-law,

Herr Max Slaten was so kind as to forward your address to me. We have not written each other in over three decades, and I was very pleased to hear that you are still alive. Hopefully you are healthy and doing well. In eight days, I will be married for twenty-eight years and eight days after that I will turn fifty-eight years old. I have three children. One son is twenty-seven and in Berlin. His name is Werner. The second's name is Herbert, twenty-six; he is married and lives in Antwerp. Then I have a little girl (*Töchterchen*), who is eighteen and a half. For two and a half years, my wife and I have been living in Palestine. I am subsisting from the sale of coffee, cacao and tea ... It is hard but I am managing to provide (*Lebensunterhalt aufbringen*) ... I would be immensely grateful if you could help us regarding my oldest son. Palestine is currently not allowing anyone to enter. Germany is a hell and innocent Jews are being persecuted. They are not allowed to live, are not allowed to work, and if things continue the way they are, Jews will vanish due to starvation. My wife Minna and I are very much concerned for our boy and don't know, due to all this excitement and trouble, what to do. Believe me, Dear Pauline, when Werner sends us a letter, our hearts tremble and we have sleepless nights. Perhaps you can give us some advice and get into touch with people who can do something ... An immediate solution is required if the boy is not to perish (*untergehen*) in Berlin ... Heartfelt greetings from your loving brother-in-law Salomon.[44]

Riemer's case shows how the distant father was unable to intervene on behalf of his children and experienced his forced passivity in the form of fear. His desperate attempt to contact a distant relative is evidence of his struggle as a father who likely had tried all other, more promising means to get his son out of Germany prior to writing this letter. Similar to the economic fears outlined above, the dealings of Jewish fathers are also reflections of how fears were recorded within a very private, intimate sphere. Either in the form of diary writing or in letter writing to a single relative, German-Jewish men confessed their fears in a sealed environment where they thought they would not lose face or at least keep the humiliation (and anticipated ridicule for being unable to fulfill their gender roles as fathers) to a minimum.

There are few records of entire families moving out of Germany together. More common were the decisions made by parents to first send their children out of Germany.[45] It was an equally troubling experience, however, to be physically disconnected from their children. In his diary, Erich Frey alludes to his fear for his daughter Miriam after she had left for Palestine in late August 1939, when her trip was interrupted by the outbreak of the war.[46] Willy Cohn also used his diary to project his inner struggle as a father who was unable to be around his child. Following the separation from his son in April 1933, Cohn wrote, "Wölfl [his son] is gone now. It was a very difficult farewell. But a father is not eager to commit to paper or express how he feels at such a moment." A year later, Cohn had not yet become accustomed to the forced separation of the family. "My separation from Wölfl weighs heavily on me, as does the shrinking prospect of me seeing him again in the foreseeable future. This feeling overwhelms me at night in particular."[47]

Frey and Cohn openly confessed their fatherly concerns about being unable to be physically close to their children and offer them support and guidance. Perhaps even more tormenting was the unknown fate of their children far away and the inability of the fathers to have any direct impact on the well-being of their offspring. In these indirect expressions of fatherly fear, the gendered norm of masculine behavior is noticeable; children, regardless of their age, are viewed as helpless, dependent humans who are in need of a strong, protective hand. Elbau wanted to keep the family together as he likely assumed that he would be able to better protect the family. Frey and Cohn felt marginalized in their roles as fathers with their children being far away and no longer under their paternal auspices.

An emphasis on fatherly concerns does not undermine the important roles women also played in keeping their families together. As Marion Kaplan and others have shown, Jewish women endured extraordinary hardship in getting their husbands out of concentration camps, or filing for emigration in various embassies, going from one government office to the next. Furthermore, many Jewish women, who had managed to send their families abroad, took on additional burdens and stayed behind to take care of their elderly parents and thus had no means to escape the murderous Nazi machine. However, what was specific to Jewish men in this context of negotiating Jewish masculinities was the (self-perceived) pressure to perform the role that has been historically ascribed to men: the role of the protector. In a logical consequence, because men were culturally assigned the role of guardian over their dependents, many felt the fear of losing agency over maintaining this role and their families' well-being.

Patently, the image and standing of these men in the public and within their families as protective heads mattered greatly to them. Elbau remembered how his father tried to avoid any panic prior to the decision for emigration. He did not want the family to worry and thus acted as the steadfast, rational decision-maker. The lawyer Kurt Rosenberg (1900–1977) noted in his diary on March 31, 1933 that he expected his arrest by the Nazis any day. He too sought to preemptively assuage his family members' concerns: "I am telling my family not to be fearful if I should not come home one day." Rosenberg's public image as the household head, evidently, stood in stark contrast to his internal fears that he could acknowledge in his diary only. In front of his family, he portrayed himself as the rational, calm and in-control leader, who showed no fear of eminent danger, while in his diary, serving as the material manifestation of his private ego, he admitted—on the same day in March 1933—his worries about wife and children: "Wife and children are a grave concern." [*Frau und Kinder sind eine ernste Sorge.*][48]

Fear of Arrest and Violence

With the beginning of the Third Reich, Nazi party paramilitary and the police immediately embarked upon physically attacking and incarcerating alleged enemies of the state. Even though the first wave of arrests in 1933 was primarily directed against the political opposition, most notably members of the Communist and Social Democratic parties as well as journalists and other intellectuals who had criticized the Nazi movement in the past, German Jews saw Hitler's rise to power with much agony and concern. Due to the relentless spread of anti-Semitic propaganda in the media and a further, palpable increase in street violence and physical assaults, it is hardly surprising that German Jews began to fear violence and the prospect of concentration camp imprisonment.[49]

Prior to the deportations of German Jewish men and women starting in 1940/1941, Nazi physical assaults and Stormtrooper hooliganism were overwhelmingly carried out on men and such violence was not restricted to single events only. Instead, Jewish men had become pariahs in the open public and could become subjected to violence for various pretexts at any time. As Claudia Koonz has asserted, "Women suffered far less from violent attacks than Jewish men until the deportations began in 1941. Before, the Gestapo, SA, police and angry mobs on the street assaulted only men."[50]

Before the war, the Nazis took relatively little notice of German-Jewish women, either in their anti-Semitic propaganda imagery or in their translation of anti-Semitism into actual "deeds." Kim Wünschmann has argued in her study of prewar Jewish concentration camp prisoners that "women, at least in the early years of the regime, were mostly spared brutal forms of abuse. Nazi propaganda vilified first and foremost the male Jew; public persecutions of the Jewish enemy stereotype were to be gendered male."[51] This gendered imbalance of direct physical violence toward Jews in the Third Reich makes a gendered analysis of fear for men's personal physical integrity and inviolability all the more necessary.

Only a few weeks after the Nazi takeover of power, Will Pressmann (b. 1914) started to vividly record in his diary his frightening experience of the pervasiveness of Nazi violence in Berlin:

> March 5, 1933: Today are the elections for the new Reichstag ... Earlier in the big traffic circle I saw two Nazis and their victim carried away on a stretcher. Maybe he was injured, maybe he was dead. I considered how dangerous it was even to walk along the streets, as I was doing. I thought to myself that I was lucky to be walking away, when I saw another victim being carried.
>
> March 23, 1933: In the streets are troublemakers and anti-Semites. You must let them have their peace without fighting or talking back ... my own mind tells me to consider getting out of Germany while I am [still] alive.

Several months later, Pressmann left for Belgium, a temporary exile, while his parents still remained in Berlin. He described it as a time of fierce arguments between him and his parents, who wanted their son to return and help in the family business. Due to Pressmann's incessant fears for his physical well-being, the numerous letters and phone calls by his parents proved to be ineffective.

> Over the phone my mother asked me to return to Berlin; I explained my position about Nazi arrests of visitors returning to Germany. Many of those in "protective custody" never returned alive. I asked them to think it over before commanding that I come home.[52]

Pressmann was not alone in his fears for his own safety already in early 1933. Willy Cohn noted in his diary on May 1, 1933, that he woke up at 3:00 in the morning, bathed in sweat. "I dreamed that I was in protective custody."[53] Walter Tausk noted bluntly in July 1933: "You have to shut up—otherwise KZ!" (*Maul halten—sonst KZ!*).[54]

In these excerpts, concerns for one's personal safety are evident. Fears for economic survival and one's family emerged gradually as they required time to mature, longer-lasting sentiments as Keith Oatley coins them. Fears based on physical violence—German Jews' realization that they could potentially become subjects to assault anytime—were reactive and emerged more abruptly.⁵⁵ Pressmann was a 19-year-old bachelor who prior to his escape to Belgium had worked in his father's textile business. Willy Cohn was a teacher and Walter Tausk a businessman. It is telling that ostensibly inconspicuous and innocent German citizens, with no criminal records and no direct interest and involvement in politics, harbored these feelings of fear and then converted them into emphatic language and practical solutions, only weeks after the Nazi takeover but many years prior to the implementation of genocide. Though anti-Semitism was rampant in the increasingly censored German media, such attacks on Jews were on the one hand not entirely novel, as anti-Semitic papers had been widely circulated in the Weimar Republic as well. On the other hand, the great majority of German Jews were not physically harassed in the early months and years of the Third Reich (unlike the political opposition). But it is certainly clear that the Nazi revolution, the creation of a Nazi dictatorship through semilegal means of terror and intimidation, transported the now ostracized social group, German-Jews, into a tense emotional state. Jews, not for unfounded reasons, anticipated violence toward them.

Jewish men were not alone in experiencing fears of physical violence, but as my discussion on the provider- and protector-related fears has relayed, their fears could take distinctly gendered forms. In the context of physical fears, it is striking that Jewish men and women were concerned about possible assaults and brutalities, but what they feared was predominantly directed at men in prewar Nazi Germany. Kurt Rosenberg, for instance, noted in his diary on April 14, 1933 that his wife was very concerned when the door rang one evening. It was a courier, but his wife immediately thought of the SA.⁵⁶ Wilhelm Buchheim noted in his diary shortly after Kristallnacht that when the SA rang their doorbell on November 10, his wife decided that she would open the door whereas he was to hide in bed and act sick. In her fear for her husband, Buchheim's wife reasoned that the Nazis would not touch an ailing man.⁵⁷ Finally, Elizabeth Freund recalled how fearful she was for her husband shortly after the war had started:

> On a Saturday night, around quarter to ten, the door rings. Good Heavens! Who can it be so late and unannounced? It cannot be Jewish acquaintances because they are not allowed to be outside after 8 o'clock. It can only be a house search. The doorbell rings a second time! What shall we do? They are going to take my husband—but where should he hide in this small apartment? Nothing helps, we have to open.⁵⁸

The accounts illustrate that the construction of Jewish masculinity was not a reserved domain for men only; women participated in the gender identity construction of Jewish masculinities and their views were equally important to Jewish men's own perception of themselves. German-Jewish constructions of a new, marginalized masculinity in the eyes of both men and women had drastically changed under the Nazis, and the male prospect of facing anti-Semitic violence was recognized and internalized by both sexes.

Physical violence against Jews continued to erupt intermittently and by the end of the decade drastically increased. Over the entire year of 1938, the Nazis amplified their attacks on German Jews. One of the affected, Paul Steiner, recalled that in May 1938—shortly after Austria's annexation—he only dared to go out onto the street for fifteen minutes and only under the protection of darkness.[59] In the summer of 1938, a nationwide *Aktion* began, targeting hundreds of Jews (and non-Jews) who were deported to concentration camps; so-called asocial elements, such as the unemployed, "work-shy" and criminals, were arrested, among them many Jews who, however, had neither been unemployed nor had any criminal records.[60] Finally, in November 1938, the *Kristallnacht* pogrom led to the arrest of more than thirty thousand Jewish men and their internment in concentration camps. In this radicalizing environment of 1938, the more abstract fear of losing physical integrity and intactness (*Unversehrtheit*) gradually shifted toward a more defined, concrete fear of concentration camp imprisonment. While violence and physical assault had been a constant yet fluctuating feared possibility, the mass arrest of Jewish men in November 1938 marked a turning point not only in Nazi anti-Semitism but also in Jewish life as well. Numerous memoirs and diaries testify to a new but pervasive atmosphere of fearing the concentration camp. Alexander Szanto (1899–1972), a journalist who had been interrogated by the Gestapo several times before, recalled that in 1938, he still had not become accustomed to the dread that rushed through his bones when he thought about being taken away from his bed at night.[61] Other men, in their fearful anticipation of arrest, went into hiding. One witness recalled, "At my aunt's, who had a two-bedroom apartment in Berlin, a total of six male relatives, my cousin included, lived there during the period of the pogroms. Others resided in the Grünewald forest, in spite of the November cold." A second report remembered: "In Berlin, it was possible to hide and between November 10 and 20, thousands of Jewish men lived an existence similar to hunted game [*gehetztes Wild*]. Some were on the go day and night, using public transportation. Many spent their nights at different places, often in the homes of already arrested Jews, often with Aryans, some of who were quite supportive. Eleven Jewish men stayed in a villa of an 'Aryan' merchant. Some of them did not even know the proprietor but were told about him by friends. In a tiny cigar shop owned by an Aryan which was about nine square meters in size, two Jews spent fourteen consecutive nights there on chairs."[62]

The impact of the 1938 outburst of anti-Semitic violence had a dramatic and lingering effect and the fear of Jewish men being caught by the Nazis did not instantly recede following the violent incident. Adolf Riesenfeld admitted to his diary in 1938 that every day following Austria's Anschluss in March he feared arrest. He had begun internalizing a worst case scenario of Nazi mistreatment. As part of his developing fears and to circumvent possible physical torture, he had requested cyanide from his pharmacist.[63] Willy Cohn attested to his enduring fear on November 20, ten days after the actual pogrom. "After dinner, I took a walk with Trudi for the first time since Friday a week ago and breathed fresh air for the first time. It did me good! A person feels like a criminal walking along empty and ill-lit alleys, hoping to avoid people who might ask how come you aren't in the camp."[64]

These excerpts show that more than imprisonment in the concentration camp was feared; the nerve-wracking anticipation, the uncertainty, the not-knowing if and when the arrest and deportation would happen were equally tormenting. In the growing anticipation of violence to be inflicted upon men, many Jewish women recalled in their postwar memoirs how even prior to the year 1938 their husbands had stopped answering the phone, opening the front door or even getting out of the house. This process of self-imposed isolation had gradually started in 1933 (see the example of Kurt Rosenberg) but was greatly aggravated in 1938 when the risk of arrest for any Jewish man had become more tangible. Later on, Jews were forbidden to be outdoors after 8:00 in the evening. Erich Bloch remembered that he was so intimidated and scared when he was once caught after the curfew that thereafter he began to avoid the public sphere altogether.[65] Victor Klemperer too tried to circumvent the danger on the street. He decided to stay at home whenever possible. "I hardly get out of the house anymore. Always the fear of the dogcatchers." "Eva [his wife] must go out today; we are completely without food and I do not have the confidence to go into town." "I am completely tied and am afraid of the street." "Only when it is absolutely necessary do I venture on to the street."[66]

Bodily Fears

In addition to Jewish men's fear of sociocultural ostracizing in the 1930s, fears materialized that pertained to the threat of physical violence. Nazi methods to crush political opposition and discriminate against German Jews were known for being ruthless and violent. Bodily fears were aggravated over the course of the Third Reich, and because in the prewar years violence was by and large directed against Jewish men,[67] it can hardly be surprising that Jewish women's primary concerns were often for the health of their Jewish men—their sons, husbands and other male relatives. Already in April 1933, Kurt Rosenberg disclosed how he was suffering from fever and permanent exhaustion, all likely due to internal agitation (*innere Erregung*).[68] Martin Hauser went even further in his diary. His fears did not just emanate from physical exhaustion; he feared the actual violence of Nazi thugs. When he had a verbal confrontation at work with a Nazi coworker and found out that this colleague had denounced him to the local Nazi chapter, Hauser wrote, "SA means ambushing and the worst possible beatings, if not more."[69] As a result, Hauser immediately left Germany.

A mental state of anxiety and nervousness was not necessarily gender-specific. In unprecedented times as these, Jewish women were also in an emotional state of agony and disdain; women too worried about the future and their families.[70] But German Jews projected their fears of possible physical maltreatment by the Nazis onto men, and when in November 1938, the arrests of thousands of Jewish men began, many went into temporary hiding to avoid the arrest and with it the associated physical brutalities that were expected to occur in Dachau, Buchenwald, and Sachsenhausen. Going into hiding was a direct corollary of the internal fear of being brutalized by the Nazi state. Max Krakauer from Leipzig remembered how he first went into hiding at a friend's place and then finally moved to the big city of Berlin where he hoped he could live anonymously.[71] Walter Tausk, on the other hand, was one of the lucky ones who were not ultimately arrested during the immediate aftermath of the pogrom. Yet, he admitted in his diary that he was still overridden by fear. On November 15, 1938, a few days after the pogrom, he wrote that he had been suffering from major sleeplessness at night and all kinds of nightmares. Even during the day, his state of anxiety (*Angstzustände*) made him suffer heat rushes and sudden headaches.[72]

If the fear and its effects on one's psyche and body pertaining to possible physical mistreatment were not enough, there is evidence that the after-effects of concentration camp imprisonment nourished further fears and anxieties among Jewish men and their families. Not everyone could overcome the trauma and shock experienced in a *KZ* after their release. For some Jewish men, the mistreatment was so dramatic and incisive that it changed their demeanor profoundly. Walter Besser recalled how his brother Heinz had been arrested already in 1933 and spent three years in Dachau where he had been subjected to solitary confinement in darkness (*Dunkelhaft*); upon his release, his brother was a different person. On the street, he would habitually look behind himself, in fear of being followed. In the trains, the metro, everywhere, he was in a permanent state of anxiety, fearing that his traumatic experiences in Dachau could be repeated.[73] Moritz Mandelkern described his adolescent son's return from Sachsenhausen in August 1940 as a blessed day for him and his wife: "But sometimes, it was strange. When he saw a soldier, on the way to the synagogue, he would jump to attention … He was so different. He might have been away five years instead of nine months."[74]

Other men refused to talk about their experiences in the concentration camps. This was partially a strategy to forget and move on with their lives, but it was also due to the fear that the SS had infused into these men.[75] Upon their release all men were explicitly warned not to talk to anyone about their imprisonment. Emil Schorsch recalled how the voice and the warning of the SS officer lingered on his mind following his release. Out of dread, Schorsch and many others never dared to speak of the horrors they experienced:

> When we were getting released, an SS officer was standing in front of
>
> us who in a toxic voice warned us: "When you are abroad and talk about Germany and your arrest, we will catch you, wherever you are!" These were his approximate words, but the tone of his voice remained in my memory forever. I had not even told my wife about the concentration camp until we got to America.[76]

Cases such as these are striking demonstrations that the gendered reality of fear for Jewish men transcended economic concerns for themselves and their families as well as sociocultural concerns over losing their social position. Jewish fears in the prewar years of the Third Reich could include manifest fears of one's physical survival and well-being. Fears for bodily integrity were voiced by both men and women, and such fears were more pronounced in specific contexts such as during the aftermath of the Nazi takeover in 1933, when for the first time, the Stormtroopers had a free hand to "conduct their business," or following *Kristallnacht* in 1938, when many Jewish men went into hiding. Bodily fears, as demonstrated, could also relate to a permanent state of anxiety that then resulted in physical and mental exhaustion as Walter Tausk and Kurt Rosenberg experienced. Lastly, renewed fear of physical integrity could be enhanced following the incarceration and traumatic treatment in a concentration camp.

Conclusion

While fears can materialize in the form of constructing a threatening group of outsiders, it is, paradoxically, the outcasts—who often represent minorities within larger societies—that are the ones who get victimized. This chapter has put the emphasis on a victim group—German Jews in Nazi Germany—and analyzed gendered dimensions of some of the fears German Jews harbored between 1933 and 1939.

This chapter is based on the premise that the cultural construct, social reality, and individual human experience of fear—real and imagined—all need to be better understood in their gendered dimensions. While fear is a basic and universal emotion that transcends gender, class and race, the imagination, construction, and perception of fear can differ significantly in gender-specific contexts and spaces. When German adolescent and adult men in the Third Reich were subjected to hyper-masculinized propaganda that portrayed "Aryan" men as hard as "Krupp steel and tough as leather," German-Jewish men found their masculinities challenged, being depicted as effeminate and unsoldierly or as sexually deviant and perverted. Following further antisemitic legislation, Jewish men confronted existential fears for themselves and their dependents. Starting in 1933, Jewish men's previous socialization and acculturation to German society—which had been deeply imbued with nationalist and veterans' codes of behavior—stood in an ambivalent contrast to the sometimes overt admissions of and the expressions of fear. They contradicted the expected gender role performativity of German men. Jewish survivors of the Third Reich, often children and wives, remembered how their husbands and fathers tried to conceal signs of fear and failure within the public and within the family.

Fear among German Jews, men and women, became an increasingly pervasive, omnipresent and more pronounced daily reality to live with over the course of the Third Reich. As a strategy to process, German-Jewish men hoped to suppress their fears in public, and allowed fears to surface only the private sphere, primarily at home and often only through the use of diaries, arguably the most intimate space of human reflection. We have seen that diaries are a particularly suitable and authentic medium through which to examine fear. They convey a sense of immediacy and authentically reflect the actual thoughts and feelings that orbited around an actual or imagined fear by the author. In these writings, Jewish men acknowledged their fears more overtly without having to face social stigmatization and possible ridicule in public society. Many confessed their struggles to fulfill some of the conventional gender roles and expectations as men, husbands, and fathers, and the growing impotence of being unable to withstand and defy the avalanche of Nazi discrimination and intimidation.

Historians have produced an important literature on women's victimization, Jewish and non-Jewish, under the Nazis during the Second World War and the Holocaust. The intention of this chapter, however, was not to construct what Gisela Bock has rightly criticized as a "hierarchy of suffering."[77] In fact, the focus of my analysis was on the fears that were experienced prior to the unprecedented and various forms of victimization of Jewish men and women under the Nazis once the war begun. While both sexes had and displayed fears before 1939, some were specifically related to gender roles and conventions and the feared inability to uphold and adhere to them.

I have discussed economic fears that troubled Jewish men in their frantic and exasperating attempts to continue providing for themselves and their families. Such fears were augmented by Jewish men in their roles as protectors and their concerns for their dependents, often children who were sent abroad. Physical bodily fears also intensified during the 1930s when Jewish men were singled out, deported, and their psyches and bodies mistreated in prisons and concentration camps. As this chapter has shown, although fear transcends gender in its universality, fears can be experienced in gendered ways. Jewish men with their gendered fears resemble what Barbara H. Rosenwein phrased an "emotional community" marked by gender-idiosyncratic fears and concerns.[78] Scrutinizing gendered fears of German-Jewish men—fears for themselves and their loved ones, fears of economic subsistence, and fears of physical attacks by the Nazi state and its organizations—allow important insights into how German Jews, both men and women, perceived and experienced their marginalization in Nazi Germany and how they in turn processed and negotiated these fears.

Notes

1 Paul Steiner, *Diary*, vol. 7 Leo Baeck Institute New York AR25208, 41.
2 Willy Cohn, *No Justice in Germany: The Breslau Diaries, 1933–1941*, ed. Nobert Conrads, trans. Kenneth Kronenberg (Palo Alto, CA: Stanford University Press, 2012), 1.
3 Edwin Landau, "My Life before and after Hitler," in *Jewish Life in Germany: Memoirs from Three Centuries*, ed. Monika Richarz (Bloomington: Indiana University Press, 1991), 312.

4 See for instance: Jan Plamper, *The History of Emotions: An Introduction* (Oxford, Oxford University Press, 2015); Ute Frevert and Thomas Dixon, eds., *Emotional Lexicons: Continuity and Change in the Vocabulary of Feeling, 1700–2000* (Oxford: Oxford University Press, 2014); Aleida Assmann and Ines Detmers, *Empathy and Its Limits* (New York: Palgrave Macmillan, 2016); Keith Oatley, *Emotions: A Brief History* (Oxford: Blackwell, 2004).

5 For literature of masculinity see: David D. Gilmore, *Manhood in the Making: Cultural Concepts of Masculinity* (New Haven, CT: Yale University Press, 1990); Raewyn Connell, *Masculinities* (Berkeley: University of California Press, 1995); George Mosse, *The Image of Man: The Creation of Modern Masculinity* (Oxford: Oxford University Press, 1996); Thomas Kühne, ed. *Männergeschichte— Geschlechtergeschichte: Männlichkeit im Wandel der Moderne* (Frankfurt am Main: Campus Verlag, 1996); John Tosh, *A Man's Place: Masculinity and the Middle-Class Home in Victorian England* (New Haven, CT: Yale University Press, 1999). See also the 2018 special edition of *Central European History* on masculinity in the Third Reich.

6 Alexandra Garbarini, *Numbered Days. Diaries and the Holocaust* (New Haven, CT: Yale University Press, 2006); Marion Kaplan, "Weaving Women's Words: Zur Bedeutung von Memoiren für die deutsch-jüdische Frauengeschichte," in *Deutsch-Jüdische Geschichte als Geschlechtergeschichte*, ed. Stefanie Schüler-Springorum and Kirsten Heinsohn (Göttingen: Wallstein Verlag, 2006).

7 Jochen Hellbeck, *Revolution on My Mind: Writing a Diary under Stalin*. (Cambridge: Harvard University Press, 2009), 3.

8 Alexandra Garbarini, *Numbered Days. Diaries and the Holocaust* (New Haven, CT: Yale University Press, 2006), 14.

9 Kaplan, "Weaving Women's Words," 261.

10 Oatley, *Emotions*, 3.

11 Ute Frevert, "Defining Emotions: Concepts and Debates over Three Centuries," in *Emotional Lexicons: Continuity and Change in the Vocabulary of Feeling, 1700–2000*, ed. Ute Frevert and Thomas Dixon (Oxford: Oxford University Press, 2014), 5. See also: Jan Plamber, *A History of Emotions: An Introduction* (Oxford: Oxford University Press, 2015), 29.

12 See for instance: Joan Ringelheim, "The Unethical and the Unspeakable: Women and the Holocaust," *Simon Wiesenthal Center Annual* (Los Angeles, CA: Simon Wiesenthal Center, 1984); Dalia Ofer and Lenore J. Weitzman, eds., *Women in the Holocaust* (New Haven, CT: Yale University Press, 1998); Judith Tydor Baumel, *Double Jeopardy: Gender and the Holocaust* (London: Valentin Mitchell, 1998); Gisela Bock, ed., *Genozid und Geschlecht. Jüdische Frauen im nationalsozialistischen Lagersystem* (Frankfurt am Main: Campus Verlag, 2005); Florian Rübener, *Frauen in Konzentrationslagern: Eine geschlechts-spezifische Studie zu Überlebensstrategien und Alltag* (Hamburg: Diplomica Verlag, 2013); Beate Kosmala,

"Überlebensstrategien jüdischer Frauen in Berlin: Flucht vor der Deportation, 1941–1943," in *Alltag im Holocaust: Jüdisches Leben im Großdeutschen Reich 1941–1945*, ed. Andrea Löw, Doris Bergen, and Anna Hájková (Munich: Oldenbourg Verlag, 2013), 29–48.

13   Sharon Gillerman, Paul Lerner, and Benjamin Maria Baader, eds., *Jewish Masculinities: German Jews, Gender and History* (Bloomington: Indiana University Press, 2012), 15. See my dissertation, Sebastian Huebel, "Stolen Manhood? German-Jewish Masculinities in the Third Reich" (PhD thesis, University of British Columbia, 2017) as well as two of my publications: "Victor Klemperer: A Jew but also a Man: The Importance of Understanding German-Jewish Masculinities in the Third Reich," *Women in Judaism* 12 no. 2 (2016). Avail.: https://wjudaism.library.utoronto.ca/index.php/wjudaism/article/view/27169 [accessed September 10, 2019]; "Disguise and Defiance: German Jewish Men and Their Underground Experiences in Nazi Germany, 1941–45," *Shofar* 36, no. 3 (Winter 2018): 110–42.

14   For a detailed study on German-Jewish life under the Nazis see: Saul Friedländer, *Nazi Germany and the Jews: The Years of Persecution 1933–1939* (New York: Harper Perennial, 1998).

15   There seems to be a consensus that at least for the duration of the prewar years, Jewish men were specifically targeted and physically victimized by the Nazis. Marion Kaplan, for instance, argues that "[Nazi] racism was not gender-neutral. In imagery and practice, the Nazi government and most Germans treated Jewish women differently from Jewish men. Nazi propaganda castigated Jewish men as cheats and traitors, depicting them as greedy bankers and pimps. The Nazis persecuted Jewish men early on, culminating with their arrests during the November pogrom. With rare exceptions, Nazi policy before the deportations bowed to taboos against physically abusing women in the public." Joan Ringelheim noted that Jewish men were the primary targets of the Nazis. "They were certainly the first Jewish victims of forced labor and in the beginning, the primary targets of the *Einsatztruppen*." See: Marion Kaplan, *Between Dignity and Despair: Jewish Life in Nazi Germany* (Oxford: Oxford University Press, 1998), 235; Joan Ringelheim, "Genocide and Gender: A Split Memory," in *Gender and Catastrophes*, ed. Ronit Lentin (London: Zed Books, 1997), 23. These findings, however, are not to undermine scholarship on the victimizations of (Jewish) women under the Nazi regime. For some of the more prominent literature on this subject see: Gisela Bock, *Zwangssterilisation im Nationalsozialismus: Studien zur Rassenpolitik und Frauenpolitik* (Opladen: Westdeutscher Verlag, 1986); Judith Tylor Baumel, *Double Jeopardy: Gender and the Holocaust* (Elstree, UK: Vallentine Mitchell, 1998); Dalia Ofer and Lenore Weitzman, *Women in the Holocaust* (New Haven, CT: Yale University Press, 1999); Rochelle Saidel, *The Women of Ravensbrück* (Madison: University of Wisconsin Press, 2004).

16 Hermann Tuggelin, "Memoir," in *Sie durften nicht mehr Deutsche sein*, ed. Margarete Limberg (Berlin: Aufbau Verlag, 2003), 29.
17 Edwin Landau, "My Life before and after Hitler," in *Jüdisches Leben in Deutschland, Vol 3: 1918–1945*, ed. Monika Richarz (Stuttgart: DVA, 1982), 311.
18 Erich Leyens, *Years of Estrangement*, trans. Brigitte Goldstein (Evanston, IL: Northwestern University Press, 1996), 9–11.
19 Daniel Wildmann, *Begehrte Körper: Konstruktion und Inszenierung des "arischen" Männerkörpers im Dritten Reich* (Würzburg: Könighausen & Neumann, 1998).
20 Some of the works published by the Reichsbund Jüdischer Frontsoldaten include *Die jüdischen Gefallenen des deutschen Heeres, der deutschen Marine und der deutschen Schutztruppen 1914–1918* (Berlin: Reichsbund Jüdischer Frontsoldaten, 1932); *Gefallene Deutsche Juden: Frontbriefe, 1914–1918* (Berlin, 1935); *Heroische Gestalten jüdischen Stammes* (Berlin, Reichsbund Jüdischer Frontsoldaten, 1937).
21 See Kaplan, *Between Dignity and Despair*; Nechama Tec, *Resilience and Courage: Women, Men, and the Holocaust* (New Haven, CT: Yale University Press, 2003).
22 Avraham Barkai, *Vom Boykott zur Entjudung. Der wirtschaftliche Existenzkampf der Juden im Dritten Reich 1933–1943* (Frankfurt am Main: Fischer Verlag, 1988).
23 Although economic fears increased unevenly over time and were contingent on socioeconomic factors such as class (wealthier Jewish families felt economic pressures less immediately), most middle-class Jews had worked either in the civil service (as teachers, notaries, judges), were in self-employment (lawyers, physicians, business-owners), or were employed in certain industries (merchandise, banking, trade). In all three sectors, Jews were driven out of employment starting in 1933. For an excellent introduction into Jewish economic life, Jewish demographics and occupational patterns see: Monika Richarz's introductory chapter of *Jewish Life in Germany: Memoirs from Three Centuries* (Bloomington: Indiana University Press, 1991).
24 Cohn, *No Justice in Germany: The Breslau Diaries, 1933–1941*, 85.
25 Ibid., 205.
26 Victor Klemperer. *I Shall Bear Witness, The Diaries of Victor Klemperer, 1933–1941*, trans. Martin Chalmers (London: Weidenfeld & Nicolson, 1998), 57.
27 Ibid., 103. Half-income refers to his pension that he still received following his forced retirement.
28 Max Krakauer, *Lichter im Dunkeln, Flucht und Rettung eines jüdischen Ehepaars im Dritten Reich* (Stuttgart: Quell Verlag, 1994), 16.
29 Hans Winterfeldt, "Memoir," in *Sie Durften nicht mehr Deutsche sein*, ed. Margarete Limberg (Berlin: Aufbau Verlag, 2003), 214.
30 Zvi Aviram, *Mit dem Mut der Verzweiflung: Mein Widerstand im Berliner Untergrund, 1943–1945*, ed. Beate Kosmala and Patrick Siegele (Berlin: Metropol, 2015), 18.

31 Inge Deutschkron, *Ich trug den gelben Stern*, 2nd ed. (Cologne: Verlag Wissenschaft und Politik, 1979), 19.
32 Monika Richarz, "Geschlechterhierachie und Frauenarbeit seit der Vormoderne," in *Deutsch-Jüdische Geschichte als Geschlechtergeschichte*, ed. Stefanie Schüler-Springorum and Kirsten Heinesohn (Göttingen: Wallstein Verlag, 2006), 96.
33 Simone Lässig, "Religiöse Modernisierung, Geschlechterdiskurs und kulturelle Verbürgerlichung," in *Deutsch-Jüdische Geschichte als Geschlechtergeschichte*, ed. Stefanie Schüler-Springorum and Kirsten Heinsohn (Göttingen: Wallstein Verlag, 2006), 63.
34 Alfred Meyer, *My Attitudes towards Germany: Memoir*, Leo Baeck Institute New York, AR 25075, 4.
35 Paul Steiner, *Diary*, Leo Baeck Institute, AR25208, Entry March 12, 1938.
36 That does not mean it did not happen, but as masculinity needs to be understood as a template of manly behavior, a set of trials that men have to perpetually undergo as David Gilmore calls it, admitting to the failure to provide for one's family would have resulted in a loss of face for many Jewish men and a self-perceived and -inflicted emasculation.
37 Victor Klemperer, *I Shall Bear Witness, The Diaries of Victor Klemperer, 1933–1941*, 103.
38 Felix Fechenbach, *Mein Herz schlägt weiter. Briefe aus der Schutzhaft*, ed. Walther Victor (St. Gallen: Kultur Verlag, 1936), 12.
39 Ludwig Marum, *Briefe aus dem KZ Kislau*, ed. Elisabeth Marum-Lunau and Jörg Schadt (Karlsruhe: Müller Verlag, 1988), 50.
40 Ibid., 74.
41 Cohn, *No Justice in Germany: The Breslau Diaries, 1933–1941*, 6.
42 With the Nazi rise to power, about 37,000 German Jews left Germany immediately. This number declined in the following years but peaked again in 1938, with new waves of violence and antisemitic agitation. In 1938, about 36,000 Jews and in 1939, another 77,000 Jews left Germany (and by then Austria). At the outbreak of the Second World War, approximately two hundred thousand Jews remained in Germany (of 525,000 in 1933) and a further fifty-seven thousand in annexed Austria.
43 Alfred Elbau, *Von Neu Tempelhof in die Welt: Erinnerungen eines Berliner Juden*, United States Holocaust Memoiral Museum, RG 10.041, 51.
44 Salomon Riemer, "Letter," United States Holocaust Memorial Museum, AC 2009.383.
45 See: Brian Amkraut, *Between Home and Homeland: Youth Aliyah from Nazi Germany* (Tuscaloosa: University of Alabama Press, 2006).
46 Erich Frey, *Tagebuch*, trans. Alfred Elbau, United States Holocaust Memorial Museum, RG 10.041, 5.
47 Cohn, *No Justice in Germany: The Breslau Diaries, 1933–1941*, 6 and 40.

48 Kurt Rosenberg, *Diaries, 1916–1939*. Leo Baeck Institute New York, AR25279, Entry March 31, 1933.
49 Some of the first published works on the physical assaults against German Jews include *Die Stellung der Nationalsozialistischen Arbeiterpartei zur Judenfrage*, ed. Centralverein deutscher Staatsbürger jüdischen Glaubens (Berlin, 1932); *Die Lage der Juden in Deutschland 1933. Das Schwarzbuch—Tatsachen und Dokumente*, ed. Comite des Delegations Juives (Paris, 1933); *Ein Appell an das Gewissen der Welt! Ein Buch der Greuel: Die Opfer klagen an. Dachau, Brandenburg, Papenburg, Königstein, Lichtenstein, Colditz, Sachsenburg, Moringen, Hohnstein, Reichenbach, Sonnenburg*, ed. anonym (Karlsbad, 1934).
50 Claudia Koonz, *Mothers in the Fatherland: Women, the Family and Nazi Politics* (New York: St. Martin's Press, 1987), 349.
51 Kim Wünschmann, *Before Auschwitz: Jewish Prisoners in the Prewar Concentration Camps* (Cambridge: Harvard University Press, 2015), 102.
52 Pressmann, *Diaries*, March 5, 1933.
53 Cohn, *No Justice in Germany: The Breslau Diaries, 1933–1941*, 2.
54 Walter Tausk, *Breslauer Tagebuch, 1933-1940*, 4th ed. (Berlin: Rütten & Loening, 1988), 87.
55 Oatley, *Emotions*, 4.
56 Kurt Rosenberg, *Diaries, 1916–1939*, Leo Baeck Institute, AR 25279, April 14, 1933.
57 Wilhelm Buchheim, *Diaries*, Leo Baeck Institute New York, ME1535, 33.
58 Elizabeth Freund, *Memoir*, Leo Baeck Institute New York, ME153 MM24, 48.
59 Steiner, *Diary*, June 15, 1938.
60 See Christian Faludi, ed., *Die Juni-Aktion 1938: Eine Dokumentation zur Radikalisierung der Judenverfolgung* (Frankfurt am Main: Campus Verlag, 2013).
61 Alexander Szanto, *Memoir*, Leo Baeck Institute New York, ME638 MM76, 105.
62 Ben Barkow, Raphael Gross, and Michael Lenarz, eds., *Novemberpogrom 1938—Die Augenzeugenberichte der Wiener Library*, trans. S. Huebel (Berlin: Suhrkamp Verlag, 2008), 131 and 459.
63 Adolf Riesenfeld, *Diaries Volume 4*, Leo Baeck Institute New York, ME787, 49.
64 Cohn, *No Justice in Germany: The Breslau Diaries, 1933–1941*, 193.
65 Erich Bloch, *Antrag auf Entschädigung wegen Schaden an Körper und Gesundheit*, Archiv Gedenkstätte Deutscher Widerstand, Berlin.
66 Victor Klemperer, *To the Bitter End: The Diaries of Victor Klemperer, 1942–1945*, trans. Martin Chalmers (New York: Modern Library, 2001), 6, 8, 28, and 58.
67 This in no way means to downplay the idiosyncratic ways women in general and Jewish women in particular had suffered during the Holocaust. Important scholarship by Dalia Ofer, Marion Kaplan, Gisela Bock, and others have enriched our understanding of gendered female suffering and the female experience during this crucial time period. As most literature has concentrated

on the war years and the Holocaust, however, an imbalance has emerged that by and large ignored the six to seven years of Nazi rule prior to the war. During these years, victims of Nazi violence were primarily men. See: Kim Wünschmann, "Die Konzentrationslagererfahrungen deutsch-jüdischer Männer nach dem Novemberpogrom 1938," in *Wer bleibt, opfert seine Jahre, vielleicht sein Leben: Deutsche Juden, 1938–1941*, ed. Susanne Heim, Beate Meyer, and Francis Nicosia (Göttingen: Wallstein Verlag, 2010); Kim Wünschmann, *Before Auschwitz: Jewish Prisoners in the Prewar Concentration Camps* (Cambridge: Harvard University Press, 2015).

68 Rosenberg, *Diaries, 1916–1939*, Entry April 2, 1933.
69 Martin Hauser, *Wege jüdischer Selbstbehauptung: Tagebuchaufzeichnungen 1929–1967* (Berlin: Bundeszentrale für Politische Bildung, 1992), 51.
70 See for instance: Erna Segal, *You Shall Never Forget: Memoir*, Leo Baeck Institute New York, ME 594. MM 69.
71 Max Krakauer, *Lichter im Dunkeln: Flucht und Rettung eines jüdischen Ehepaars im Dritten Reich* (Stuttgart: Calwer Verlag, 1994), 16.
72 Tausk, *Breslauer Tagebuch*, 165.
73 Walter Bresser, *Vernehmungsprotokoll des Zeugen Walter Bresser*. Der Generalstaatsanwalt der Deutschen Demokratischen Republik May 9, 1963. Gedenkstätte Deutscher Widerstand Berlin.
74 Moritz Mandelkern, "In Our Hope," in *We Survived: Fourteen Histories of the Hidden and Hunted in Nazi Germany*, ed. Erich Boehm (New York: Basic Books, 2003), 222.
75 Kaplan, *Between Dignity and Despair*, 123.
76 Emil Schorsch, *Memoir*, Leo Baeck Institute New York, ME 575 MM 67, 11.
77 Gisela Bock, ed., *Genozid und Geschlecht: Jüdische Frauen im nationalsozialistischen Lagersystem* (Frankfurt am Main: Campus Verlag, 2005), 8.
78 Barbara H. Rosenwein, "Worrying about Emotions in History," *American Historical Review* 107, no. 3 (June 2002): 821–45.

8

Gangs in the Forest: The Construction of the Criminal Archetype in Post–Second World War Western Germany

Thomas J. Kehoe

Histories of post–Second World War Germany are replete with lurid descriptions of crime and social disorder, which has in turn frequently been blamed on non-Germans under the euphemism "DPs," short for "displaced persons."[1] That DPs are imagined to have committed crime frequently or that they comprised many (if not most) of the criminals in postwar Germany has only rarely been questioned.[2] Instead, assertions of excessive foreign criminality have followed the logic underpinning depictions of a more generalized crime wave: that war destroyed the social fabric and societal infrastructure that ensured lawfulness, resulting in widespread theft and looting, proliferation of gangs and group violence, and other forms of more insidious crime that together made for a slow and painful recovery after the Nazi surrender on May 7, 1945.[3] The "social disintegration" account is intuitively satisfying when considered against the destruction caused by the Second World War. Its explanatory power lay in supporting contradictory narratives fitting, for instance, both a "Zero Hour" (*Stunde Null*) interpretation of the end of war in which society came to a halt on May 7, and a continuity thesis of conflict and trauma continuing past surrender. The ubiquity of "social disintegration" has hindered its close interrogation, including of its origins, the historical phenomena it instantiates, and the emotional realities that may underlie it, all of which would be revealed by closer inspection.[4]

Of import, laying the blame for much of postwar crime on "vengeful DPs" and "DP gangs" is deeply problematic, though this interpretation partly derives from their frequent appearance in contemporary reports and documentation from the Allied military governments, German police and government reports, the

British and American press, and the rumors and complaints of civilians.[5] Fear of crime and foreign-perpetrated crime, in particular, were pervasive and almost universally felt. But extensive criminological and psychological scholarship suggests reasons to be skeptical of such claims, no matter how commonly or formally they were made. The emotional dimension to crime assessments is well established. People's beliefs about crime bear little relationship to the actual rate at which it occurs or the identities of the perpetrators.[6] On the broader social disintegration portrayal of postwar Germany, a few scholars have eroded the Hobbesian picture of postwar crime using military, court, and police documents. In so doing, they have shrunk the supposed duration of *en masse* disorder from years (1945–8), to between hours and months. But the psychological and emotional dimensions to postwar crime reporting remain largely unaddressed including the evident fixation on DP criminals by Germans and the Allied occupation forces.[7]

Inquiry is, therefore, required into the shared German-Allied focus on foreign criminality and the emotional realities it reflected. In this chapter I focus primarily on the British Zone of occupation, though shared command structures and preinvasion planning mean that any examination of the western occupation will necessarily touch on the Americans. In so doing, I examine the German and western Allies' construction of a foreign crime threat. In particular, why did Germans and the western Allies fix on a foreign crime threat and what did foreign criminals represent? And, why did the Allied occupiers seemingly endorse German constructions of foreign criminals as thuggish Poles, greedy Jews, and thieving Gypsies, each of which bore striking resemblance to Nazi caricatures?

As this chapter reveals, the focus on foreign "DP" criminals was not a straightforward extrapolation of German or the western Allies' fears derived from preexisting xenophobia and ethnic animosities. Nor did the Allies simply adopt Germans' long-standing ethnicized and racialized fears, which had been further cultivated by the Nazis during their thirteen years in power. Rather, the postwar construction of a threat from foreign and DP criminals derived from historical antecedents original to the Allies and the Germans, and the interaction of these respective ideas within the challenging postwar context. The profound psychological trauma, economic upheaval, social and societal fragility, and an absence of German national sovereignty together shaped new fears that mingled with the old, and in turn fostered new fantasies about the identity of criminals and their crimes.

Amidst the Disorder: Allied Crime Assessments in 1945

On July 30, 1945, British military government (MG) detachment 622 replaced detachment 808 and took responsibility for Cologne. These "detachments" were specialized units comprising officers that had received specific training in foreign civil affairs and occupation management, and they were responsible for administering the occupation of Germany. By design and necessity they were small, consisting of between five and thirty officers, and an equal number of enlisted personnel. Detachment size was contingent on the population of the urban (*Stadt-*) or rural district (*Landkreis*) to which each was assigned. They were also granted near full autonomy for district governance, wielding power over everything from local criminal justice, to housing and street repair. In keeping with the primary demands of ongoing war, their first objective was pacifying the local population.[8]

Civil order remained a priority through the entirety of the postwar occupation, which helps explain the initial attention detachment 622 gave to lawlessness. On arrival in Cologne, the MG officers (MGOs) quickly discovered that crime remained a major problem in the city. There were 153 arrests made in the detachment's first week and social disorder was hindering reconstruction. The German "Kripo" (criminal police) were in disarray, denying the British effective help. Detachment 808 had uncovered the city's German police records, but they were in "great disorder" and offered little useful information on repeat offenders or preexisting criminal networks. Not that Nazi-era intelligence would have been very helpful to the British. They viewed crime in the city as a post-conflict event deriving from removal of Nazi-era controls and the liberation of the regime's former slaves and persecutes. "Eastern DPs" were believed to be the primary criminals. This euphemism—along with "Ausländer," (from "foreigner" in German) and the generic "DP"—was an Allied catchall for non-Germans. It primarily denoted former Nazi victims such as Poles, other Slavs, Jews, and Gypsies. In Cologne, even three months after the end of the war, offenses by this broad group of non-Germans allegedly "still remained high."[9]

There are good reasons to be skeptical of these British assessments of crime in Cologne and its supposed DP perpetrators. For one, while the Nazis had fanned long-standing German bigotries toward these groups, the British and the Americans carried similar prejudices into Germany. Britain had a long history of oscillating between semi-acceptance and rejection of Jews, and anti-Gypsy and -Slavic feelings were entrenched.[10] In the United States, anti-Semitism was more embedded in the national consciousness, and the influx of immigrants in the late nineteenth and early twentieth centuries had exported old world ethnic animosities, while simultaneously fanning new anti-immigrant sentiments in the existing American populace.[11]

War and occupation created a new context for these preexisting prejudices. Contrary to detachment 622's assessment, Cologne's crime problem actually began well before the British occupation. The city was a major industrial center and six years of war had left it a blasted wreck in 1945. The Allies had bombed it nearly three hundred times through the war and as Nazi Germany was strangled in late 1944 by assaults on three fronts, resources became thin leading to petty crime and the emergence of a massive black market. The Nazis responded harshly to all crime, classing even minor offenses as "defeatism," an offense punishable by death. Mass public executions became common as the end of the war neared, but such displays did nothing to assuage basic human needs or dissuade survival-driven crime.[12] And then, during the final battle for Cologne, the Americans and the British laid siege before American forces assaulted. The city became essentially hell on earth during March 1945 as starving Germans were forced by ardent Nazis on the threat of summary execution to fight to the death against an inevitable American victory. The carnage was worse just to the north where the Americans and the British formed the infamous "Ruhr Pocket," sealing German civilians and the remaining military forces inside Nazi Germany's industrial heartland. Social disorder and reciprocal Nazi violence became routine, and American records from the units enforcing the perimeter show patterns of mass looting bleeding into the surrounding territories.[13]

Although offering some of the more extreme examples, events in Cologne and the Ruhr were part of a pattern that unfolded across Germany during the Allies' invasion from the west. As conquest became imminent, petty crime rose, and it was met by extreme retaliatory violence by the remaining committed Nazis. Daily life effectively stopped during combat, but in its immediate aftermath disorder reigned. Violence and crime by former Nazi slaves was just one part of a much larger wave of criminality that included Germans and Allied soldiers who looted, assaulted, raped, and even committed murder.[14] Stepping into this maelstrom, MG detachments' first task was to restore a semblance of order, which was an especially mammoth undertaking in the cities and frequently led to MGOs' reporting it a near impossibility.[15]

In cities like Cologne, instability continued for months after the initial occupation. Cities also became collection centers for the masses of transient DPs and internal German refugees. Every day, urban MG detachments like 622 faced new arrivals of former victims of the Nazi regime, Germans returning home, and internally displaced peoples, all of whom needed food and shelter. MGOs lacked any means of predicting the number of new arrivals each day. The relative autonomy each detachment enjoyed in its district meant limited communication with neighboring detachments and, consequently, a frustrating reality of being solely responsible for an area under constant pressure from an unknown external world.[16]

While the humanitarian crisis hindered the restoration of order in the cities, the situation was different in the countryside where the transfer to Allied control had often occurred peacefully and the war left few physical scars. However, the comparative normality of rural Germany created its own problems. Local Germans worried about transient DPs and gangs that could raid travelers and small communities and then melt back into the woods. MGOs were concerned that pro-Nazi partisans could do the same. When it quickly became apparent that there was no organized German resistance, MGOs turned their attention to the potential threat from violent criminals and gangs. Such concerns stemmed from MG training, which taught MGOs to preemptively identify and prevent sources of disorder. Yet, crime was rarely a major issue in the countryside. Military court records, intelligence reports, and police investigation files reveal little genuine disorder. Most offenses were minor violations of Allied restrictions on civil controls including curfews and on travel. Within days—at most weeks—the primary concern for rural MG detachments was restoring basic administrative functions and local infrastructure.[17]

Despite often taking longer in the cities, routine administrative issues quickly came to dominate detachments' daily concerns over the summer of 1945. Even so, in both the cities and the countryside, a pervasive fear of crime and a more fundamental social disorder remained. Postwar society appeared fragile. MGOs consistently reported concerns about a failing recovery and threats from nearly every quarter including widespread petty crime and a ubiquitous black market. They also near uniformly divided their reporting of arrests and prosecutions into Germans and DPs. This division became standard across the British Zone by mid-1946. Detachments also tended to consider crime as 622 did in Cologne; they linked DPs as a group to a generalized threat, which remained at the fore of MGOs' thinking even as reconstruction progressed peacefully.[18]

Such attribution helps explain why DPs have tended to bear the brunt of criminal responsibility in historical writing, though links between the psychology of postwar space and actual social conditions is also instrumental. For many historians, the Second World War and the resulting violent conquest of Germany created such profound societal instability and a depth of psychological trauma that peace could not easily be restored in the aftermath. Moreover, trauma has often been conceptually tied to social interactions, such that "social disintegration" becomes an instantiated historical phenomenon reflective of individual and group psychic damage. It follows this logic that DPs were supposedly more prone than Germans to participate in criminal and disorderly behavior. The Nazis had brutalized the major ethnic groups that became DPs. These people had been torn from their families and the social and societal networks that provided security and a sense of personal identity. After the war, they were displaced, homeless, and continued to lack many of the structures that the Nazis destroyed.[19]

This extrapolation of psychic injury to social behavior provides a (subtly) confirmatory framework for interpreting the plethora of German and MG reports, and stories in the press on DP crimes and gangs. Such reasoning is evident in many of the earliest histories of the postwar, which uncritically take as *fait accompli* Allied and German testimonies of newly liberated DPs exacting vicious, drunken revenge on victimized Germans. Such framing further instantiates in the historical record gangs of DPs disconnected from German social and societal structures that were so powerful they threatened the Allies' military forces.[20] The first studies of postwar crime conducted in the late 1940s by Adolf Schönke and Karl S. Bader fix on such gangs as indicators of a wider breakdown in social order and law enforcement.[21] It is perhaps understandable that such imagery was propagated at the time, but it has also since remained a staple of postwar narratives. Herbert Kosyra's claim that "no one anywhere was safe" from roaming gangs that committed armed robberies, rapes, and murder is in the mainstream rather than on the fringe. Authors including Christoph Klessmann, Alexander Häusser, and Gordian Maugg, popular writers Giles MacDonogh and Keith Lowe, and even Richard J. Evans portray postwar Germany as nearing a Hobbesian state of disorder in which gangs ruled.[22]

Predictions, Crisis, and the Allies' Fear

MGOs' concerns about disorder during the occupation in part grew from predictions made prior to the invasion. It was common in briefing materials to suggest that severe social unrest would follow Nazi Germany's defeat. Such thinking derived from assumptions about the results of large-scale war and Nazi brutality. The Allies were aware of the Nazis' forced labor programs and extensive concentration camp network, and after the Americans, British, and

Soviets agreed at Casablanca in January 1943 to seek the total defeat of Nazi Germany, military planners in London and Washington began preparing for a full occupation and its humanitarian consequences. From late 1943, the Supreme Headquarters Allied Expeditionary Forces (SHAEF)—the supra-Allied command structure in the west covering American, British, Commonwealth, and other Allied forces—developed instructional manuals and handbooks warning MGOs that they would likely encounter human blight in Germany. Slave laborers, and so-called racial and ideological enemies of the Nazi state would be desperate and volatile when liberated, planners predicted. MGOs were told that if not properly controlled these desperate people could and would wreak havoc on efforts to ensure the peace.[23]

To the British and American militaries, such humanitarian strife was nearly as problematic as active German resistance. Long colonial experience had taught the British that persistent disorder—regardless of its cause—could become the ferment for native partisans.[24] The Americans reached similar conclusions from their own overseas experiences.[25] And the first incursions into Germany in September 1944, around Aachen on the Dutch-Belgian border, appeared to confirm these predictions. Streams of German civilians and liberated slave laborers crowded the advancing Allied forces creating logistical obstacles.[26] There was not anarchy, though SHAEF told officers to prepare for disorder and armed resistance once the initial "shock" of combat had dissipated. These warnings became more earnest as preparations for the final assault into Nazi Germany were made over the winter of 1944–5. MGOs in rear staging areas were told to expect generalized disorder and active Nazi resistance, and to do virtually whatever was necessary to prevent both.[27]

The level of destruction frequently shocked MGOs once they arrived in German cities. It was difficult to imagine that social disorder did not accompany the wreckage, an inference that extended from their concerns about ensuring the peace in a fragile postwar society. For the MGOs of detachment 622, their first shock came in late 1944. At that time, the detachment was stationed on the German–Dutch border and found the black market, "exist[ing] on a far larger scale than [the officers] at first believed." Despite "insufficient rations" being an understandable cause for illegal trade, the detachment commander was quick to label participants "parasites" and all such activity an "evil," evidence of a more profound post-conflict social decay. "A nation ensnared in the black market has no future left," he wrote.[28]

Such feelings about the danger of criminality complemented detachments' interpretation of their orders to quell dissent and resistance, and maintain order. MGOs formulaically applied civil controls including curfews and travel restrictions on occupied Germans, and made arrests for minor infractions, often regardless of mitigating circumstances.[29] But beyond this assertion of strict martial law, they also proactively searched for hidden sources of disorder. Among these were potential anti-Allied partisans such as former Nazis who hid their party affiliations and also criminals and centers for criminal activity; though preventing crime became the more pressing concern as fear of German resistance diminished.[30]

MG's security priorities and their enforcement raise questions about more hyperbolic historical assessments of postwar disorder arising from—what one collection of authors from the RAND Corporation calls—a "law and order gap."[31] This is not to say postwar conditions in the west were peaceful. Law breaking was ubiquitous throughout much of the occupation, driven in large measure by a thriving black market. People struggled on inadequate rations that at times fell as low as 1,000 calories per day. Classic strain theory could explain the crime that emerged during this time, though the near universality of the postwar strain created a unique environment where rather than behaviors being driven by the "loftier" goals—such as social status—posited in the original theory, everybody sought basic survival and engaged in whatever behavior was necessary to live.[32] As one observer wrote at the time, "nearly everyone" turned to illegal trade and petty crime in order to supplement their rations and stay alive.[33] Within the context of strictly enforced martial law, even petty law breaking led to frequent collisions with MG criminal justice, so much so in fact that there were frequently backlogs for MG courts. Especially in heavily war-damaged cities like Cologne, there were numerous arrests and the frontline MG "summary" courts often heard upwards of fifty cases per day for curfew violations and violations of travel restrictions, along with minor thefts, possession of stolen property (typically Allied food rations), and black market participation.[34]

But this strain on occupation administration does not support claims of anything like postwar anarchy, though to the authorities at the time, the frequency of minor offenses suggested a dangerous willingness among civilians to flout the law. More serious offenses only exacerbated these fears, becoming evidence of a more profound social and moral rot underneath the apparent criminality.[35] There was also sufficient foreign-perpetrated crime to sustain MGOs' concerns about DPs. In the tumult surrounding the end of the war and over the months that followed, some DPs did loot German homes; commit armed robberies and assaults; and perpetrate violent crimes including rape and murder. To the Allies, a disproportionate number of criminals and gang members appeared to be DPs, a fact confirmed by their overrepresentation in the higher MG courts. Only the most serious cases were referred to the higher "intermediate" and "general" MG courts for trial. During detachment 622's first month in Cologne, there were eleven defendants tried and convicted in the city's highest MG court—the Cologne General Court—for illegally possessing a firearm. Five were Poles and they received lengthy sentences in prison. Another Pole was tried and convicted of murder and sentenced to death.[36]

As in virtually any setting, serious and violent crimes had an outsized impact on popular impressions of criminality, from which MGOs were not exempt. For instance, 35-year-old Pole Felix Sikowski was brought to trial in the Cologne General Court on September 29, 1945 charged along with three other gang members with committing multiple thefts and armed robberies. Their hearing immediately followed that of two other young Poles charged and convicted for illegally possessing firearms. The same panel of British officers sat as judges in both cases. They had given the first two men three-year prison sentences. Sikowski and his compatriots were also convicted. Sikowski was deported to Poland and the other two were each sentenced to five-years imprisonment.[37]

British MGOs recorded the ethnicities of these defendants in the registers primarily for practical purposes. DPs were classed as United Nations Personnel and for their protection exempted from German criminal justice. Foreigners could also be deported. But when aligned with the overwhelming focus on DP criminals in weekly, monthly, and quarterly reports from all levels of MG—often in contrast to figures showing a far greater number of German-perpetrated offenses –identifying non-German criminals also likely contributed to beliefs about a DP crime wave.

Higher-level court cases represented only a tiny proportion of overall criminality, most of which was comparatively minor. MGOs nonetheless routinely inferred that those arrested merely reflected the tip of the iceberg. As the detachment commander of 622 wrote in late 1944, for MGOs, serious crimes— no matter how infrequently they actually occurred—became an exemplar of the deeper social disintegration in Germany, which was demonstrated by widespread black market trade and extensive petty criminality. That DPs were overrepresented in trials for serious crimes no doubt further helped sustain beliefs about an unseen serious crime problem.[38]

German Fears

Violent crimes by DPs similarly helped support the German fixation on foreign criminality. At the end of July 1945, German police in Hanover reported that "90 percent of all crime [in the city was] the work of DPs." Moreover, crime remained "particularly high" in July 1945, though it had "reached its peak during the period just before and immediately after the occupation." Police provided a list of reported incidents for the seven-week period from May 15 to July 1 that suggested staggering levels of crime. Violent offenses included twenty-nine murders and manslaughters, forty-four incidents of "grievous bodily harm," and seven more assaults resulting in death. There were additionally fifty-one rape cases and nineteen "indecent assaults." Extrapolated to a yearly incidence for a population estimated to be between 280,000 and 300,000, the rate of criminal killings alone (murders, manslaughters, and "grievous bodily harm resulting in death") would have been approximately 95 per 100,000 ([36/7 weeks x 52 weeks]/280,000 x 100,000 = 95) against historic trends in Germany of between 1 and 4 per 100,000.[39] The rate of offenses against property was supposedly even worse. In the same period there had allegedly been 680 cases of "plundering," 2,895 robberies, 4,606 armed robberies, 1,186 "serious thefts," and 508 cases of "simple larceny."[40]

The Hanover police knew where the burden of responsibility lay: "It is thought that the high crime incidence can be attributed mainly to (a) the activities of DPs and the lack of control the German police have over these individuals, (b) the disarming of the German police, and (c) the lack of preventive and protective police measures during curfew hours."[41] The data they provided and their claims of insufficient ability to police DPs provide context for their asserting that DP crime not only "continue[d] to be high" in late July, but that it included, "the usual murder, rape, and wholesale looting of food stuffs."[42] Moreover, in the view of the police, this crime represented devolution of the social order into something like anarchy: "In some areas, looting expeditions [were being] conducted as minor military operations." DP looting parties were allegedly "covered by an armed flank guard" that "did NOT [capitals in original text] hesitate to open fire to cover a withdrawal."[43]

There are again good reasons to treat such claims cautiously. For one, it is difficult to imagine such extreme disorder existed alongside MG's rigid enforcement of social order, a picture maintained in Hanover's MG court data. The majority of the defendants in Hanover's MG courts were German and most offences were minor violations of curfews and other civil restrictions.[44] That the assertions were also made on the basis of relatively few salient criminal incidents further suggests a considerable distance between the police perception of crime and the picture that emerges from the available criminal justice data. For the period from July 19 to July 31, 1945, for instance, Hanover police reported that "Russians" had robbed employees of the Reich postal service on numerous occasions. Though making sweeping claims of a foreign crime epidemic, they cited just two examples. One employee was stabbed with a bayonet, and his bicycle and mailbag were stolen. Another was robbed of everything he had, including the clothes he was wearing. The victims, and in turn the police chief and the city mayor, claimed these crimes were the work of Russian DPs; yet no perpetrators were caught and evidence for their ethnicity was based entirely on inferences made by the victims.[45]

Such deviation between claimed conditions and the available examples could be indicative of weak law enforcement, such that most perpetrators escaped prosecution and, therefore, crimes do not appear in the available criminal justice data. Court and police data is always a subset of the actual rate of crime, which is a well-known problem in criminological studies and even more so in analyses of historic crime. Other evidence can shore up conclusions however, and in his exploration of postwar rural policing in Bavaria, Jose Canoy found a similar pattern of German crime reporting deviating significantly from the other available data. He argues that Germans quickly "foreignized" crime and attributed virtually all of it to non-Germans. The result was greater police attention to foreign criminality and consensus around foreign responsibility for most unsolved offenses.[46]

There are many other examples of this process of targeting specific groups in response to beliefs about their criminal inclinations; such behavior rarely reflects deliberate manipulation of evidence or an attempt to vindicate a group at the expense of another. Rather, confirmatory bias writ large appears to drive the process and only limited salient examples are required to spur the continuation of such perceptions.[47] In the postwar west, German police priorities reflected popular beliefs about extensive foreign criminality, deriving from what Richard Bessel notes was the very presence of DPs being evidence for "a world turned upside down" in which former Nazi victims were now masters.[48] The fear this inversion provoked helped drive beliefs about crime best reflected in the rumors that abounded about rampaging criminals, imminent social collapse, and the handover of the western Zones to the Soviets, among others.[49] All of these fear-driven stories frustrated MGO's attempts to ensure the peace by upsetting locals who were rarely assuaged by counterarguments. Officers, however, tended to understand that Germans' absence of knowledge about wider conditions or their national future created fertile ground for fearful speculation. Occupation planners predicted the problem and made "dissemination of any rumor calculated to alarm or excite the people" punishable under the MG legal code by any prison term up to and including life, though even the threat of lengthy imprisonment rarely prevented such stories circulating.[50] For the most part, MGOs were forced to monitor them and offer factual counters when facing questions from locals, though problematically, local MGOs were often little better informed than the Germans they governed.[51]

Inability to stem the tide of virulent rumors meant that stories about foreign criminals circulated widely, frequently, and were readily accepted, even if they were largely detached from observable conditions and based on multiplications of single events or even pure fantasy.[52] For instance, in response to rumors about violent DP gangs roaming the countryside, farming families would routinely take turns standing watch over their properties, convinced the threat from these criminals was imminent. Germans were nearly always portrayed as the victims in these crime stories, suffering horrific depredations at the hands of Poles, Jews, and other traditional foci for their ethnic animosities. Such claims—especially in the frequency of crime they asserted—were rarely substantiated. More often than not, purveyors of rumors were two or three steps removed from an alleged criminal incident. The disconnection between the horrors described in these rumors and the account of conditions available from other contemporary evidence suggested to Canoy that rumors were likely multiplying salient criminal incidents.[53] This was not an intentional process but rather an emergent one in keeping with the spread of crime wave beliefs in other societies. Its identification did, however, lead Canoy to question how accurately rumors and stories described crime in postwar Germany and whether it "was really that violent a place in historical terms?"[54]

His question can be more broadly applied to the problem of DP crime. Outside the German context, fear-driven rumors have frequently been the antecedents of "crime wave" hysteria and "moral panics," but rumors about crime also tend to have deeper roots that are historic- and contextually-specific.[55] In postwar western Germany, repeated assertions by the Hanover police of their inability to exercise control over DPs is revealing of German resentment about their lack sovereignty under Allied rule. The police were more emphatic in a document from late July 1945. In their view, the DP crime they believed was occurring was largely due to German police having "NO [capitals in original text] jurisdiction at that time [over DPs]."[56]

Police were frustrated by Allied restrictions that prevented them from being in a position to protect ordinary German civilians from real or imagined threats, but their expression of these feelings also expose the deeper ethno-nationalist origins of Germans' fixation on DP criminals, which subjugation to foreign military rule exacerbated. The labels German police and administrators applied to criminals, such as "DP" and "gangs," were interchangeable with more specific references to "Polish criminals" and "marauding Polish gangs," itinerant and thieving Gypsies, and deceitful "Jewish DPs." This official terminology aligned with the rumors circulating in the wider community about German victimization. In the immediate aftermath of the Third Reich, the parallel proliferation of fear about foreign criminality expressed as rumors and racialized terminology is unsurprising. Postwar xenophobia extended racialized tropes that Nazi propagandists had carefully curated and cultivated. The Nazis' classification of these non-Germans as "subhuman" (*Untermenschen*) became the basis for their exclusion from Nazism's "Aryan" racial national community (*Volksgemeinschaft*) and, ultimately, for their enslavement and extermination.[57]

Such thinking was not original to the Nazis, who instead tapped a deep well of German ethnic, religious, and nationalist tensions. Anti-Semitism has a long history in Germany and its racialization predated Hitler's particular conception of it, and it was certainly part of the conceptualization of postwar DP criminals.[58] But the postwar fixation on Poles, Slavs, and Gypsies provides insight into the extent to which old concepts of German *Kultur* shaped construction of the archetypal DP criminal for ordinary Germans. In the postwar west, non-German peoples were negatively contrasted with Germans. They were demonized as lacking civility and moral character, and were therefore by default believed to be more prone to criminal behavior. These groups had, like Jews, been consistent targets of German animosities for centuries, though in a somewhat different fashion. Rather than living among Germans, they were cast as ethnic enemies at the borders of German civilization and condemned for their supposedly "uncivilized" way of life. As Charissa Kurda shows in her chapter in this book, during the late nineteenth century, successive *Kaiserreich* governments made repeated efforts to stop Gypsy itinerancy and force them to accept a settled lifestyle.[59] These efforts followed other policies designed to "Germanize" the empire—notably Otto von Bismarck's *Kulturkampf* against Poles during the 1870s—that voiced a similar fear of encroachment into German linguistic and cultural space.[60]

Official government policies reflected a deeper German fascination and fear of the "Slavic" east (though this is now an understandably problematic term). Germans who ventured to the Prussian frontier were, according to Kristin Kopp, believed to be in danger of moral debasement. Fictional stories abounded of German encounters with the wild, uncultured, and amoral peoples believed to exist there on the edge of German society. Such fears have clear parallels with the postwar construction of criminality as a foreign tide swamping the traditional German heartland in the west.[61]

Postwar fears drew from these older ideas about invasion and direct antecedents in the Nazi period. As Jeffrey Herf argues, the Nazis formulated racial policies on belief in Aryan supremacy and from a place of genuine existential fear about the threat non-German peoples posed to Germany's racial and national integrity.[62] They turned to these fearful underpinnings of their ideology when attempting to steel Germans against Allied invasion. In the closing months of the war, Nazi propaganda portrayed "subhuman" Russians, Slavs, and black American and French colonial soldiers raping and murdering Germans in the event of an Allied victory. The Nazis also claimed that the Allies would release Germany's enslaved racial enemies, who would in turn exact revenge. This propaganda and the prospect of defeat brought to the fore a sublimated culture of anxiety about foreign domination and the prospects for Germans in a post-Nazi world.[63]

Agreement

Although having different origins, the Allies' concerns and German fears coalesced into a shared fixation on foreign criminality early in the occupation. This was a profound change for western Allied soldiers (perhaps particularly the British), many of whom were initially deeply antagonistic toward Germans for the war, and sympathetic to Nazism's victims. But within months of the war's end, it was common for American and British MGOs to praise German traits—fortitude, respect for authority, and apparent willingness to abide by martial law—in contrast to DPs who were cast as the antithesis. Such thinking only became more entrenched. By mid-1946, assertions like that of the MG detachment in Oldenburg in Lower Saxony were typical: that local German discipline and work ethic "was always … good."[64] Such laudatory assessments were juxtaposed against DP's propensity for disorder and crime. The same report from Oldenburg documented the imposition of greater restrictions on DP camps because of the negative effects that bad behavior by the inhabitants was having on local Germans. According to the German police, "Residents in the immediate vicinity of the camps" were complaining about "being constantly pestered by Latvians." DPs were engaged in selling various black market items including illegal distilled alcohol from an "illicit distillery."[65]

Simplified perceptions of each group's behavior bolstered a dichotomized view of "law-abiding Germans" versus disorderly non-German DPs.[66] Context also facilitated this meeting of the minds. As Robert Abzug and more recently Susan Carruthers point out, the roots of the western Allies' particularly negative feelings toward DPs extended beyond preexisting prejudices and began at their first encounters in Germany in 1945. Liberating Nazi forced labor and concentration camps created complex and variegated responses among American and British soldiers. The Nazis had badly mistreated their forced laborers and concentration camp inmates, and then left them in a terrible state, and Allied soldiers frequently felt sorry for them and/or pitied them. But the liberators were often simultaneously horrified by the inmates' stench, appearance, and their wanton celebrations of liberty, which included everything from drinking and eating until passing out, to open fornication. The disgust such sights engendered was difficult to overcome and many of the occupiers' lasting impressions were shaped by these initial encounters.[67]

DPs were then separated from Germans and privileged above them in the Allies' criminal justice system. Official segregation reinforced DPs' separation from ordinary German society, which was especially problematic in an occupation that devolved power to near-autonomous district-level MG detachments. These small detachments relied on Germans for nearly every aspect of local governance beyond criminal justice, and increasingly that too from mid-1946 onward.[68] Such reliance required close working relationships that tended to foster positive assessments among Allied officers. As the British Frontier Control Service—responsible for monitoring the zonal borders—noted in its praise of German officers, their efficiency was "generally increasing due to closer working relations with local British officers." DPs, however, were permanently outside this collaborative governance and they also tended to create logistical and managerial problems due to their transience.[69]

Virtually any crime by a DP separated them further. And, as has frequently been shown in criminological studies, only a few crimes are required to motivate crime fears and seed a mythology about a particular minority group's propensity for criminal behavior.[70] Even though fear of crime led Germans and the Allies to exaggerate the frequency of DP crimes, there were more than enough serious offenses by DPs to maintain the perceptions. DP riots and fights with local Germans, for example, were not uncommon. One of the most sensational occurred in Paderborn, North Rhein-Westphalia on July 19, 1945. Approximately hundred residents of the local DP camp raided the town following a rumor that Germans had victimized several of their number. Carrying an assortment of makeshift weapons, they burned homes, assaulted Germans, and murdered seven. Nearly fifty DPs were arrested when British forces arrived to quell the disturbance and thirty-nine were found guilty of various crimes including murder. Four were sentenced to death.[71]

Although highlighting the degree of reciprocal tensions between DPs and Germans, rioting and similar offenses were still comparatively rare. More typical serious and violent crimes committed by DPs were somewhat more common. Yugoslav Rade Julic, for instance, appeared in the Oldenburg General Court on July 3, 1945 charged with murder for "killing a person in a malicious and cruel manner." The court took only a few hours to convict the 18-year-old and then sentenced him to death, though his punishment was later reduced to life imprisonment and, eventually, to five years.[72] In February the following year, two Poles Antoni Stochniatck and Josef Glinski were tried in the Hanover General Court for multiple offenses including looting, illegal firearm possession, and rape. These crimes were not only terrible, they indicated to the court the perpetrators' recidivism, and both were convicted and received seven years in prison.[73]

Although these crimes were horrific and DPs appeared to be overrepresented, they too were comparatively rare. Each incident nonetheless fed narratives of German victimization and appeared to confirm belief in a broader postwar social instability. Both of these narratives in turn sprang from a more strident fear among Germans about the very integrity of their society during the occupation. Conquest had appeared to wipe away police and governmental structures, the bases of a traditional authoritarian culture that had for centuries reinforced feelings of personal, familial, and community security. As Brian Chapman shows in his formative work on the history of German policing, the German *Polizeistaat* was different from the term "police state," as it is now commonly used as a pejorative. Historically in Germany, the *Polizeistaat* was a legitimate form of government, reflecting the exercise of executive control over the predominately rural society of the eighteenth and nineteenth centuries. It can be found in its nascent form under Prussia's Frederick the Great but was solidified across Germany during Napoleon's occupation. During French rule, the *gendarmerie* was the only connection between the citizenry and the state, and its officers reflected executive power. There were rarely more than one or two officers in most villages and small towns, but they were responsible for regulating social interactions to maintain the social order, which required enforcing moral as well as legal standards. This form of *Polizeistaat* was maintained following Napoleon's expulsion and then through the *Kaisereich*.[74]

Small *gendarmerie*-style police forces could not simply enforce citizens' compliance. They instead relied on community-aided surveillance to maintain their authority and assure state control. With the help of local citizens laterally observing their neighbors, a few officers were able to monitor their communities. The Nazis capitalized on these existing authoritarian systems and culture to facilitate policing, and bend the people to their own warped moral and social aims. Sheila Fitzpatrick and Robert Gellately lead a valuable literature exploring how a culture of denunciation aided popular adherence to Nazi rule. Neighbors and family members helped the regime by invading and observing private space, and in turn propagating a seemingly outsized presence of the police—especially organizations like the Gestapo—that promoted a general terror.[75]

Fitzpatrick and Gellately point out that there is a fine line between neighbor observation and "denunciation." Broadly defined, the latter is a more public act of official condemnation. To go one step further, denunciation also ingratiates the denouncer with the authorities in contrast to the denounced person who is publicly ostracized. It is worthwhile drawing these distinctions, lest we fall into a conceptually bizarre space where more benign forms of neighborhood watch are considered essentially the same as the denunciation that frequently occurs in authoritarian and totalitarian regimes. But the two are not so distinct in practice, instead existing on a sliding scale of magnitude, which is guided by the demands of the state and the sociohistorical context. Informing on potential criminal acts is good civic duty in a benign society, and may result in an investigation and prosecution if the identified person has violated the law. In a Nazi-like state, informing police potentially carries more extreme consequences, especially if denouncing an "illegal" person and could result in summary execution. When reduced to their bases, each is an example of informing on a potential violation of civic norms and is underpinned by the same lateral, community-based observation. It is the nature of the norms and consequences that differ, and that should for the potential informer guide the moral calculus.[76]

MG readily satisfied a powerful desire among Germans for a continuation of the underlying pre-Nazi culture of authoritarianism and its accompanying societal structures. In early 1946, MG in the American Zone lifted civilian curfews in an effort to boost what the authorities saw as flagging German morale. As in the British Zone, curfews had been strictly enforced and were widely disliked. But, in a surprise to American authorities, the move instead provoked outrage among Germans. Local governments speaking on behalf of their constituents claimed that the curfews curtailed DP gangs roaming and pillaging at night, and, therefore, made communities safer. Their objections were so furious that within weeks Zonal MG returned discretion to impose curfews to local MG detachments on a case-by-case basis and many restored them.[77]

Despite German fears, MG maintained the central features of authoritarian culture and policing, for instance, like prior German governments, MG relied on civilian assistance to detect crime.[78] Germans regularly attempted to aid investigations, raising their suspicions about DP criminals and unknown persons that had moved into the local area. Informants were so emphatic that MGOs were sometimes reticent to embrace such seemingly antidemocratic behaviors or endorse them. For the most part though, German authoritarian culture was a boon for military control. Civilian surveillance aided intelligence gathering, and existing German police priorities and patterns of behavior aligned with MG's strict civil controls. German police understood how to meet MG's aim of monitoring and controlling civilian movements, registering new arrivals, identifying non-residents, and conducting surveillance on suspected criminals.

Continuation of an authoritarian culture further helps explain an outsized fear of foreign criminals and its particular fixation on DP gangs. Police and civilian surveillance ensured non-Germans were identified and collectively labeled aliens. Ascribing a propensity for gang behavior to them solidified their otherness, applying to them the worst characteristics of being outside regular German society. Such reinforcing progressions in logic are all too common when minority groups are associated with criminality, known in the criminological literature as "group criminalization." Gangs are not only threatening in the violence and amorality inherently ascribed to them; but they also represent an alternative societal structure in opposition to the majority, which in turn reinforces the ostracism of the broader minority group associated with them. And similar to virtually all crime fear, fear of gangs is bolstered by any incident vaguely attributable to the overarching group, and though perhaps rare in the sweep of postwar criminality, there were again just enough salient group cases to support such fear-driven inferences because, as the literature on group criminalization shows, often just one incident is sufficient to maintain prejudiced, fear-driven beliefs.[79]

Fragility, Recovery, and Persistent Fear

MGOs and Germans remained concerned about societal fragility even after the founding of the Federal Republic of (West) Germany in 1949, and Allied diplomatic oversight replaced the military occupation. In January 1950, the British Army of the Rhine (BAOR) conducted an investigation into "criminal activity in DP camps in the British Zone."[80] Most of the nearly seven million DPs moving around Germany in 1945 were repatriated by that Christmas or through 1946, and as the BAOR report notes, there were only between 150,000 and 180,000 DPs left in the British Zone in 1950 against a German population of 24 million.[81] These remaining DPs had few options. They either could not—or would not—return East to their former homes under Soviet control, or they were stateless. All were seeking asylum in the west and most would eventually end up far afield in places like the United States, Canada, and Australia.[82] In Germany however, camp life was bleak. They were for the most part well provided for in the camps, but they had little opportunity for work or entertainment, and their movements were heavily restricted. Such conditions tend to breed social disorder, and in western Germany many DP camps had thriving black markets and petty crime was common.[83]

But while deserving attention, the BAOR's primary concern was not DPs' living conditions or crime *inside* the camps. They instead focused on charting "the extent to which criminal activities [across the Zone] [could] be traced to DP camps." The analysis extended the bifurcation of crime analysis between Germans and non-Germans that had existed from early in the occupation, and when divided, the available data appeared to support British concerns about DP behaviors. According to the report: "Police statistics on crime show that on a ratio basis the percentage of crimes by DPs [exceeded] that of the indigenous (German) population." DPs were also arrested at a rate for their population that vastly exceeded that for Germans. And worryingly for the British, "The more serious the crime the greater the disparity."[84]

From early in the occupation crime statistics provided powerful evidence to the Allies that DPs were more criminal than Germans. And by 1950, each set of new findings tended to reinforce existing thinking. As the BAOR report notes, "There is little doubt that this greater incidence of crime among the DPs may be traced to the fact that these unhappy people, having been torn away from their homes and countries and subjected to hardship and ill-treatment over a number of years have now psychologically come to believe that the German is 'fair game.'" In the British assessment, camp life only entrenched this psychological damage because it did "little to instill any feeling of civic responsibility." Although at once a seemingly fair sociological explanation of how trauma and camp conditions could lead to resentment and higher levels of criminal behavior, this reasoning also managed to (not so subtly) bend the experience of Nazi brutality into a rationale for DPs' criminal predispositions, while simultaneously casting Germans as victims.[85]

Nor did structural and historical explanations for DP crime significantly mitigate DPs' culpability, in the British view. After recognizing that camp life could motivate crime, the BAOR report posits that an improving German economy would only likely increase serious crime by DPs because it would lead to "declining profits from the black market." The problem, apparently, was that ingrained criminal inclinations would necessitate recidivism. It was an insight highlighted by the assertion that economic improvement would expose "habitual criminals" who, "knowing that they are unacceptable for resettlement [outside of Germany], and must remain in Germany, [would be] prepared to go to greater lengths to attain their ends."[86]

The British were not talking about all foreigners in this report. Its subsequent ethnic-racial discussion explicitly demonstrates the alignment of euphemistic terms like "DP" for specific ethnic groups. While offering the qualifier that it was impossible, "to break down the [crime] statistics by nationality" and that "it would be generally dangerous to impute responsibility to any particular group or camp, or to judge any particular group by the behavior of a minority," the authors proceeded to do both. According to the report, the "Baltic group"—from what is now Estonia, Latvia, and Lithuania—were "a well behaved community, whereas on the other hand, there were undoubtedly a number of hardened criminals among the Poles, the most numerous group." The greatest problems were among the Jews at the camp at Hohne (in Lower Saxony between Hanover and Wolfsburg), "known to be the center of large scale black market activities."[87]

The authors attempted to moderate the generalizations implied in these assessments by concluding, "It would however be entirely wrong to regard DPs generally as a criminal class." It was a statement revealing of the western Allies' cognitive dissonance when assessing DP crime. There was a powerful imperative for the western Allies to appear equitable and non-discriminatory in the administration of criminal justice in contrast to the Nazis. Even prior to the occupation it was thought that a "democratic" approach to law and order would help Germans accept Allied rule and, further, would form the basis of a new German society. Such ambitions were, however, at odds with the differential assessments of DP versus German crime that had quickly become embedded in Allied thinking at the outset of the occupation.[88]

Entrenched perceptions of DP criminality soured even the better-intentioned Allied policies regarding DPs. In 1950, the British were preparing to lift DPs' special protections and return them to the jurisdiction of the German criminal justice system. Rather than assessing the potential dangers of this transfer, the British instead hoped to prevent "allowing DPs to regard themselves in any way as a separate or privileged class."⁸⁹ It is highly unlikely that by 1950 any DPs felt "privileged" in postwar western Germany. Most certainly felt separate. Not only were they far fewer in number than the Germans, they were heavily scrutinized by MG, German police, civilians, and the press, meaning any deviation—no matter how small—was more likely to be detected. Their confinement made the very premise of tracing most crime back to the DP camps nearly absurd. Yet in a cyclical logic, any identified DP-perpetrated crime reinforced their association as a group with criminality in the view of Germans and the Allies.⁹⁰

Conclusions and Future Directions

Fear of crime pervaded postwar western Germany and for Germans and the Allies, it largely fixed on foreign DP perpetrators. In the British Zone, local German governments, police, and British MGOs at the local and upper-levels of MG repeatedly claimed astonishing levels of DP crime. Violent DP criminals were believed to stalk the streets. Powerful DP gangs were believed to threaten the ability of MG to protect rural communities. These assertions came laden with depictions of itinerancy, greed, a-morality, a propensity for violence, and other nefarious qualities long ascribed to Gypsies, Jews, Poles, and other "Eastern" Slavic peoples. It should, therefore, give us pause that these assertions so clearly extended existing racialized tropes and, further, bore little connection to the available criminal justice data, or the nature of MG's strict administration of martial law, which was designed to ensure civilian pacification and the general security.

This deviation between contemporary reporting of DP criminality and the other available evidence suggests the rapid emergence of a deep and pervasive, socially emergent subtle fear of crime that warped perceptions and in turn legitimized extreme assertions about the extent and nature of all crime, and foreign-perpetrated crime in particular. This is not to say that crime did not occur, or that DPs were not responsible for some of it. Rather, it is to point out that the rate of DP criminality was greatly exaggerated. These narratives about violent foreign criminality nonetheless give important insight into the dominant emotions that existed in postwar western Germany. The instantiation of a foreign crime threat gave voice to preexisting prejudices and xenophobia refracted through the particular context of the western Allies' military occupation. Western Germany was a deeply unpleasant place after the Second World War. Years of bombing and wartime economic strain, the brutality of Nazi rule, and the final battles for the homeland in 1944–5, created a space riven by physical and psychological trauma. Horrific Nazi programs created millions of DPs in the war's aftermath, many of Jewish, Gypsy, and Slavic origins. These people had to find solace in battered Allied-controlled territory among local Germans with long-standing prejudices against them, which had been cultivated and exacerbated by 13 years of Nazi rule. And, the western Allies had their own prejudices toward these groups.

But preexisting bigotries only partly explain the emergence of shared German-Allied fears about foreign criminality. The context of the postwar occupation was instrumental. In the months before Germany's defeat, racialized Nazi propaganda fixed on foreign revenge for the war, voicing a deep anxiety felt by virtually all Germans about the future for country, family, and self. Occupation meant the end of German sovereignty with no clear prospects for the future. Following the Nazi defeat, the Allies overturned the Nazis' racial social system, releasing forced laborers and concentration camp inmates, and elevating them to a privileged place in postwar society, exempt from German criminal justice. The Allies' apparent removal of traditional authoritarian systems further heightened the impact of such radical changes to German society.

The Allies' desire for civil pacification and order guided MG throughout the occupation. MG's first concern was preventing resistance, notably ardent Nazi partisans. But neither a Nazi threat nor any other systematic German resistance materialized, and MG's next priority was proactively maintaining the peace. Monitoring DP behavior was an important part of this broader goal. Their approach was shaped by the initially negative feelings Allied soldiers felt on encountering DPs. And in the context of small detachments reliant on German collaboration for governing, it also ensured entrenchment of perceived differences between Germans and DPs, and an in-group/out-group dichotomy of the Allies-Germans on the one hand against DPs on the other.[91]

Preexisting prejudices, wartime trauma, and fears about societal fragility facilitated a strong tendency toward confirmatory bias when Germans and members of the Allies assessed crime. Establishment of a clear out-group and the fixation on security resulted in a tendency to make unsubstantiated inferences about wider unseen conditions from the available salient crime reports, and to be more accepting of rumors and other less reliable sources of information that seemed to confirm their fear-drive beliefs about crime. Again, this was not an intentional process but an emergent one, in keeping with "crime wave" hysteria and "moral panics" that have occurred in many other societies through history.[92]

Even when their own arrest and court records were directly contradictory, both the Allies and the Germans routinely failed to check whether multiplication of reporting was distorting crime data, or question the veracity of civilian claims. Germans and MGOs were also equally subject to the same exaggeration of crime fears that affect all people. A few salient cases appearing in MG courts, and in German and MG arrests provided continuing fodder for distorted beliefs. Problematically, the distorted account of excessive serious, foreign-perpetrated crime complements common intuitions about postwar social disintegration and resulting criminality fits nearly every postwar narrative, whether resulting from a "zero hour" caesura or the continuation of wartime trauma. Crime and disorder have therefore powerfully endured in the literature as instantiated historical phenomena, though we are instead more likely seeing an emergent emotional and psychological condition resulting from the trying experience of postwar life.

The association of Poles, Jews, Gypsies and other non-Germans with crime in the postwar years derived from a long history of ethnic antagonism and fear of foreign threat refracted through thirteen years of ideological Nazi rule. And while fear was the dominant feeling for nearly every German in the closing months of the war, the preexisting threads of xenophobia, and religious and racial bigotry were reweaved during the occupation into a new totalizing crime fear. Allied conquest meant the release of so-called racial enemies and an abolition of German sovereignty, which removed the societal structures and protections long provided by the authoritarian state. Petty crime and black marketeering proliferated, and DPs were not only free, they were ostensibly privileged above ordinary Germans. Postwar society not only appeared fragile, war and conquest had weakened it in many important and fundamental ways: people had little knowledge of the world outside their districts, the economy was in a dire state, and infrastructure had often been largely destroyed. In this immediate context, and with the weight of preexisting prejudices, fixing on foreign (DP) crime provided a language through which to express deep fears about unseen threats to the foundations of German life and, for the Allies, to the success of their reconstruction project.

Notes

1 Dexter L. Freeman, *Hesse: A New German State* (Frankfurt am Main: Druck- und Verlagshaus Frankfurt am Main GmbH, 1948), 20–3; Christoph Klessmann, *Die*

doppelte Staatsgründung. Deutsche Geschichte 1945–1955 (Göttingen: Vandenhoeck & Ruprecht, 1982), 46–53; Giles MacDonogh, *After the Reich: The Brutal History of the Allied Occupation* (New York: Basic Books, 2009), 378.

2 Jose Raymund Canoy, *The Discreet Charm of the Police State: The Landpolizei and the Transformation of Bavaria, 1945–1965* (Leiden: Brill, 2007), 107. On important analysis of interactions between DPs, Allies (Americans), and Germans see: Adam Seipp, "Refugee Town: Germans, Americans, and the Uprooted in Rural West Germany," *Journal of Contemporary History* 44, no. 4 (2009): 675–95; Adam R. Seipp, *Strangers in the Wild Place. Refugees, Americans, and a German Town, 1945–1952* (Bloomington: Indiana University Press, 2013), 8–9.

3 Alan Kramer, "'Law Abiding Germans?' Social Disintegration, Crime and the Re-imposition of Order in Post-war Western Germany, 1945-9," in *The German Underworld: Deviants and Outcasts in German History*, ed. Richard J. Evans (London: Routledge, 1988), 238.

4 Michael Ermarth, "Introduction," in *America and the Shaping of German Society, 1945–1955*, ed. Michael Ermarth (Providence, RI: Berg, 1993), 3–4; Herbert Kosyra, *Nach der Stunde Null. Die deutsche Kriminalpolizei in den Jahren 1945–1955* (St. Michael: J. G. Bläschke Verlag, 1980). The *Stunde Null* is pervasive, see for example: Curtis F. Morgan, Jr., *James F. Byrnes, Lucius Clay, and American Policy in Germany, 1945–1947* (New York: Edwin Mellen Press, 2002), 63. On continuity see: Richard Bessel, *Germany 1945: From War to Peace* (New York: HarperCollins, 2009), 184; Mark Mazower, *Hitler's Empire. Nazi Rule in Occupied Europe* (London: Penguin Books, 2009), 524–5.

5 Bessel, *Germany 1945*, 321; Richard J. Evans, *Rituals of Retribution: Capital Punishment in Germany, 1600–1987* (Oxford: Oxford University Press, 1996), 748–9; Kosyra, *Nach der Stunde Null*, 12–13; MacDonogh, *After the Reich*, 74.

6 On crime fear in crime reporting: Michael O'Connell and Anthony Whelan, "The Public Perception of Crime Prevalence, Newspaper Readership and 'Mean World' Attitudes," *Legal and Criminological Psychology* 1 (1996): 179–95. There are many other studies of the phenomenon of perceiving more crime than exists. For one example of exaggeration see: Don Weatherburn, Elizabeth Matka, Bronwyn Lind, *Crime Perception and Reality: Public Perceptions of the Risk of Criminal Victimisation in Australia* (Sydney: Bureau of Crime Statistics and Research New South Wales, 1996). Avail.: http://search.informit.com.au/documentSummary;dn=91674727884 1078;res=IELHSS [accessed July 17, 2014]. See also an interesting study on support for the police extending from persistent fear of crime: Richard L. Block, "Fear of Crime and Fear of the Police," *Social Problems* 19, no. 1 (Summer, 1971): 91–101.

7 Thomas J. Kehoe, "Control, Disempowerment, Fear, and Fantasy: Violent Criminality during the Early American Occupation of Germany, March-July 1945," *Australian Journal of Politics & History* 62, no. 4 (2016): 566–70; Kramer, '"Law Abiding Germans?"' 254–5.

8   Rebecca Boehling, *A Question of Priorities. Democratic Reform and Economic Recovery in Postwar Germany. Frankfurt, Munich, and Stuttgart under US Occupation 1945–1949* (New York: Berghahn Books, 1996), 31, 117 [see chapter 5 particularly, beginning p. 156.]

9   Headquarters Military Government Stadtkreis Koln, "Weekly Summary for Period 31 Jul–7 Aug 45," August 9, 1945, The British National Archives, Kew, London (abbrev. TNA), WO 171 8039, 1.

10 On anti-Gypsy feeling in Britain see: Mike Cole, "A Plethora of 'Suitable Enemies': British Racism at the Dawn of the Twenty-First Century," *Ethnic and Racial Studies* 32, no. 9 (2009), 1674–5. For the classic work on anti-Semitism in Britain see: Colin Holmes, *Anti-Semitism in British Society, 1876–1939* (London: Routledge, 2015). For an examination of shared prejudices between Britain, Germany, and the United States toward Poles and Slavs see: Leo Lucassen, "The Great War and the Origins of Migration Control in Western Europe and the United States (1880–1920)," in *Regulation of Migration: International Experiences*, ed. Anita Böcker, Kees Groenendijk, Tetty Havinga, Paul Minderhoud (Amsterdam: Het Spinhuis, 1998), 45–72.

11 On anti-Semitism in the United States see: Leonard Dinnerstein, *Anti-Semitism in America* (Oxford: Oxford University Press, 1995). For a brief history of the links between anti-Semitism and anti-Polish bigotry in the United States see: Alan Dundes, "A Study of Ethnic Slurs: The Jew and the Polack in the United States." *The Journal of American Folklore* 84, no. 332 (April–June, 1971): 186–203 [esp. 193–4 on Jewish stereotypes].

12 Malte Zierenberg, *Berlin's Black Market, 1939–1950* (London: Palgrave Macmillan, 2015), 111.

13 Mazower, *Hitler's Empire*, 524–5. On Nazi treatment of "defeatism" see: Steven R. Welch, "Securing the German Domestic Front in the Second World War: Prosecution of Subversion before the People's Court," *Australian Journal of Politics and History* 53, no. 1 (March, 2007): 44–56.

14 On the outbreak of crime see: Ralf Dahrendorf, *Law and Order* (London: Stevens, 1985), 3; Kehoe, "Control, Disempowerment, Fear, and Fantasy." On Allied soldier crime see: Miriam Gebhardt, *Als die Soldaten kamen: Die Vergewaltigung deutscher Frauen am Ende des Zweiten Weltkriegs* (Deutsche Verlags-Anstalt, 2015); Thomas J. Kehoe and E. James Kehoe, "Crimes Committed by US Soldiers in Europe 1945–1946," *Journal of Interdisciplinary History* 47, no. 1 (Summer 2016): 53–84; Thomas J. Kehoe and E. James Kehoe, "A Reply to Robert Dykstra's 'Evident Bias in Crimes Committed by US Soldiers in Europe 1945–1946," *Journal of Interdisciplinary History* 47, no. 3 (Winter 2017): 385–96. The Kehoes provide new estimates of crime in the American Zone. Gebhardt has questionable quantitative methods, so it is unclear whether we can rely on her estimates for British crime. But qualitative

data suggests there was a similar problem among British soldiers. See: 821 (L/R) Det Mil Gov (Obernburg) "Activity Report," n.d., TNA, WO 171/8084, 2.

15 Headquarters Third Infantry Division, "Report of Operations," June 10, 1945, NACP, RG 407, Entry 427, Box 5402, 9.

16 Kehoe, "Control, Disempowerment, Fear, and Fantasy," 570-3.

17 Public Safety Branch, Land Commissioner's Office Schleswig-Holstein, "Public Safety Report Schleswig-Holstein," November 21, 1952, TNA, FO 1050/581, 1-2.

18 Headquarters Military Government Stadtkreis Koln, "Report for Month Ending 31 Aug 45, by 622 (SK KOLN) Det Mil Gov," August 31, 1945, TNA, WO 171 8039, 5; Headquarters Military Government Stadtkreis Koln, "Appendix D issued with 116/Gen Rep/D/5 dated 28 Nov 45 for period 28 Oct to 27 Nov 45," November 28, 1945, TNA, WO 171 8039, 2.

19 On the experiences of the people who became DPs see: Mark Wyman, *DP: Europe's Displaced Persons, 1945-1951* (Philadelphia, PA: Balch Institute Press, 1989).

20 Oliver J. Frederiksen, *The American Military Occupation of Germany: 1945-1953* (Europe: Historical Division, Headquarters, United States Army, 1953), 61; Freeman, *Hesse: A New German State*, 20-3.

21 Karl S. Bader, *Soziologie der Deutschen Nachkriegskriminalität* (Tübingen: J.C.B. Mohr, 1949), 168-77; Adolf Schönke, "Criminal Law and Criminality in Germany of Today," *Annals of the American Academy of Political and Social Science* 260, Postwar Reconstruction in Western Germany (November 1948): 137-43.

22 Evans, *Rituals of Retribution*, 748-9; Alexander Häusser and Gordian Maugg, *Hungerwinter: Deutschlands humanitäre Katastrophe 1946-47* (Berlin: Propyläen, 2009), 20-5; Klessmann, *Die doppelte Staatsgründung*, 46-53; Kosyra, *Nach der Stunde Null*, 12-13; Keith Lowe, *Savage Continent: Europe in the Aftermath of World War II* (London: Viking, 2012), xiii.

23 War Department, *FM 27-5. United States Army and Navy Manual of Military Government and Civil Affairs*, December 22, 1943, 14-15.

24 Douglas Botting, *In the Ruins of the Reich* (London: George Allen & Unwin, 1985), 148.

25 Kehoe, "Control, Disempowerment, Fear, and Fantasy," 565.

26 For a good (if slanted) discussion of the fall of Aachen see: Harry D. Condron, "The Fall of Aachen," n.d. (presumed November 1944), NACP, RG 407, Entry 427A, Box 19023.

27 These orders were reiterated in April 1944 and included depopulating and destroying towns and cities if necessary, though no such actions were ever taken. See: Office of the Chief of Staff, SHAEF, "Reprisals," April 1945, NACP, RG 331, Entry 27, Box 82.

28 Headquarters Military Government Stadtkreis Koln, "War Diary of 622(A) Det C.A.," January 19, 1945, TNA, WO 171/8039, 2.

29 There are frequent notes in the MG court registers of people being arrested and convicted of curfew and travel violations with plausibly reasonable explanations. They were almost never released. See registers in British Military Government Court Records, TNA, FO 1060.

30 Thomas J. Kehoe, *The Art of Occupation: Crime and Governance in American-Controlled Germany, 1944–1949* (Athens: Ohio University Press, 2019) [part 1, esp. chapter 3].

31 James Dobbins, John G. McGinn, Keith Crane, Seth G. Jones, Rollie Lal, Andrew Rathmell, Rachel M. Swanger, and Anga R. Timilsina, *America's Role in Nation-Building: From Germany to Iraq* (Washington, DC: RAND, 2003), 9–10.

32 On the original formulation of strain theory see: Robert Merton, "Social Structure and Anomie," *American Sociological Review* 3, no. 5 (1938), 672–82. For the newer see: Robert Agnew, "Building on the Foundation of General Strain Theory: Specifying the Types of Strain Most Likely to Lead to Crime and Delinquency," *Journal of Research in Crime and Delinquency* 38, no. 4 (2001): 319–61.

33 Victor Gollancz, *In Darkest Germany* (London: Victor Gollancz, 1947), 24.

34 Cologne Military Government Court Registers, TNA, FO 1060/2061, 2461. Cologne had a population in 1945–6 of approximately five hundred thousand (reduced from 1 million prior to the war).

35 Headquarters Military Government Stadtkreis Koln, "Appendix D issued with 116/Gen Rep/D/5 dated 28 Nov 45 for period 28 Oct to 27 Nov 45," 2.

36 Cologne General Court Register, TNA, FO 1060/2061, cases 9–16.

37 Ibid., cases 37–8.

38 Ibid.

39 Eric A. Johnson, "The Crime Rate: Longitudinal and Periodic Trends in Nineteenth- and Twentieth-Century German Criminality, from *Vormärz* to Late Weimar," in *The German Underworld: Deviants and Outcasts in German History*, ed. Richard J. Evans (London: Routledge, 1988), 159–88.

40 J. Timmerman, "Report on Kripo Leitstelle Hannover (*sic*)," July 1945, TNA, FO 1050/315, 1.

41 Ibid.

42 "Appendix A to Second Fortnightly Report from Mil Gov Hanover Region Covering the Period 19 Jul 45 to 31 Jul 45," n.d. (presumed July 31, 1945), TNA, WO 171 7955, 1.

43 Ibid.

44 Thomas J. Kehoe and E. James Kehoe, "Civilian Crime during the British and American Occupation of Western Germany, 1945–1946: Analyses of Military Government Court Records," *European Journal of Criminology*. DOI: 10.1177/1477370819887516 [2019].

45 "Appendix A to Second Fortnightly Report from Mil Gov Hanover Region," 5.

46 Canoy, *Discreet Charm of the Police State*, 107.

47 On faulty reconstruction of memory and the exaggeration of threat see: Amos Tversky and Daniel Kahneman, "Availability: A Heuristic for Judging Frequency and Probability," *Cognitive Psychology* 5, no. 1 (1973): 207–33; Elizabeth F. Loftus, *Eyewitness Testimony* (Cambridge, MA: Harvard University Press, 1996). These processes contribute to "group criminalization." For a clear analysis see: Pamela Preston and Michael P. Perez, "The Criminalization of Aliens: Regulating Foreigners," *Critical Criminology* 14, no. 1 (2006): 43–66.
48 Bessel, *Germany 1945*, 262.
49 Seipp, *Strangers in the Wild Place* [particularly the example on p. 105].
50 *Military Government Handbook Germany. Section 2M*, Proclamation No. 1, Article II, Sec. 40.
51 On MGOs' lack of knowledge about wider conditions see: Kehoe, *Art of Occupation* [chapter 4].
52 Ibid., 115.
53 Andrew H. Beattie, "Die allierte Internierung im besetzen Deutschland und die deutsche Gesellschaft: Vergleich der amerikanischen und der sowjetischen Zone," *Zeitschrift für Geschichtswissenschaft* 62 (2014): 239–56; Canoy, *Discreet Charm of the Police State*, 116; Kehoe, "Control, Disempowerment, Fear, and Fantasy," 571.
54 Canoy, *Discreet Charm of the Police State*, 131.
55 Jeffrey S. Adler, "The Making of a Moral Panic in 19th-Century America: The Boston Garroting Hysteria of 1865," *Deviant Behavior* 17, no. 3 (1996), 259–78. For the classic work on "moral panic" (another term for "crime wave hysteria") see: Victor E. Kappeler and Gary W. Potter, *The Mythology of Crime and Criminal Justice*, 5th ed. (Long Grove, IL: Waveland Press, 2018).
56 "Appendix A to Second Fortnightly Report from Mil Gov Hanover Region," 5.
57 Michael Burleigh and Wolfgang Wippermann, *The Racial State, Germany 1933–1945* (Cambridge: Cambridge University Press, 1991), see chapters 2 and 3 [pp. 23–73].
58 William Brustein, *Roots of Hate* (Cambridge: Cambridge University Press, 2003), 101. For Hitler's famous quote in reference to seeing a Jewish man, "is this a German?," see: Adolf Hitler, *Mein Kampf*, trans. Ralph Manheim (London: Hutchinson, 1973), 52.
59 Charissa Kurda, "Gypsy Hysteria in 19th Century Germany: A Biopolitical Response," in *Reflections of Fear in the German-Speaking World, 1600–2000*, ed. Thomas J. Kehoe and Michael Pickering (London: Bloomsbury, 2020), 87–122.
60 Matthew Fitzpatrick, *Purging the Empire: Mass Expulsions in Germany, 1871–1914* (Oxford: Oxford University Press, 2015).
61 Kristin Kopp, "Constructing Racial Difference in Colonial Poland," in *Germany's Colonial Pasts*, ed. Eric Ames, Marcia Klotz, and Lora Wildenthal (Lincoln: University of Nebraska Press, 2005), 80–6.
62 For more on Nazi paranoia see: Jeffrey Herf's argument on "Radical Antisemitism," in *The Jewish Enemy: Nazi Propaganda during World War II and the Holocaust*,

ed. Jeffrey Herf (Cambridge, MA: Belknap Press of Harvard University, 2006), 6 [pp. 1–8].
63   Christian Goeschel, "Suicide at the End of the Third Reich," *Journal of Contemporary History* 41, no. 1 (2006): 159–60.
64   Frontier Control Service, "Report of Proceedings No. 2. For August 1946," n.d. (presumed September 1946), TNA, FO 1073/37, section D, 2.
65   Ibid., section N, 4.
66   Kramer, '"Law Abiding Germans?'"
67   For initial American reactions to victims of Nazi brutality see: Robert H. Abzug, *Inside the Vicious Heart* (Oxford: Oxford University Press, 1985), 142–7; Susan L. Carruthers, *The Good Occupation: American Soldiers and the Hazards of Peace* (Cambridge, MA: Harvard University Press, 2016), 151–4 [see: chapter 5 on Displaced Persons]; Wyman writes of the shock that the Allies felt at first seeing the behavior of DPs, including open fornication. See: Wyman, *DP*, 38–9.
68   Geoffrey Best argues that this "arch-occupier" approach to governance was predicated on the assumption that local population would necessarily acquiesce to foreign military rule during wartime. See: Geoffrey Best, *Humanity in Warfare. The Modern History of the International Law of Armed Conflicts* (London: Weidenfeld & Nicolson, 1980), 180.
69   Frontier Control Service, "Report of Proceedings No. 2. For August 1946," section D, 2.
70   Kappeler and Potter, *Mythology of Crime and Criminal Justice*, 41–62 [also on crime myths see: pp. 29–35].
71   This case has been addressed in detail by Evans, *Rituals of Retribution*, 751–2.
72   Oldenburg General Court Register, TNA, FO 1060/3597.
73   Hanover General Court Register, TNA, FO 1060/2944.
74   Brian Chapman, *Police State* (Westport, CT: Praeger, 1970), 47–8.
75   Sheila Fitzpatrick and Robert Gellately, "Introduction to the Practices of Denunciation in Modern European History," *Journal of Modern History* 68, no. 4 (December 1996); Sheila Fitzpatrick and Robert Gellately, *Accusatory Practices: Denunciation in Modern European History, 1789–1989* (Chicago, IL: University of Chicago Press, 1997); Robert Gellately, "Denunciations in Twentieth-Century Germany: Aspects of Self-Policing in the Third Reich and the German Democratic Republic," *Journal of Modern History* 68, no. 4 (1996), 931–67. Also see the newer work by Andrew Szanadja on prosecution of those who denounced others during the Nazi period, particularly the extent to which they contributed to Nazi crimes: Andrew Szanadja, *Indirect Perpetrators: The Prosecution of Informers in Germany, 1945–1965* (Lanham, MA: Lexington Books, 2010), 3–5.
76   Fitzpatrick and Gellately, "Introduction to the Practices of Denunciation in Modern European History," 747.

77 Peter Vacca, "Weekly Intelligence Report, No. 9," January 31, 1946, 13. From collection: Peter Vacca, Office of Military Government for Bavaria Intelligence Branch, "Weekly and Periodic Intelligence Reports," NACP, RG 260, Entry A1 899, Boxes 168 and 169.

78 Canoy, *Discreet Charm of the Police State*, 37–8.

79 Criminologists have repeatedly demonstrated the fear-generating processes that allow links to be drawn between certain minorities and non-locals to crime, most famously with persistent anxiety about African-American gang crime in the urban United States, but the same is true of everything from Scottish soccer fans and the mentally ill, to refugees in many different contexts. See: Ted Chiricos, Michael Hogan, and Marc Gertz, "Racial Composition of Neighborhood and Fear of Crime," *Criminology* 35, no. 1 (February 1997), 107–31; Craig St. John and Tamara Heald-Moore, "Fear of Black Strangers," *Social Science Research* 24 (1995): 262–80; Wendy Fitzgibbon, "Risikoträger oder verletzliche Individuen: über die präemptive Kriminalisierung von Menschen mit psychischen Problemen," in *Risiko Gesundheit: Über Risiken und Nebenwirkungen der Gesundheitsgesellschaft* (Wiesbaden: VS Verlag für Sozialwissenschaften, 2010), 227–40; Michael Lavalette and Gerry Mooney, "The Scottish State and the Criminalisation of Football Fans," *Criminal Justice Matters* 93, no. 1 (2013): 22–4.

80 "G" Section, Office of the Chief of Staff, B.A.O.R., "Criminal Activity in DP Camps in the British Zone," January 1950, TNA, FO 1060/44.

81 Wyman, *DP*, 17 [dropped to 1.8 million, p. 37]. Estimates of the DP population vary within the report, though there were 149,000 registered with the International Refugee Organization for assistance and of these 106,202 were living in DP camps. Presumably some were not registered and were living among the regular German population. See: "G" Section, Office of the Chief of Staff, B.A.O.R., "Criminal Activity in DP Camps in the British Zone."

82 Ibid.

83 It is difficult to draw a direct comparison to the camp condition, but the broad findings on the relationship between increased poverty and higher crime is clear. For overviews see: Ralph C. Allen, "Socioeconomic Conditions and Property Crime: A Comprehensive Review and Test of the Professional Literature," *American Journal of Economics and Sociology* 55, no. 3 (1996): 293–308.

84 "G" Section, Office of the Chief of Staff, B.A.O.R., "Criminal Activity in DP Camps in the British Zone," 1–2.

85 Ibid., 2.

86 Ibid.

87 Ibid., 3.

88 Eli E. Nobleman, *American Military Government Courts in Germany: Their Role in the Democratization of the German People* (S. J. D., New York University, 1950), i.

89 "G" Section, Office of the Chief of Staff, B.A.O.R., "Criminal Activity in DP Camps in the British Zone," 1.
90 Intense scrutiny had begun early. From 1945, American and British guards systematically questioned all DPs who left the camps for the day, arresting those found with contraband and even those who appeared to have violated the law. By 1946, only 10 percent of DPs were allowed to leave the camps at any given time. For these orders see: "Weekly Report for Military Government for Land Bayern," No. 31, December 6–13, 1945, NACP, RG260, Entry A1 141, Box 532, 10. For an example of the stories in the press about DP crime see: "Germany's Economic Chaos: Local Self-Sufficiency in Food Breaking Down," *Manchester Guardian*, May 31, 1945, 5; "DP's Warned on Crime: Army Says those in Germany are getting Bad Reputation," *New York Times*, February 24, 1948, 11. On Polish efforts to challenge these characterizations see: "Polish DP Charge Rebuffed by UN," *New York Times*, May 17, 1949.
91 Thomas J. Kehoe and Elizabeth M. Greenhalgh, "'An Indispensable Luxury': British American Tobacco in the Occupation of Germany, 1945–1948," *Business History* 61, no. 8 (2019): 1326–51.
92 Adler, "Making of a Moral Panic in 19th-Century America."

9

Fear of Falling: German Discussions of Poverty from 1945

Christoph Lorke

In 2010, two years after the Global Financial Crisis (GFC), the German Institute for Economic Research (*Deutsches Institut für Wirtschaftsforschung*) identified a remarkable "downward mobility," a shrinking of the middle class that was resulting in "status panic."[1] It was just one of countless examples from recent years indicating middle class Germans' fear of social decline. Sociologists Holger Lengfeld and Jochen Hirschle similarly found a remarkable fear of social relegation, especially among the mid and lower segments of the middle class. The study surprised researchers because the German middle class was generally regarded as being comparatively stable and well protected from economic downturn, including a resulting lack of education and long-term unemployment.[2] The question for middle class Germans after the GFC had become: would they experience a social decline similar to, say, the United States, among other countries, where the middle class had seen a steady decline in power and status since the 1970s? In 1989, Barbara Ehrenreich's bestseller dealt with this latent fear of social decline among Americans.[3] The book became a classic in "falling literature," dealing directly with the "discreet anxiety of the Bourgeoisie."[4] The book was translated into German in 1992 (and again in 1994), and enjoyed considerable success in Germany as well.[5]

Eherenreich's thesis seemingly had new salience for middle class Germans in 2010, articulating essentially the same fear that Lengfeld and Hirschle identified: a fear of deteriorating social status among a certain social group. Fear as a collective feeling—as a driving and motivating force—can be a motivator of social action and thus deserves careful consideration by historians.[6] Fear is a basic and constitutive emotion, which may be interpreted as a response to an objective or perceived security deficit.[7] As Nehring, among others, notes, fear can be interpreted as the inverse to a sense of security.[8] This chapter explores the fear of social decline and of falling into poverty in West and East Germany—the Federal Republic of Germany (FRG) and the German Democratic Republic (GDR)—after 1945. Following Nehring's insight, the first question is: to what extent were the ruling powers in both Germanys successful in providing their population with appropriate answers in their "search for security?"[9] Did these answers legitimize their (social) politics? Second, it has often been supposed that public, political, and media narratives and discourses of fear have shaped and influenced public imagination. It can be assumed with sufficient probability that the (working) middle class in both Germanys was the main addressee of social narratives, fear narratives, and moral verdicts. The fact that fear (both imagined and real) could be easily mobilized in pursuit of political agendas highlights a permanent anxiety about social decline, downward demarcation, and status competition,[10] which reciprocally made it easier to propagate images of specific enemies (*Feindbilder*).[11] While mass media has a central function in the communicative processing of fear, the following chapter seeks to illustrate the production, conjuncture, and circulation of fear within the public, and especially via media debates in divided Germany.

By no means can it be considered obvious to take into consideration both the FRG and GDR when analyzing the social and emotional order, and the perception of it. For many years, historians regarded the structural differences between East and West Germany as insurmountable, wherefore an integrated German–German postwar history was characterized as highly complicated and "bulky."[12] For a long time the trenches seemed too wide for a controlled and historically sensible, summarized approach. In the past ten years or so, however, the topic has attracted more attention and a range of historians has demanded further efforts in this field. Christoph Kleßmann's dictum "between interdependence and demarcation" within an "asymmetrical intertwined parallel history"[13] has become a key point of reference. In all these studies, at least three main topics were emphasized that suggest a deeper analysis of the social relevance and potency of emotions in a historical German–German perspective: the comparable starting point after the end of the Second World War and the legacy of National Socialism, the respective handling of worldwide trends—including, among others, the oil crisis and globalization—and, ultimately, reunification.[14]

When we ask about the politics of fear, we must carefully discuss the question: who sets the tone in contemporary debates about fear?[15] Mass media—meaning here the sum of journal and newspaper articles, radio broadcasts, and audio-visual artifacts—do not simply display emotions but rather influence and change the interpretation, construction,[16] and practice of feelings. Mass media plays an important role, not only in the process of producing and intensifying emotions but also in social standardization.[17] Certain emotions can be evoked and generated through public discourse, and thus stabilized by it. In order to understand better which fear narratives became especially powerful, it is useful to look at, first, the historical context and circumstances in which contemporaries used the term *poverty* and which expectations and fears were mentioned regarding social inequality[18], and, second, the social and symbolic functions of these ways of talking. By deconstructing the forms of official and public communication, we may be able to trace certain discourses and narratives of fear and their relation to social decline. This further provokes the question of the role of these socially "toxic" issues in the emergence of certain sentiments such as fear.[19]

While the constant threat of unemployment and poverty, or anxiety about the collective (social) future have long been widespread, it is surprising that the fear of social failure as a specific emotion has not been the subject of historical research until now.[20] On the one hand, historians understandably have a conceptual and methodological fear of contact with the "power of emotions."[21] The concept of *fear* is a complex and a difficult psychological and social category to "measure" empirically, which has at least three consequences: (1) fear is self-evident, but the different relations between significance and meaning, and the changeability of semantics of fear throughout history, offers heuristic challenges.[22] (2) It is methodologically dubious to project from statements directly to a protagonist's feelings, and in turn to the entirety of the "middle class."[23] (3) Research on the media's impact on socially experienced emotions faces different methodological challenges, which are too extensive for discussion here. Suffice it to say, they further muddy the conceptual waters.[24] In addition, using the term "poverty" is also complicated. It is an emotionally charged and multidimensional term, and thus difficult to define.[25] "Poverty" is not an *ex post* external label for a stable phenomenon but even among the contemporaries it could influence feelings.[26] Hence, it has, therefore, been decided (1) to follow sociologist Georg Simmel's guide and apply a socially constructive understanding of *poverty* that requires concentration on the contemporary definitions and attributions regarding the label "poor."[27] This also applies to contemporary constructions of fear. In which contexts and how were representations of *poverty* explicitly interwoven with representations of fear? Furthermore, it is barely sufficient (2) to reduce statements of fear and poverty to their verbal dimension.[28] Instead, this chapter will concentrate on their public representations and thus on the processes of social and moral engineering. These representations were orchestrated mainly by mass media. In addition to having an entertainment aspect, mass media contained meaningful symbolic material and needed to fulfill a "social mission" by communicating shared values, norms, and habits. We can also understand them as a mirror and a manifestation of effective public attention to—and perception of—social dissent and "fear communication" about this dissent. Therefore, understanding them may help to dismantle contemporary constructions of both the social and symbolic order in the two German states after 1945.[29]

Postwar Years: Reducing Risks, Reducing Fears, Avoiding "Poverty" Communication (1956–60)

Both Germanys had opportunity for a new beginning after the Second World War, especially concerning social and welfare policy. The first step was to handle the many urgent challenges they shared, such as the payment of war damages, hunger, unemployment, homelessness, and the integration of refugees and displaced persons.[30] In West Germany, the occupying powers and, later, the Adenauer government addressed these pressing tasks and the people's need (*Volksnot*)[31] with pragmatic social policies. Prominent examples include the Emergency Aid Act (*Soforthilfegesetz, Gesetz zur Milderung dringender sozialer Notstände*) of 1949 and the Burden Sharing Act (*Lastenausgleichsgesetz*) of 1952.[32] At that time, consciousness of a disturbance in the internal social order was constantly present. According to the historian Meike Haunschild, "The contemporaries were still well aware of the situation in the Weimar Republic, where economic crises, political unrest and social dislocations had completely destabilized [the] social order," which may, in turn, explain the common desire for social security and orderly politics.[33] In the following years, prudent economic policy was the best way to save individuals from the risk of falling into poverty and guarantee "prosperity for everybody."[34] The slogan "no experiments" during the 1957 election, when the ruling party CDU celebrated an overwhelming victory, can also be interpreted as a reflexive response to the fear of economic and social imbalance.[35] In 1957, these social safety promises were extended to a major reform of the pension system. Until then, poverty among pensioners was one of few examples in which poverty was directly mentioned in the public and media sphere: "material misery" was one of the most common associations connected with the process of aging[36], and "there was near panic about the retirement age" among West German employees.[37] Visual representations of this fear in those years were, however, at best an exception, such as a female pensioner who could afford meat only once per week.[38] Adenauer's reforms were both real, as well as symbolizing "social pacification," and thus "social justice as [a] motivational norm" became crucially important.[39] As a consequence, in the following years more affirmative modes of depicting the social situation of old age became common.[40]

The circulation of visual representations via mass media was crucial for the persistence of these social images—and likely even more so for the emotions and sentiments they presumably evoked. It is rather obvious that certain, often stable and positive, images of the "worthy" poor (e.g., old pensioners or war-damaged individuals) were expected to serve as "fear-breakers," offering audiences an optimistic portrait of future social situations. There was little public or political imperative among the consensus-oriented mass media of the Adenauer era to portray social misery, poverty, and society's "losers." Instead, "poverty" was ousted, and narratives of *Trümmerfrauen* (women of ruins)[41], social climbing, or sentimental movies[42] were intensively promoted (and desired) within the public sphere. These narratives referred to the "postwar emotional regime(s)" characterized by control, restraint, and anti-intensity[43], and expressed the widespread desire for "normalization" after years of privation. According to this demand, the scholarly social self-conception within the FRG was dominated by conceptions of a broad and stable middle class, which was reflected in popular and powerful representations such as Helmut Schelsky's *nivellierte Mittelstandsgesellschaft* (leveled middle class society)[44]—much more a program than a "reality" and thus no less than a societal self-harmonization.[45] This was the characterizing model for West Germany's social structure from the 1950s until the 1970s. During times of economic prosperity, the overemphasis of society's "middle" has been connected to a promise of social integration and upward movement, and thus supported the process of "poverty's" fading from the public sphere. However, from the policymaker's point of view, addressing poverty, social misery, and inequality within a broader public and societal context had the considerable potential for de-legitimization, which was connected with the omnipresence of the second German state, the GDR.

In the Eastern part of Germany, the Soviet occupiers and then the Socialist Unity Party of Germany (SED) pursued the paternalistic-authoritarian traditions of the German welfare state, which endured through the Empire and the Weimar Republic. According to Marxist-Leninist ideology, "poverty," "social inequality," and generally speaking all forms of social grievance were regarded as relics of the capitalist relations of production and therefore as "foreign" to socialism. All remaining social problems would soon be obsolete—at least according to the ideology's self-description and vision of the future. This highly incontrovertible self-perception also meant that representations of endemic forms of "poverty" had to be absent from the public sphere. Remaining social difficulties were individualized, a process that was supported by a rigid welfare policy. Moreover, the social standing and achievements of each country's own citizens were incessantly contrasted with the alleged failures of the other's: references to capitalistic class differences, the "militaristic authoritarian state," or the occurrence of beggars, outlined the superiority of the GDR's socialist system, which was able to guarantee citizens the necessary rights for a decent livelihood. In her reflections on social care in 1959, head of the main department of social services in the Ministry of Health Care Käthe Kern praised the achievements of the socialist system. In her view, being released from the fear of crisis and unemployment, the livelihood of the working people was no longer threatened as it was in West Germany.[46] Such thinking not only highlighted a competition for labor; it also showed that the impact of the Cold War. Intra-German competition evoked a fear of becoming outdated and backward. In the context of social policy, both Germanys wanted to avoid being labeled the "inhuman state." The mutual and permanent observation of social policy had retroactive effects, even though it remains an open question as to how this fear influenced political decision-making regarding such policies, and even if the fear relation was mainly an asymmetric one. The fear of communism in the West[47] never found an analogous complement; welfare capitalism grew strikingly in response to the expansion of socialistic security systems in the East.[48] At least until the construction of the Berlin Wall in 1961, both German states acted as comparative cases, opponents, and (secret) role models.[49] Comparing the sociopolitical developments of one state with its counterpart could also mean increasing the pressure to prove its ability to handle social groups and the poor more appropriately, and to offer adequate solutions. Against the background of the Cold War and this perpetual competitive pressure, it was a logical consequence that "poverty" was transformed from an emotive word into a taboo.[50] In both countries, social politics contributed to the state's legitimation, and it was highly symbolically charged—winning the audience's and citizens' trust implied offering more successful safety nets against social risk and the loss of social status.[51]

Overall, in the first postwar decade in neither East nor West Germany were social problems a broader topic for discussion in politics, general discourse, or in the media. Leading politicians in both states were aware of existing deficits, but they tended to see social imbalances as transitional phenomena and were confident they could overcome them via their own respective strategies. These strategies were only different on cursory inspection. Instead, in both the East and the West, the guiding category of "labor" (and further, the ability and willingness to work) was central to explaining, interpreting, and constructing social deprivation and poverty. Thus, the "adopted" implicit classification of the "worthy" and "unworthy" poor remained a crucial means of social and symbolic hierarchy.[52] Presumably, referring back to the longstanding and well-tried division could help in gaining an overview of a confusing and complex postwar situation that extended far beyond social considerations. Social commentators used traditional definitions of poverty and characteristics suspected of endangering the whole society—including an inability to think rationally and logically, an aversion to work, "animal sexual instincts," moral waywardness, lack of education and culture, and so on—when talking about their "own" poor. However, "real poverty" was not usually situated within their own borders but rather within the "capitalistic sphere," in the case of East Germany or in the "Third World," in the case of West Germany. This communicative strategy of "outsourcing" was addressed to the audience as well, "verifying" a successful reconstruction and a stable social system, and minimizing the vague feeling of threat: the political and media policy of an "extra-territorialization" of poverty permitted conclusions about the desired social order within each state's own boundaries[53]—a quite stable feature of the negotiation of "poverty" in divided Germany until 1989, when new forms of security were created anew.

Booming Years: Discovering Poverty, Fear of Transfer, Fear of Decline (1960–75)

While securitization in reference to an opposing system was the dominant mode of poverty communication in the first postwar years, the system of coordinates would change in the early 1960s. In East Germany, the construction of the Berlin Wall led to an intensified scholarly focus on society's fringe groups, such as pensioners and large families. In West Germany, the passing of the *Bundessozialhilfegesetz* (federal social security law) strengthened the faith that poverty would finally be overcome. An example of the almost humorous handling of the remaining poor in the context of an "economic miracle" is an article by the journalist Peter Brügge, who explored "poverty" in West

Germany in 1961—and could hardly find any trace of it.[54] Full employment, an "affluent society," and a comprehensive system of social benefits against "the ups and downs of life" were commonly seen as the best instruments against the loss of social status. The possibility for social advancement and increasing mobility was one of the major promises of that time, characterized by Ulrich Beck as the "trickledown effect."[55] Nevertheless, it is questionable whether this period can be characterized as the "latency period"[56] of academic and public "poverty" communication and, further, whether its description as a phase of "displacement of the poverty problem"[57] can be fully shared, particularly in the context of the production and circulation of new patterns of fear. Instead, the 1960s were a decade of politicization and emotionalization.[58] As a result, experts and journalists called attention to the problems of different social minorities. Little by little, journalists in particular promoted a visualization of the social. Thus, it is possible to talk about a first wave of the medicalization of "poverty," which also affected the fear regimes. These tendencies of the new, extended rules of "sayability," (*Sagbarkeit*) according to Michel Foucault,[59] and demonstrability were reinforced through the 1968 Movement and the change of federal government one year later to a social-liberal coalition. In clear contrast with his predecessors in office, Chancellor Willy Brandt explicitly identified fear as an issue in modern social policy during an official statement on behalf of his government in 1973: "Eliminating the fear of material need and social decline is no longer enough; social policy should strive for a more just cause, so that there is more real freedom in our society."[60] This quote refers not only to the (re-) discovery of poverty but also to increased political attention after more than a decade of relative silence.

As a consequence of this development, numerous examples of advocacy and tolerant interpretation could be found in mass media. There were also contrasting reactions.[61] The latter were often connected by concerns about the deleterious effects of "affluence." In the context of the discovery of the poor in the 1960s, it was not uncommon for social scientists such as criminologists or sociologists to characterize the poor as hedonistic, fiscally irresponsible, or unable to survive without state relief—an approach that was not specific to West Germany but was evident in other western industrial countries at the time.[62] According to Barbara Ehrenreich, the poor represented "what the middle class feared most in itself," mainly a "softening of character, a lack of firm internal values."[63] People in emergency shelters in particular were seen and depicted as the "other," the altering part of society, because they did not lean on the typical values of the middle class such as self-regulation and -control, ambitiousness, steadiness (*Sesshaftigkeit*), stability, and steadiness. In terms of a "culture of poverty,"[64] it was therefore proposed that children be saved from following in their parents' footsteps, and thus from being infected with socially undesirable characteristics. In the media, as well as in scientific studies, it was not uncommon for authors to highlight the promiscuous attitude of the poor and, consequently, to suggest the free delivery of contraceptives.[65] The frequent voyeurism of many media accounts from that period presumably could have led to a further symbolic debasement of this social group. Here we should think more about the role of the journalists[66]—most of whom were socialized within a bourgeois milieu—that adopted (whether intentionally or not) a particular perspective between empathy and disgust.[67] Furthermore, there is another reason for the heavily underrepresented and highly selective mode of media reporting about "poverty"—what scholars of communication call the "circle of marginality":[68] there is little media interest (because, perhaps, of the evocation of fear) on the topic of poverty on the part of the typical spectator because, as a radio documentary from 1975 presumed, "Those standing in the light do not want to know much about the others, because they are afraid of finding themselves in the shadows unexpectedly, too."[69] This example not only refers indirectly to Ehrenreich's concepts, it impressively proves also the ambivalence of (1) lacking or, later, (2) misconceived, or one-sided, emphasis of the topic in the eyes of contemporary media analysts.

Representations of the "unreliable" succeeding generation most likely evoked emotions regarding an unstable social order, and personal failure was a popular point of reference: above all, homeless persons and persons of no fixed abode (*Nichtsesshafte*) were frequently depicted as biographical (and moral) counter-concepts to the standard, "normal" (work) biographies. Depictions of submissively crouching beggars in pedestrian zones referred to long-lasting iconographic traditions and can be seen as a compressed visualization of individual social decline.[70] To what extent media consumers felt fear, or were deterred, motivated, or incited because of such representations, has not been decisively clarified. As we have seen, during times of prosperity and wellbeing, there were many societal reflections regarding the reasons for the existence of "residual paupers."[71] From a (neo-)Marxist point of view, new considerations were brought into the discussion: the poor were essential due to their useful feature—namely, the production of fear. With only their mere existence, they could keep millions in check, embodying the threat of absolute nothing.[72] This interpretative pattern, which outlined not only political omissions but also systemic (capitalistic) failures in general, would celebrate its comeback several years later.

In the GDR, the modes of verbal-symbolic inclusion and exclusion of certain social groups functioned in a slightly different way. As in West Germany, the 1960s were also a period of a remarkable shift toward internal problems and a discovery of the social margins there. Legal measures such as the passing of a new penal code with the famous paragraph 249 for "A-sociality,"[73] the huge number of scholarly publications in the context of a "scientification of the social" (*Verwissenschaftlichung des Sozialen*)[74]—the increasing problematizing of social processes as academic questions and the permeation of different processes of socialization—and, finally, the media adaptation of "the social" were clear signs of a paradigm change. After the construction of the Berlin Wall and the physical containment of "harmful" western influences via contamination, different contemporaries pointed out the deficits of socialist collectivization.[75] As a result, many scholarly studies—only published within the GDR—examined the societal margins, with the objective of finding out where, and why, the enforcement of sociopolitical targets regarding the process of social reproduction was not "satisfactorily solved."[76] These studies pointed out significant distance between pensioners, large families, and single-mother-households, whether in terms of material, monetary, or cultural dimensions. As a consequence, observers noted a specific fear among the concerned: at the end of the 1960s, many GDR citizens were afraid of reaching retirement age.[77] This fear was not baseless: an internal survey from 1972 revealed that half of all large families and more than one third of all pensioners in the GDR could be regarded as "poor."[78] This result had to be kept secret, and only functionaries and select parts of the scholarly community were informed; but they certainly regarded the findings as an unprecedented and potentially explosive social and political force, especially after the events of the Prague Spring in 1968. As a consequence, a strategy of social pacification was sought through Honecker's 1971, "unity of economic and social policy" (*Einheit von Wirtschafts- und Sozialpolitik*), and the sociopolitical efforts were intensified. The fear of disclosing social inequalities was great. Instead, the claim that all forms of poverty had been eliminated was an essential and integral part of the inward legitimization of sovereignty and an outward sign of the superiority of socialism. These communication strategies in terms of "social insecurity" remained a significant structural element at that time. It seemed that the permanent reference to, and visualization of, the "capitalistic" failures was used to define the benefits of socialism *ex negativo*: the supposed, constant fear of becoming unemployed and/or homeless and, in general, the "unsocial" system as a whole—where elderly people and large families were socially oppressed—could be found in regular weekly media cycles.[79] On the other hand, the sociopolitical measures for each country's own "underprivileged" population coincided with symbolic up-valuations: in mass media, social figurations that "proved" the successful regime were the order of the day. Representations of happy, sprightly "veterans of work" or well-ordered, disciplined, and perfectly educated children in large families, helped establish the two most important symbolic counter-terms of social fear and anxiety among the GDR public: safety and security (*Sicherheit und Geborgenheit*). These were highly symbolic and didactically presented in positive model biographies. The symbolic forms discussed above needed a symbolic counterpart: that of socially deviant families or individuals. Since the late 1960s, in many internal sociological, criminological, or medical studies, one could find indications of the fear of decline and of losing social status on the part of party functionaries and others, as was already the case in the early labor movement. This old discourse regarding the demarcation between the *lumpenproletariat* and the real, orderly, and honest worker can be found in these scientific attributions and categorizations as well, and it referred to a pronounced fear, disgust, and abhorrence of the "lowest (social) class."[80] The terms *a-sociality* and *dissociality* (*Dissozialität*) were expressions for these tendencies, which were in many respects quite "bourgeois": large families and/or unskilled or low-skilled workers, in particular, who did not fit into the desired socialistic framework of behavioral and moral principles, were accused of being parasitic, egoistic, inefficient, and irresponsible. Within these social descriptions, a continuation of a traditional, petty bourgeois set of values[81] can be found, usually including laziness, alcoholism, the breakdown of universal moral norms, and the neglect of one's household, children, and family. The fear of an intergenerational transfer to the younger generation was also often mentioned explicitly.[82]

The discussion was similarly, slightly transformed within the media and public spheres. Narratives about the "undeserving poor"—which were highly individualized and usually neglected all potential systemic errors—introduced the socialist anti-type to a substantial audience through TV genres like the contemporary crime serials *Polizeiruf 110* and *Der Staatsanwalt hat das Wort*,[83] as well as through semi-fictional court documentaries in newspapers. Alliterative stories about the 'labile Lutz' or 'idle (*arbeitsscheue*) Annelene'[84] again refer to a symbolic and performative dimension. The presentation of both positive and negative model biographies had an important function in stabilizing rules and mobilizing spectators in two different ways: (1) symbolizing security and safety by offering instructions for the appropriate handling and negotiating of desired values like virtue, modesty, diligence, and an appropriate work moral; (2) referring to the potential consequences of "abnormal" patterns of behavior by reviving older standards and norms. There are various indications that these semantics were primarily addressed to the working (middle) class, as scenarios of social loss and symbolic degradations could (assumedly) or should (presumably the wish of political and media elites) support the determination of their imagines and real (social) location.

Crisis Years: Old and New Semantics of Fear (1975–90)

Since the mid-1970s, certain forms of crisis were increasingly shaping both German states. The energy crisis in 1973 sounded the bell for the end of the postwar economic boom.[85] Both German states had to recognize in the following years that the vision of a predictable and designable society and social order would be difficult to achieve.[86] It was not that the basic (symbolic and real) handling of socially marginalized groups had changed completely, but that noticeable changes could be observed, particularly in regard to the "undeserving poor" in West Germany. In the context of the political rediscovery of poverty in the mid-1970s[87] and, one decade later, in the debate about the "new poverty" (*Neue Armut*),[88] a remarkable revival of exclusionary rhetoric became quite conspicuous. Some of the politicians and media outlets now openly condemned social fraud, laziness, and "shirkers."[89] The famous symbol of the (social) hammock as a metaphor for the overly generous welfare state united all these supposed features of indolence. This (verbal and visual) symbol was used by critics of the welfare state, who insisted that more attention should be paid to wage labor and the wage gap (*Lohnabstandsgebot*), and that social benefits should be lower than the going wage. Calls were also made for a reduction in social contributions, like unemployment benefits. As a side effect of the highly generalized and pithy presentations, the motif of the fear of social decline and material need was publicized, especially through the high-circulation daily newspaper *Bild*.[90] Within the more nervous public climate of the 1980s, narratives of former civil servants who were now, in the context of mass unemployment, the unforeseen "clients" of second-hand clothing stores and soup kitchens, allegorized a transformation of the perception and representation of poverty, which now included warnings of a new "underclass."[91]

On the whole, a stronger concentration on the individual fates of the poor reflects the renewed value placed on sensitivity in Western industrial countries since the 1970s.[92] The living situation of (poor) pensioners once again received focused when set alongside the potential social risks faced during people's working life. As discussed previously, there was consistent and widespread attention given to the "worthy poor," but representations of the "elderly poor" took on a new life: during this period, the poor and starving female pensioner, eating dog food or searching for leftovers at the weekly market, became the archetype for poverty.[93] Such images were normally accompanied by sharp appeals to separate these "bashful poor," from the "welfare scroungers" and "parasites." The depiction of meager flats and sparse diets not only symbolically outlined their social respectability; it also reflected the intensified societal engagement with demographic developments and the risks of insufficient individual and state pension schemes.[94]

The highly self-reflective discussion about the context of "fear" and "poverty" reached a peak in the mid-1980s, when the unemployment rate reached more than two million and sociopolitical legislation was reduced.[95] The connection between both terms was explicitly outlined from different political and ideological directions: "Inequality is necessary," stated the 1974 Nobel Memorial Prize Winner in Economics Friedrich August von Hayek in 1981. These comments received significant attention in West Germany. According to him, inequality is not regrettable but rather required for society because it serves as an additional motivating factor in generating the social product. The individual decides freely if he or she wants to perform better or not[96]—a neoliberal criticism of the welfare state, according to which inequality acts as a driving force for the functioning of capitalist society, or in short: "Every man is the architect of his own fortune."[97] Taking up this idea, "leftist" or Marxist critics of the welfare state also discussed these ideas, including the social scientist Wolf Wagner, who regarded the constant "fear of falling" as one of the most decisive factors of everyday actions.[98] Political scientist Ernst-Ulrich Huster described poverty as a "nightmare"—as an indispensable component, incentive, and negative pole of the performance-oriented society, which would deter demotivation and laziness.[99]

Meanwhile, there were similar discussions taking place in the GDR. As a reaction to economic stagnation and noticeable socio-economic problems due to, *inter alia*, the Soviet Union's control of oil and increasing restriction of supplies, several sociologists claimed that larger income differentials could act as additional driving forces (*Triebkräfte*) for society. Doubts could be observed, according to which the "convergence of the classes" became steadily less convincing.[100] Moreover, internal studies increasingly looked beyond the failings of the individual, to the failures of society and its structural deficits. But these voices never reached the attention of the broader public. Instead, the hegemonic representation was of a GDR free from the fear of the workplace and social decline, a representation that was even appropriated by West German observers.[101] Until 1989, fear of the internal "other" fulfilled an important moral function in the GDR system of emotions. As before, affiliation and non-affiliation were regulated via language and depictions, which helped to identify internal and external enemies on the one hand—and on the other, to conjure the image of an "orderly" collective of citizens. In this context, language and representation were highly ritualized and morally oriented.[102] Simultaneously, the crisis in the West offered the media and politics welcome points of reference in order to highlight the supposed supremacy of each state's system: countless media examples could be found that discussed long-term unemployment, the greed for profit, homeless persons, fear about wages and food, and the individual fates of social relegation and hopeless situations in the context of the "new poverty."[103] In many respects, the media communication strategies from this period were similar to those in the 1950s—but times had changed, and it seemed that these narratives could not motivate the desired effect. For Germans in the GDR, even the socio-economic situation of the poorer classes of West German society was regarded as sufficiently promising.[104]

Conclusion and Outlook

In West and East Germany, the "fear of falling" and social relegation was closely linked to the fear of the destruction of internal order.[105] In this context, fear had an important segregationist function, dividing society into homogenous communities of social equals, and demarcating between being endangered and being dangerous.[106] The reduction of insecurity via social policy[107] was one of the major tasks of the respective governments in the West and East, and this policy had to be propagated insistently. Moreover, aside from the sociopolitical measurements, there was a durable presence of a symbolic dimension that was promoted by politicians, scholars, and the media. Apart from the constant public imagining of the "worthy" poor, their symbolic opposition—the "unworthy" poor—was an inherent part of the public communication of social mobility and the desirable social structure: homeless people, large families, and certain social welfare recipients (in the case of the FRG), and "a-socials," "dissocials," and also large families (in the case of the GDR) allegorized socially undesirable and unacceptable behavior. In the press, social and juridical documentaries, and crime movies, the images of social "otherness" were remarkably consistent. The presence of "welfare scroungers" and "parasites" was a very important feature of the West and East German media landscapes from at least the 1960s. These images were transformed during the subsequent decades and appeared in different forms, depending on context, such as the economic situation.

It should not be forgotten, of course, that it is very difficult to trace the effective power of scenarios of social relegation and images of social threat, especially in historical retrospective. Taking into consideration the aforementioned brief sketch of fear in divided Germany along with its differences and analogies, at least three points can be noted for now. (1) The communicative functions of the production and distribution of "fear" changed over time. (2) It can be reasonably assumed, according to Barbara Rosenwein, that both "social communities"—the FRG and GDR—established specific "systems of feeling"[108] with a primary functional task: the public and media narratives of "poverty" were meant to handle the "nervousness of the middle."[109] And, (3) even though the "middle" was not precisely the "middle" and the fear of impoverishment varied considerably,[110] recourse to history may allow a better understanding of the present: the privatization of the public sector and other fields of work; cutbacks in social security benefits; flexible working arrangements; increasing temporary employment; and a return to normal working arrangements, are all hallmarks of the postmodern world of work.[111]

Following the sociologist Heinz Bude, the fear of social failure is the driving force of the "zero-error principle" in the late twentieth and early twenty-first centuries, which resulted in numerous publications of "self-optimization," but also a slavish self-exploitation. Eventually, the result would be a society of permanently exhausted and depressed individuals.[112] Even though this assessment seems exaggerated, the supposed constant stress and pressure could explain certain recent observations. These include, the controversies about social welfare connected to Thilo Sarrazin's book *Germany Is Doing Away with Itself* (2010);[113] the term *social tourism* as the 2013 "nonword" of the year; the debates in the context of the European migrant crisis and the resulting (real or imagined) conflict about the distribution of social resources;[114] or various publications regarding the German "underclass," the "unnecessary,"[115] or the "precariat" (*Prekariat*),[116] which frequently contained a mixture of compassion, voyeurism, merrymaking, and outrage. These publications shape particular images of an, "underclass" and—based on their success in the marketplace—the public clearly thirsts for them. The reasons for their success cannot yet be decisively clarified, but the deflection of each country's own "fear of falling" and the uncertainty permeating large sections of each population could be plausible explanations. Even the party *Alternative für Deutschland* (AfD, Alternative for Germany) currently knows how to profit from the (social) fears and insecurities of many people, and there are various reasons why this works even better in the former East Germany. Therefore, the "fear of falling" highlights not only long-term patterns of argumentation, epistemic figures, and topoi but also current issues with very real social and political importance.

Notes

1 Lisa Erdmann and Anna Reimann, "Gesellschaft in der Krise: Die Angst vorm Abstieg," *Spiegel Online*, June 6, 2010. Avail.: http://www.spiegel.de/politik/deutschland/gesellschaft-in-der-krise-die-angst-vorm-abstieg-a-699777.html [accessed June 19, 2016].

2 Holger Lengfeld and Jochen Hirschle, "Die Angst der Mittelschicht vor dem sozialen Abstieg. Eine Längsschnittanalyse 1984–2007," *Zeitschrift für Soziologie* 38, no. 5 (2009): 394.

3 Barbara Ehrenreich, *Fear of Falling: The Inner Life of the Middle Class* (New York: Pantheon Books, 1989).

4 Jefferson Morley, "Review of Barbara Ehrenreich, Fear of Falling," *New York Times*, August 6, 1989.

5 Barbara Ehrenreich, *Angst vor dem Absturz: das Dilemma der Mittelklasse* (München: Kunstmann, 1992); Barbara Ehrenreich, Angst vor dem Absturz : das Dilemma der Mittelklasse (Reinbek bei Hamburg: Rowohlt, 1994).

6 For an overview of the discussion from the past fifteen years see *inter alia*: Ute Frevert, "Angst vor Gefühlen? Die Geschichtsmächtigkeit von Emotionen im 20. Jahrhundert," in *Perspektiven der Gesellschaftsgeschichte*, ed. Paul Nolte (München: Beck, 2003), 95–111; Nina Verheyen, "Geschichte der Gefühle, Version: 1.0," *Docupedia-Zeitgeschichte*, June 18, 2010; Alexandra Przyrembel, "Sehnsucht nach Gefühlen. Zur Konjunktur der Emotionen in der Geschichtswissenschaft," *L'Homme* 16 (2005): 116–24; Martina Kessel, "Gefühle und Geschichtswissenschaft," in *Emotionen und Sozialtheorie*, ed. Rainer Schützeichel (Frankfurt am Main: Campus-Verlag, 2006), 29–47; Frank Biess, et al., "History of Emotions: Forum," *German History* 28, no. 1 (2010): 67–80; Jonas Liliequist, ed., *A History of Emotions: 1200–1800* (London: Pickering & Chatto,

2012); Jan Plamper, *Geschichte und Gefühl. Grundlagen der Emotionsgeschichte* (München: Siedler, 2012); Jan Plamper, *The History of Emotions: An Introduction* (Oxford: Oxford University Press, 2017); Barbara H. Rosenwein, *Generations of Feeling: A History of Emotions, 600–1700* (Cambridge: Cambridge University Press, 2016). For a critical appraisal see: Rüdiger Schnell, *Haben Gefühle eine Geschichte? Aporien einer "History of Emotions"* (Göttingen: V&R unipress, 2015).

7   Pierre-Frédéric Weber, *Timor Teutonorum: Angst vor Deutschland seit 1945. Eine europäische Emotion im Wandel* (Paderborn: Schöningh, 2015).

8   Holger Nehring, "Angst, Gewalterfahrungen und das Ende des Pazifismus. Die britischen und westdeutschen Proteste gegen Atomwaffen, 1957–1964," in *Angst im Kalten Krieg*, ed. Bernd Greiner, Christian Th. Müller, Dierk Walter, et al. (Hamburg: Ed Hamburger, 2009), 436–64.

9   Eckart Conze, *Die Suche nach Sicherheit. Eine Geschichte der Bundesrepublik Deutschland von 1949 bis zur Gegenwart* (München: Siedler, 2009); Eckart Conze, "Sicherheit als Kultur. Überlegungen zu einer 'modernen Politikgeschichte' der Bundesrepublik Deutschland," *Vierteljahrshefte für Zeitgeschichte* 53 (2005): 357–80; Eckart Conze, *Geschichte der Sicherheit: Entwicklung – Themen – Perspektiven* (Göttingen: Vandenhoeck & Ruprecht, 2018).

10 Stefan Hradil, "Armut in einer modernen Gesellschaft," in *Arm und Reich. Zur gesellschaftlichen und wirtschaftlichen Ungleichheit in der Geschichte*, ed. Günther Schulz (Stuttgart: Steiner, 2015), 15–24.

11 For theoretical background see: Christoph Jahr, Uwe Mai, and Kathrin Roller, eds., *Feindbilder in der deutschen Geschichte: Studien zur Vorurteilsgeschichte im 19. und 20. Jahrhundert* (Berlin: Metropol Verlag, 1994). For the GDR see: Silke Satjukow and Rainer Gries, eds., *Unsere Feinde: Konstruktionen des Anderen im Sozialismus* (Leipzig: Leipziger Universitäts-Verlag, 2004).

12 Regarding the differences between democracy and social market economy vs. dictatorship and planned economy see: Christoph Kleßmann, "Verflechtung und Abgrenzung. Aspekte der geteilten und zusammengehörigen deutschen Nachkriegsgeschichte," *Aus Politik und Zeitgeschichte* 29/30 (1993): 30–41. Kleßmann was the pioneer in this field See: Christoph Kleßmann, *Die doppelte Staatsgründung. Deutsche Geschichte 1945–1955* (Göttingen: Vandenhoeck & Ruprecht, 1982); Christoph Kleßmann, *Zwei Staaten, eine Nation. Deutsche Geschichte 1955–1970* (Göttingen: Vandenhoeck & Ruprecht, 1988); Christoph Kleßmann, *The Divided Past: Rewriting Post-war German History* (Oxford: Berg, 2001); Christoph Kleßmann and Georg Wagner, eds., *Das gespaltene Land. Leben in Deutschland 1945–1990. Texte und Dokumente zur Sozialgeschichte* (München: Beck, 1993); Christoph Kleßmann and Peter Lautzas, eds., *Teilung und Integration: Die doppelte deutsche Nachkriegsgeschichte als wissenschaftliches und didaktisches Phänomen* (Schwalbach am Taunus: Wochenschau-Verlag, 2006).

13 Christoph Kleßmann, "Spaltung und Verflechtung—Ein Konzept zur integrierten Nachkriegsgeschichte 1945 bis 1990," in *Teilung und Integration*, ed. Christoph Kleßmann and Peter Lautzas (Schwalbach am Taunus: Wochenschau-Verlag, 2006), 20–37.
14 With no claim of being complete: Konrad H. Jarausch, "'Die Teile als Ganzes erkennen.' Zur Integration der beiden deutschen Nachkriegsgeschichten," *Zeithistorische Forschungen/Studies in Contemporary History* 1 (2004): 10–30; Udo Wengst and Hermann Wentker, eds., *Das doppelte Deutschland. 40 Jahre Systemkonkurrenz* (Berlin: Links, 2008); Tobias Hochscherf, Christoph Laucht, and Andrew Plowman, eds., *Divided, but Not Disconnected. German Experiences of the Cold War* (New York: Berghahn Books, 2010); Detlef Brunner, Udo Grashoff, and Andreas Kötzing, eds., *Asymmetrisch verflochten? Neue Forschungen zur gesamtdeutschen Nachkriegsgeschichte* (Berlin: Links, 2013); Frank Bösch, ed., *Geteilte Geschichte. Ost- und Westdeutschland 1970–2000* (Göttingen: Vandenhoeck & Ruprecht, 2015).
15 Benjamin Lazier and Jan Plamper, "Introduction," in *Fear. Across the Disciplines*, ed. Benjamin Lazier and Jan Plamper (Pittsburgh, PA: University of Pittsburgh Press, 2012), 12, 1–14. See also: Michael Laffan and Max Weiss, eds., *Facing Fear: The History of an Emotion in Global Perspective* (Princeton, NJ: Princeton University Press, 2012).
16 Rom Harré, ed., *The Social Construction of Emotions* (Oxford: Blackwell, 1986).
17 Lars Koch, "Einleitung. Angst als Gegenstand kulturwissenschaftlicher Forschung," in *Angst. Ein interdisziplinäres Handbuch*, ed. Lars Koch (Stuttgart: Metzler, 2013), 2, 1–4. For the connection between media and emotions see also: Frank Bösch and Manuel Borutta, eds., *Die Massen bewegen. Medien und Emotionen in der Moderne* (Frankfurt am Main: Campus, 2006).
18 Paul Nolte, *Die Ordnung der deutschen Gesellschaft. Selbstentwurf und Selbstbeschreibung im 20. Jahrhundert* (München: Beck, 2000), 14.
19 See for example: Ute Frevert, "Was haben Gefühle in der Geschichte zu suchen?" *Geschichte und Gesellschaft* 35, no. 2 (2009): 183–208, here 198–9; Ute Frevert, ed., *Gefühlswissen: Eine lexikalische Spurensuche in der Moderne* (Frankfurt am Main: Campus, 2011).
20 C.f. the research overview: Bettina Hitzer, "Emotionsgeschichte—ein Anfang mit Folgen," *H-Soz-Kult*, November 23, 2011. Avail.: http://www.hsozkult.de/literaturereview/id/forschungsberichte-1221 [accessed June 20, 2016].
21 Alf Lüdtke, "Macht der Emotionen—Gefühle als Produktivkraft. Bemerkungen zu einer schwierigen Geschichte," in *Rausch und Diktatur. Inszenierung, Mobilisierung und Kontrolle in totalitären Systemen*, ed. Árpád von Klimó and Malte Rolf (Frankfurt am Main: Campus, 2006), 44–55.
22 Koch, "Einleitung."

23 Hans-Ulrich Wehler, "Emotionen in der Geschichte: Sind soziale Klassen auch emotionale Klassen?," in *Europäische Sozialgeschichte. Festschrift für Wolfgang Schieder*, ed. Christof Dipper, Lutz Klinkhammer, and Alexander Nützenadel (Berlin: Duncker & Humblot, 2000), 461–73. For a sociological point of view see: Jürgen Gerhards, *Soziologie der Emotionen. Fragestellungen, Systematik und Perspektiven* (München: Juventa, 1988), 11–23.
24 Heinz Bonfadelli and Thomas N. Friemel, *Medienwirkungsforschung* (Konstanz: UVK, 2000).
25 Hans-Ulrich Wehler, *Deutsche Gesellschaftsgeschichte, Vol. 5: Bundesrepublik und DDR: 1949–1990* (Bonn: Bundeszentrale für politische Bildung, 2009), 162.
26 Verheyen, "Geschichte der Gefühle."
27 Georg Simmel, *Soziologie. Untersuchungen über die Formen der Vergesellschaftung* (Leipzig: Duncker & Humblot, 1908), 371–2.
28 William Reddy, *The Navigation of Feeling. A Framework for the History of Emotions* (Cambridge: Cambridge University Press, 2001), 34–111, 108–37. For different approaches see: Schnell, *Gefühle*, vol. 1, 77–104.
29 This chapter is mainly based on my dissertation thesis. For a more detailed account of the following see: Christoph Lorke, *Armut im geteilten Deutschland. Die Wahrnehmung sozialer Randlagen in der Bundesrepublik und der DDR* (Frankfurt am Main: Campus, 2015). For recent research in historiography on this topic see also: Meike Haunschild, *"Elend im Wunderland." Armutsvorstellungen und Soziale Arbeit in der Bundesrepublik 1955–1975* (Marburg: Tectum, 2018); Raphael Lutz, ed., *Poverty and Welfare in Modern German History* (New York: Berg, 2017). For an overview see also: Winfried Süß, "Die Geschichte der Sozialpolitik als Teil der Neueren und Neuesten Geschichte/Zeitgeschichte," *Deutsche Rentenversicherung* 72, no. 2 (2017): 224–36.
30 Kleßmann, *Zwei Staaten*, 37–9; Paul Erker, "Hunger und sozialer Konflikt in der Nachkriegszeit," in *Der Kampf um das tägliche Brot. Nahrungsmangel, Versorgungspolitik und Protest 1770–1990*, ed. Manfred Gailus and Heinrich Volkmann (Opladen: Westdeutscher Verlag, 1994), 392–408; Petra Schmolling, *Die Armut in der Bundesrepublik Deutschland im Kontext gesellschaftlicher und politischer Entwicklungen* (Dissertation, Hamburg: Universität Hamburg, 1994), 147.
31 Deutscher Verein für öffentliche und private Fürsorge. *Aufgaben der Fürsorge zur Überwindung der deutschen Volksnot. Bericht über den Deutschen Fürsorgetag des Deutschen Vereins für öffentliche und private Fürsorge in Frankfurt/ Main am 13. Mai 1946* (Berlin: Urban & Schwarzenberg, 1947).
32 Friederike Föcking, *Fürsorge im Wirtschaftsboom: die Entstehung des Bundessozialhilfegesetzes von 1961* (München: Oldenbourg, 2007); Eike Geisel, *Lastenausgleich, Umschuldung. Die Wiedergutwerdung der Deutschen. Essays,*

Polemiken, Stichworte (Berlin: Edition Tiamat, 1984); Michael L. Hughes, "Lastenausgleich unter Sozialismusverdacht. Amerikanische Besorgnisse 1945–1949," *Vierteljahrshefte für Zeitgeschichte* 39 (1991): 37–53.

33 Meike Haunschild, "Freedom versus Security. Debates on Social Risks in Western Germany in the 1950s," *Historical Social Research* 41, no. 1 (2016): 180–1.

34 Ludwig Erhard, *Wohlstand für alle* (Düsseldorf: Econ-Verlag, 1957).

35 Axel Schildt, "'German Angst.' Überlegungen zur Mentalitätsgeschichte der Bundesrepublik," in *Geschichte als Experiment. Studien zu Politik, Kultur und Alltag im 19. und 20. Jahrhundert*, ed. Daniela Münkel and Jutta Schwarzkopf (Frankfurt am Main: Campus, 2004), 95, 87–97.

36 Ludwig von Friedeburg and Friedrich Weltz, *Altersbild und Altersvorsorge der Arbeiter und Angestellten* (Frankfurt am Main: Europäische Verlagsanstalt, 1958), 21.

37 Arthur Killat, "Problematik einer Reform der deutschen Sozialversicherung," *Gewerkschaftliche Monatshefte* 4 (1953): 90.

38 Anon. "Los, Bonn!," *Das grüne Blatt* 53 (1955): 12.

39 Cornelius Torp, "The Adenauer Government's Pensions Reform of 1957—A Question of Justice," *German History* 34, no. 2 (2016): here 252 and 256. C.f. also: Hans Günter Hockerts, *Der deutsche Sozialstaat. Entfaltung und Gefährdung seit 1945* (Göttingen: Vandenhoeck & Ruprecht, 2011), 71–85.

40 Anon. "Darauf haben Tausende in Hamburg gewartet: Tag der Rentner," *Bild-Zeitung*, April 11, 1957. See Lorke, *Armut*, 74–80.

41 Leonie Treber, *Mythos Trümmerfrauen. von der Trümmerbeseitigung in der Kriegs- und Nachkriegszeit und der Entstehung eines deutschen Erinnerungsortes* (Essen: Klartext, 2014), 241–76.

42 Bernd Hey, "Zwischen Vergangenheitsbewältigung und heiler Welt. Nachkriegsdeutsche Befindlichkeiten in deutschen Spielfilmen," *Geschichte in Wissenschaft und Unterricht* 52 (2001): 237.

43 Frank Biess, "Feelings in the Aftermath: Toward a History of Postwar Emotions," in *Histories of the Aftermath: The legacies of the Second World War in Europe*, ed. Frank Biess (New York: Berghahn Books, 2010), 34–7, 30–48.

44 Helmut Schelsky, "Die Bedeutung des Schichtungsbegriffs für die Analyse der gegenwärtigen deutschen Gesellschaft (1953)," in *Auf der Suche nach Wirklichkeit*, ed. Helmut Schelsky (Düsseldorf: Diederichs, 1965), 331–6.

45 Hans Braun, "'Helmut Schelskys Konzept der ‚nivellierten Mittelstandsgesellschaft' und die Bundesrepublik der 50er Jahre," *Archiv für Sozialgeschichte* 29 (1989): 199–223; Rüdiger Schmidt, "Kein Zeitalter der Extreme. Die Mitte als gesellschaftliches Leitbild in der Bundesrepublik," in *Soziale Ungleichheit im Visier: Wahrnehmung und Deutung von Armut und Reichtum seit 1945*, ed. Eva M. Gajek and Christoph Lorke (Frankfurt am Main: Campus), 85–99.

46 Käthe Kern, "Zehn Jahre Sozialfürsorge in der DDR," *Arbeit und Sozialfürsorge* 14 (1959): 629.
47 Georg Schild, "Kommunisten-Phobie. Angst und Hysterie in den USA im Kalten Krieg," *Gefühl und Kalkül. Der Einfluss von Emotionen auf die Politik des 19. und 20. Jahrhunderts*, ed. Birgit Aschmann (Stuttgart: Steiner, 2005), 86–100; Bernd Greiner, "Antikommunismus, Angst und Kalter Krieg: eine erneute Annäherung," in *"Geistige Gefahr" und "Immunisierung der Gesellschaft": Antikommunismus und politische Kultur in der frühen Bundesrepublik*, ed. Stefan Creuzberger (München: Oldenbourg, 2014), 29–41.
48 Marcus M. Payk, "Kalter Krieg," in: Koch, *Angst*, 325–31, here 327–9; Friederike Brühöfener, "'Angst vor dem Atom'. Emotionalität und Politik im Spiegel bundesdeutscher Zeitungen 1979-1984," in *Den Kalten Krieg denken: Beiträge zur sozialen Ideengeschichte*, ed. Patrick Bernhard (Essen: Klartext, 2014), 285–306.
49 Lorke, *Armut*, 112.
50 Christoph Butterwegge, *Armut in einem reichen Land. Wie das Problem verharmlost und verdrängt wird* (Frankfurt am Main: Campus, 2009), 105.
51 Conze, *Sicherheit*, 172.
52 Hartmut Kaelble, "Das europäische Sozialmodell – eine historische Perspektive," in *Das europäische Sozialmodell. Auf dem Weg zum transnationalen Sozialstaat*, ed. Hartmut Kaelble and Günther Schmid (Berlin: Edition Sigma, 2004), 31–50, 33; Gerhard K. Schäfer, "Geschichte der Armut im abendländischen Kulturkreis," in *Handbuch Armut und soziale Ausgrenzung*, ed. Ernst-Ulrich Huster, Jürgen Boeckh, and Hildegard Mogge-Grotjahn (Wiesbaden: VS, 2008), 221–41, 221, 229; Lorke, *Armut*, chapter I. 4.
53 Adalbert Evers and Helga Nowotny, *Über den Umgang mit Unsicherheit: Die Entdeckung der Gestaltbarkeit von Gesellschaft* (Frankfurt am Main: Suhrkamp, 1987), 109.
54 Peter Brügge, "'Unsere Armen haben das nicht nötig'. Elend im Wunderland," *Der Spiegel*, December 20, 1961.
55 Ulrich Beck, *Risikogesellschaft. Auf dem Weg in eine andere Moderne* (Frankfurt am Main: Suhrkamp, 1986), 121–60.
56 Stephan Leibfried, Lutz Leisering, and Petra Buhr, et al., *Zeit der Armut. Lebensläufe im Sozialstaat* (Frankfurt am Main: Suhrkamp, 1995), 217.
57 Petra Buhr, Lutz Leisering, Monika Ludwig, et al., "Armutspolitik und Sozialhilfe in vier Jahrzehnten," in *Die alte Bundesrepublik. Kontinuität und Wandel*, ed. Bernhard Blanke and Hellmut Wollmann (Opladen: Westdeutscher Verlag, 1991), 530.
58 For a summary see: Axel Schildt and Detlef Siegfried, eds., *Dynamische Zeiten. Die 60er Jahre in den beiden deutschen Gesellschaften* (Hamburg: Christians, 2003).
59 Achim Landwehr, *Geschichte des Sagbaren. Einführung in die historische Diskursanalyse* (Tübingen: ed. diskord, 2004).

60 Government declaration, Willy Brandt, January 18, 1973 ("Moderne Sozialpolitik handelt nicht mehr nur davon, die Furcht vor materieller Not und sozialem Abstieg zu beseitigen. Sie strebt nach mehr Gerechtigkeit und sie will bewirken, daß in unserer Gesellschaft mehr reale Freiheit herrscht."). See Klaus Stüwe, ed., *Die großen Regierungserklärungen der deutschen Bundeskanzler von Adenauer bis Schröder* (Opladen: Westdeutscher Verlag, 2002), 193.

61 For example see Josef Berres, "Zur Frage der Obdachlosen," *Nachrichtendienst des Deutschen Vereins für öffentliche und private Fürsorge* 43 (1963): 164–70; Werner Schlotmann, *Die Fruchtbarkeit im asozialen Milieu im Vergleich zum Durchschnitt in der Gesamtbevölkerung* (Dissertation, Düsseldorf: University Düsseldorf, 1968).

62 For France see: Christiane Reinecke, "Localising the Social: The Rediscovery of Urban Poverty in Western European 'Affluent Societies,'" *Contemporary European History* 24 (2015): 555–76. For the United States: Claudia Roesch, *Macho Men and Modern Women. Mexican Immigration, Social Experts and Changing Family Values in the 20th Century United States* (Berlin: De Gruyter Oldenbourg, 2015).

63 Ehrenreich, *Fear*, 51.

64 Oscar Lewis, "The Culture of Poverty," *Scientific American* 215 (1966): 19–25.

65 Schlotmann, *Fruchtbarkeit*; Anon., "Empfängnisverhütende Spritzen für obdachlose Frauen," *Frankfurter Allgemeine Zeitung*, February 17, 1970.

66 Michael Schanne, "Armut in den Medien," in *Gesellschaftliche Risiken in den Medien. Zur Rolle des Journalismus bei der Wahrnehmung und Bewältigung gesellschaftlicher Risiken*, ed. Werner A. Meier and Michael Schanne (Zürich: Seismo, 1996), 185–206, 201; Lorke, *Armut*, 300–2.

67 Winfried Menninghaus, *Ekel. Theorie und Geschichte einer starken Empfindung* (Frankfurt am Main: Suhrkamp, 2002).

68 Richard Stang, "Armut und Öffentlichkeit." Huster, Boeckh, and Mogge-Grotjahn *Handbuch Armut*, 577–88; Kurt Luger, "Das Bild der Dritten Welt in Österreichs Öffentlichkeit," *Medien Impulse* 7, no. 26 (1998): 16.

69 Florian Sattler, "Kommentar zum Randgruppenbericht der Bundesregierung, Das Notizbuch." *Bayerischer Rundfunk*, August 11, 1976, protocol, Bundesarchiv Koblenz, B 189/21991.

70 Christoph Sachße and Florian Tennstedt, *Bettler, Gauner und Proleten. Armut und Armenfürsorge in der deutschen Geschichte. Ein Bild-Lesebuch* (Reinbek bei Hamburg: Rowohlt, 1983); Gottfried Korff, "Bemerkungen zur aktuellen Ikonographie der Armut," in *Armut im Sozialstaat. Gesellschaftliche Analysen und sozialpolitische Konsequenzen*, ed. Siegfried Müller and Ulrich Otto (Neuwied: Luchterhand, 1997), 281–301; Kelly S. Johnson, *The Fear of Beggars. Stewardship and Poverty in Christian Ethics* (Grand Rapids, MI: Eerdmans, 2007).

71 Anton Burghardt, "Über residualen Pauperismus," *Zeitschrift für die gesamte Staatswissenschaft* 124 (1968): 349–68.

72 Wolfgang Röhl, "Armut in der Bundesrepublik." *Konkret*, January 13, 1969, 20–5, here quoting a spokesperson of the *Inner Mission*.
73 See: Sven Korzilius, *"Asoziale" und "Parasiten" im Recht der SBZ/DDR. Randgruppen im Sozialismus zwischen Repression und Ausgrenzung* (Köln: Böhlau, 2005); Johannes Raschka, "Mobilisierung zur Arbeit. Die Verfolgung von 'Parasiten' und 'Asozialen' in der Sowjetunion und in der DDR 1954–1977." *Zeitschrift für Geschichtswissenschaft* 53 (2005): 323–44.
74 Lutz Raphael, "Die Verwissenschaftlichung des Sozialen als methodische und konzeptionelle Herausforderung für eine Sozialgeschichte des 20. Jahrhunderts." *Geschichte und Gesellschaft* 22 (1996): 165–93.
75 Lorke, *Armut*, 147–53.
76 As for example in Rainer Ferchland, *Probleme der Annäherung von Arbeiterklasse und Intelligenz in der Industrie der Hauptstadt der DDR* (East Berlin: Akademie für Gesellschaftswissenschaften beim ZK der SED), 1981, 52.
77 Lorke, *Armut*, 153–4.
78 Hans Mai, *Zur quantitativen Widerspiegelung notwendiger individueller Bedürfnisse der Arbeiterklassen, dargestellt am Beispiel eines Vier-Personen-Arbeiter-Angestellten-Haushaltes* (Berlin: Institut für Konsumtion und Lebensstandard, Hochschule für Ökonomie, 1972, unpublished manuscript); Günter Manz, *Armut in der "DDR"-Bevölkerung. Lebensstandard und Konsumtionsniveau vor und nach der Wende* (Augsburg: Maro-Verlag, 1992), 85.
79 For example: Anon., "Weiße Kreise machen Mieter zum Freiwild," *Neues Deutschland*, July 2, 1966.
80 Michael Schwartz, "'Proletarier' und 'Lumpen.' Sozialistische Ursprünge eugenischen Denkens," *Vierteljahrshefte für Zeitgeschichte* 42, no. 4 (1994): 544.
81 Sven Korzilius, "Arbeitsethik, Sozialdisziplinierung und Strafrecht in der sowjetischen Besatzungszone und in der DDR – Kontinuität oder Diskontinuität," in *ausgesteuert – ausgegrenzt ... angeblich asozial*, ed. Anne Allex and Dietrich Kalkan (Neu-Ulm: AG-SPAK-Bücher, 2009), 213, 209–22.
82 Fritz Ahnert, *Untersuchungen über die Sozialstruktur dissozialer Familien im Kreis Kalbe/Milde* (Magdeburg: Medizinische Akademie Magdeburg, Dissertation, 1969), 51; Lorke, *Armut*, 157–66 for further examples. See also as an example for the later years: Hans Szewczyk, "Die Frühkriminalität Jugendlicher und der circulus vitiosus der Dissozialität," in *Humangenetik und Kriminologie. Kinderdelinquenz und Frühkriminalität*, ed. Hans Göppinger and Rainer Vossen (Stuttgart: Thieme/Enke/Hippokrates, 1984), 61–70. For Hans Szewczyk see also: Greg Eghigian, *The Corrigible and the Incorrigible. Science, Medicine, and the Convict in Twentieth-Century Germany* (Ann Arbor: University of Michigan Press, 2016).
83 Christoph Lorke, "Depictions of Social Dissent in East German Television Detective Series, 1970–1989," *Journal of Cold War Studies* 19, no. 4 (2017): 168–91.

84　Helge Hinrichs, "Arbeitsscheue Annelene warf niemanden hinaus," *Neue Zeit*, 8 August 1984; "Im Gerichtssaal notiert: Der labile Lutz," *Wochenpost*, 30 January 1987. See: Lorke, *Armut*, 340.

85　Anselm Doering-Manteuffel and Lutz Raphael, *Nach dem Boom. Perspektiven auf die Zeitgeschichte seit 1970* (Göttingen: Vandenhoeck & Ruprecht, 2010); Anselm Doering-Manteuffel, Lutz Raphael, and Thomas Schlemmer, eds., *Vorgeschichte der Gegenwart.Dimensionen des Strukturbruchs nach dem Boom* (Göttingen: Vandenhoeck & Ruprecht, 2016); Frank Bösch and Rüdiger Graf, eds., *The Energy Crises of the 1970s. Anticipations and Reactions in the Industrialized World* (Köln: GESIS, Leibniz Inst. for the Social Sciences, 2014).

86　Charles S. Maier, "Two Sorts of Crisis? The 'Long' 1970s in the West and the East," in *Koordinaten deutscher Geschichte in der Epoche des Ost-West-Konflikts*, ed. Hans Günter Hockerts (München: Oldenbourg, 2014), 49–62.

87　Heiner Geißler, *Die neue soziale Frage. Analysen und Dokumente* (Freiburg im Breisgau: Herder, 1976).

88　C.f. Marie Sophie Graf, *Die Inszenierung der Neuen Armut im sozialpolitischen Repertoire von SPD und Grünen 1983–1987* (Frankfurt am Main: Lang-Ed., 2015); Christoph Lorke, "Die Debatte über 'Neue Armut' in der Bundesrepublik. Konstruktion einer Kampagne und Strategien ihrer Zurückweisung (1983–1987)," *Zeitschrift für Geschichtswissenschaft* 63, no. 6 (2015): 552–71.

89　For more contextual information, see: Martin Jörg Schäfer, "Arbeitslosigkeit," in Koch, *Angst*, 359–65.

90　Thomas Riedmiller, *Arbeitslosigkeit als Thema der Bild-Zeitung* (Tübingen: Tübinger Vereinigung für Volkskunde, 1988), 77, 118.

91　Erika Martens, "Klassengesellschaft neuer Art? Als Folge der Wirtschaftskrise bildet sich in der Bundesrepublik eine neue Unterschicht," *Die Zeit*, May 24, 1985.

92　Frank Biess, "Die Sensibilisierung des Subjekts: Angst und 'neue Subjektivität' in den 1970er Jahren," *Werkstatt Geschichte* 49 (2008): 51–72. See also: Andreas Reckwitz, *Das hybride Subjekt. Eine Theorie der Subjektkulturen von der bürgerlichen Moderne zur Postmoderne* (Weilerswist: Velbrück Wissenschaft, 2006); Sabine Maasen, et al., eds., *Das beratene Selbst. Zur Genealogie der Therapeutisierung in den "langen" Siebzigern* (Bielefeld: Transcript-Verlag, 2011).

93　Lorke, *Armut*, 301–2.

94　Cornelius Torp, ed., *Challenges of Aging. Pensions, Retirement and Generational Justice* (Basingstoke: Palgrave Macmillan, 2015).

95　Marcel Boldorf, "Die 'Neue Soziale Frage' und die 'Neue Armut' in den siebziger Jahren. Sozialhilfe und Sozialfürsorge im deutsch-deutschen Vergleich," in *Das Ende der Zuversicht. Die siebziger Jahre als Geschichte*, ed. Konrad H. Jarausch (Göttingen: Vandenhoeck & Ruprecht, 2008), 138–56.

96　Friedrich August von Hayek, "Ungleichheit ist nötig," *Wirtschaftswoche* 11 (1981): 36–41.

97 George F. Gilder, *Reichtum und Armut* (Berlin: Severin und Siedler, 1981).
98 Wolf Wagner, *Die nützliche Armut. Eine Einführung in die Sozialpolitik* (Berlin: Rotbuch-Verlag, 1982).
99 Ernst Ulrich Huster, "Die Leistungsgesellschaft braucht Armut als Schreckgespenst." *Frankfurter Rundschau*, January 28, 1983; Lorke, *Armut*, 294–6.
100 Manfred Lötsch, "Soziale Strukturen als Wachstumsfaktoren und als Triebkräfte des wissenschaftlich-technischen Fortschritts," *Deutsche Zeitschrift für Philosophie* 30, no. 6 (1982): 721–31.
101 Marlies Menge, "Hier hat keiner Angst um seinen Arbeitsplatz," *Die Zeit*, August 5, 1977.
102 Ralph Jessen," Einschließen und Ausgrenzen. Propaganda, Sprache und die symbolische Integration der DDR-Gesellschaft," in *Politische Wechsel – sprachliche Umbrüche*, ed. Bettina Bock, Ulla Fix, and Steffen Pappert (Berlin: Frank & Timme, 2011), 135–52.
103 Just four examples: Werner Goldstein, "Dauerarbeitslos – sozialer Abstieg. Sog kapitalistischer Krise zerrt immer mehr Menschen ins Elend," *Neues Deutschland*, February 7, 1978; Anon., "Profitgier als Krebsübel," *Neues Deutschland*, August 9, 1978; Barbara Beissert, "Unterwegs im Saarland," *DDR-F-1* (television), March 5, 1980, Deutsches Rundfunkarchiv Babelsberg, IDNR 018758; Regina Drosdatis, "Das hätten sie sich nicht träumen lassen. Menschenschicksale in der BRD," *DDR-F-1* (television), February 19, 1986, Deutsches Rundfunkarchiv Babelsberg,., IDNR 018548.
104 Jens Gieseke, "Ungleichheit in der Gesellschaftsgeschichte der DDR," *ZeitRäume. Potsdamer Almanach des Zentrums für Zeithistorische Forschungen* (2009): 48–57; Jürgen Wilke, *Presseanweisungen im zwanzigsten Jahrhundert. Erster Weltkrieg – Drittes Reich – DDR* (Köln: Böhlau, 2007), 256–309.
105 Schildt, "German Angst," 89.
106 Thor Hvidbak, Lars Thorup Larsen, and Thomas Lemke, eds., *Fear*. Special Issue of Distinktion: Scandinavian Journal of Social Theory 12 (2011): 113–14.
107 David Denney, *Living in Dangerous Times: Fear, Insecurity, Risk and Social Policy* (Chichester: Wiley-Blackwell, 2009).
108 Barbara H. Rosenwein, "Worrying about Emotions in History," *American Historical Review* 107 (2002): 821–45, here 842.
109 Berthold Vogel, *Wohlstandskonflikte. Soziale Fragen, die aus der Mitte kommen* (Hamburg: Hamburger Edition, 2009).
110 Lengfeld and Hirschle, *Angst*; Olaf Groh-Samberg and Florian R. Hertel, "Abstieg der Mitte? Zur langfristigen Mobilität von Armut und Wohlstand," in *Dynamiken (in) der gesellschaftlichen Mitte*, ed. Nicole Burzan and Peter A. Berger (Wiesbaden: VS, 2010), 137–58.
111 Oliver Nachtwey, *Die Abstiegsgesellschaft. über das Aufbegehren in der regressiven Moderne* (Berlin: Suhrkamp, 2016); Berndt Keller and Hartmut Seifert, "Atypische

Beschäftigungsverhältnisse und Flexicurity," in *Flexicurity. Die Suche nach Sicherheit in der Flexibilität*, ed. Martin Kronauer and Gudrun Linne (Berlin: Ed. Sigma, 2005), 127–47.

112 Heinz Bude, *Gesellschaft der Angst* (Hamburg: Hamburger Ed., 2014); Alain Ehrenberg, *Das erschöpfte Selbst: Depression und Gesellschaft in der Gegenwart* (Frankfurt am Main: Suhrkamp, 2008). For self-optimization see: Ulrich Bröckling, *Das unternehmerische Selbst: Soziologie einer Subjektivierungsform* (Frankfurt am Main: Suhrkamp, 2007).

113 Michael Haller and Martin Niggeschmidt, eds., *Der Mythos vom Niedergang der Intelligenz: Von Galton zu Sarrazin. Die Denkmuster und Denkfehler der Eugenik* (Wiesbaden: VS, 2012).

114 Michalis Lianos, *Dangerous Others, Insecure Societies. Fear and Social Division* (Farnham: Ashgate, 2013).

115 Heinz Bude and Andreas Willisch, eds., *Exklusion. Die Debatte über die "Überflüssigen"* (Frankfurt am Main: Suhrkamp, 2008).

116 For an overview with numerous media examples see: Karl August Chassé, *Unterschichten in Deutschland: Materialien zu einer kritischen Debatte* (Wiesbaden: VS, 2010).

10

German Angst after 1945 as Fear of the Fear

Pierre-Frédéric Weber

Reinterpreting "German Angst" after 1945

Since the end of the Second World War, Germany has been, for many Europeans, a source of post-traumatic fears, some of which also go back to previous historical experience. Germany was seen as a threat to European and world security twice within less than half a century, due to its aggressive policies. Since 1945 it has been considered as a potential challenge to peace and order as a result of the Cold War situation, which split the country in two states divided by the Iron Curtain and, later, the Berlin Wall. Indeed, the so-called German question, long left unsettled, poisoned international relations until the successful reunification process of 1989/1990 when it became once again the most divisive European issue, especially with regard to the expected preponderance of German power in the European Economic Community (EEC)/European Union (EU). Margaret Thatcher's hostility was quite symptomatic of this perception. In fact, the German question was a stress factor no matter whether it was left open or a solution was sought: despite differences, there was, in both cases, a destabilizing effect perceived by Germany's neighbors.[1]

In addition, given the scale of Nazi crimes, Germany became a symbol of absolute evil and, as a consequence, a surrogate for many different fears and related emotions in Cold War Europe. States and societies projected some of their fears on Germany: fear of loss (of territory), fear of asymmetry or imbalance (in influence), fear of satellization (regarding sovereignty), and so on. These fears were not homogeneously distributed among Europeans; it is even possible to outline a certain territoriality governing fear(s) of Germany in Europe. Furthermore, this emotion was not equally and constantly present; it ebbed and flowed, and endured the adoption of different emotional temporalities and regimes[2] with regard to Germany by different "emotional communities."[3] Whatever the intensity, duration, and repetition of certain patterns of fear, this emotion was among those that dominated Europe during the postwar and Cold War periods, along with others: fear of communism, fear of nuclear war, and fear of apocalypse.

The perceptions and emotions of other nations could not but influence the Germans' self-perception, as well as their own emotional culture, after 1945. Much has been written about the political, ideological, and societal changes Germany experienced following its defeat in the Second World War, during the occupation regime (1945-9) or later, in both the Federal Republic of Germany (FRG) and the German Democratic Republic (GDR). Both the Allies' postwar program of disarmament, demilitarization, denazification, and democratization ("4D") and the later historiographical assessment of the results it actually achieved usually tend to present Germany's transformation as a change in civilization (in spite of some continuities—e.g., as far as elites were concerned). Peter Sloterdijk in particular uses the concept of *metanoia* to describe the transformation. He defines it as "the willingness to transform the cultural rules ascertained as detrimental to behavioral patterns of a less harmful form. ... [T]he term 'metanoia' ... does not mean ... Christian repentance but pragmatic relearning in order to increase civilizational viability."[4] Obviously this short definition does not contain all of the relevant elements constituting the process of *metanoia*, lacking especially the *emotional* dimension of the transformation. In this particular case, the structural change of Germany's international behavior was supposed to activate emotions such as shame[5] (about the past) and fear (of the future).

The consciousness of Nazi crimes, initiated by the Nuremberg trials and subsequently consolidated—especially as of the end of the 1960s and the beginning of the 1970s—led to a unique kind of reflection about German responsibility. In the FRG, the so-called *Vergangenheitsbewältigung*, a core element of the *metanoia* process, exerted a deep influence on the Germans' emotional culture. In an attempt to create the "first Workers' and Peasants' State on German soil," the GDR adopted an ideologically different position that biased the process, despite actually deeper and farther-reaching denazification, by assigning the responsibility to a class, that is, the capitalists rather than considering it in a broader national-societal frame.[6] Austria in turn evaded the process for almost forty years, stressing its "victimhood" rather than its co-responsibility, thus assuring itself an emotional security that was denied to Germany.[7]

The second element of the emotional aspect of (West) Germany's *metanoia* after 1945 concerned the Germans' position in international politics. This chapter intends to propose an interpretation of the centerpiece of German foreign policy after 1949 (when both German states were created), underlining in particular the case of the FRG: *self-limitation* (*Selbstbeschränkung*), primarily associated with the process of binding (West) Germany in the Western camp (*Westbindung*) in geopolitical, military, and economic dimensions.[8] Self-limitation would also include West Germany's refraining from any step possibly jeopardizing the Four Powers' rights concerning Germany as a whole. There is evidence that West Germany's subsequently cautious attitude in international politics, first conditioned chiefly by external factors (i.e., the states in charge of the German question: the United States, USSR, the UK, and France), became a self-imposed behavioral characteristic *sustained by a particular emotional culture/regime*. The deciding emotion fuelling this culture was a specific kind of fear: mirrored fear, or *fear of other nations' fear of Germany's territorial and/or economic ambitions*. As a matter of fact this chapter proposes a more interactive interpretation of "German Angst" that goes beyond the primary postwar fear and societal anxiety traditionally attributed to Germans since 1945. From Konrad Adenauer to Helmut Kohl, the FRG's decision-makers generally conducted the country's foreign policy while paying attention to other countries' possible emotional reactions. While this characterized the FRG's self-representation through foreign cultural policy,[9] it could be observed especially in situations in which the FRG had to choose a geopolitical path: Chancellor Adenauer's slogan "*Keine Experimente!*" was one of the most revealing examples of this attitude, which was also motivated by the fear of communism. After years, this emotional norm showed a strength that even surpassed earlier political expectations, when, for instance, the fear of the fear (along with common fear of a nuclear war) became internalized at a broader societal level through the pacifist movement growing stronger in the late 1970s.

Germany as an Historical Fear Factor in Europe

Before exploring Germany's role as a perceived political, economical, or military risk[10] for its European neighbors in the second half of the twentieth century, attention should first be paid to the farther origins of this collective emotional phenomenon. In international relations, fears can concern different types of risks in various areas. The main fear usually comes from the real or perceived risk of territorial loss. Here it is worth remembering that Germany began to play such a role in relation to its neighbors only in the second half of the nineteenth century, as for most of its *histoire longue*, Germany was not a unified space of power creating a single threat to other European agents (states). The Peace of Westphalia (1648) had not only brought the Thirty Years' War to an end but also meant a profound reorganization of international relations in Europe. The nation-state started becoming the main agent, which supposed a growing secularization of the concept of sovereignty once theologically attributed to God.[11] The sovereign state took this principle over and promulgated it in terms of its own territoriality. This was indeed a key moment, as the spatialization of sovereignty would also concern fears related to a possible loss of sovereignty. State territory would become a core attribute of modern sovereignty. This in turn would lead to a "resacralization" of secularized space: the territory was given the status of a sanctuary to be protected from outer aggression, violation, or annexation.[12] Both the highly emotional protection of a given state-agent's own territory and the (almost holy) fear of a loss of that territory led states to consider space as the highest good. This spatial materialization of sovereignty eventually led state-agents to develop a geopolitical mindset centered on the search for more space as a reaction to the fear of losing some of it. It also strengthened the importance of borders and redrawing of the "mental maps"[13] of European decision-makers—and crystallized to an even greater extent with the rise of modern nationalism in the nineteenth century and beyond.[14]

Germany's position as a nation-state was assured from 1871 following Prussia's victory over France and the creation of the Second Reich. This was also the moment when a unified German nation-state started playing the part of one of the main stress factors for its European neighbors. Actually, a kind of mutually stressing effect could be observed between Germany and states such as France or the UK. The frenzy of German foreign policy to catch up with other European powers,[15] especially after the Berlin Conference of 1884/1885, in terms of the establishment of its own colonial territory, was a source of risk for the interests of countries that had consolidated their possessions earlier. This fear would lead to a typical case of security paradox[16]: while trying to contain the expansion of German diplomacy in and beyond Europe through a net of trans-European military security alliances, state-agents such as France, the UK, and Russia conversely increased German fears of encirclement and strengthened the perception of the risk of a two-front war for Germany—Chancellor Bismarck's well-known "nightmare of coalitions." As a consequence, the quest for security and sovereignty became a source of greater insecurity. One of the best examples concerns the entanglements of German-French relations in that era.

Conscious of the stressing effect of Prussia's repeated successes in the 1860s (the wars against Denmark in 1864 and Austria in 1866) and eager to realize the project of a German nation-state from the North Sea to the Alps, Bismarck did not try to minimize French fear or other negative collective emotions. On the contrary, he took strategic steps leading to the intensification of French suspicions against Prussian intentions. Eventually, the crisis provoked around the so-called Ems Dispatch (1870) led Paris to taking the initiative and declaring war against Berlin. This plan to quash Prussia before it became hegemonic in Europe quickly backfired for France. Although the shock linked to an unexpected and shameful defeat was experienced by the French side after Prussia's victory (Napoleon III was captured and the German Empire founded while Paris was both under Prussian siege and in the throes of civil war), the success of Bismarck's strategy did not entirely appease German fears. France's post-traumatic stress as well as French embitterment in the wake of the territorial loss of Alsace and part of Lorraine would fuel an explosive mix of shame and resentment contained in Léon Gambetta's famous line, "*Y penser toujours, n'en parler jamais.*"[17] Pronounced with regard to the above-mentioned lost and contested territories, it announced the will for revenge—necessarily a source of concern for the newly united German state in the following years.

The Franco-Prussian war initiated a strongly negative emotional relationship between the two countries. One of the best concepts to characterize the complexity of contacts and conflict between France and Germany between 1870 and 1945 can be taken from the sociology of emotions: the two agents were emotionally interwoven through a "feedback loop" or "spiral."[18] The idea of "loops" offers indeed the advantage of showing both the self-dynamic and mimetic dimensions of emotional interaction. Thomas Scheff describes such "loops" as a particular case of feeling trapped, in which shame unleashes anger (rage), which in turn leads to shame again. Yet, in my opinion, one should not forget another fundamental emotion linking the first two and adding some complexity to the emotional dynamics: fear. What can be observed is in fact an emotional triangle including and relating anger, fear, and shame. Fear either incited shame to explode into rage, which I would call the "Ems spiral"—in allusion to the case of 1870 when the French Second Empire fearing to become Prussia's "underdog" reacted with rage to a (perceived as) shaming humiliation (the Ems Dispatch), declaring war to Prussia; or, on the contrary, fear blocked aggression and activated shame, which would be sort of a "Nuremberg spiral": the (channeled) anger expressed during the early Nazi period through mass events with torchlight processions in Nuremberg, for example, got unleashed in the

Second World War; after the Third Reich's defeat and collapse, the same city became emotionally symbolic again (*pars pro toto* for Germany as a whole), this time concentrating fear of the winners' justice and eventually first signs of German collective shame after the Nuremberg trials (in which France was, of course, not the only agent). In between, the conflict of the First World War was both an expression of mutual rage (and also French revenge) concluding the first so-called Ems spiral, as well as a main trigger for the "Nuremberg spiral" (stirring up German shame, and anger again).[19] These loops, however, did not presage the endless repetition of the relationship in question. They also bore the potential for change. This occurred after the end of the Second World War, the paroxysmal and final stage of the two entangled French–German emotional spirals I have described.

En route to Germany's *Metanoia*

The cycle of violence between France and Germany was only the most outstanding part of the conflict opposing Germany to Western Europe. From a naval and commercial perspective, the shared perception of a major reciprocal threat by Germany and the UK would appear by the end of the nineteenth century.[20] However, France represented a much stronger challenge to the German territories and communities, especially since the French Revolution and its subsequent export throughout Europe with the Napoleonic Wars. As Europe's main stress factor from 1789 to 1815 (and even later, if one considers the slower rhythm of changes in collective mentality), France was a major source of German fears. This prolonged stress exposure was later converted into aggression (rage). In fact, there would be two contradictory collective feelings directed toward France: the country and its culture were both awful and awe-inspiring. Or, as expressed in German: they caused *Furcht* as well as *Ehrfurcht*. Yet, as Sloterdijk underlines, this was not an emotional one-way system; the German-French relationship was "something fatal, something that had been more than just a relationship going back at least as far as the era of the Napoleonic Wars whereby the Germans and the French had, culturally and politically, become caught up in an endless cycle of mimicry, imitation, one-upmanship and projective empathy with each other. This began acutely with the French importing German romanticism with Germaine de Staël's influential book *De l'Allemagne* of 1813 and the Prussians importing the Napoleonic art of war through Clausewitz's book *Vom Kriege* (posthumous 1832-34)."[21] The same author, chronologically resuming where Scheff ended, calls the process by means of which both countries—or both nations—began to change their mutual perception after 1945, from "fascination" to "de-fascination" (*Entfaszinierung*) and "disentanglement" (*Entflechtung*), a cultural phenomenon of *metanoia*.[22] This deep cultural change was made possible only thanks to a fundamental collective transformation of the emotional norm in the social communities concerned, particularly the German. Whereas until the very end of the Second World War, a general atmosphere of hatred and aggression had prevailed as the legitimate norm of the German so-called *Volksgemeinschaft* with regard to its perceived enemies, this once tightly state-controlled rage mostly visible in Nazi propaganda material and mass meetings had eventually to undergo a determinant evolution or, rather, a rupture. This change included a strong emotional dimension that became obvious in particular in the Allied Forces' postwar projects for Germany.

The decisions made at the Potsdam conference in early August 1945 have often been summed up as the "4D" program. Defeated Germany had lost its sovereignty and would have to be transformed according to four (sometimes extended to five) main principles: *d*emilitarization, *d*enazification, *d*emocratization, *d*ecentralization (and *d*ecartelization).[23] The root idea was to reeducate the German nation, to inculcate in the Germans norms and models that would break up with the perceived German "*Sonderweg*" and move closer to the norm-setting patterns of Western liberalism. As such, the postwar evolution in (West) Germany was an important stage on the "long way towards the West" described by H. A. Winkler.[24] In fact, this civilizational shift was not only a question of rational social norms, discourses, and practices. It included and was even—I daresay—sustained by strong emotional dynamics. Indeed, if one considers Germany as an, "emotional community," it appears that German society also went through a profound transformation process leading from an "emotional regime"[25] dominated by pride and aggression to a radically different one characterized by shame—and fear. Of course, circumspection is required here in order not to resort to abusive generalization. The main "emotional climate" during the Hitler regime[26] would not exclude the expression of other, sometimes divergent feelings. It even might have included emotional contents which had been obvious in the case of the Nazi leisure organization called *Kraft durch Freude* ("Strength through Joy"): inculcating the German people with the Third Reich's ideology and uniting the society around the new cult of strength and pride presupposed on one side a regime of fear directed outward (and also inward, against actual or potential opponents) and on the other a set of positive emotions fostering social cooperation and collective acceptance.[27] Group happiness through organized trips and other leisure activities was one of the means applied by the Nazi state as an emotional norm-setter.[28]

At the end of the war in 1945, "Germany's Zero Hour" also meant a profound emotional disruption. Fear, which had already started its rise to a major collective emotion in Germany as the Allied Forces' carpet bombing of many German cities grew heavier, eventually dominated the emotional climate when the war was over. It is worth reflecting on the question of which experience(s), both individual and collective, Germany's postwar emotional regime was rooted in.

"German Angst": The Emotional Origins of Germany's Postwar Collective Behavior

During the winter of 1945, reports on the reality on the front lines (especially in the east) based on private experience were more and more in dissonance with the official discourse of Nazi propaganda. Contrary to the compulsory optimism about the imminent implementation of a "wonder weapon" capable of bringing the Third Reich final victory, more and more Germans had to cope with the destruction caused by Allied air attacks on German territory. Moreover, farther to the east in Germany, information about the successes of the Red Army and its soldiers' excesses and crimes (e.g., against German women[29]) also contributed to delegitimize Germany's heretofore dominant emotional regime of pride and confidence. Against the will of Nazi officials, many Germans living close to the approaching eastern front decided to flee westwards so as to escape from the Soviet "barbarians." The Germans' disregard for nations depicted in earlier years as inferior to the "Aryans" was transformed into fear of revenge.[30]

The first great shock in the closing stage of the Second World War thus concerned German populations in Central and Eastern Europe, especially those settled in territories bordering interwar Poland or constituting to that point a part of Czechoslovakia. These Germans were forced to abandon their homelands, either because they were fleeing from the Red Army rolling over the Wehrmacht or because they were expelled and subsequently forced to emigrate by the postwar regimes in Poland, Czechoslovakia, and other states in the region in accordance with the Potsdam agreements.[31] Taking with them, for the most part, only what they would be able to carry themselves, they had to leave their houses, farms, cattle, and other property in order to escape. Many of the refugees heading for the central and western parts of the Third Reich were women, children, and elderly people, who were not directly involved in the war.[32] Their justified fear and direct experience of loss was probably the first collective German emotion determining later emotional patterns and evolution in postwar Germany. This initial, spontaneous fear did *not* reflect the causality between Nazi aggression and the revenge of the victim states (and nations). For several decades (sometimes even up to our times),[33] German expellees tended to see themselves as innocent victims, which was a result of their inability to see the link between German responsibility and the loss of German territories (and their homes) in the east. This was quite obvious especially in expellees' claims for their so-called right to homeland (*Recht auf Heimat*), which would often blend out the very reason why so many Germans had had to abandon their native regions in Central Europe and lead to criminalizing postwar expulsion (or to emphasizing blind acts of revenge actually committed against some of the expellees by Poles or Czechs, e.g., during the forced migration process). This interpretation was seen as legitimate in the FRG until the late 1960s, when the expellees' lobby gradually lost its influence on both domestic and foreign policies.[34]

With the collapse of the Nazi state system, overrun from the east and from the west by the Allies in the spring of 1945, the experience of loss, fear, and despair struck more and more Germans. These negative feelings were intensified by the behavior of the occupying troops, not only, but especially, Soviet soldiers. Recent research has showed that the last weeks of the Second World War and the first months of the postwar period brought an unprecedented number of suicides in the German population. There were many cases of collective suicide, in which a whole family chose death instead of hardship and dishonor (rape). Even if Christian education and tradition forbade suicide, which must have had its consequences in terms of the will to hide the reality of this massive social phenomenon, the observed rise in mortality—a death toll linked not only to war and privation—could not but indicate it.[35] Of course, this collective anxiety and hopelessness did not characterize the German population alone; it was present also—sometimes even more so—among the former victimized nations. What Huber calls the "smell of fear"[36] was pervasive throughout the European continent after years of mass destruction and murder. This sort of "Great Fear" was not like the *Grande Peur*, a collective panic attack overwhelming the French people in 1789,[37] in the early stages of the Revolution; it was rather a lasting feeling of powerlessness in a life-endangering postwar environment, as described, for example, by Marcin Zaremba in terms of the Polish case.[38]

However, one additional factor characterized the emotional climate—and, soon, the emotional regime—in (West) Germany: shame over the crimes committed during the Second World War in Europe. The liberation of the concentration and extermination camps established by the Nazis in occupied Central and Eastern European countries from 1939 to 1945 revealed to the Allied Forces the actual scale of terror to which the Nazi ideology had led during the war. This strengthened their will to "denazify" Germany by punishing war crimes and would eventually lead to the long and unprecedented Nuremberg trials.[39] The German postwar population belatedly (in the case of most average citizens) discovered if not the reality, at least the tremendous scale of the abysmal crimes that had been perpetrated due to the German people's indifference, acceptance, and/or participation. This shock needed some time to be absorbed and to lead to new, emotionally structured, collective behavior.

Fear of the Fear (1): *Vergangenheitsbewältigung*

In the first postwar years, Germans lived in an occupied, disorganized, and partially devastated country with no sovereignty of its own. All the attention of postwar populations is usually concentrated on the satisfaction of their main (i.e., minimally necessary) needs. In situations of life-threatening crisis the realm of emotion tends to be limited to strong basic feelings, among which fear is probably dominant, temporarily leaving little space for more sophisticated emotions. After a total war like the Second World War, symptoms reminding of what we call today post-traumatic stress disorder (PTSD) would affect not only war veterans[40] but also many civilians (in bombed cities for example), driving many individuals and groups into a state of more or less pathological emotional blunting.[41] This comes to expression in particular through the difficulty of mourning even their own relatives, let alone other victims—a social phenomenon best described in the Mitscherlichs' classical study of post-Nazi Germany.[42] Hitler's leader cult in particular had had a powerful impact on the collective emotional regime dominating Germans during those years: by concentrating in one person all their "emotional effort"[43] toward collective pride and disdain for feebleness or despair, the Nazis had practically rendered sorrow taboo. Reduced to a mostly individual and often nonverbal practice, mourning became a sort of barely possible "emotional refuge"[44] bearing a high risk (and thus fostering fears) of exclusion from the only norm-setting collectivity of the time—the Germanic *Volksgemeinschaft*. Yet an important part would be played by the Churches in postwar Germany in order to articulate the complex relationship to the recent past and, for example, to help German expellees cope with the loss of former German territories in the east (as in the so-called *Ostdenkschrift* published by the EKD, Protestant Church in Germany).[45]

Though the German expellees from Central and Eastern Europe became an essential part of the FRG's memorialization of the Second World War from the 1950s to the early 1970s, they first had to force their way into the somehow "anti-emotional," emotional climate of German postwar society. There actually existed something like German-German racism that socially and *emotionally* ostracized German expellees.[46] This social phenomenon (which did not mean exactly that the very experience of expulsion was taboo, as per an opinion often present in past and even recent research) led Kossert to use the expression "cold homeland" to sum up the emotional dimension of the encounter between German expellees and Germans in the Allied occupation zones (later the FRG and GDR).

Nevertheless, the activation of what I would choose to call the past-bound aspect of the German "fear of the fear" required both an external emotional trigger and an internal shift in emotional norms. After the war, a collective emotional backlash turned the fear of German aggression into anger against defeated Germany. This led first to isolation of the Germans, whose country was considered by most Europeans a pariah nation because of its responsibility for the war and the scale of destruction it had brought. As natural and understandable on a human level as this emotional reaction was, it did not, however, prohibit exceptions: some would quickly acknowledge that to leave the Germans alone in that explosive state of emotional numbness which temporarily hid their fears, resentment, hatred, and shame could create far-flung and once again devastating consequences for their neighbors as well. As pointed out by one of the representatives of such a (re)conciliatory attitude toward the Germans, Joseph Rovan[47], as early as in October 1945, the winner's role, as a reeducator of the defeated German society, was also to "show respect and esteem for the German spirit" so as to set Germany on the right path; "the future of Germany w[ould] depend on our merits too."[48] The *metanoia* process thus required an adequate gesture from Germany's victims. Both the massive stress of isolation (admittedly reduced by the new imperatives of the Cold War) *and* the somewhat distant hope for reintegration into the community of Europe's nations appeared useful in leading to the indispensable change of norms in Germany.

This is where the second factor came into effect. The emotional climate in Germany could not have been transformed without the action of the Germans themselves—if not of society in general then at least of some trailblazing norm-setters or "norm-entrepreneurs."[49] These pioneers were responsible for the definition of a new emotional regime accompanying the process of societal *metanoia* set in motion by the Allies. The will for change found expression in different ways: the GDR elaborated a mix of ostentatious denazification, a *tabula rasa* founding myth, and performative albeit not necessarily disingenuous discourse[50] concerning friendship—especially with regard to the country's eastern neighbors (and socialist kin states). Austria chose to escape into invented self-victimization and neutrality. The FRG, however, took another route. Although, for both organizational and (geo)political reasons, denazification did not go as far as expected, profound ideological and structural transformations were actually prompted and led by the Allied occupation forces that prepared the creation of the new West German state. The Basic Law (*Grundgesetz*) of the FRG started with the laconic but clear acknowledgment of Germany's guilt for past crimes, assuring the world that the German people were "conscious of their responsibility before God and man." This foundation, along with the Christian Democratic orientation of the first chancellor, Adenauer, paved the way for the FRG's long-lasting and unique "policy of reconciliation."[51] Bilateral treaties played a key role in this process, as did symbolic gestures and emotionally fuelled performative speech acts,[52] including the reconciliation mass celebrated by Adenauer and the French president, General Charles de Gaulle, in Reims in 1962; Willy Brandt's genuflection in front of the Warsaw Ghetto memorial in 1970; another mass attended by Chancellor Helmut Kohl and Poland's first noncommunist prime minister Tadeusz Mazowiecki in Krzyżowa/Kreisau (Silesia) in 1989; and, for example, Chancellor Angela Merkel's speech in the Knesset in 2008.

These norm-setting events determined the emotional regime of the FRG, structuring it on a complex feeling of shame, remorse, and awe toward the victims of Nazism in general and the Jews in particular (especially from the 1970s on). By seeking ways to come to terms with their past—the very meaning of the concept of *Vergangenheitsbewältigung*[53]—(West) Germans took an important step toward the structural transformation of the German political culture. As the new emotional regime became more stable and dominant, the social and international risk of not respecting it became greater and was linked to even stronger fears of loss: other countries' potential fear of an unteachable Germany would feed the Germans' fear of that fear.[54]

Fear of the Fear (2): *Selbstbeschränkung*

The *metanoia* process was not, however, exclusively bound to the past. As West Germans looked back on their own responsibility as a fear-causing factor in Europe and thus tried to avoid sparking their neighbors' fearful and/or angry reactions, they also carefully considered how to implement an adequate foreign policy. While seeking an emotionally appropriate definition of the FRG's international goals, West German decision-makers were clearly interested in developing fear-relieving behavior. I argue that this new trend in (West) Germany's international role was an emotional effect of the *metanoia* process described above. The perception of other European countries' post-traumatic fear and anger toward the Germans in general incited the latter—especially the FRG—to adopt their aims and methods. However, this was not strictly a rational choice; given the dynamics of "emotional feedback loops," the observed reaction was motivated to some extent by the new emotional regime, which was generally characterized by a state of anxiety.[55] This was the real emotional dimension of self-limitation in foreign policy.

The foundation of the FRG's foreign policy was defined by Adenauer in the early years of the new state: *Westbindung*.[56] Its aim was to bind the FRG to the West and the Western alliance, as the Cold War had just started. It is clear that the emotional trigger here was not only a German fear of the others' (post-traumatic) fear of Germany. There were also specific German fears: of the east, of the Soviet Union (or "the Russians"), of communism, of atomic Armageddon, and even of the US cultural domination. "German Angst" was a mixture of all of these, but the definition of the emotional regime would largely depend on political, and sometimes tactical, factors. It is true, indeed, that the use of fear for political reasons is a method applied rather by authoritarian states than by liberal democratic ones. However, as Corey Robin correctly puts it, any state enjoys "considerable leeway to define ... the objects of fear that [will] dominate public concern."[57] The West German state's commitment to democracy did not thus rule out political management of fear. In fact, there would be a definition of priorities according to the FRG's state interests that would consider certain fears and the resulting need for security more pressing than others.

As one of the founding fathers of the FRG's political culture, Adenauer, too, exerted a strong influence on the definition of its emotional regime. This was visible especially when this regime was about to be challenged and redefined by other norm-entrepreneurs, as happened, for example, during the parliamentary elections of 1957 when Adenauer's Christian Democratic Party (CDU) succeeded in presenting the Social Democratic Party's (SPD) foreign policy proposals as an uncalculated risk for the FRG. This was the main function of the CDU's slogan, "No experiments!" (*"Keine Experimente!"*).[58] What Adenauer had to deal with was the rise of the West Germans' fear of atomic war when it came to protecting the FRG by stationing NATO nuclear weapons on its territory. Pacifism would grow even stronger in the following years, the 1960s and 1970s, as a particular form of military self-limitation expressing fear of the (others') fear. Adenauer, however, considered the risk of Soviet aggression against the FRG much more probable than any nuclear escalation. There was a struggle in order to define the main risk and thus legitimize the stronger of the two fears mentioned: "It is not a fight against the opposition. That was settled in the Bundestag. Now it is a fight against fear, because fear also concerns our people, those who usually adhere to us. That is why in my opinion it is possible to cast out the fear only with another, greater fear."[59]

Paradoxically, Adenauer's resolve to bind the FRG to the West could appear less self-limiting than the political left's wish to avoid any military solutions, even prophylactically dissuasive ones. With the SPD gaining more and more influence in the definition of Bonn's foreign policy in the 1960s,[60] prudence became a core trait of the FRG's international behavior, especially with regard to their Eastern Bloc neighbors. Political restraint was clearly motivated by the wish not to worry these European counterparts. What Egon Bahr, the spin doctor of the SPD's *Ostpolitik*, once expressed as a foundation of inter-German relations (i.e., between the FRG and GDR) was in fact a leitmotif in West Germany's contacts with the Eastern Bloc in general. It was up to the FRG to "make the definitely justified worries of those regimes wane."[61] This emotional concern was best summed up in the so-called New Eastern Policy's slogan "change through rapprochement" ("*Wandel durch Annäherung*").

"German Angst" after 1945 was often the result of a fundamental tension between specific German fears on one side, and the Germans' fear of the fear they (had) inspired in neighbor nations on the other. The SPD, too, had to cope with this dilemma when the Cold War entered a second revival phase after years of détente between East and West. The question of whether to place American, or NATO's, nuclear weapons on the FRG's territory in order to assure West Germany's and Western Europe's security in case of Soviet aggression became of utmost relevance by the end of the 1970s.[62] Given the strong pacifist movement in West German society, especially among left-wing and social-democratic sympathizers and voters, there was a moment of confidence crisis between the latter and the ruling SPD (with Chancellor Helmut Schmidt). Eventually, the internalization of the emotional culture of self-limitation had penetrated so deep into West Germany's "emotional community" that it happened to outperform even the goals of the political warrantors of the *metanoia* process initiated in 1945.

However, as a core element of the FRG's collective identity, the emotional culture of restraint was mostly in accordance with the regime prevailing in West

German foreign policy. This would last beyond reunification (1990). Even if the end of Germany's postwar partition opened the way to a normal German state, the reunified "Berlin Republic" neither rejected nor abandoned the behavior that had prevailed between 1949 and 1989/1990. The possibility of German military intervention abroad, let alone beyond NATO territory, would remain taboo for several years. Germany's participation in the NATO campaign in Kosovo was a first step,[63] the active presence of the Bundeswehr in Afghanistan a second[64]— of outstanding importance as well for the definition of the new German state's emotional regime, of the position accorded to foreign fears, and of their effect on "German Angst."

Mirroring German "Mirror Fears" Again and Again?

This chapter has presented fear and fear of the fear as being two facets of "German Angst" since 1945. As there are basically no limits to so-called mirroring effects, attention should therefore be drawn also to the emotional consequences of (West and reunified) Germany's multiple fear to their European neighbors. This prompts to pose a paradox: the contrast between Germany's rising economic power in Europe and the European Community (subsequently the EU), on one hand, and the lasting German restraint in foreign policy, on the other, appeared to trigger sometimes unexpected fearful reactions in various European countries. In fact, whereas reunification made Germany a normal state after almost half a century of double German statehood, the new "Berlin Republic" did not really behave the way that international standards would lead one to expect of a state as powerful as Germany had become by the end of the twentieth century. Fear of the fear as a particular expression of "German Angst" began to appear suspicious to some European partners who considered it a possible strategy to keep Germany out of international commitments while maximizing the economic advantages of such political and military restraints. French officials have repeatedly expressed their concern over the past few years, a time when German participation in the settlement of regional crises such as, for example, Mali[65] or Chad remained very modest.

When it comes to Germany's role in Europe as one of the key players in the EU, fear has been fuelled by the perception of a German state not willing (or fearing) to accept the burden of leadership in times of economic turmoil and geopolitical upheaval. By the end of 2011, Poland's foreign minister Radosław Sikorski confessed: "I fear German power less than I am beginning to fear German inactivity."[66] But accepting international activity and taking initiatives is not enough: since fall 2015, the Syrian refugee crisis has shown that for Germany's neighbors the main stress factor is perhaps German unpredictability or (perceived) desultoriness.[67] It is actually quite ironic that Germany is starting to provoke fear again at the very moment when, in the eyes of its neighbors, its foreign policy might seem to be turning away from the cultural stereotype of German meticulousness. Could it be, then, that, at least for some Europeans, a fearless Germany would be too frightening a perspective?

Notes

1 See comparative case studies in: Rainer Fremdling, Hans Lodder, Rob Wagenaar, and Friso Wielenga, eds., *Die überwundene Angst? Die neun Nachbarländer und die deutsche Einheit* (Groningen: Forsten, 1994).
2 See: Pierre-Frédéric Weber, *Timor Teutonorum: Angst vor Deutschland seit 1945. Eine europäische Emotion im Wandel* (Paderborn: Ferdinand Schöningh Verlag, 2015), 181–229.
3 The concept is taken from Barbara H. Rosenwein, *Emotional Communities in the Early Middle Ages* (Ithaca, NY: Cornell University Press, 2007), 2.
4 Peter Sloterdijk, *Theory of the Post-war Periods. Observations of Franco-German Relations since 1945* (Vienna: Springer, 2009), 14. Originally published in 2008 in German: *Theorie der Nachkriegszeiten*.
5 In other situations, shame can be, of course, a powerful trigger of conflicts, see: Thomas J. Scheff, *Bloody Revenge: Emotions, Nationalism and War*, 2nd ed. (Lincoln: Authors Guild Backinprint, 2000).
6 This was true even before the foundation of the GDR, during Soviet occupation, see: Jörg Osterloh, "'Diese Angeklagten sind die Hauptkriegsverbrecher.' Die KPD/SED und die Nürnberger Industriellen-Prozesse, 1947–1948," in *NS-Prozesse und deutsche Öffentlichkeit: Besatzungszeit, frühe Bundesrepublik und DDR*, ed. Clemens Vollnhals and Jörg Osterloh (Göttingen: Vandenhoeck & Ruprecht, 2011), 107–29.
7 See: Peter Utgaard, *Remembering and Forgetting Nazism: Education, National Identity, and the Victim Myth in Postwar Austria* (New York: Berghahn Books, 2003), 1–24; Sabine Loitfellner, "Hitlers erstes und letztes Opfer? Zwischen 'Anschluss' und Auschwitz-Prozess; zum Umgang Österreichs mit seiner NS-Vergangenheit," in *Kriegserfahrung und nationale Identität in Europa nach 1945: Erinnerung, Säuberungsprozesse und nationales Gedächtnis*, ed. Kerstin von Lingen (Paderborn: Schöningh, 2009), 150–69.

8   See: Helga Haftendorn, *Deutsche Außenpolitik zwischen Selbstbeschränkung und Selbstbehauptung 1945-2000* (Stuttgart: Deutsche Verlags-Anstalt, 2001), 56-60 and 61-2. For *Westbindung* see: Heiner Timmermann, *Adenauers Westbindung und die Anfänge der europäischen Einigung* (Sankt Augustin: Konrad Adenauer Stiftung, 2009).

9   See: Johannes Paulmann, "Representation without Emulation: German Cultural Diplomacy in Search of Integration and Self-Assurance during the Adenauer Era," *German Politics and Society* 25, no. 2 (2007): 168-200.

10 I use the concept of "risk," not "danger," see: Niklas Luhmann, *Soziologie des Risikos* (Berlin: de Gruyter, 2003), 30 et seq. "Danger" corresponds to a threat not linked to potential decisions made by the agents.

11 See: Jean B. Elshtain, *Sovereignty: God, State, and Self* (New York: Basic Books, 2008), 57-76.

12 This is reminiscent of the concept of "heterotopia," the difference between the nature of a sacralized space and others. See: Michel Foucault, "Des espaces autres [1984]," in *Anthologie zum Städtebau, Bd. 3: Vom Wiederaufbau nach dem Zweiten Weltkrieg bis zur zeitgenössischen Stadt*, ed. Vittorio M. Lampugnani (Berlin: Mann, 2005), 519-26.

13 See the definition of mental maps by Alan K. Henrikson, "The Geographical 'Mental Maps' of American Foreign Policy Makers," *International Political Science Review* 4, no. 1 (1980): 498: "Mental map means an ordered but continually adapting structure of the mind—alternatively conceivable as a process—by reference to which a person acquires, codes, stores, recalls, reorganizes, and applies, in thought or action, information about his or her large-scale geographical environment, in part or in its entirety."

14 The consciousness of a national community of people—a *nation*—was generally strongly in favor of territorial unification. In Europe, this also concerns the creation of "belated" nationstates, such as Italy or Germany.

15 See: Michael Stürmer, *Das ruhelose Reich. Deutschland 1866-1918* (Munich: Bassermann, 2004), 143-93.

16 See: Ken Booth and Nicholas J. Wheeler, *The Security Dilemma: Fear, Cooperation and Trust in World Politics* (Basingstoke: Palgrave Macmillan, 2008), 62-80.

17 "Think of it ever, speak of it never," Léon Gambetta (1838-1882).

18 See: Thomas J. Scheff, *Bloody Revenge. Emotions, Nationalism and War*, 2nd ed. (Lincoln: Authors Guild Backinprint, 2000), 113-17.

19 See: Pierre-Frédéric Weber, "Cultures of Fear in International Relations: Contribution to an Historical Sociology of Emotions," in *Die Ambivalenz der Gefühle. Über die verbindende und widersprüchliche Sozialität von Emotionen*, ed. Jochen Kleres and Yvonne Albrecht (Wiesbaden: Springer, 2015), 187-204, 200 et seq.

20 This was visible even far from Europe, where German and British interests came into conflict. For example see: Heinrich Walle, "Deutschlands Flottenpräsenz in Ostasien 1897–1914. Das Streben um einen 'Platz an der Sonne' vor dem Hintergrund wirtschaftlicher, machtpolitischer und kirchlicher Interessen." *Jahrbuch für europäische Überseegeschichte* 9 (2009): 127–58.
21 Sloterdijk, *Theory of the Post-war Periods*, 45.
22 Ibid., 45. For a definition, see footnote no. 4 in this chapter.
23 For example see: Nicholas Pronay, ed. *The Political Re-education of Germany and her Allies after World War II* (London: Croom Helm, 1985). As far as Germany is concerned, the authors consider decentralization as present in both the political and economical intentions expressed by the Allies, and they choose the stronger concept of "deindustrialization" instead of mere "decartelization."
24 Heinrich A. Winkler, *Der lange Weg nach Westen*, vols. 1 and 2 (München: C. H. Beck, 2000).
25 As defined in William M. Reddy, *The Navigation of Feeling. A Framework for the History of Emotions* (Cambridge: Cambridge University Press, 2001), 129: "Emotional regime: the set of normative emotions and the official rituals, practices, and emotives that express and inculcate them; a necessary underpinning of any stable political regime."
26 As used in Jack Barbalet, *Emotion, Social Theory, and Social Structure* (Cambridge: Cambridge University Press, 1998), 159 et seq.: "Emotional climate therefore includes emotional tones and patterns which differentiate social groups or categories by virtue of the fact that they are shared by their members and unlikely to be shared with non-members. ... An emotional climate is not a blanket which equally covers each member of the group associated with it."
27 See: Götz Aly, "Die Wohlfühl-Diktatur," *Der Spiegel* no. 10 (2005): 56–62.
28 I understand norms in a constructivist approach, as leading practices defining a given culture; the latter can be seen as socially shared knowledge. In the context of international relations, see in particular: Alexander Wendt, *Social Theory of International Politics* (Cambridge: Cambridge University Press, 1999).
29 See: Svetlana A. Alexievich, *War's Unwomanly Face* (Moscow: Progress, 1988), 33.
30 See: Helga Hirsch, *Die Rache der Opfer: Deutsche in polnischen Lagern 1944–1950* (Berlin: Rowohlt, 1998).
31 See US Department of State, *Foreign Relations of the United States*. Article XII stipulates: "The transfer to Germany of German populations, or elements thereof, remaining in Poland, Czechoslovakia and Hungary, will have to be undertaken. ... [A]ny transfers that take place should be effected in an orderly and humane manner."
32 This was visible in the structure of the expelled German population, especially in the Soviet occupation zone after 1945, where men able to work represented

only about 22 percent of the expellees, see: Torsten Mehlhase, *Flüchtlinge und Vertriebene nach dem Zweiten Weltkrieg in Sachsen-Anhalt. Ihre Aufnahme und Bestrebungen zur Eingliederung in die Gesellschaft* (Münster: LIT, 1999), 147; Peter-Heinz Seraphim, *Die Heimatvertriebenen in der Sowjetzone* (Berlin: Duncker & Humblot, 1954), 56.

33 The first years of the twenty-first century gave rise to several misunderstandings between Poland and Germany due to remembrance projects proposed by the main organization of German expellees, *Bund der Vertriebenen*. See: Stefan Troebst, "The Discourse on Forced Migration and European Culture of Remembrance," *The Hungarian Historical Review* 1, no. 3/4 (2012): 397–414.

34 Yet, this discourse would still find advocators among the expellees long after, see for example: Heinz Nawratil, *Vertreibungs-Verbrechen an Deutschen. Tatbestand, Motive, Bewältigung* (Munich: Universitas, 1982).

35 This was also confirmed by private war diaries. See: Florian Huber, *Kind, versprich mir, dass du dich erschießt. Der Untergang der kleinen Leute 1945* (Berlin: Berlin Verlag, 2015).

36 Ibid., 208 et seq.

37 See: Georges Lefebvre, *La grande peur de 1789* [first published in 1932] (Paris: Colin, 2014).

38 See: Marcin Zaremba, *Die große Angst 1944–1947. Leben im Ausnahmezustand* (Paderborn: Ferdinand Schöningh Verlag, 2016). Originally published in 2012 in Polish as *Wielka Trwoga*.

39 See: Arieh J. Kochavi, *Prelude to Nuremberg: Allied War Crimes Policy and the Question of Punishment* (Chapel Hill: University of North Carolina Press, 1998).

40 This phenomenon was also reappraised for the First World War: Stefanie C. Linden, Volker Hess, and Edgar Jones, "The Neurological Manifestations of Trauma: Lessons from World War I," *European Archives of Psychiatry and Clinical Neuroscience* 262, no. 3 (2012): 253–64.

41 Bombing alone, however, would not lead to the constitution of "German Angst," nor did it impede later resilience, as has been found in: Martin Obschonka, Michael Stützer, P. Jason Rentfrow, Jeff Potter, and Samuel D. Gosling, "Did Strategic Bombing in the Second World War Lead to 'German Angst'? A Large-Scale Empirical Test across 89 German Cities," *European Journal of Personality* 31, no. 3 (2017): 234–57.

42 See: Alexander Mitscherlich and Margarete Mitscherlich, *Die Unfähigkeit zu trauern: Grundlagen kollektiven Verhaltens* (München: Piper, 1967), 36 et seq., 77 et seq.

43 See: William M. Reddy, *The Navigation of Feeling. A Framework for the History of Emotions* (Cambridge: Cambridge University Press, 2001), 129: "Maintaining a goal or action plan in spite of rising suffering due to goal conflict."

44 Ibid., 129: "A relationship, ritual, or organization (whether informal or formal) that provides safe release from prevailing emotional norms and allows relaxation of emotional effort, with or without an ideological justification, which may shore up or threaten the existing emotional regime."
45 See: "Seeking Reconciliation."
46 See: Andreas Kossert, *Kalte Heimat. Die Geschichte der deutschen Vertriebenen nach 1945* (Bonn: Bundeszentrale für politische Bildung, 2008), 71-86.
47 Joseph Rovan (1918-2004), a French historian of Jewish-German origin, survived Dachau and started working for French-German reconciliation just after the Second World War.
48 Joseph Rovan, "L'Allemagne de nos mérites," *Esprit* 13, no. 115 (1945): 529-40 (Translation: PFW).
49 See: Martha Finnemore and Kathryn Sikkink, "International Norm Dynamics and Political Change," *International Organization* 52, no. 4 (1998): 887-917.
50 As originally conceptualized in: John L. Austin, *How to Do Things with Words*, The William James Lectures delivered at Harvard University in 1955, ed. James Opie Urmson and Marina Sbisà (Cambridge: Harvard University Press, 1962).
51 See: Lily G. Feldman, *Germany's Foreign Policy of Reconciliation. From Enmity to Amity* (Lanham, MD: Rowman & Littlefield, 2012). The author chose to analyze in particular the cases of France, Israel, Poland, and Czechoslovakia.
52 See: Danielle Celermajer, *The Sins of the Nation and the Ritual of Apologies* (Cambridge: Cambridge University Press, 2009), 56.
53 There is by now extensive literature available on this topic, so that we choose to draw attention to only one of the latest publications in English concerning the subject, with particular concern for the burden of the Holocaust: Caroline Sharples, *Postwar Germany and the Holocaust* (London: Bloomsbury Academic, 2016). The author describes the path from confronting and acknowledging the Holocaust to its memorialization through culture and education.
54 What we are considering here are the emotional aspects, not exactly the question of a "moral cudgel" (*Moralkeule*), as evoked, for example, by Martin Walser in 1998: the writer posed the controversial argument that German guilt for Auschwitz had often been used as kind of a thought-terminating cliché against Germany and the Germans.
55 See: Wolfgang Sofsky, *Das Prinzip Sicherheit* (Frankfurt am Main: S. Fischer, 2005), 32: "Anxiety is a state that completely overwhelms the person experiencing it. It determines sensations, biases perception, blocks action, and alights on life like a nightmare. ... Eventually it stiffens to a personal mindset. Pusillanimity and nervousness become character traits. As anxiety has its source in imagination, there are no limits to threats" (Translation: PFW).
56 For a definition, see footnote no. 8 in this chapter.

57 See: Corey Robin, *Fear. The History of a Political Idea* (New York: Oxford University Press, 2004), 33.
58 See: Günter Buchstab, "'Keine Experimente.' Zur Geschichte eines Wahlslogans," in *Ein Eifler für Rheinland-Pfalz*, ed. Johannes Mötsch, vol. 2 (Mainz: Gesellschaft für Mittelrheinische Kirchengeschichte, 2003), 689–97.
59 Quoted in Hans-Peter Schwarz, ed., *Konrad Adenauer. Reden 1917–1967* (Stuttgart: Deutsche Verlags-Anstalt, 1975), 353–60 (Translation: PFW).
60 Willy Brandt (SPD) was foreign minister from December 1966 to October 1969, then chancellor until May 1974.
61 Egon Bahr, "Wandel durch Annäherung," *Deutschland-Archiv* 8 (1973): 862–5. (Translation: PFW).
62 See: Stephan Layritz, *Der NATO-Doppelbeschluß. Westliche Sicherheitspolitik im Spannungsfeld von Innen-, Bündnis- und Außenpolitik* (Frankfurt am Main: Peter Lang, 1992).
63 See: Helga Haftendorn, "Einsatz im Kosovo 1999: das vereinte Deutschland und die Welt," in *Deutschland in der Welt. Weichenstellungen in der Geschichte der Bundesre publik*(Göttingen: Vandenhoeck & Ruprecht, 2010), 131–44.
64 See: Stephan Bierling, *Vormacht wider Willen: deutsche Außenpolitik von der Wiedervereinigung bis zur Gegenwart* (München: C. H. Beck, 2014), 80–106.
65 See: Alexandre Pouchard, "Les désaccords militaires entre la France et l'Allemagne se multiplient," *Le Monde*, January 21, 2013. Avail.: http://www.lemonde.fr/international/ article/2013/01/21/les-desaccords-militaires-entre-la-france-et-l-allemagne-se-multiplient_1819968_3210.html [accessed March 23, 2015].
66 Radosław Sikorski, *Poland and the Future of the European Union, Berlin 28th November 2011*. Deutsche Gesellschaft für Auswärtige Politik, 2011. Avail.: https://dgap.org/sites/default/files/event_downloads/radoslaw_sikorski_poland_and_the_future_of_the_eu_0.pdf [accessed March 23, 2015].
67 See: Thomas Schmid, "Europas Angst vor dem planlosen Deutschland," *Die Welt*, December 17, 2015. Avail,: http://www.welt.de/debatte/kommentare/article 150069598/Europas-Angst-vor-dem-planlosen-Deutschland.html [accessed April 7, 2015].

11

Conclusions

Thomas J. Kehoe and Michael G. Pickering

The far-right political party *Alternativ für Deutschland* (AfD) gained international attention during the 2017 federal election in Germany by portraying itself as the protector of German culture in opposition to Islam. One AfD poster showed the backs of two (presumably German) women in bikinis with the tag, "'Burkas?' We prefer bikinis" (*"Burkas?" Wir steh'n auf Bikinis*). Another more explicitly contrasted German culture against the so-called Islamic way of life. Over the image of a piglet was the question and answer: "'Islam?' It does not suit our kitchen" (*"Der Islam?" Passt nicht zu unserer Küche*). Fear is evident in these bigoted appeals to ethno-cultural exclusivity, though the xenophobia inherent in such messages is partially masked by braggadocio. The AfD was more assertively hateful in other posters, casting Islam as an invading force. In one, under a black and white picture of three women in burkas read the statement, "Stop Islamization" (*Islamisierung Stoppen*). But even such blunt characterization of otherness was not as dark as the portrayals of Muslims as a threat to the deeper ethnic character and cultural values of Germany. Over the picture of a smiling pregnant woman lying on her back was the question and answer, "'New Germans?' We do it ourselves" (*"Neue Deusche?" Machen wir selber*). Such messages accompanied demands for *"Islamfreie Schulen!"* (Islam-free schools!). To the AfD, Muslims are a threat to German children, women, and the very ethno-cultural identity of the German nation.[1]

This particular message of bigoted, nationalist misogyny has, unfortunately, resonated with a growing portion of the population. The AfD gained ground in 2017, winning 12.4 percent of the vote and ninety-four seats in the *Bundestag*, the first time it had ever passed the 5 percent necessary to seat representatives.[2] In the press, and in much of the scholarly discourse since, these appeals have been interpreted as reflecting contemporary local and geopolitical events. There have long existed anti-Islamic sentiments in Central Europe, but the past five years has seen an influx of Muslim refugees from civil wars in Libya, Syria, and Iraq, the persistent political unrest elsewhere in the Middle East, and, of course, the brutal and expansionist Islamic State of Iraq and Syria—better known as ISIS—that sought to exterminate nonbelievers and other "sinners" under its extreme interpretation of Sharia law.[3]

The masses of refugees that fled these areas for Europe challenged the divided instincts of Europeans and those in the German-speaking world, humanitarian on the one hand and ethno-nationalist on the other. In 2015, the crisis became a domestic political issue in Germany by threatening the integrity of the European Union (EU). German chancellor Angela Merkel adopted an expansive, Euro-focused view of her nation's role. For her, Germany's failure to ease an unmanageable humanitarian crisis in one of the smaller member states would weaken the EU's claims to legitimacy as a supranational political entity that offered its constituents mutual benefit.[4] Germany and the German-speaking world in Central Europe could have remained largely removed from the refugee crisis, protected by a string of nations that bordered the Middle East and the Mediterranean from Greece to Spain. Eschewing isolation and geographic protection, Merkel made a strident argument for a shared EU approach to the calamity and in 2015 welcomed over one million Middle Eastern refugees into Germany.[5] For their part, the Austrians and the Swiss also welcomed more refugees.[6]

The political ramifications were profound. In the 2016 presidential elections in Austria, far-right populist Norbert Hofer of the Freedom Party of Austria (*Freiheitliche Partei Österreichs*, FPÖ) barely lost on an explicitly nationalist, anti-Islamic, anti-immigration platform.[7] For all the generosity of spirit and heartwarming videos of refugees being welcomed at the Munich central station, there were also political consequences for Merkel.[8] She struggled to a narrow victory in the 2017 elections and it subsequently took months to establish a ruling coalition. Then, in the summer of 2018, she barely weathered a concerted attack from her more conservative coalition partner—the Christian Social Union in Bavaria (CSU)—which sought to curtail the existing open door policy on refugees, primarily in response to the prospect of losing electoral ground to the AfD. In July, press stories abounded with summaries like "German Chancellor Angela Merkel is trying to keep the European Union together, but in doing so, she's slowly tearing Germany apart."[9] The incidents in these reports may have been unreasonably framed in giving credence to the xenophobia she sought to counter, but the latter half of 2018 saw a more assertive and confident far right in

Germany. In August, mobs hunted foreigners through the streets of Chemnitz, and there were violent clashes in the city center between right-wing extremists and counterprotesters.[10] Later in 2018, the far right sought to march in many major cities on the eightieth anniversary of *Kristallnacht*.[11]

The far right's particular brand of xenophobia—exemplified in portrayals of non-Germans (however they are characterized) as a pernicious threat to the nation's cultural and biological integrity—harkens discomfortingly to twentieth-century history, as does rioting and violence against targeted minorities. There are clear similarities between these events and those described in Berg and Scully's chapter on the Nazi SA, particularly the combination of hateful propaganda and violent street demonstrations. One could extend such comparisons further and through the chapters in this book trace a deep fear of foreign invasion and the threat posed by aliens to local culture, whether defined religiously, linguistically, and/or culturally. But doing so would likely be far too reductive and elevate versions of the *Sonderweg* narrative, which spuriously tries to find simple developmental answers for complex phenomena that are culturally, socially, and psychologically emergent.

Fear is, of course, central to Germany's very recent history, shaping both political positions and policies in response to perceived popular sentiments, and conversely, having been cultivated by reactionary parties to win electoral support. Moreover, the corollaries to the historic examples explored in this book are difficult to miss. Current fears of refugees appear to instantiate many of the same fear-guided narratives that have emerged repeatedly in the history of the German-speaking world that we have explored here, including fear of invasion and cultural change, "others" bringing danger—e.g., terrorism—and the porousness of national borders resulting from the geography of Central Europe. Alarmist political messaging taps intense feelings among the general population and in turn highlights them. These include, among others, a growing xenophobia, a fear of foreign incursion and cultural dilution, and a sense of abandonment by government in favor of foreign groups. The anti-Islamic messages of far-right parties across Germany share ideological affinity with the FPÖ's *Heimat* principle (for "homeland"), which holds the party as the protector of "Austrian identity."[12] These parties portray refugees as invaders coming *en masse*, different in religion, culture, and language, and as in the AfD posters, they are painted as threatening to change the fabric of the world into which they seek entry.

The current demonizing of Muslim refugees fits the pattern revealed in the collected chapters of this book, which show a recurring connection between fear of invasion/infiltration and the construction of particular fear-carrying archetypes. Current fears of Muslims, for instance, are little different in outward form to the anxieties about the Ottoman border, or the perceived danger of the French, the Poles, and Jews. Indeed, concerns about vampires on the Habsburg-Ottoman border in the eighteenth century, Gypsies in the nineteenth century, and foreign criminals after the Second World War gave voice to anxieties about incursion into and corruption of the inner cultural, social, and political "heartland" of the German-speaking world. While fears analogous to these can indeed be found outside German-speaking Central Europe, some tentative, contextual connections unique to it are evident. The fear described in Kirsten Cooper's chapter of losing German culture to the French voices the persistent geographic pressure on German peoples in Central Europe from neighboring powers. This region was in many ways a transient space, its borders consistently unfixed and threatened by groups that were culturally, religiously, and linguistically different. A consequent fear about the loss of national sovereignty is, therefore, more understandable, especially so when considered against a history of successive wars and occupations by foreign powers including the Ottoman Empire, the French, and in 1945, the complete supplanting of German rule by former ethnic and racial enemies, notably Russians and Slavs from Eastern Europe who implemented Soviet occupation. This regional malleability helps explain the persistent fears of incursion and cultural degradation that emerge in the collected chapters.

The nebulous geography of the "German-speaking world" may also explain the emergence of fear-carrying archetypes that, while ostensibly different, share many similar characteristics. Vampires and caricatures of Gypsies and Jews personified the more intangible fears born of geographic porousness. As Charissa Kurda describes, the very idea of transience was anathema in the German Empire, believed to threaten the settled Germanic culture. Put another way, the movement of Gypsies highlighted the weakness in concepts of territorial and cultural cohesion within a defined space. That some of these constructed entities were believed to hide their true identities and pass as accepted members of the community enhanced their threat. In their true form, they were thought to lurk in the hidden places on the peripheries of society, threatening it, undermining it, never fully visible, yet ever-present. As such, these archetypes voiced a deep fear about the fragility of a "German" area in Europe.

Sebastian Huebel's chapter exploring the Nazis' destruction of German-Jewish concepts of masculinity takes up this theme of "the enemy within." It is important to remember that while one element of genocidal ideation concerns those anxieties driven by fantasies about imminent threat from unseen enemies within a society, there is not a straight line from fear to such genocidal horror, as Mahmood Mamdani argues in the context of discussing the Rwandan genocide.[13] Exploring the implications of such fantasies from the point-of-view of the oppressed, Huebel shows how fears on the part of Jewish men in the Third Reich could possess deeply gendered dimensions and could also be bound up with acts of resistance. Indeed, while the well-known attempts of the Third Reich to demonize and vilify Jews in general reflected the construction of a particular *Feindbild*, the dynamics of fear on the part of persecuted Jewish males revealed the personal and particular ways in which such processes were internalized and negotiated.

A closely related theme that this collection has explored concerns the spaces in which the fantastical instantiation of fears occurred. *Der Wald*, for instance, figures as both a literal and metaphorical space in which such enemies were sometimes imagined to dwell. In the early-modern period, satanic rites and witch rides were imagined to literally occur in the woods that surround many German towns and villages. After the Second World War, the woods became the space in which gangs of Polish, Jewish, and other non-German "Displaced Persons" (DPs) were believed to hide and from there raid German travelers and farmsteads. As Frey suggests, these fantasies about instantiated threats created a fixed point for collecting and mentally negotiating the anxieties of daily life and the less comprehensible fears about political and social events far beyond one's control.

A useful caveat to the foregoing discussion is that while there appears to be a consistency in these patterns of expression, it is nonetheless difficult to concretely define the phenomenon at hand. This is because fear, as we have considered it, is both socially and textually emergent, reminiscent of William Reddy's "emotives"[14]; it is a fluid construction that can change from context to context. As various examples in this collection have shown, fear is also socially contingent, existing between people and communities, and it is this aspect that we have emphasized. Further, while engaging with the matter of individual anxieties and fears, the general focus of this collection has been to examine constructions and representations of fears.

Avoiding the pitfalls and outmoded assumptions underpinning essentialist conceptions of the emotions, it needs to be acknowledged that there is almost certainly a universally human dimension to the fears explored in this book. Social scientists have firmly established the innate human ability to form "in-groups" and "out-groups," and to regard fearfully those cast as "others," often constructing them as fear-carrying archetypes, especially when they are minorities in a given society. However, as the contributions to this collection remind us, expressions and constructions of fear are strongly conditioned by their historical, social, and cultural contexts. Indeed, the social constructivist approach is in no sense new. What we set out to do was to investigate whether a longue durée perspective might reveal any commonalities in the culturally and geographically conditioned constructions of fear in the German-speaking world. In so doing, we have added a spatial dimension to an otherwise temporal conceptual lens. The apparent transtemporal consistency in the appearance of certain expressions of fear in the German-speaking world bolsters Barbara Rosenwein's rejection of previous grand narratives that sought to establish a qualitative distinction between modern and premodern emotional expression.[15] Far from imposing a different sort of grand narrative, our observations support the increasingly popular notion that a useful analytical lens for the study of emotions is that of space: the ways in which not only distinct places but also broader social and cultural conceptions of space can influence the expression of emotions and their construction.

Although merely initial efforts, the chapters here have together begun what should be a long-running exploration of the expressions and formative influence of fear in the German-speaking world over the past four hundred years and, more broadly, the cultural, linguistic, and geographical context for their origin, experience and expression. Far more work is required. Future studies might explore the influence of the Napoleonic invasion and could also stretch back to examine the important relationship between fear and the Thirty Years' War. The division of Europe during the Cold War was undoubtedly important and, though touched on here in the final chapters, could be explored in significantly more depth. The avenues for future research are too numerous to recount fully here. Suffice it to say that it is difficult to overlook how influential fear has been on the history of the German-speaking world and how culturally-contextualized fears continue to shape current events in Central Europe.[16]

Notes

1   Kirsten Kortebein, "In Pictures: Keeping (Some) AfD Posters Just Out of Reach," *Politico*, September 23, 2017. Avail.: https://www.politico.eu/interactive/in-pictures-keeping-some-afd-posters-just-out-of-reach/ [accessed May 17, 2018].

2. Cas Mudde, "What the Stunning Success of AfD Means for Germany and Europe," *The Guardian*, September 25, 2017. Avail.: https://www.theguardian.com/commentisfree/2017/sep/24/germany-elections-afd-europe-immigration-merkel-radical-right [accessed May 16, 2018].
3. For a scholarly analysis of ISIS see: Joana Westphal, "Violence in the Name of God? A Framing Processes Approach to the Islamic State in Iraq and Syria," *Social Movement Studies* 17, no. 1 (2018): 19–34.
4. Kelly M. Greenhill, "Open Arms behind Barred Doors: Fear, Hypocrisy and Policy Schizophrenia in the European Migration Crisis," *European Law Journal* 22, no. 3 (2016): 317–32.
5. Ibid.
6. For statistics on refugee intake see: "Refugee Population by Country or Territory of Asylum," 2018, *The World Bank*. Avail.: https://data.worldbank.org/indicator/SM.POP.REFG [accessed July 27, 2018].
7. Philip Oltermann, "Austria Rejects Far-Right Candidate Norbert Hofer in Presidential Election," *The Guardian*, December 5, 2016. Avail.: https://www.theguardian.com/world/2016/dec/04/far-right-party-concedes-defeat-in-austrian-presidential-election [accessed March 3, 2018].
8. Kate Connolly, "Germany Greets Refugees with Help and Kindness at Munich Central Station," *The Guardian*, September 3, 2015. Avail.: https://www.theguardian.com/world/2015/sep/03/germany-refugees-munich-central-station [accessed March 15, 2018]; Ben Knight, "Munich Sees Massive Impromptu Help for Refugees," *Deutsche Welle*, September 2, 2015. Avail.: https://www.dw.com/en/munich-sees-massive-impromptu-help-for-refugees/a-18688838 [accessed March 15, 2018].
9. Lisa Millar and Roscoe Whalan, "Germany's Angela Merkel at a Crossroads as Anti-Immigrant Sentiment Grows," *ABC News*, July 9, 2018. Avail.: http://www.abc.net.au/news/2018-07-08/angela-merkels-migrant-problem/9953192 [accessed July 24, 2018].
10. Kate Connolly, "German Police Criticised as Country Reels from Far-Right Violence," *The Guardian*, August 28, 2018. Avail.: https://www.theguardian.com/world/2018/aug/28/german-police-criticised-as-country-reels-from-far-right-violence [accessed November 20, 2018]; Kate Connolly, "Chemnitz Riots Spark Calls for AfD to Be Put under Surveillance," *The Guardian*, September 4, 2018. Avail.: https://www.theguardian.com/world/2018/sep/04/chemnitz-riots-spark-calls-for-afd-to-be-put-under-surveillance-neo-nazi [accessed November 21, 2018].
11. Rachel Loxton, "Update: Hundreds to Stand Against Far-Right March Planned on 80th Anniversary of Kristallnacht," *The Local*, November 9, 2018. Avail.: https://www.thelocal.de/20181109/thousands-to-attend-counter-protest-against [accessed December 12, 2018].

12 Duncan Morrow, "Jörg Haider and the New FPÖ: Beyond the Democratic Pale?," in *The Politics of the Extreme Right: From the Margins to the Mainstream*, 2nd ed., ed. Paul Hainsworth (London: Bloomsbury, 2016), 60.

13 On genocidal ideation see for example: Dominik J. Schaller, "From Conquest to Genocide: Colonial Rule in German Southwest Africa and German East Africa," in *Empire, Colony, Genocide: Conquest, Occupation, and Subaltern Resistance in World History* (New York: Berghahn Books, 2008), 296–324 [esp. pp. 302–6]. For Mahmood Mamdani's discussion see: Mahmood Mamdani, *When Victims Become Killers: Colonialism, Nativism, and Genocide in Rwanda* (Princeton, NJ: Princeton University Press, 2001), 200.

14 William M. Reddy, *The Navigation of Feeling: A Framework for the History of Emotions* (Cambridge: Cambridge University Press, 2001), 128.

15 Barbara H. Rosenwein, "Worrying about Emotions in History," *American Historical Review* 107 (June 2002): 821–45.

16 This connection, while examined to some extent in the following publication, has not been exhausted: Jennifer Spinks and Charles Zika, eds., *Disaster, Death and the Emotions in the Shadow of the Apocalypse 1400–1700* (London: Palgrave, 2016).

Contributors

Jacob Berg is conducting a joint PhD candidature at the University of St Andrews, Scotland and the University of New England, Australia. He examines the investigation of radical paramilitary organizations and political parties in Germany from 1919 to 1945, centering on two key issues: the Nazi Party's use of the *Sturmabteilung* as a visual image in German propaganda and, in turn, the way that image allows us to further understand the way political parties use propaganda to bolster their ideology, mythos, and culture.

Kirsten L. Cooper finished her doctorate in the Fall of 2019 at the University of North Carolina at Chapel Hill. Her research and publications focus on political rhetoric and pamphlets to explore how ideas of cultural and national belonging were understood in seventeenth- and eighteenth-century Europe and often mobilized in the service of dynastic interests. Her dissertation focuses specifically on the use of national rhetoric in pamphlets written during the many conflicts between France and the Holy Roman Empire during the wars of Louis XIV. She has also published on the politics of national dishonor in the Journal of the Western Society for French History, and how dynasty and nation were inextricably intertwined in eighteenth-century understandings of political sovereignty for the forthcoming *A Cultural History of Memory in the Eighteenth Century* (Bloomsbury, 2020).

Dennis Frey is Associate Professor of History at Lasell University, Massachusetts. His research revolves around the socioeconomic and cultural history of *Handwerker* (i.e., artisan–craftspeople) in the German hometown of Göppingen during the eighteenth and nineteenth centuries. His findings have wider ramifications for how historians and social scientists view socioeconomic and cultural change over time. Inspired by the work of Pierre Bourdieu, Frey's research avoids the intractable and misleading dichotomies between conservatism and innovation, structure and agency. Recently, he has expanded his interest in nonhuman animals in Göppingen. He has published in the *International Review of Social History*, *Central European History*, and *Money in the German-Speaking Lands* (Berghahn Books, August 2017). He is a fellow of the Fulbright foundation and the Deutsche Akademischer Austausch Dienst (or German Academic Exchange Service). In 1990, he was also awarded a Younger Scholar Summer Research Grant in 1990 by the National Endowment for the Humanities.

Sebastian Huebel finished his doctorate at the University of British Columbia in the Fall of 2017. His dissertation concentrates on German-Jewish masculinities in Nazi Germany. He has published a gender study of Victor Klemperer's diaries in *Women in Judaism: A Multidisciplinary Journal* and, more recently, an article, "Disguise and Defiance: German Jewish Men and Their Underground Experiences in Nazi Germany, 1941–45," in *Shofar: An Interdisciplinary Journal of Jewish Studies*. His main areas of interest include twentieth-century Germany, gender history, and the history of the Holocaust and modern genocide. He immigrated to Canada from Germany with his family in 2003. He teaches at the University of the Fraser Valley and Alexander College in Vancouver.

Thomas J. Kehoe is postdoctoral research fellow in the School of Humanities, Arts, and Social Sciences at the University of New England. He specializes in German and American history, with interests in crime, policing, and military governance, genocide studies, and the history of emotions. He completed his postgraduate degrees at the Universities of Sydney and Melbourne and has published on propaganda, military justice, and occupation in prestigious journals including the *Journal of Genocide Research*, the *Journal of Interdisciplinary History*, *War in History*, and the *Journal of the History of Sexuality*. He is fellow of the German Academic Exchange Office (DAAD) and a sole-authored monograph based on the research conducted on that fellowship exploring crime and governance during the American occupation of Germany after the Second World War was released in Fall 2019.

Charissa Kurda is a PhD candidate in modern European history at Flinders University in Adelaide, South Australia. Her research focuses on the persecution of Gypsies in Germany, Austria, and Switzerland from 1870 to 1945. Her doctoral thesis primarily considers whether a general biopolitical campaign was waged against the Gypsies across Central Europe by assessing the interactions between Switzerland and Austria alongside the development of German Gypsy policies. It further evaluates the approaches of Michel Foucault, Giorgio Agamben, and Roberto Esposito in relation to the history of the *Porrajmos* (the Nazi genocide of Gypsies).

Kurda is a fellow of the German Academic Exchange Service (DAAD), which in 2016–17 provided support for study at the University of Paderborn and extensive archival research throughout Central Europe including the *Geheimes Staatsarchiv Preussischer Kulturbesitz*, the *Bayerisches Hauptstaatsarchiv*, and the *Bundesarchiv Berlin*.

Christoph Lorke completed his PhD at the University of Münster in 2013 and since then has been a researcher and instructor at that university. He specializes in German and European history, particularly that of post-1945 Germany, and has researched poverty and migration during the division of Germany. His dissertation examined poverty in East and West Germany between 1945 and 1989. Currently, he explores the impact of borders and border-crossings on marriages between Germans and non-Germans. He has published widely in German and in English, and has recently had articles published in prestigious international journals including the *Journal of Migration History* and the *Journal of Cold War Studies*.

Michael G. Pickering is subject leader and lecturer at Trinity College, University of Melbourne. A graduate of the University of Melbourne, his research focuses on magic in the early German Enlightenment. His doctoral thesis examined the so-called vampire debate of the 1730s, utilizing it as a conceptual lens through which to examine shifting ideas about the perceived limitations and capacities of magical power in the early eighteenth century. His postdoctoral research, funded in 2019 by the Herzog August Bibliothek, Wolfenbüttel, examines the connections between *magia naturalis* and the healing arts, 1670–1750.

Richard Scully is Associate Professor in Modern European History at the University of New England, Australia. The author of *British Images of Germany: Admiration, Antagonism & Ambivalence, 1860–1914* (2012), he focuses on the First World War in his undergraduate and postgraduate teaching and has explored aspects of transnational war-work and service by cartoonists, nurses, cartographers, and soldiers in: *The Great War and the British Empire: Culture and Society* (2017); and the journals *War & Society* (2016) and *Imago Mundi* (2010). He is currently undertaking a study of the wartime service of G. M. Trevelyan; while a three-volume study of *Eminent Victorian Cartoonists* was published in 2018. His current research projects relate to other aspects of political cartoon history (internationally, as well as in Australian contexts), arising from a 2013–15 Australian Research Council Early Career Research Award.

Pierre-Frédéric Weber is currently associate professor at the University of Szczecin, Poland. His research fields include the history of twentieth-century international relations and postwar processes in Europe, and the history and sociology of emotions. He studied German and European Studies at the French Universities of Angers and Paris III–Sorbonne Nouvelle, where he completed a PhD on German–Polish relations in the 1960s and early 1970s. His dissertation was published as *Le triangle RFA-RDA-Pologne 1961–1975: guerre froide et normalisation des rapports germano-polonais* (2007). His latest publication (and second book), *Timor Teutonorum: Angst vor Deutschland seit 1945. Eine europäische Emotion im Wandel* (2015), explores fear of Germany in Europe after 1945.

Index

Aberglaube (superstition) 58
Abrahamson, Heinz 173
Abzug, Robert 208
Academia Naturae Curiosorum 53
acculturation 186
Adenauer, Konrad 10, 231, 255
Agamben, Giorgio 90
aggression 123
Aichele, Hermann 92, 107
Aktion 182
à la Françoise 23
Albrecht, Angelika 110 n.11, 111 n.14
alcohol abuse 72
alcoholism 70, 72, 73, 74, 78, 80, 237
Alternative für Deutschland (AfD) 242, 275
Angstzustände see anxieties
anti-Allied partisans 202
anti-capitalist ideology 141
anti-fear campaign 171
anti-French pamphleteers 17 *see also* pamphleteers' strategies
anti-French rhetoric 28
anti-Gypsy feelings 197
anti-Gypsy measures 89
anti-Gypsy policies 89, 99, 101, 103, 113 n.24 *see also* Gypsies
    Aichele's systemization of 115 n.44
anti-Jewish boycotts 173
anti-Nazi parties 133
anti-Nazi poster imagery 142
anti-republican force 131
anti-Semitism 176, 179, 181, 182, 197, 207, 219 n.11
    discrimination 166
Antiziganismus (anti-Gypyism) 90
anxieties 7, 43, 57, 184 *see also* fear(s); geopolitical anxieties
    "discreet anxiety of the Bourgeoisie" 227
    and nervousness 184
Apostolidès, Jean-Marie 32 n.20
Appell am 23. Februar 1933 155

Arnold, Hermann 113 n.28
"Aryan" manhood 9, 171, 186, 208
a-social elements 182
a-sociality 236, 237, 241
assimilation 93
    Gypsies 93–4, 96, 108
Aulic War Council in Vienna 46
"Ausländer" 197
Austrians 10, 276
    identity 277
    immigrations 104

Bader, Karl S. 200
Bahn frei! Für Liste 1 Sozialdemokraten 138
Bähr, Andreas 69
    fear and anxiety 69
Bahr, Egon 266
Baltic group 214
Barbalet, Jack 270 n.26
Barbara, Anna 72–4, 80
Battle for Berlin 130
Battle of Tannenberg 133
Bauman, Zygmunt 4, 7
Baumel, Judith Tylor 189 n.15
Bavaj, Riccardo 129
Bavarian anti-Gypsy policy 94 *see also* Gypsies
Bavarian bureaucracy 97
Bavarian Interior Ministry 107
Bavarian movement 130
Bavarian People's Party 148
Beck, Ulrich 234
Beier, Johannes 57
Belgrade administration 46
Bengel, Johann Albrecht 68
Bennecke, Heinrich 157 n.5
Berg, Jacob 9, 123
Berlin Conference of 1884/1885 256
Berlin Republic 267
Berlin Voran: Dritter Märkertage, 29–30 Sept 1928 135, 136

Berlin Wall 253
Bibliothèque national de France 19
biopolitics 90–1
Bismarck, Otto von 100, 256, 257
black market 198, 199, 201–3, 208, 213
   crime in 217
   German–Dutch border 201
   participation 202
Bloch, Erich 183
Block, Martin 113 n.28
bloodsuckers 47 *see also* vampire
Bock, Gisela 189 n.15, 192 n.67
Bohn, Thomas 58
Bonn's foreign policy 266
Bourke, Joanna 3, 6, 7, 17, 26, 31 n.17
Brandt, Willy 248 n.65, 264
Brecht, Martin 68
British Army of the Rhine (BAOR) 212–13
British assessments of crime in Cologne 197
British Frontier Control Service 209
British military government (MG) detachments 197
British Zone of occupation 196
Brüder! Sammelt Euch in der Deutschen Staatspartei 145
Brügge, Peter 233
Brüning, Heinrich 127
Buchheim, Wilhelm 181
Bude, Heinz 241
Bundessozialhilfegesetz (Federal Social Security Law) 233

Carruthers, Susan 208
cataloguing system 107
cemetery 48
Charles VI 58
Christian Democratic Party (CDU) 265
Christian Social Union in Bavaria (CSU) 276
Christoph Kleßmann 243 n.12
circle of marginality 235
civilizing process 5
Civil War 156
   psychology 141
class 190 n.23
Cohn, Willy 165, 172, 174, 175, 181
Cold War 10, 232, 253, 263–6, 280

Collegia pietatis 68
Cologne General Court 203
Cologne's crime problem 198
commercium 47, 51, 52
Communist party 132
concomitant loss of status 166
conservative anxieties 4
contagions medicus 46, 51
contagious disease 42
contemptus mundi 5
Cooper, Kirsten 1, 8, 58
Copia des vom Hern Frombald 58 n.2
Cordon 43
Cordon Sanitaire 45
   stretching 42
Cottaar, Anne-Marie 113 n.25
crime assessments 196
"crime wave" hysteria 206, 216
criminal archetype, construction *see* displaced persons (DP)
criminality 89, 94, 109, 195, 196, 202, 203, 205, 207, 208, 212
criminalization 97
cultural construct 186
cultural fear 22
cultural frameworks 1
cultural infiltration
   rhetoric of 26–9
   threat of 21–6
culture of poverty 235
Czechoslovakia 260

d'Adorno, Botta 48
Dampfnudeln 70
Dauerarbeitslos 251 n.103
de-fascination 259
defeatism 198
DeJean, Joan 38 n.88
Delumeau, Jean 4
*Denkschrift über die Bekämpfung der Zigeunerplage*Harster (Theodor) 105
denunciation 211
Der S.A. Mann ist die sich immer erneuernde Kraft der Bewegung 152, 153
Der Staatsanwalt hat das Wort 237
Dessert, Daniel 31 n.18
detachments 197–8
Dhampir 54

diaries 167
Diebitsch, L. 152
Diehl, Paula 156 n.3
Die Lebensbeschreibung der Ertzbetrü gerin und Landstörtzerin Courasche and *Der seltsame Springinsfeld* (von Grimmelshausen) 87
Die Stunde ist da! 151
Die Zigeunerfrage mit besonderer Berücksichtigung Württembergs (Aichele) 92
Dillmann, Alfred 88, 92, 105
disarmament, demilitarization, denazification, and democratization (4D) 254, 259
disentanglement (*Entflechtung*) 259
displaced persons (DP) 195–6
  agreement 208–12
  allied crime assessments in 1945 197–200
  crime 215
  fragility, recovery, and persistent fear 212–15
  gangs 195
  German fears 203–8
  predictions, crisis, and Allies' fear 200–3
  riots and fights 209
  violent crimes by 203–4
Dissertation of the Gipsies (Grellmann) 91
dissociality (*Dissozialität*) 237, 241
dissuade survival-driven crime 198
domestic Gypsies 100
downward demarcation 228
downward mobility 227
DP *see* displaced persons (DP)
"4D" program *see* disarmament, demilitarization, denazification, and democratization (4D)
Dritter Märkertag 135, 136
dueling 35 n.67
Duke Karl 75
Dunlop, Ian 30 n.6
Dutch–Belgian border 201

East Germany 3, 10, 228, 233, 240, 242
Eber, Wilhelm Emil (Elk Eber) 154
economic crisis in Germany, 1932 127, 141

economic depression 127
economic fears 190 n.23
  of facing unemployment 166
economic hardship 3
economic interest 4
"economic miracle" 233
Edict of Nantes 16
'ego document' 67
Ehrenreich, Barbara 227, 234
Ehrenreich's concepts 235
Elbau, Alfred 176
elemental emotion 1
Elias, Norbert 5
emotions
  analysis of 3
  analytical category 165
  attitudes 165
  behaviors 165
  cultural history of 166
  defined 1
  elemental 1
  generic human emotions 1
  of Germanic cultural history 2
  in historical writing 4
  perceptions 165
emotional climate 259
  of German postwar society 263
emotional communities 5, 254, 266
emotional feedback loops 265
emotionalization 234
Emotional Lexicons: Continuity and Change in the Vocabulary of Feeling 1700–2000 (Frevert) 7, 79
emotional refuge 262
emotional regime(s) 231, 259–67
emotional restraint 5
Emperor Josef II 76
employment (*Erwerbstätigkeit*), 174
Ems Dispatch 257
Ems spiral 257
enemies (*Feindbilder*) 228
Erblande 51
ethnic purges 2
ethno-cultural exclusivity 275
ethno-cultural identity 275
ethnolinguistic Germanic culture 1
Ettmüller, Michael Ernst 53
euphemism 197
Europäischer Niemand 45

European Economic Community (EEC) 253
European resistance to Louis XIV's expansionism 15
European Union (EU) 253, 276
Evans, Richard J. 126, 127, 200
expulsion 89, 93, 94, 96, 100, 102, 104, 106
extra-territorialization of poverty 233
extremist political groups 127

fait accompli 200
Faithful Executioner, The (Harrington) 67
falling literature 227
famine *(Hungersnot)* 70, 73, 78, 80
fantasies 8, 11 n.1
  of decimation 44
fascination 259
fear-allaying strategy 57
fear-breakers 231
fearless fear 73
fear of the fear
  Selbstbeschränkung 264–7
  Vergangenheitsbewältigung 262–4
fear(s) 57
  and anxiety 7, 77
  of arrest and violence 179–83
  bodily 183–5
  communication 229
  concept of 229
  cultural 22
  of decline 233–8
  defined 1, 227
  economic 172–6, 190 n.23, 230
  eighteenth-century, Southwest German Hometown 65–80
  emotional experience 2–3
  factor in Europe 255–8
  for the family 176–9
  fearless 73
  of foreign invasion 1
  gendered themes of 165–85
  German-Jewish masculinities in Third Reich 165–85
  German-speaking world 3
  in Germany 18
  Germany's *metanoia* 258–60
  of Gypsy itinerancy 87–109
  Habsburg Monarchy, intersectionality on periphery of 41–58
  of infiltration/incursion 42–3
  instrumentality of 6
  invasion and cultural change 277
  manipulation of 17
  "mirror fears" 267–8
  Pickering's analysis 8–9
  political (*see* political fear during wars of Louis XIV)
  power relations 6, 18
  production of 235
  religious 20
  of satellization 10, 253
  semantics of 238–40
  of social decline among Americans 227
  of social imbalance 230
  of social relegation 227
  Sturmabteilung (SA) 123–56
  of transfer 233–8
  of vampires 8
Fechenbach, Felix 174, 175
Federal Republic of Germany (FRG) 228, 254
  Basic Law *(Grundgesetz)* of 264
Federal Republic of (West) Germany 212
Feindbild 43, 279
fetishization of sexual murder 3
fire 66, 68, 75, 77, 78, 88
Fischer, Conan 125, 159 n.40
Fitzpatrick, Matthew 99
Fitzpatrick, Sheila 211
Flückinger, Johann 44–56
  autopsy 52
foreign criminals 206
foreign investment 127
foreignness 43
Fort mit den Stützen des Finanzkapitals — wählt nationalsozialistisch 139, 140
Foucault, Michel 234
  model of biopolitics 90
FPÖ's *Heimat* principle 277
France *see also* Germany
  policy of "reunions" 16
  Protestantism in 16
  Truce of Ratisbon, 1684 16
Franco-Dutch War (1672–8) 15, 27, 28, 30 n.3
Franco-Imperial conflicts 27
Franco-Prussian war 257
Freedom of Movement Act 98

Freedom Party of Austria 276
French armies of Louis XIV 8
French cultural infiltration 17
French hobbies and pastimes 23
French invading soldiers 165
French language 23
French Revolution 258
Freund, Elizabeth 181
Frevert, Ute 6, 79, 168, 242 n.6
Frey, Dennis 8–9
Frey, Erich 178
Friedrich II 58
Fritsche, Johann Christian 62 n.74
Frombald 41
Frontbann 129
Fulda, Bernhard 141
Furcht (fear) 7 *see also* fear

Gambetta, Léon 257
gangs in forest *see* displaced persons (DP)
Garbarini, Alexandra 168
Gaulle, Charles de 264
Gellately, Robert 211
gender conventions and responsibilities 168
gendered masculine fears 166
geopolitical anxieties 8, 42, 43, 44, 45
"German Angst" after 1945 11, 253–5
    fear factor in Europe 255–8
    Germany's *metanoia* 258–60
    Germany's postwar collective behavior 260–2
    "mirror fears" 267–8
    Selbstbeschränkung 264–7
    Vergangenheitsbewältigung 262–4
German authoritarian culture 211
German-born Gypsies 99
German culture in opposition to Islam 275
German Democratic Party 133
German Democratic Republic (GDR) 228, 254
German Federal Election, 1928 128
German-Frenchmen 25
German–French relationship 258
German–German postwar 228
Germanic communities 2
German Institute for Economic Research 227

German-Jewish masculinities in Third Reich 165–9
    bodily fears 183–5
    economic fears 172–6
    fear of arrest and violence 179–83
    fears for the family 176–9
    gendered themes of fear 169–72
German Jews 181, 192 n.49
    in Nazi Germany 186
German "Kripo" (criminal police) 197
Germanness 26, 27
German *Polizeistaat* 210
German Reichstag elections, 130 130
German romanticism 258
German soldierly manhood 171
German victimization 207, 210
Germany 30 n.1 *see also* France
    fear in 18
    historical fear factor in Europe 255–8
    internal conflict in 21
    location influenced territorial fear 10
    Nazi Germany 3
    post–First World War 3
    post–Second World War 2
    sovereignty 10
    systemic culture 123
Germany Is Doing Away with Itself (Sarrazin) 241
"Germany's Zero Hour" 260
Gilmore, David 168, 191 n.36
Glaser, Johann Friedrich 46–7, 50
Glinski, Josef 210
Global Financial Crisis (GFC) 227
Goebbels, Joseph 123, 128, 136, 156 n.1
Goldstein, Werner 251 n.103
Göppingen, Kirchenregisteramt 72, 81
Grande Peur 261
Grand Tours *(Kavalierstouren)* 22
Grellmann, Heinrich 91, 93, 113 n.28, 115 n.38
group criminalization 212
growing secularization 256
Gypsies 8, 9, 87–91, 109 n.1
    assimilation 93–7, 108
    bands 97
    biopolitical persecution 89–90
    centralization and transnationalism 102–8
    children 100

criminal activity 98
culmination of Bavaria's biopolitical management of 97–9
deportation 99
domestic 100
dumping 101
ethnicity and culture 113 n.25
foreign 96
"Gypsy nuisance" 93, 102–8
"Gypsy plague" 90, 92, 95, 99–102, 114 n.28
"Gypsy question" *(Zigeunerfrage)* 90
hysteria 89
immigration of 99–100, 118 n.72
intelligence 103, 105
itinerancy 207
naturalization 105
nomadic lifestyle 87, 88–9
nuisance and harassment 97, 101, 103–4
population 93
prohibition of camping 101
racial construction 91–4
racial mixing 94
romanticization 87–8
thieving 207
threat of nomadism 91
vengeance 101

Habsburg Monarchy 8, 41–58
  administration 55
  bureaucracy 44, 59 n.11
  territories 42
Hancock, Ian 110 n.9
Harster, Theodor 105–6
hausen 71
Hauser, Martin 184
Haushaltung 71, 74, 78
Häusser, Alexander 200
Hayek, Friedrich August von 239
Healy, Róisín 59 n.14
Hehemann, Rainer 111 n.14
Heimatprinzip 112 n.15
Helberg, Iris 132
Hellbeck, Jochen 167
Henrikson, Alan K. 268 n.13
Herf, Jeffrey 3, 208
Heuss, Herbert 111 n.14
hierarchy of suffering 187
Hilfspolizei (Auxiliary Police) 154
Hirschle, Jochen 227

Hitler, Adolf 163 n.133
Hitler's Stormtroopers 125
Hock, Stefan 60 n.27
Hofer, Norbert 276
Hofkriegsrat 46
Hofmann, Eulau 139
Holocaust 2, 169, 192 n.67
Holy Roman Empire 1, 8, 15, 16, 18, 22, 29
homo sacer 90
Huber, Florian 261
Huebel, Sebastian 9, 165
humanitarian crisis 199, 276
Hunt, Lynn 80
Huster, Ernst-Ulrich 239
hyper-masculinized propaganda 186

illicit distillery 208
Illustrierter Beobachter 135, 136, 137
Illuzzi, Jennifer 90, 99, 112 n.22, 113 n.24, 118 n.74
Imperial coalitions 16
Imperial Provisor Frombald 45
inequality 229, 231, 239
infectious illness 54
infiltration/incursion 2, 51, 54, 278
  cultural 8, 17, 21, 24–9, 39 n.96
  fear of 42–3
  Habsburg territories 42
instrumentality 3, 4, 6
internal German refugees 198
intimidation 125, 126, 130, 170, 181, 187
invasion/infiltration 278
Islamic State of Iraq and Syria (ISIS) 276

Jacob, Ernst 73
Jarausch, Konrad H. 244 n.14
Jew *see also specific enteries*
  of Nazism 2
  physical violence against 182
Jewish masculinity 8, 169, 181
Jewish women 184
Jewish World War One veterans' organization 171
Johnson, Eric 125–6
Julic, Yugoslav Rade 210

Kaiserreich 89, 90, 108, 210
  governments 9

Kampfzeit 123
Kaplan, Marion 177, 189 n.15, 192 n.67
Kasparek, Michael 45
Kehoe, Thomas J. 1, 12 n.7, 165
Kershaw, Ian 154
Kisolova 57
Klaniczay, Gábor 60 n.25
Klemperer, Victor 173, 174, 183
Kleßmann, Christoph 200, 228
Klingenberg, Heinz 152
Kohl, Helmut 11, 255, 264
Kommunistische Partei Deutschlands (KPD) 124, 142, 148
Koonz, Claudia 179
Koranic law 276
Kosyra, Herbert 200
Kraft durch Freude 259
Krakauer, Max 173, 174, 184
Kreuter, Peter 45, 49, 54, 60 n.26
Kristallnacht 185, 277
Kristallnacht pogrom 182
Kuklina 53
Kultur 207
Kulturkampf (von Bismarck) 207
Kurda, Charissa 9, 207

Laffan, Michael 4
Landau, Edwin 165, 170
Lässig, Simone 173
latency period 234
Lazier, Benjamin 4
League of Augsburg 16, 28
legal discrimination 176
Lehmann, Hartmut 68
leitmotif 165
Lengfeld, Holger 227
Leopold I 16
Leopoldina 53
Lewy, Guenter 111 n.14
Leyens, Erich 171
liberal revolution 3
Liebich, Richard 91
liquid blood *(liquides geblüet)* 50
Lisola, François-Paul de 15, 30 n.4
Lombroso, Cesare 92, 114 n.31
Lorke, Christoph 10, 227, 245 n.29
Louis XIV 58 *see also* political fear during wars of Louis XIV
  attacked Palatinate 16
  invasion in 1672 29 n.1

military power 15, 28
persecution of French Protestants 27–8
sworn enemy of Christ 20
threat to Christendom 20
Lowe, Keith 200
Lucassen, Leo 89, 111 n.14, 113 n.24, 113 n.25, 116 n.47
Luxembourg 16
Lynn, John A. 30 n.2

MacDonogh, Giles 200
magical pestilence 52–4
Malssen, P. J. W. van 19
Mandelkern, Moritz 185
"marauding Polish gangs" 207
Margalit, Gilad 87
Marquardt, Fred 81
martial law 202
Martins-Heuß, Kirsten 87
Marum, Ludwig 174, 175
Marx, Wilhelm 133
Marxist-Leninist ideology 231
mass media 228–9
  consensus-oriented 231
mass unemployment 238
material misery 230
Matt, Susan 6
Maugg, Gordian 200
Mazowiecki, Tadeusz 264
McCullough, Roy L. 30 n.9
medicalization of the vampire body 55
Medvedja 41–7, 57
Mein Kampf (Hitler) 146, 163 n.133
men, gender conventions and responsibilities 168
mental maps 268 n.13
Mercy, Claudius Florimund Graf von 44
Merkel, Angela 264, 276
metanoia 254–5, 258–60, 263, 264–5
Meyer, Alfred 174
MG detachments 198–9
MG officers (MGOs) 197, 201, 212
middle class Germans 227
Militärgrenze (military border) 43, 44, 49
Miliza 42, 44
"mirror fears" 267–8
mirroring effects 267–8
Mjölnir cartoon 151
modernization 11

moral panic 222 n.55
"moral panics" 206, 216
mortality 261
Mosse, George 168
Müller, Yves 132
Münchner Neueste Nachrichten 88
Munich Conference, 1911 91, 107
Munich Putsch 134
Muslim refugees, demonizing of 277

Nachzehrer 43
Napoleonic Wars 258
Napoleon's occupation 210
national boycott against Jewish businesses 170
national corruption 26
National Socialism 123, 129, 146, 228
National Socialist agenda 143
National Socialist symbol 135
National-sozialismus: Der Organisierte Wille der Nation 149, 150
Nazi
  aggression within West Germany 10
  anti-Semitism 182
  authoritarian systems 211
  brutality 200, 213, 223 n.67
  crimes 10, 253
  dictatorship 170
  intimidation 170
  mistreatment 183
  movement 125, 131, 148, 179
  parlance 146
  physical assaults 179
  racial and ideological enemies of 201
  racism 189 n.15
  revolution 181
  Stormtroopers 134, 139
  surrender 195
  victims 205
  violence 170, 180, 183, 198
  Werewolves 216
Nazi Germany 3
  humanitarian consequences after defeat 201
Nazi Party 12 n.7, 127, 129
Nazism 2, 12 n.6, 129
  boycott, impact of 170
  opponents of 133

Nehring, Holger 227
New Eastern Policy 266
"new poverty" *(Neue Armut)* 238 *see also* poverty
nightmare of coalitions 256
Nine Years' War (1688–97) 15, 16, 27, 28, 30 n.3
nivellierte Mittelstandsgesellschaft (Schelsky) 231
non-German "Displaced Persons" (DPs) 279
normalization 231
Nowosadko, Jutta 59 n.15
nuclear escalations 266
Nuremberg spiral 257

Oatley, Keith 168
O'Connell, Michael 218 n.6
Oetinger, Christoph 68
Ofer, Dalia 192 n.67
Öffentlichkeit concept 157 n.10
Öhman, Arne 79
Ostdenkschrift 262
ostentatious denazification 263
Ottoman-controlled regions 42
Ottoman Empire 20, 57–8
Ottomans 8, 44
  invasion 16
  provenance 43

pamphleteers' strategies 17–25, 28
pamphlets 17–22, 28
pater familias 176
Paule, Arnout 41–2
Peace of Westphalia 256
penal colonies 106
persecution 166
Pfister, Jakob 104
physical brutality 168–9
Pia desideria (Spener) 68
Pickering, Michael G. 1, 59 n.15, 165
  analysis of fears 8–9
Pietism 68–70
Pietistic conventions 79
Pietistic hymnals 68, 69
Plagojevitz, Peter 41, 45
plague 42
Plamper, Jan 4
police targeting 2

Polish criminals 2, 207
political fear during wars of Louis
    XIV 15–18
    cultural infiltration, threat of 21–6
    inventing fear 26–9
    reflecting fear 18–21
politicization 234
Polizeiruf 110 237
Pope Pius VI 76
post–First World War Germany
    ultranationalist movements 3
post–Second World War Germany 9
    see also Germany
post-traumatic stress disorder
    (PTSD) 262
postwar criminality 212
postwar emotional regime 231
postwar occupation 197
postwar society 199
postwar xenophobia 207
postwar years 230–3
Pott, August 113 n.28
poverty 10, 229, 231, 232
    "bashful poor" 239
    communication 233
    culture of 235
    definitions of 233
    discovering 233–8
    extra-territorialization 233
    medicalization 234
power relations 6, 7, 18, 57
"precariat" *(Prekariat)* 241
pre-Nazi culture of authoritarianism 211
Pressmann, Will 180–1
prognostications 21
programmatic argumentation 18
pro-Hindenburg election poster,
    1932 123–4
pro-Nazi partisans 199
Protestants 20, 27
    German 41
    protestantism in France 16
Prussian Interior Ministry 99
public imagination 228

rabble-rousing anti-Semitic rhetoric 169
Rache (revenge) 132
racial enemies 130
racism 189 n.15

radical paranoia underpinning Nazi
    ideology 3
radical Pietism 68
RAND Corporation 202
rapes 20
recidivism 210
reciprocal Nazi violence 198 *see also* Nazi,
    violence
Red Army 260
Reddy, William M. 270 n.25, 279
Red Front Fighters 142
Red Front Fighters League 130, 139
Reich 101
Reichardt, Sven 156 n.2
Reichsfeind 27
Reichstag elections 132
Reich-wide economic crisis 94
Reimar, Walter 133
Reinhardt, Jakob 104
resacralization 256
reunification 228
Richarz, Monika 173
Riemer, Salomon 177
Riesenfeld, Adolf 183
right to homeland 261
Ringelheim, Joan 189 n.15
Ritter, Robert 92
roaming gangs 200
Robin, Corey 29, 31 n.16, 265
Röhm, Ernst 125
Roma 109 n.1
Rosenberg, Kurt 179, 181, 183, 184, 185
Rosenhaft, Eve 139
Rosenwein, Barbara H. 5, 187, 268 n.3
Roter Frontkämpferbund (RFB) 124
Rovan, Joseph 263
Ruhr 126
Ruhr Pocket 198
Rwandan genocide 279

Sachße, Christoph 248 n.70
Sarrazin, Thilo 241
Sawyer, Jeffrey K. 19
Scheff, Thomas 257
Schelsky, Helmut 231
Schicketanz, Peter 68
Schluss Jetzt mit Hitlers Volksverhetzung!
    Wählt Hindenburg 123–4
Schmidt, Daniel 132

Schmidt, Frantz 67
Schmitt, Carl 90
Schönke, Adolf 200
Schuman, Dirk 124
Schweitzer, Hans 149
Scully, Richard 9, 123
Second World War 10
Selbstbeschränkung 264–7
self-imposed isolation 183
self-limitation *(Selbstbeschränkung)* 255
  in foreign policy 265
self-optimization 241
self-victimization 264
sentimental movies 231
Serbia 43
Seven Years' War 18
Sheehan, James J. 30 n.1
Siege of Vienna 16
Siemens, Daniel 125
Sikowski, Felix 203
Simmel, Georg 229
Sinold, Philipp Balthasar 45
Sinti 109 n.1
Skoll, Geoffrey 127
Sloterdijk, Peter 254, 258
social bonding 168
social climbing 231
social communities 5
social Darwinian ideas 9
social decline 228
Social Democratic Party (SPD) 133, 137, 265
social-democratic sympathizers 266
Social Democrats (SPD) 133, 142, 148
social disintegration 195, 200
  postwar Germany 196
social disorder 198
social equals 240
social harassment 176
social humiliation 166
social inequality 229, 231, 239
social insecurity 236
socialism
  superiority of 236
socialist collectivization 236
Socialist Unity Party of Germany (SED) 231
socialization 186
social justice 231
social-liberal coalition 234

social mobility 240
social "otherness" 241
social pacification 231, 236
social reality 186
societal fragility 212, 216
societal self-harmonization 231
sociocultural ostracism 183
Soll, Jacob 32 n.19
Sonderweg 2, 259
Soviet and communist invasion 10
Soviet-communist occupiers 165
Soviet occupation 268 n.6
Spätzle 70
Spener, Philip Jakob 68
Spinks, Jennifer 6
sporadic violence 2
Staatskanzlei in Vienna 45
Stadtbrand 77
Starobinski, Jean 6
status competition 228
status panic 227
Stearns, Peter 5, 174
Steiner, Paul 165, 174, 182
Stochniatck, Antoni 210
Stormtroopers 125–6, 129, 154, 170
  Stormtrooper hooliganism 179
strain theory 221 n.32
Strasbourg 16
stringent police surveillance 95
Sturmabteilung (SA) 123–56
"subhuman" *(Untermenschen)* 207, 208
Sun King *see* Louis XIV
superiority of socialism 236
superstition 58
Supreme Headquarters Allied Expeditionary Forces (SHAEF) 201
Swett, Pamela 130
symbolic degradation 166
Szanto, Alexander 182

Tatar, Maria 3
Tausk, Walter 181, 184, 185
Tennstedt, Florian 248 n.70
territorial sovereignty 8, 43–4, 57
terrorism 277
Third Reich 9, 92, 94, 149
  bodily fears 183–5
  economic fears 172–6
  fear of arrest and violence 179–83
  gendered themes of fear 169–72

German-Jewish masculinities in 165–9
Third Reich 9, 92, 94, 149
Thirty Years' War (1618–48) 20
threats
  by Gypsies 89
  by Muslims 275
  of physical violence 183–4
  of unemployment and poverty 229
Titanic syndrome 7
torrent of emotions 80
trading licenses 99
transformation 11
Treaty at Passarowitz 50
Treaty between Austria-Hungary,
  Germany, and Switzerland,
  1870 103
Treaty of Versailles 126
Trebbin 130
"trickledown effect" 234
Troeltsch, Walter 67–8, 70, 74
Trotz Hass und Verbot Nicht Tot 147
Truce of Ratisbon, 1684 16
Trümmerfrauen (women of ruins) 231
Tuggelin, Hermann 170

unemployment 168–9
Universal-Lexicon (Zedler) 7
universal monarchy 33 n.32
Utgaard, Peter 268 n.7

vampires 41
  autopsy 52
  bodies with medical signification 56
  debate 44
  and demons 165
  emergence of 43
  Habsburg military personnel 42–3
vampirism 41–2, 49, 51
  encroachment of 58
  Habsburg–Ottoman border 44
  instances of 44
  magical origin for 53
  supernatural dimensions of 53
  in Transylvanian regions of Habsburg
    Monarchy 44
Vayhinger, Ernst Jacob 65, 70, 76
  Barbara, Anna 71
  uxor propter Bibendum 70
  wife's alcoholism 72, 74
vengeful DPs 195

Vergangenheitsbewältigung 254,
  258–60, 262–4
violence 123
violent offenses 204
violent political climate 124
visum et repertum 52, 53, 55
Volksgemeinschaft 146, 259, 262
Volksstimme 142
Vom Kriege (Clausewitz) 258
von Bismarck, Otto 207
von Grimmelshausen, Hans Jakob
  Christoffel 87
von Haller, Albrecht 68
von Hindenburg, Paul 127, 133
von Köttwitz, Ensign 53, 54
von Puttkamer, Robert 99
Vukanovic, T. P. 53

Wagner, Wolf 239
Wählt Hindenburg [Vote Hindenburg]
  144
Wallachia 42
Wallmann, Johannes 68, 83 n.17
War of Devolution (1667–8) 15, 30 n.3
War of the Reunions (1683–4) 30 n.1
War of the Spanish Succession
  (1701–15) 30 n.3
wars of Louis XIV, political fear 15–18
  cultural infiltration, threat of 21–6
  inventing fear 26–9
  reflecting fear 18–21
wartime trauma 217
*Was steckt hinter dieser Maske? Also wählt
  Marx* 134
weaver 65, 67, 70
Weber, Pierre-Frédéric 10
Weimar *Öffentlichkeit* 123–6
  antidote to fear 151–5
  posters and distribution of fear
    133–51
  SA violence and terror 128–33
  social and economic disorder 126–8
Weimar Republic 126, 128, 141, 142, 156,
  181, 230, 231
Weiss, Max 4
welfare capitalism 232
welfare scroungers 241
Wessel, Horst 152
Westbindung 265
Western "guilt" culture 5

West Germany 10–11, 228, 230–9, 255, 261, 265, 266
Whaley, Joachim 30 n.11
Whelan, Anthony 218 n.6
Wienerisches Diarium 46
wife's mismanagement 70, 72, 80
Willems, Wim 113 n.25
Winkler, H. A. 259
Winterfeldt, Hans 173
Wir Schaff en das neue Deutschland! Denkt an die opfer Wählt Nationalsozialisten Liste 1 146, 147
witch 52
women's victimization 187
worsted-wool weaver *(Zeugmacher)* 65
Wrede, Martin 31 n.14
Wünschmann, Kim 179
Württemberg 45, 67, 99, 104, 106, 107, 118 n.72

xenophobia 3, 277

Zamoyski, Adam 3–4
Zaremba, Marcin 261
Zedler, Johann 7
Zeller, Eberhard 68
Zentralpolizeiblatt 95
Zentrum Partei 133
zero-error principle 241
"Zero Hour" *(Stunde Null)* interpretation 195, 217
Zeugmacher 65, 67, 70
Zigeuner see Gypsies
Zigeunerbuch (Dillmann) 88, 92, 99, 104, 107, 118 n.72
Zigeunerplage (Gypsy nuisance) 9, 87, 89
Zigeunerzentrale 98, 105
Zika, Charles 6

www.ingramcontent.com/pod-product-compliance
Lightning Source LLC
Chambersburg PA
CBHW070018010526
44117CB00011B/1618